what is a world?

Frontispiece: William Kentridge for *The Refusal of Time*, 2012 (detail). Courtesy the artist.

PHENG CHEAH **what is a world?**

ON POSTCOLONIAL LITERATURE AS WORLD LITERATURE

DUKE UNIVERSITY PRESS *Durham and London* 2016

© 2016 Duke University Press
All rights reserved
Printed in the United States of America
on acid-free paper ∞
Designed by Amy Ruth Buchanan
Typeset in Minion Pro by Westchester
Publishing Services

Library of Congress Cataloging-in-Publication Data
Cheah, Pheng, author.
What is a world? : on postcolonial literature as world
literature / Pheng Cheah.
pages cm
Includes bibliographical references and index.
ISBN 978-0-8223-6078-0 (hardcover : alk. paper)
ISBN 978-0-8223-6092-6 (pbk. : alk. paper)
ISBN 978-0-8223-7453-4 (e-book)
1. Postcolonialism. 2. Literature and society.
3. Literature and globalization. 4. Literature,
Modern—History and criticism. I. Title.
PN56.P555C44 2016
809'.05—dc23
2015028568

Cover art: William Kentridge, video still from *The
Refusal of Time*, 2012. 5-channel video installation with
breathing machine. Courtesy the artist, Marian Goodman
Gallery (New York, Paris, London), Goodman Gallery
(Johannesburg, Cape Town) and Lia Rumma Gallery
(Naples, Milan).

CONTENTS

ACKNOWLEDGMENTS

Even though it puts into question the equation of the world with the spatial extensiveness of the globe, a book that takes as its subject something as large as the world and literature's relation to the world is necessarily the product of intellectual conversations that have stretched across the globe. Special thanks to Jonathan Culler, Elizabeth Grosz, and David Wang Der-wei for reading the manuscript, Benedict Anderson and Caroline Hau for invaluable feedback on the epilogue, Wendy Larson for her insightful comments on chapter 7, and Zachary Manfredi for his careful reading of chapters 4 and 5. Peter Fenves and Simon Gikandi were exemplary manuscript reviewers. This book is stronger because of their incisive comments. Nuruddin Farah and Amitav Ghosh patiently answered factual questions about their writing.

Earlier versions of chapters were presented at the Beijing Foreign Languages University, Binghamton University, Birkbeck, University of London, the University of British Columbia, Cornell University, Ehwa Woman's University, Florida State University, Georgetown University, Goldsmiths, University of London, the University of Hong Kong, Indiana University, the University of Wisconsin at Madison, the University of Manchester, National Chung-hsing University, National Taiwan University, the National University of Singapore, New York University, Northwestern University, the University of Oregon at Eugene, Oxford University, Peking University, the University of Pennsylvania, Seoul National University, Shanghai Jiaotong University, Stanford University, Thammasat University, the University of Washington at Seattle, and the University of Zürich. I would like to thank my interlocutors on these occasions, especially Samuel Weber, Susannah Gottlieb, Costas Douzinas, J. Hillis Miller, Andrea Riemenschnitter, Rita Felski, Ramon Saldivar, Dai Jinhua, Franco Moretti, David Damrosch, Haun Saussy, Annu Jalais, Elizabeth Anker, Natalie Melas, Robert Young, Rajeswari Sunder Rajan, Sneja Gunew, Ankhi Mukherjee, Elleke Boehmer, Alessia Ricciardi, Vicente Rafael, Laurie Sears, Walter Cohen, Neil Saccamano, Leslie Adelson, Robin Goodman, Vinay Dharwadker, Susan Stanford Friedman, Robert Guay, Jini Kim Watson,

Chris Berry, Gina Marchetti, Jackie Stacey, Felicia Chan, Gyan Prakash, Lisa Rofel, David Goldberg, Sven Trakulhun, Ralph Weber, Sanjay Subrahmanyam, Chris Lee, Mary Bryson, Hector Hoyos, Jed Esty, Simon Richter, Liao Hsien-hao, Guy Beauregard, Bennett Fu, Chiu Kuei-fen, Thanet Aphornsuvan, Visarut Phungsoondara, Yukti Mukdawijitra, Lamia Karim, Claudia Berger, Eileen Julien, Benjamin Robinson, Jonathan Elmer, Kenneth Dean, Peggy Cho, Kang Woosung, Chon Sooyoung, and Nicole Rizzuto.

I received research support from my home institution, the University of California at Berkeley, in the form of a Townsend Center Initiative Grant for Associate Professors in the spring of 2007. My thanks to Gillian Hart, my faculty counterpart, who patiently listened to my critique of critical geographical theories of the world. I also received a Humanities Research Fellowship for the spring and fall of 2008. My thanks to Janet Broughton, Humanities Dean at that time, for facilitating the research leave. Colleagues at Berkeley who have given me intellectual sustenance during the writing of this book include Suzanne Guerlac, Deniz Gökturk, Martin Jay, Tony Kaes, Hsing You-tien, Trinh Minh-ha, Michael Mascuch, David Cohen, Candace Slater, and Charles Briggs. I also thank my editor, Courtney Berger, for her cheerful attentiveness and help.

Quite appropriately, much of this book was written in Asia. I am grateful for the research support I received from the Asia Research Institute at the National University of Singapore, where I was visiting research professor from August 2012 to August 2013 and from the School of English at the University of Hong Kong, where I have been a visiting research professor in the summer months since May 2012. Prasenjit Duara was an exemplary host as Director of the Asia Research Institute, and Chua Beng Huat was a wonderful leader of the Cultural Studies Research Cluster. The intellectual friendships that were formed and strengthened with Wendy Larson, Bill Callahan, Andrea Riemenschnitter, Lim Song Hwee, and Felicia Chan during my year in Singapore will always be an important part of my scholarly life. The University of Hong Kong School of English has been a second institutional home. Elaine Ho, Chris Hutton, Douglas Kerr, Wendy Gan, and Adam Jaworksi have been extremely congenial colleagues.

The book draws on material previously published in the following articles: "What Is a World? On World Literature as Cosmopolitanism," in special issue on cosmopolitanism, *Daedalus* 137, no. 3 (summer 2008), 26–38 (reprinted in *Routledge Handbook of Cosmopolitan Studies*, ed. Gerard Delanty (London: Routledge, 2012), 138–49 (reprinted by permission of Routledge),

"World against Globe: Toward a Normative Conception of World Literature," *New Literary History* 45, no. 3 (summer 2014), 303–29, and "Of Other Worlds to Come," in *Delimiting Modernities: Conceptual Challenges and Regional Responses*, ed. Sven Trakulhun and Ralph Weber (Lanham, MD: Lexington Books, 2015), 3–23.

Missed Encounters

Cosmopolitanism, World Literature, and Postcoloniality

In a recent video installation, *The Refusal of Time*, the South African artist William Kentridge brilliantly captures a key premise of this book: the hierarchical ordering and control of the world as we know it is based on technologies of temporal calculation. Kentridge shows how the cartographical organization of the capitalist world-system relies on Northern- and Eurocentric regimes of temporal measurement. The subordination of all regions of the globe to Greenwich Mean Time as the point zero for the synchronization of clocks is a synecdoche for European colonial domination of the rest of the world because it enables a mapping that places Europe at the world's center. This tethering to the uniform march of European standard time is a form of imprisonment that smothers lived local temporalities (see this book's frontispiece).

> The perfection of chronometers had long been the aim of geographers, to fix more precisely the positions of islands and continents in relation to Europe. With the spread of cables under sea and over land, that followed the development of electric telegraphy, time was taken from the master clocks of London and Paris and sent to the colonies.
>
> The lines on maps were miniature renderings of the real lines of cables that snaked round continents, or drew great arcs across the floors of oceans. Sending and receiving stations followed the cable and marked the end of lines tethering the center to the satellite colony. The clock and the colonial observatory completed the mapping of the world.
>
> The strings of cables, these birds' nests of copper, turned the world into a giant switchboard, for commerce and control. The world was covered by a huge dented bird cage of time zones, of liens of agreement of control, all sent out by the clock rooms of Europe. Local suns were shifted further and further from local zeniths.[1]

In a section entitled "Blowing up the Meridian," Kentridge suggests that all acts of resistance to colonial rule are revolts against the pervasive control of imposed European time. They express the demand "Give us back our Sun. As if blowing up a train line could blow up the pendulum of the European clock, which swung over every head."[2] "In colonial terms, this refusal was a refusal of the European sense of order imposed by time zones: not only literally, but this refusal also referred metaphorically to other forms of control as well."[3]

The mapping of the world by temporal calculations is premised on a conceptualization of the world as a spatial category, namely, an object of the greatest possible spatial extension that can be divided into zones of quantitatively measurable time. *World*, however, is originally a temporal category. Before the world can appear as an object, it must first *be*. A world only is and we are only worldly beings if there is already time. The unity and permanence of a world are thus premised on the persistence of time. This book explores how the conceptualization of the world in temporal terms provides a normative basis for transforming the world made by capitalist globalization and how this normative understanding of the world leads to a radical rethinking of world literature as literature that is an active power in the making of worlds, that is, both a site of processes of worlding and an agent that participates and intervenes in these processes.

My redefinition of world literature has two main implications. First, it orients world literature so that it addresses a fundamental contradiction of the modern capitalist world-system. As Marx pointed out, the globalization of capital creates the material conditions for a community of the greatest possible extension. However, the capitalist world-system also radically undermines the achievement of a human community of global reach, that is, a genuine unity of the world. For Marx, the world is a normative category that exceeds the global market. This book explores the normative dimension of worldliness from the perspective of narrative literature from the postcolonial South that attempts to remake the world against capitalist globalization.

Second, understanding world literature as a world-making activity clarifies the connections it has to cosmopolitanism that existing scholarship has obscured. Modern cosmopolitanism has largely been an affair of philosophy and the social sciences. Whether one thinks of the ideal ethical projects of worldwide solidarity of the eighteenth-century French *philosophes* or Kant, or of more recently emerging discourses of new cosmopolitanism in our era of economic globalization, transnational migration, and global communications, literature appears to have little pertinence to the formulation of normative cosmopolitan principles for the regulation of institutional actors on the global stage or to the study of the proliferating associations and networks that envelop the entire globe. Indeed, cosmopolitanist discourse seems only to refer to literature in disparagement. Kant frets that his teleological account of world history, which aims to establish a world federation of states, will be taken for a fanciful fiction: "It is admittedly a strange and at first sight absurd proposition to write a *history* according to an idea of how world events must develop if they are to conform to certain rational ends; it would seem that only a *novel* could result from such a perspective [Absicht]."[4] A cosmopolitan vision cannot be expressed in literary representation because literature can only render an ideal picture that has at best a tenuous relation to the world.

Contemporary theories of world literature have been equally hesitant about connecting world literature to cosmopolitanism perhaps because they have identified cosmopolitanism with an abstract universal normative view of the ideal unity of the world, whereas they are concerned with how literary texts attain worldliness as a result of the establishment of multiple concrete attachments through circulation.[5] The deeper reason for the missed encounter between world literature and cosmopolitanism is that neither field of study has carefully examined the key concept common to them, *the world*. Cosmopolitanism is about viewing oneself as part of a world, a circle of political belonging that transcends the limited ties of kinship and country to embrace the whole of deterritorialized humanity. However, since one cannot *see* the universe, the world, or humanity, the cosmopolitan optic is not one of perceptual experience. It should be evident that we should not take the presentation of the world for granted because, at the very least, it is given to us by the imagination.

Theories of world literature take the concept of world for granted in a different way. They equate the world with circulatory movements that cut across national-territorial borders. They are primarily concerned with the impact of these spatial movements on the production, reception, and interpretation of literary texts instead of world literature's impact qua literature on the world. As I will show, they reduce the world literature's normative force to the barest minimum.

Cartographies of the Spatial World

My account of world literature as a force of world-making should be distinguished from two other intellectual approaches to the world: the argument in literary studies that literature constitutes a possible world and the view that each discipline of knowledge produces its own cartography of the world. The first approach draws on the theory of possible worlds from analytical philosophy and formal semantics to correct the excessive formalism of structuralist approaches to literature that dispense with literary reference and thematic content. It argues that literature creates a world, a totality with its own consistency, by appropriating elements from the referential world. As Thomas Pavel puts it, "freed from the constraints of the textualist approach, theory of fiction can respond again to the world-creating powers of imagination and account for the properties of fictional existence and worlds, their complexity, incompleteness, remoteness, and integration within the general economy of culture."[6] Although this approach suggests that literature, especially realist literature, has the power of creating a world, the literary world's ontological status is one of virtuality. It depicts a "genuinely possible alternative" to the actual world qua base.[7] Hence, although literature does not just reflect the actual world, its creativity is not a causal power in the actual world. It is limited to the construction through diegesis and mimesis of a world with sufficient consistency in its events to be a possible world.

In the second approach, a given discipline projects a cartographical image of the world according to specific criteria and principles of knowledge- and information-production. A mapping of the world in political economy may highlight global capital investment flows, whereas an anthropological mapping may emphasize migration flows. These cartographies divide the globe up hierarchically and map relations of power and inequality. They have an important impact on human existence, especially its social, economic, and political dimensions. For example, the cartography of the Failed States Index of the Fund for Peace is intended to promote "greater stability worldwide" by giving early warning to the international community about weak and failing states that pose a threat to global security so that effective policies can be formulated.[8]

Such cartographies can have a critical edge. Public international law scholarship has highlighted the trajectory of the spread of international law and human rights from European colonial expansion in the Americas, Africa, and the Pacific, with its hierarchical assumptions of civilizational, religious, and national differences, to the contemporary United Nations system with its regime of international human rights law based on the principles of national sovereignty and individualism.[9] In a more methodologically progressive vein, anthropologists of inter-Asia have urged us to move beyond the territorial nation-state-bounded dynamics of anti-imperial discourse and study the thick transnationalism of transregional networks across Asia. It is argued that research of an intermediate scale above the nation-state and below the world-system will help us evade the abstractions of global analysis and the myopic focus on minute detail yielded by local studies within a nation-state frame.[10] Intermediate-level interconnections created by religious movements, diasporas, trade exchanges, artistic production, and relocations exceed and escape the homogenizing, totalizing tendency of global forces. They generate frictions and offer immanent resources for resisting Northern- and Western-centric capitalist globalization.[11]

Recent theories of world literature employ a similar cartographical approach, although they do not approach the sophistication and suppleness of anthropological analyses of transnational networks and flows. As I will show in this book's first chapter, these theories map flows of literary exchange across national boundaries and through global circuits. They define the world in terms of the circulation of commodities, that is, as the expression, field, and product of transnational market exchange. The world is a spatial category, determined solely in terms of extension. Although there are merits to understanding literary phenomena beyond the nation-state framework, the fundamental shortcoming of equating the world with a global market is that it assumes that globalization creates a world. This leads to a restricted understanding of the relation between literature and capitalist globalization that places literature in a reactive position. Instead of exploring what literature can contribute to an understanding of the world and its possible role in remaking the world in contemporary globalization, theories of world literature have focused on the implications of global circulation for the study of literature.[12] They have turned away from questions about literature's worldly causality and avoided examining the normative dimension of worldliness. This book seeks to ask more of literature: Is there a normative worldly force immanent to literature? What are its key features?

A Normative Theory of World Literature: Temporalizing the World

This book develops a normative theory of world literature. By this, I mean an account of world literature that does not merely describe and analyze how literary works circulate around the world or are produced with a global market in mind but that seeks to understand the normative force that literature can exert in the world, the ethicopolitical horizon it opens up for the existing world. This requires careful elucidation of both terms in the phrase "normative force." "Normativity" refers to what ought to be. We conventionally understand norms and their related cognate, values, as ideals that practical reason prescriptively projects onto reality to transform it in the image of human ends or as principles immanent to collective human existence that will unfold and actualize themselves. The force of a norm comes from its universal validity. A norm with universal force can move human agents to worldly action. The normative force of world literature refers to its power or efficacy to change the world according to a normative ethicopolitical horizon. This concept of normativity informs all spiritualist accounts of the world. To take the most pertinent example, in his inaugural account of world literature, Goethe argued that the literary products of different nations are the diverse manifestations and expressions of an ideal universal humanity and the normative vocation of world literary exchange is to reveal this underlying ideal.

As opposed to a descriptive theory, a normative theory of world literature is based on an understanding of the world as a temporal category. Here we should take a leaf from Goethe, who characterized the world's normativity in temporal terms. Although wider human intercourse is initially enabled by material connections, literary exchange generates a spiritual world that transcends spatial networks. The members of this higher world hope that in due time, through historical progress, the ideal humanity that literary intercourse reveals will be actualized in the existing world. The first two parts of this book elucidate the normative force of world literature by means of two temporal concepts: *teleological time* and *worlding*.

Since its inception, the normative project of *Weltliteratur* has been augmented by teleologies of history that see the world as the horizon of humanity's universal historical progress toward the normative end of freedom. Today, teleology is viewed as an outmoded and even pernicious way of thinking because it constrains history by prescribing a universal end. Strictly speaking, however, teleology is simply the doctrine that events in the world are driven by immanent ends. Any kind of rational human action, for example means-ends relations and final causality, is teleological. A teleological world history understands the world's normativity in terms of teleological time, a phrase I have adapted from Amihud Gilead's provocative argument that Kant's Third Critique establishes a systematic unity between time and teleology.[13] Teleological time is the time of incarnation in which rational ends are actualized in the empirical world. It functions to bridge the mechanical natural world and the realm of freedom, defined as a sphere of rational spontaneity that characterizes the rational human being's power of self-determination. As distinguished from the linear time of mechanical causality that governs nature, where cause and effect follow each other in an irreversible sequence of succession, teleological time is circular and self-returning. Final causality is the actualization of a rational end in existence. In a teleological history, the end or final cause is not external but originally immanent to its effect. Its effect is the unfolding of, the return to, and the completion of an immanent end. In a modern mechanistic worldview, where all ends are externally prescribed by human reason, the only possible example of final causality in nature is the temporal structure of a living organism's causality as a self-organizing being in which its very life is generated by a complete reciprocity between parts and whole such that they are both the cause and effect of each other. Because an organism's epigenetic processes resemble the final causality of human reason, the entire tradition of German idealism viewed the teleological time of organic life as an apposite analogue for human freedom and saw this resemblance as grounds for the hope that human actors can actualize moral ends in the world.[14] Accordingly, human cultural progress (*Bildung*) was understood in terms of teleological time. As evidenced by its teleological view of historical progress, Marxist materialism inherits this legacy.

The contemporary distrust for teleology is often part of a larger critique of normativity that questions the coercive and exclusionary character of universalistic ideas of humanity and their historical alignment with class exploitation, patriarchal domination, Eurocentrism, and Western imperialism. In his critique of the ethical and moral ideals of bourgeois philosophy such as civil and human rights, Marx characterized these norms as ideological abstractions generated by the autonomization of reason from concrete material life. Notwithstanding this qualification, a "normative" horizon remains in Marx's materialist account of the world, namely, the universal fulfillment of concrete human needs by the cooperative social regulation of productive forces.

Unlike the discursive cartographies of the social sciences and recent accounts of world literature, cartographies of the world generated by teleological time are patently normative. Chapters 2 and 3 of the book examine how Hegelian idealism and Marxist materialism conceptualize the world within the eschato-teleological framework of universal progress. For example, the world proletarian revolution is the end of human history in two senses. It is the highest achievement of historical progress, the fullest development of history's rational purpose, and also its terminal horizon, the point at which history concludes because there is nothing else to be achieved. Here, the world's normative force is the transcendence of temporal finitude and the creation of a higher world by rational human action that overcomes the particularity and limitations of the present world.[15]

In describing worlding (*welten*), the second temporal concept I use to construct my normative theory of world literature, "normative force" must be used with even greater qualification. Unlike teleological time, worlding, which originates from Heideggerian phenomenology, has some currency in literary theory. It refers to how a world is held together and given unity by the force of time. In giving rise to existence, temporalization worlds a world. Gayatri Spivak introduced the term to postcolonial theory as shorthand to describe how European imperialist cultural representations constructed the geography of colonies. These processes of imperialist discursive cartography, which include canonical literature, are a form of epistemic violence that shapes how colonized subjects see themselves. These processes continue to play a role in the "worlding" of the Third World and its native inhabitants after decolonization.[16] Spivak referred to Heidegger's essay *The Origin of the Work of Art* as the source of the idea of "the 'worlding of a world' upon what must be assumed to be uninscribed earth" and drew an analogy between worlding and imperialist cartography.[17] Imperialism inscribed worlds that were inhabited prior to European conquest as the uninhabited space of *terra nullius*. Accordingly, "when the Heideggerian concept-metaphor of earth and world is used to describe the imperialist project, what emerges out of the violence of the rift . . . is the multifarious thingliness of a represented world on a map."[18]

Spivak acknowledges that postcolonial theory's use of worlding is a "vulgarization." Indeed, her analogy obscures what is truly valuable about Heidegger's concept for understanding the relation between world literature and globalization. Chapters 4–6 explore the concept's implications through a study of Heidegger, Arendt, and Derrida. For Heidegger, a world is precisely what cannot be represented on a map. Worlding is not a cartographical process that epistemologically constructs the world by means of discursive representations but a process of temporalization. Cartography reduces the world to a spatial object. In contradistinction, worlding is a force that subtends and exceeds all human calculations that reduce the world as a temporal structure to the sum of objects in space. Imperialist cartography is a calculation in the sphere of geopolitical economy that objectifies the world as a temporal process. It constructs a world insofar as its discursive representations enable us to determine and shape the world that temporalization opens up. Processes of discursive construction are worldings in a derived sense. They imbue the objective world with value and significance. But they are also processes of unworlding because by reducing the world to something spatial, they obscure its worldliness.

The relation between teleological time and worlding is as follows: teleological time worlds in the narrow sense by spiritually and materially shaping the world through the prescription of normative ends. To return again to the example of Marx, the proletarian revolution is a progressive force that intervenes in the existing world, reinscribing it through alternative discursive constructions in order to actualize a higher world. However, worlding in the derived sense presupposes worlding in the general sense, the prevailing of a world that follows from the sheer persistence of time. The world is linked to transcendence. But unlike teleological accounts, the world is not generated by the transcendence of finitude. Instead, time itself is the force of transcendence that opens a world. Better yet, temporalization constitutes the openness of a world, the opening that is world. In situations where progressive teleological cartographies are leveled off by capitalist globalization, this openness is an unerasable normative resource for disrupting and resisting the calculations of globalization. It opens up new progressive teleological times.

My characterization of worlding as a normative force is almost a catachresis, the use of a phrase because of the lack of better words that puts its usual meaning under erasure. Heidegger's account of the world not only problematizes the concepts of causality and force. It is also a sharp critique of teleology and normative value because it rejects the view of the world as a human community in which rational subjects give meaning to objective reality by prescribing values and norms. Teleological time is a rational calculation and appropriation of time that reshapes time in the image of human reason by suggesting that the historical course of worldly events is in harmony with the final causality of human action. In contradistinction, Heidegger argues that the emergence of the rational subject as the giver of normative value is premised on temporal processes that precede and exceed the human subject. We can only create normative value if we exist in a world with other beings and have access to them. The unifying power of temporalization is precisely a force of worlding, the precipitous ushering into a world, a meaningful whole that brings all beings into relation. When we fixate on values and norms, we obscure this prior meaningfulness and reduce other beings to what is valuable for us. Insofar as it precedes the rational subject from which normative value originates, worlding is not a normative process. Yet it also has everything to do with normativity because without this opening that puts all beings into relation, we would not have access to other beings and no value could be formed. Worlding is a "normative force" because it gives rise to the totality of meaningful relations that is the ontological condition for the production of values and norms.

Arendt's revision of Heidegger's idea of worlding suggests that natality, the force by which we come into the world, is the ground of our world-making capacities. As free subjects, we have the power to begin something new and to fabricate the world through our actions. Whereas Heidegger and Arendt view the destruction of world in capitalist modernity as a fall from an authentic condition, Derrida suggests that the relation between worlding in the general and narrow senses is aporetic. Worlding in the general sense carries with it the irreducible risk of unworlding because rational agents are guided by determinative calculations that specify the world's direction. However, because all calculations presuppose the persistence of time and this is incalculable, every unworlding points to the irreducible possibility of the opening of another world. As the basis of (un)worlding, the incalculable gift of time is a principle of real messianic hope immanent to the world.

What then is the connection between literature and the "normative force" of worlding such that we can speak of world literature as literature that worlds a world? Here the distinction between the two senses of worlding is crucial. The spiritualist and idealist accounts of the world (Goethe, Kant, and Hegel) I discuss in chapters 1 and 2 suggest that as an aesthetic and cultural process, literature creates a higher spiritual world. In contradistinction, Marx's materialist account of the world, the subject of chapter 3, poses an insurmountable obstacle to world literature. By characterizing spiritual products as phantomatic superstructures that are devoid of efficacy in making the real world, Marx deprives literature of any worldly normative force. Marxist critical theories of space and critical geography (Lefebvre and Harvey) go some way toward a materialist understanding of literature's power to shape the world through representational cartography because they offer a dynamic account of the making of space that gives an important role to cultural and aesthetic processes. However, in the final analysis, this shaping is directed at the world as something spatial. It is worlding in the narrow sense. In contradistinction, literature has a more fundamental relation to the world in phenomenological and postphenomenological accounts. The world's reality is neither objective nor subjective because it is a process grounded in the force of temporalization. Literature has a similarly curious ontological status: it is not something objective and so cannot be reduced to the subject's rational powers of determination and calculation. The radical indeterminacy of literature's meaning also means that it exceeds the subject's powers of interpretation. Hence, literature does not merely map the spatialized world and give it value and meaning. Rather, its formal structures enact the opening of a world by the incalculable gift of time. We may therefore speak of the world as having a "literary" structure that is more fundamental, more infrastructural, to adopt Marx's language, than the material reality of economic production. For the early Heidegger, literature discloses how temporalization holds the world together because it is a meaningful whole that is prior to the subject. Arendt and Derrida connect this literary structure to action in their respective elaborations of it as a web of stories without an author and the condition of possibility of narrative that opens a world.

Understanding world literature in terms of literature's connection to worlding and the coming of time points to immanent resources for resisting capitalist globalization. Capitalist accumulation needs and takes time. Capital is augmented by rational technologies and calculations that appropriate and manage time for the maximal extraction of surplus value. But capital can neither give itself time nor destroy it and, moreover, does not want to destroy it. This means that an irreducible principle of real messianic hope is always structural to capitalist globalization. The persistence of time is infrastructural to capital and cannot be destroyed. As an enactment of the opening of worlds by the coming of time, world literature points to something that will always exceed and disrupt capital.

My discussion of spiritualist, materialist, and phenomenological accounts of the world is intended as a progression toward a richer understanding of literature's worldliness. A later account of the world does not invalidate prior accounts but critically supplements them. We can then view a given work of world literature as the locus where different processes of worlding are played out in a historically specific field of forces, and we can analyze the complex relations, antagonisms, and aporetic tensions between these processes.

Postcolonial World Literature: A Critique of Heterotemporality

The third part of the book introduces a third term to the encounter between cosmopolitanism and world literature: postcoloniality. Literature of the postcolonial South is an important modality of world literature defined as literature that worlds and makes a world because the sharp inequalities created by capitalist globalization and their devastating consequences for the masses of postcolonial societies make the opening of other worlds a matter of the greatest imperativity. Put another way, the tension between cosmopolitanism and globalization, world and globe, is most acute in postcoloniality because far from holding a world together, capitalist globalization incorporates peoples outside the European world-system by violently destroying their worlds. Unlike teleologies of world history, the unity at stake here is not that of the whole of humanity. It is more modest and fragile: the gathering- and holding-together that maintains a place of habitation in the face of the leveling violence of global technologies of temporal calculation. The survival of these worlds is necessary to the constitution of a larger world of humanity that is truly plural.

For more than a decade, critical social science concerned with the postcolonial South has been arguing that the world is made up of multiple temporalities that can only be liberated by exploding Western capitalist modernity's linear time. Boaventura de Sousa Santos, a sociologist of international law and an active participant in the World Social Forum, suggests that we need to replace "the monoculture of linear time" with "the ecology of temporalities" to release alternative realities and generate different experiences of contemporaneity. "Societies are constituted of various temporalities. Many practices are disqualified, suppressed, or rendered unintelligible because they are ruled by temporalities that are not contained in the temporal canon of Western capitalist modernity. Once these temporalities are recuperated and become known, the practices and socialities ruled by them become intelligible and credible objects of argumentation and political debate. The expansion of the present occurs, in this case, by the relativization of linear time and the valorization of other temporalities that may articulate or conflict with it."[19] In the humanities, postcolonial theory has likewise explored the complicities between the teleological time of Western modernity's universal narrative of progress, colonial violence, and the linear time of capitalist exploitation. Dipesh Chakrabarty's theory of heterotemporality suggests that non-Western temporalities coexist with the time of modern progress and are important resources for resisting and subverting Western teleological time and the bases of alternative modernities to capitalist globalization.

We cannot, however, undo the history of Western imperialism and colonialism by nostalgically recuperating romanticized precapitalist pasts. We must instead patiently search for extant resources for reworlding the world. Part III is devoted to the study of narrative literature from the postcolonial peripheries that draws on alternative temporalities from the Caribbean, the South Asian subcontinent, Africa, and the Philippines to contest the world created by different flows of global capital. Michelle Cliff's Clare Savage novels, Amitav Ghosh's *The Hungry Tide*, Nuruddin Farah's *Gifts*, Ninotchka Rosca's *State of*

War, and Timothy Mo's *Renegade*, respectively, track the calculations of sugar and tourist capital, environmental movements and ecotourism, humanitarian aid, and military and economic neocolonialism in collaboration with the crony capitalism of a patrimonial state. Despite its reliance on slavery, colonial capital justified itself as a civilizing mission. United States economic and military neocolonialism during the Cold War similarly masked itself under the name of development within the security framework of protection from communism. Contemporary flows of money, especially humanitarianism and environmental and world preservation funds, present themselves as attempts to humanize the world. The novels studied expose how these global flows violently destroy worlds despite their humanizing claims. Cliff's Clare Savage novels, the subject of chapter 8, are concerned with the socioeconomic and political problems caused in Jamaica by sugar capital and the tourist industry. Chapter 9 discusses the portrayal of the tragic dispossession of subaltern populations from the Sundarbans by environmental and world heritage preservation movements in Ghosh's *The Hungry Tide*. Chapter 10, on Farah's *Gifts*, is concerned with humanitarian dehumanization in Somalia: the dehumanizing impact of transnational humanitarian aid on a receiving people. The novels by Rosca and Mo discussed in the epilogue are concerned with the devastating impact of economic corruption and political authoritarianism in the Philippines under US neocolonialism.

These novels are examples of literature that seeks to have a worldly causality in contemporary globalization. With the exception of *Renegade*, the source of literature's worldly force is the heterotemporality of precolonial oral traditions that have survived the violence of slavery, folk practices, subaltern rituals and practices of survival, religious ethics, and even the geological time of the landscape. Although the thesis of heterotemporality presents itself as a rejection of the universalizing teleological narrative of Western capitalist modernity, alternative temporalities are in fact varieties of teleological time in a smaller case. They are nonuniversal or local teleologies because they are governed by a dynamic of self-return in which a given postcolonial people or social group achieve self-determination through their own practices. They can be divided into two categories: *revolutionary time*, where the cultivation of a revolutionary consciousness takes place with the aim of transforming a given country from a subordinate part of the homogeneous abstract space of the global capitalist system into a place of belonging where local populations and groups can freely thrive (Cliff and Rosca), and *worldly ethics*, the ethos or practice of inhabiting a world with others in a conjuncture where the world is constantly being eroded by global processes and revolutionary transformation is no longer a plausible alternative (Ghosh, Farah, and Mo). Certain forms of cultural and linguistic translation, relations of generous giving that respect the self-determination of the recipient, practices of care and concern for others, and above all the telling and receiving of stories are important elements of worldly ethics.

My studies of these novels are examples of how to analyze world literature as the interplay of different processes of worlding. I take issue with the theory of heterotemporality by arguing that the alternative teleologies enacted by the novels are fundamentally problematic. Because their attempts at reworlding are repeatedly undermined by global and national capitalist calculations, the heterotemporalities they stage can only be sustained by conjuring with the incalculable and inhuman gift of time as the original opening of a world. These novels are obsessed with the story. With the help of Benjamin's essay on the storyteller, the epilogue speculates on the connection between storytelling and finitude that makes the story the most appropriate narrative form for communicating the openness of world.

The organization of this book can give the wrong impression of a division of labor between European philosophy and literature from the postcolonial South, where postcolonial literary texts have the subordinate function of illustrating the ontological and normative problems concerning worldliness that European philosophy elaborates. In fact, no such division exists. This is a work of literary theory where I study philosophical conceptions of world that are insufficiently theorized or simply missing in existing theories of world literature in order to construct a normative theory of world literature. My analyses of postcolonial world literature are not merely examples of this theory. They inflect and deepen the theory by exploring concrete postcolonial sites where the opening of new worlds is of the greatest urgency. The philosophical and literary texts are concerned with the same issues of the world's reality, literature's worldly force, and the corrosive impact of (colonial and neocolonial) global modernity on the temporalities of human worlds, especially the exclusionary character of communities in globalization. Thus, each chapter in parts I and II contains a discussion of literature's place in a given philosophical conception of the world. Conversely, there is a striking intertextual resonance between the novels studied in part III and the philosophical ideas of world explored in earlier chapters. For example, Rilke, whose poetry fascinated Heidegger and Arendt, provides much of the conceptual vocabulary and imagery of Amitav Ghosh's *The Hungry Tide*, thereby indicating the pertinence of the idea of worlding to ethicopolitical problems in the postcolonial world. Indeed, the impact of the history of colonialism on literary and intellectual production has made it impossible to clearly separate Europe from the postcolonial world and to say dogmatically that texts produced in different places do not share thematic and stylistic continuities and enter into debate with each other. Texts from different disciplinary discourses are part of world literature in the narrow sense.

My characterization of postcolonial literature as world literature will inevitably face objections. I experienced such resistance directly when I taught a graduate seminar on postcolonial world literature for the English Department of the University of California, Berkeley, in the spring of 2009 that was largely based on the plan of this book. We read many of the European philosophical and postcolonial literary texts I discuss later. The seminar had a healthy enrollment of students from various humanities departments. The comments in course evaluations by graduate students in English were worrying.[20] Although they all found the theoretical part of the class stimulating, they complained about the literature. One student wrote: "The novels themselves often seemed wanting." Another student, who planned to study nineteenth- to twentieth-century American poetry, commented: "The novels were less interesting as they mostly thematized issues about 'world.' I could think of many more interesting pieces of fiction / poetry to be read alongside this strong theoretical foundation. In the end, this class was successful at enabling me to think of aesthetics in a broader way." Another similar comment read: "Theoretical readings for the class were great. . . . The novels were a different matter. Some were not very good and one had the feeling that more interesting work could have been assigned." The harshest criticism was that "the literature chosen for the course was quite frequently terrible and insufficiently motivated under the rubric of the course to warrant overlooking that poor quality. There are many novels that would be applicable to the concept that are not pieces of worthless garbage from a strictly aesthetic viewpoint (this is not a subjective judgment but rather an objective evaluation that claims universality)."

These comments are disturbing because we read authors who are widely celebrated. V. S. Naipaul is a Nobel laureate, and Farah is rumored to be a perennial Nobel contender. Ghosh, Cliff, and Mo are regarded as strong examples of world literature. My students' comments are patently Eurocentric. They favor European philosophy and dismiss literature about the non-Western world by writers of non-Western origins. Their criticisms include the charge that seminar discussion had focused too much on thematic issues at the expense of literary form. "Theme" is implicitly associated with the crudeness and simplicity of postcolonial politics and "form" with universal aesthetic value. Here, the assertion of "objective" aesthetic judgment with universal validity is clearly an expression of the arrogance of what Gayatri Spivak has called the "sanctioned ignorance" of the culture of imperialism.

What precisely counts as "interesting" from a literary standpoint? In terms of thematic content, I would have thought that ethical and political issues arising from the impact of contemporary global capitalism on a large part of the world's population would be of interest in a seminar on contemporary world literature. But this would require readers to step outside their comfort zones of familiarity with canonical English literature and learn more about other parts of the world, especially from nonliterary discourses. Without this effort, we cannot grasp that these material conditions are part of the processes of worlding in which the novels are immersed and which they participate in and actively contest. Moreover, the sharp separation of aesthetic form from referential content is dogmatic and reductive. The formal features of these novels— for example, the kind of realism employed or the genre, rhetorical forms, and narrative style of a literary work—emerge in response to the social and political issues that are thematized. Indeed, their formal aspects often present solutions to their thematic concerns. Because the central problem of how to remake a world being destroyed by capitalist globalization refers us to the "literary" structure of worlding, literary form is precisely where the force and ground of worldly intervention is intimated.

Here some comments about my choice of novels are in order. The theory of world literature I propose suggests that the world is a normative temporal category and not the spatial whole made by globalization. Because world literature has the normative vocation of opening new worlds, its study cannot merely consist of historiographical or sociological analyses of how literary texts circulate globally and the effects of circulation at the level of form and style. This does not, however, mean that literature that thematizes or represents globalization is not world literature in the normative sense. To the contrary, I have chosen literary narratives concerned with the world-destroying consequences of various modalities of capitalist globalization in order to show that the opening of new worlds against the globalizing grain is something real that remains even in the most devastating scenarios such as the incapacitation of an aid-receiving people by humanitarianism or the destruction of subaltern worlds by world-heritage preservation and ecotourist capital. In the first place, a thematic portrayal or mapping of globalization is not merely a passive reaction that reflects and confirms the status quo. It can also be a form of critical resistance that brings the attention of the wider world to the plight of peoples impacted by global forces and their struggles to safeguard a future for their worlds.

More important, because the novels I study are interested in alternative temporalities, they traffic with the opening of worlds by the gift of time in their intense preoccupation with questions of narrativity and time. They thereby foreground the fact that the force of worlding is immanent to and subtends globalization. It would be utopian to claim that the opening of new worlds in postcoloniality can occur through a clean break from global processes. This is my critique of the theory of heterotemporality. Rather, the opening of new worlds takes place within processes of globalization because globalization involves the calculative management and appropriation of time. It follows that the temporal force of worlding is immanent to globalization and constitutes a real power that resists and undermines it, thereby opening different temporalities and worlds. To be "immanent" is to be part of the circuits of globalization, to subtend them as an irreducible part of their structure and to exceed them from within by drawing on what constitutes them as an effective resource for opening new worlds. There are no already-existing transcendent worlds from which to resist and counter capitalist globalization. But the sheer opening that is the coming of time is always already there.

There are at least three stages in the interplay between literary form and content that correspond to the relations between the two senses of worlding. I schematically outline some protocols for reading postcolonial world literature that enable us to track these stages. First, the novels undertake a cognitive mapping of the situation in question to render a fuller accounting of the issues at stake. For example, they map the calculations of different types of global capital and their unworlding of the world, the ruin and destruction they bring. The cases of unworlding the novels thematize include colonial slavery and its legacy, humanitarian imperialism, manufactured famine, the displacement of subaltern populations, and so on. As readers, we facilitate this mapping by learning more empirical knowledge about the settings of the novels.

Second, the novels employ formal means to revive non-Western temporalities in the present that can aid in worlding the world otherwise. Put another way, they generate alternative cartographies that enable a postcolonial people or a collective group to foster relations of solidarity and build a shared world in which self-determination is achieved. Literature's worldly force is here one of constructive interpretation or critical mimesis that deploys various forms of realism, allegory, and symbolism. It contests (neo)colonial and capitalist cartographies of the world with the normative aim of creating more progressive mappings. Postcolonial world literature is here a transformative representation of the world in the narrow sense.

These cognitive mappings often involve an active intertextual rewriting of canonical European literature. The most obvious case is Cliff's reinscription of motifs and characters from *The Tempest*, *Jane Eyre*, and *Great Expectations*. On the one hand, colonial education, insofar as canonical European literature had an important function in it, may have been the first widespread institutionalization of world literature outside Euro-America. Hence, world literature in the narrow sense of literature that circulates globally is historically complicit with the epistemic violence of imperialism. On the other hand, *The Hungry Tide* creatively transposes Rilke's *Duino Elegies* to understand the Sundarbans and reworld it for its subaltern inhabitants. In a similar vein, *Gifts* draws on Marcel Mauss's famous essay on the gift to explore how Somalian folk practices of giving and storytelling constitute a worldly ethics.

Third, in their different ways, the novels suggest that these heterotemporalities are only sustainable by negotiating with the incalculable gift of time as their abyssal ground. Because it subtends and disrupts the calculations of global capitalist accumulation, the gift of time is the persistent opening of other worlds. But at the same time, its sheer incalculability also undermines the sovereign intention at work in the novels in their staging of new teleological times. This incalculability is the sheer openness of worlding in the general sense. It breaks open the eschato-teleological frame of the world in the derived sense. The intimation of the gift of time is registered at the level of narrative form by types of self-reflective narrative where intense preoccupation with the novel's narrativity suspends the telos of narrative ending. Here, literature's worldly force is no longer mimetic or constructive but an enactment of worlding by the gift of time.

The force of world literature is fragile. But it nevertheless persists as a real immanent promise because without the openness of the world, nothing can take place. Because literature intimates this force of opening, it is difficult to specify what I have called world literature without the analysis of singular examples. The cases of postcolonial world literature discussed here are illustrative. The openness of world they enact is not cosmopolitanism as we commonly understand the word, the community of human beings that stretches across the globe. It is rather its ground. The world in a normative sense refers to the being-with of all peoples, groups, and individuals. It is the original openness that gives us accessibility to others so that we can be together. Global capitalism, however, incorporates peoples and populations into the world-system by tethering them to Western modernity's unrelenting march of progress and capitalist time and violently destroying other worlds and their temporalities. Attempts to characterize contemporary literature as cosmopolitan on the basis of the global character of literary production, circulation, and style only lead to a facile cosmopolitanism devoid of normative force. I am proposing a more rigorous way of understanding world literature's normativity as a modality of cosmopolitanism that responds to the need to remake the world as a place that is *open* to the emergence of peoples that globalization deprives of world.

the world of world literature in question

CHAPTER 1

The New World Literature

Literary Studies Discovers Globalization

The intensification of globalization in the past two decades has led to debates within literary studies about reinventing the discipline of comparative literature and the subfield of world literature in a manner that is ethically sensitive to the cultural differences and geopolitical complexities of the contemporary age. As illustrated by the volume published in response to the 1993 Bernheimer Report to the American Comparative Literature Association, *Comparative Literature in the Age of Multiculturalism* (1995), and its successor volume, *Comparative Literature in an Age of Globalization* (2006), and other discussions in their wake, the debate within comparative literature has focused on wrenching the comparative enterprise away from its Eurocentric home in the trans-Atlantic fraternity of English, German, and French national literatures.[1] It has been suggested that the history of colonialism and contemporary globalization has brought many different cultures into jarring proximity so that the comparative enterprise has become necessary and also more anxiety-ridden. For example, one must examine the global production of Western cultures and literatures, particularly from the perspectives of empire and postcoloniality, and include the literatures of formerly colonized regions written in European languages. The comparative enterprise should also take into account postcolonial literatures or orature in non-European vernacular languages in a study of transcolonialism. It has also been argued that contemporary globalization has created a genuinely transcultural zone that undermines the territorial borders of cultural and literary production, thereby leading to the emergence of a global consciousness.[2] Accordingly, the units of comparison can no longer be merely national. One must also consider how the local both enters into and is traversed by the global.

The comparative study of literature is generally distinguished from the study of world literature on the grounds that the former requires deep knowledge of various languages whereas world literature is merely literature in translation and is usually studied only in English.[3] Such a distinction, however, overlooks the close connections between the two forms of literary study. In the first place, world literature presupposes a prior comparative moment since the availability of something in translation requires a comparative judgment of the value of the original so that it can be translated. Second, comparative literature also presupposes translation in a very pragmatic sense. Since comparative studies of literature are written in one language, they generally involve the translation of quotations from the studied literatures into the language of the scholarly text so that the study is intelligible to a readership who may not possess all the languages the comparatist has. In this regard, comparative literary studies are also part of the enterprise of world literature, which in addition to translating foreign literatures, includes their study and criticism. But third and most important, the internal link between comparative literature and world literature is seen in the fact that comparative activity and the injunction to rethink comparative literature has become more urgent precisely because the multiplication of global connections integrates all of us into a shared world. Comparative activity makes no sense unless we are part of a common world. The world is therefore both the substrate and the end of comparison. Hence, an exploration of what constitutes a world should be prolegomenal to rethinking the agenda of both comparative and world literature.

What exactly is "the world" in recent attempts to rethink world literature in the North Atlantic academy? The primary way of asserting literature's worldliness today is to treat it as an object of circulation in a global market of print commodities or as the product of a global system of production either literally or by analogy. There is the obligatory nod to Goethe's historical lead in his use of the market analogy in his brief comments on *Weltliteratur*, but one mainly senses the shadow of Marx, particularly in the incorporation of the vocabulary of center and periphery from world-systems theory to describe literary phenomena.

When one compares the recent revival of world literature to earlier attempts to selectively appropriate and transform Goethe's idea of *Weltliteratur* in the post–World War II era, such as Erich Auerbach's exemplary essay "Philology and *Weltliteratur*" (1952), what is especially striking is the hollowing out of the humanist ethos that had been world literature's traditional heart and core.[4] Auerbach emphasized that *Weltliteratur* was governed by two principles. First, it presupposed the idea of humanity as its rational kernel. Humanity, however, was not something naturally given but a telos to be achieved through intercourse across the existential plurality and diversity of human traditions and cultures whose individuality must be maintained and whose unique historical development must be respected. "*Weltliteratur* does not merely refer to what is generically common and human; rather it considers humanity to be the product of the cross-fertilization of the manifold [als wechselseitige Befruchtung des Mannigfaltigen]. The presupposition of *Weltliteratur* is a *felix culpa*: mankind's division into many cultures."[5] World literary intercourse enables the fabrication of humanity because the philological study of the unique development of specific linguistic traditions as manifested in the world's different literary cultures can help us compose a universal history of the human spirit that underlies these literatures.

Second, *Weltliteratur* has an irreducible temporal dimension. According to Auerbach, Goethe related *Weltliteratur* to "the past and to the future," to world history. The humanism of *Weltliteratur* is "historicist," Auerbach stressed. Its concern "was not only the overt discovery of materials and the development of methods of research, but beyond that their penetration and evaluation so that an inner history of mankind—which thereby created a conception of man unified in his multiplicity [in ihrer Vielfalt einheitlichen Vorstellung vom Menschen]—could be written."[6] The universal history of the human spirit facilitates the making of humanity by serving as a specular structure, a mirror in which all human individuals can recognize, become conscious of, and contemplate their humanity and its potential because it gives them a spectacular vision of the achievements of the human species organized into a narrative of universal progress. Hence,

> within worldly actuality [Weltwirklichkeit], history affects us most immediately, stirs us most deeply and compels us most forcibly to a consciousness of ourselves. It is the only object in which human beings can step before us in their wholeness. Under the object of history one is to understand not only the past, but the progression of events in general; history therefore includes the present. The inner history of the last thousand years is the history of mankind achieving self-expression: this is what philology, a historicist discipline, treats. This history contains the records of man's mighty, adventurous advance to a consciousness of his human condition and to the actualization of his given potential [Möglichkeiten]; and this advance, whose final goal . . . was barely imaginable for a long time, still

seems to have proceeded as if according to a plan, in spite of its twisted course. All the rich tensions of which our being is capable are contained within this course. A drama [Schauspiel] unfolds whose scope and depth sets in motion all the spectator's powers [Kräfte], enabling him at the same time to find peace in his given potential by the enrichment he gains from having witnessed the drama.[7]

In Auerbach's view, the temporal dimension of *world* literature and its connection to world history gives it a normative force. To use an Aristotelian but also a Kantian word, this force is a type of *causality*, a form of action that actualizes or brings something into actuality. This causality is not efficient in character. The history in question is "an inner history," and it stimulates and forms consciousness and the spiritual dimension of human existence. It compels us to see our humanity, and what it shows us moves us to action because it allows us to see that we can actualize our potentialities. This normative force is the vocation of world literature. Only the study of literary traditions governed by it deserves to be called *Weltliteratur*.

If we compare Auerbach's account of world literature to the more prominent theories of world literature today, the causality of literature that is at stake in the contemporary reinvention of world literature is necessarily a much weaker force. In these new theories, the world has been almost completely emptied of its normative vocation. World literature has lost its temporal dimension by being sundered from what is regarded as an effete idealist humanist philosophy of world history. As I will show, the defining characteristic of the world in recent accounts of world literature is spatial extension. It refers to the extensive scope and scale of the production, circulation, consumption, and evaluation of literature. Simply put, "world" is extension on a global scale, where world literature is conceived through an analogy with a world market's global reach. What is worldly about literature is its locomotion or movement in Mercatorian space according to the mathematical coordinates of Euclidean geometry. Where literary history is broached, time is viewed in similarly spatial terms. Accordingly, as a form of intercourse, world literature is now restricted to a purely spatial dimension. It is the exchange or circulation of an object between subjects, the object's movement across flat spatial distance in time conceived spatially. It no longer opens up the temporal horizon that Auerbach calls "the inner history of mankind."

Consequently, the normative content remaining in the concept of the world is minimal. It consists of the erosion of the limitations imposed by national boundaries on the production, circulation, reception, and evaluation of literature as a result of globalization. Auerbach had also written of the "decaying" of "the inner bases of national existence," but he regarded globalization as a process of leveling and standardization that destroyed diversity and individuality.[8] In a vicious irony, globalization would bring about the unity required for a world literature even as it eradicated the plurality equally requisite to a world literature: "Man will have to accustom himself to existence in a uniformly organized earth, to a single literary culture, in an equally short time, to only a few literary languages, and perhaps even a single literary language. And herewith the thought of *Weltliteratur* would be at once actualized [verwirklicht] and destroyed."[9] In contradistinction, recent theorists of world literature are more sanguine that the globalization of literary production and consumption has led to the proliferation of differences and struggles against homogenization.[10]

One can speculate that the ascendance of a spatial conception of the world in literary studies is part of a broader attempt to reckon with the implications of globalization for the study of literature. These new theories of world literature arise in a time of the delegitimation of the humanities in universities and public consciousness in the North Atlantic, and this necessarily creates pressure on literary studies to justify the value of literature as an object of study, especially its efficaciousness in the production of value, material or spiritual.[11] While the work of a corporate lawyer, accountant, or software engineer has practical utility and economic value because it is directly part of the process of economic production, literary criticism's role in the production process is unclear, other than the part it may play in the generation of cultural capital and, more indirectly, in social reproduction and the augmentation of human capital. Exploring how a global approach can transform the parameters and the very object of literary studies (for example, the style and formal features of literary works) as well as the bearing of globalization on the normative consequences of literary studies (for example, exposing the ethical limitations of national literary traditions) may be a fruitful way of bringing out literature's place in and causal relation to our contemporary global existence and, which is not quite the same thing, the worldly aspect of literature. The causality of literature is also at stake here, but in a very different way from what Auerbach had in mind. For theorists of the new world literature, it is a matter of how literature operates as a real object of exchange and circulation in the world and constitutes a world of its own that transcends national boundaries and operates with its own specific laws and logic.

However, instead of affirming the causal power of literature, the analogy between world literature and the circulation of commodities in a global market unwittingly has the opposite effect of diminishing literature's worldly force and, therefore, its causality in relation to the world globalization creates. For what can the logical consequence of such an analogy be other than to make world literature a transmitter of global social forces? To think of the dynamics of world literature in terms of those of a global market is precisely to think of world literature as mimicking these global forces, of being a displaced and delayed communication of socioeconomic forces at work in the real world. In the final analysis, literature's worldliness would derive from its being a passive reflection of the forces at work in a global market in the specificity of its own sphere.

Literature's Worldliness: The Allure of the Market Metaphor and the Force of Globalization

Let us examine more closely the consequences of viewing world literature by analogy with market exchange. The primary allure of the market metaphor for understanding literature's worldliness is the promise of negative freedom: the liberation from a national framework's stifling strictures on appreciating and studying literature and the reductive aesthetic and evaluative criteria imposed by ossified national literary traditions on writers and the public criticism of literature. Just as contemporary global markets and the liberalization of trade and financial flows have brought about the erosion of national-state regulated economies and the thorough privatization of the means of production and the revolution in technology and communications has undermined state control over information and knowledge, thereby leading to genuinely global economic interdependence, as opposed to the independent sovereignty of national-state economies, so too the globalization of literary exchange and production is said to lead to the emergence of world literature, a form of literature that has rendered merely national literature obsolete and illusory.[12] The "world" is thus an adjective attached to the noun "literature" to qualify it. "World literature" is contrasted with merely national literature. The main consequence of this approach is that it takes the world for granted. It conflates the world with the globe and reduces the world to a spatial object produced by the material processes of globalization.

For example, in David Damrosch's pragmatic definition of world literature as "all literary works that circulate beyond their culture of origin, either in translation or in their original language," the world is regarded as a spatio-geographical category, a container within which literature has to circulate, the terrain in which it has to make its way, if it is to be worldly.[13] In Damrosch's view, "a work enters *into* world literature by a double process: first, by being read as literature; second by circulating out *into* a broader world beyond its linguistic and cultural point of origin."[14] The two prepositions I have emphasized are especially significant because they indicate literature's passage into a larger horizon, namely, a world. A literary work is therefore seen as being like a traveler, even a protagonist of a bildungsroman. It enters into a horizon wider than its immediate home. It evolves and grows as it makes its way across the world just as the protagonist gains enlightenment in a developmental process of maturation. Through an implied analogy between literary semiosis and capitalization, Damrosch regards circulation as a process in the augmentation of a literary object's value. Because literary language is not merely denotative, a literary work gains in depth and meaning through circulation, especially when it involves translation and undergoes a process of transculturation. A literary work's passage into a wider space is simultaneously a changing of its form. By being transported into another horizon, a larger sphere of being, the work of literature itself is transfigured. It is lifted up and attains a higher, more complex form. Hence, the circulated work does not only enter into the larger space of world literature. It *becomes* world literature. As Damrosch puts it, "literature stays within its national or regional tradition when it usually loses in translation, whereas works become world literature when they gain on balance in translation, stylistic losses offset by an expansion in depth as they increase their range."[15] "In its most expansive sense, world literature could include any work that has ever reached beyond its home base: . . . a work only has an effective life as world literature whenever, and wherever, it is actively present within a literary system beyond that of its original culture."[16]

It is important to note that for Damrosch, unlike the sociological approaches to world literature I will discuss later, the main agency for this potentially infinite capitalization of or exponential increase in literary meaning is the act of reading. A literary work's circulation beyond its national origin transports it to different locations and to different readers. It changes the framing conditions and cultural contexts of a work's reception and interpretation. In their encounter and interplay with a foreign work, these new readers can revitalize the work. Because they see it in a different imaginative light, they can elicit new meanings from it.[17] The fact that circulation is the fundamental material condition that enables the hypertrophy of literary meaning clearly attests to Damrosch's identification of worldliness with global circulation. The conflation of worldliness with globalization is also succinctly expressed in his claim that "the dramatic acceleration of globalization since [the era of Goethe, Marx, and Engels] has greatly complicated the idea of a world literature."[18] Franco Moretti is of the same persuasion. In his view, "the world literary system," his name for the formation of world literature that comes into being from the eighteenth century onward, "is the product of a unified market."[19]

There is a similar conflation of globalization and worldliness in an essay by John Pizer on world literature published at the beginning of the twenty-first century in *Comparative Literature*, the official journal of the American Comparative Literature Association.

> Literature is becoming *immanently* global, that is, . . . individual works are increasingly formed and constituted by social, political, and even linguistic trends that are not limited to a single nation or region. Thus, it has become increasingly difficult to regard contemporary texts as simply the products of, for example, German, Nigerian, or Chinese writers, or even of European, African, and Asian authors. With the globalization of the world economy, a true world literature, which is to say a *global* literature, is being created.[20]

> At the outset of the new millennium, such a reinvention must subtend the immanent character of world literature, the circumstance that cultural globalization is informing the structure, content, and even language of individual works themselves. This is largely due to the increasingly globalized character of literary marketplaces and to the capacity for instantaneous worldwide exchanges.

Here, too, we see a patent conflation of the globe, a bounded object in Mercatorian space, with the world, a form of belonging or community. This understanding of worldliness in terms of the material processes of globalization leads to a deficient understanding of the normativity of world literature in two respects. On the one hand, because the relation between world literature and global culture is not elaborated, the vulnerability of world literature to the techniques of the global culture industry remains unacknowledged. Insofar as the emergence of world literature is bound to a globalized print culture industry, it is vulnerable to the negative cultural consequences of what David Harvey calls space-time compression—the manipulative constitution of taste, desire, and opinion by the global commodity circuits of image production.[21] Since postindustrial techniques of marketing, advertising, and value-adjudication form a seamless web in the production, reception, interpretation, and criticism (academic or otherwise) of any given work of world literature, these techniques necessarily shape that work's form and ideational content and the kind of world it enables us to imagine. On the other hand, collapsing the world into a vast geographical entity is tacitly premised on the reduction of literature to an epiphenomenon of a material base. It is assumed that literature mirrors political-economic forces and relations in a straightforward manner: a globalized economy gives rise to a global culture and a literary transnationalism or world literature. World literature in this sense cannot be autonomous since it reflects and is conditioned by the global character of political economy.

Despite the new openings created by locomotion beyond national and regional borders, what is closed off is precisely the opening of a normative horizon that transcends present reality, such as the connection to world history Auerbach regarded as world literature's defining feature. This normative deficit becomes even more pronounced in Pascale Casanova's and Franco Moretti's sociological accounts of world literature, which are influenced by theories of social force derived, respectively, from Pierre Bourdieu and Karl Marx. Casanova and Moretti seek to explain how literature functions as a social force. However, the lack of a normative dimension in their conceptualization of world literature has problematic consequences.

In *The World Republic of Letters* and subsequent work, Casanova emphasizes that her object of study is not a collection of literary works called world literature but a transnational web of relations that exceeds nation-state boundaries. Texts are produced by authors as part of this dynamic global landscape and have literary value attributed to them according to a complex set of discursive rules.[22] Hence, it is not a matter of "analyzing literature on a world scale" but of clarifying "the conceptual means for thinking literature *as* a world."[23] To elucidate the worldliness specific to literature, Casanova borrows the commercial metaphors Goethe employed to describe *Weltliteratur*. The usefulness of these metaphors, she observes, lies in their emphasis on the market as a terrain of competitive strife. They show us that the global circuit of symbolic production where the recognition of literary value and the attribution of aesthetic-cultural capital take place is thoroughly permeated by power relations. Just as the existing system of global political economy is characterized by an uneven distribution of capital and power between core and peripheries, the transnational economy of literary value is also characterized by an unequal and hierarchical distribution of literary capital and the power to adjudicate on the standards of literary value. Hence, the production of literature involves *struggles* for recognition and over literary standards by individual writers, readers, researchers, critics, publishers, and so on.

The specificity of literature's worldly dimension means that the world republic of letters is an autonomous sphere. But its autonomy is of a peculiar kind. Because transnational literary relations are relations of power and domination, their autonomy is clearly not that of an enchanted and peaceful world of pure aesthetic creation, the conventional caricature of Kant's account of the disinterested character of aesthetic judgment. Their history "is one of incessant struggle and competition over the very nature of literature itself—an endless succession of literary manifestos, movements, assaults and revolutions."[24] However, literary power relations, Casanova insists, also do not have an immediate link to political rivalries or national cultural prejudices. Transnational literary space is autonomous in the sense that it is not a mere superstructure of geopolitics. Accordingly, Casanova also distinguishes the agonistic space of literature as a world from the homogenizing processes of cultural globalization. "The internationalization that I propose to describe here therefore signifies more or less the opposite of what is ordinarily understood by the neutralizing term 'globalization,' which suggests that the world political and economic system can be conceived as the generalization of a single and universally applicable model. In the literary world, by contrast, it is the competition among its members that defines and unifies the system while at the same time marking its limits."[25]

Yet, notwithstanding Casanova's emphasis on the complex autonomy and the agonistic character of transnational literary space, its worldly force is severely limited by the governing concept of relative autonomy. Transnational literary space is "another world . . . with its own laws, its own history, its specific revolts and revolutions; a market where non-market values are traded, within a non-economic economy; and measured . . . by an aesthetic scale of time."[26] Its struggles obey an autonomous literary logic, which is registered in changes to literary form and cannot be reduced to an ideological reflection of economic or political power.[27] In Casanova's view, the central shortcoming of postcolonial theory is that it does not elucidate literature's proper worldliness. It seeks to overcome the postulate of literature's autonomy by reductively linking literature to the real world. This reduces transnational literary struggles to real-world political struggles and sacrifices literature's specificity. "Post-colonialism posits a direct link between literature and history, one that is exclusively political. From this, it moves to an external criticism that runs the risk of reducing the literary to the political, imposing a series of annexations or short-circuits, and often passing in silence over the actual aesthetic, formal or stylistic characteristics that actually 'make' literature."[28]

It is important to emphasize that the autonomy of transnational literary space is merely relative. When Casanova discusses the production of post-colonial literature, she also refers international forms of literary dependency back to the structures of international political domination. In her words, "because the newest nations are also the ones that are the most vulnerable to political and economic domination, and because literary space is dependent to one degree or another on political structures, international forms of literary dependency are to some extent correlated with the structures of international political domination."[29] For Casanova, postcolonial theory's error is that it posits a link between literature and the real world that is *too* immediate and direct.

The concept of relative autonomy leads to a twofold inefficacy of literature as a force. On the one hand, the relative autonomy from political and economic forces of the world republic of letters means that it is only a weak force with a highly circumscribed role in the making of the world. It is so weak that it falls into a position of abject vulnerability in relation to the commercial type of world literature generated by the global culture industry. In Casanova's view, "a world literature does indeed exist today, new in its form and its effects, that circulates easily and rapidly through virtually simultaneous translations and whose extraordinary success is due to the fact that its denationalized content can be absorbed without any risk of misunderstanding. But under these cir-cumstances a genuine literary transnationalism is no longer possible, having been swept away by the tides of international business."[30] Hence, despite her rejection of literature as a realm of pure art, she ironically ends up nostalgi-cally yearning for a literary transnationalism that remains uncontaminated by market forces, a pristine space remarkably similar to that of pure art.

On the other hand, because transnational literary space is to a degree de-pendent on political and economic structures and its relations are referred back to geopolitical rivalries in the last instance, its dynamics derive from and repeat in a refracted form the dynamics of real political struggles.[31] Trans-national literary space is therefore a secondary manifestation of more funda-mental forces, which are the site of a struggle that is more real. Its agonistic rela-tions are merely a quasi-Bloomian struggle over literary standards, recognition, and influence, where the positions of father and ephebe are occupied by writers from the world republic of letters' center and peripheries. What cannot be en-tertained within this conceptual framework is an agonistic relation between an ethicopolitically committed world literature and one produced by the commercial market, where both compete as alternative attempts in the ongoing making of the real world.

The examples of recent theories of world literature I have discussed use market exchange as a paradigm for understanding the worldliness of literature. The market is, however, merely a metaphor for the circulation and production of literature. Franco Moretti's contribution to this debate is striking because he literalizes the market metaphor. In contrast to Casanova's focus on the psychical agonistics of influence and recognition between central and peripheral writers, he examines how market forces, such as printing presses, readers as paying consumers, libraries, channels of circulation, and so on, create the concrete material conditions of literary production. Literary intercourse and production are not merely analogous to market processes. They require market forces in order to take place. By the same token, the generation of literary meaning and cultural value is not only similar to the processes of commodification and capitalization. Literary works are literally made as goods for exchange in a mass market for pecuniary profits. Accordingly, whereas Casanova remained fixated on literature as high art, Moretti extends world literature's scope to include middle- and low-brow books. He also pays greater attention to form, which he understands through an analogy with the biological forms or morphological arrangements studied by evolutionary science. One would logically expect world literature to possess a greater force in this view. But Moretti's account diminishes its force even further because by literalizing the market metaphor, he reduces the force of literature to a refraction of social forces.

Moretti's account of literature's worldly force is deeply entrenched in a Marxist base-superstructure model. The model's influence is condensed in his provocative claim (via an aphorism from biological science) that "form is a diagram of forces" and "perhaps, even, as nothing but force."[32] This is, in his view, "a materialist conception of form. . . . Form as the most profoundly social aspect of literature: form as force."[33] The form of literature refers primarily to genre. Moretti is interested in the popularity of certain genres, the historical fact of their survival, and therefore their victory or hegemony over other genres in competitive market relations. The measure of the force of a literary genre is not aesthetic value but the quantity of books published. Such an approach to world literature, understood as the study of the spread of literary genres throughout the world, has the benefit, Moretti suggests, of constructing a more nuanced, empirically based picture of the complex flows of influence and adaptation that is attentive to the specific details of geographical location. It enables us to see that world literature is an unequal and uneven world-system of cultural dependency where literary influence flows from western European core cultures to peripheral cultures, but in a variegated manner such that the development of literary forms elsewhere does not follow that of a prototypical or modular western European path of development.[34]

In Moretti's view, the survival of literary form can be explained through an account of form as an "abstract of social relationships."[35] Literary forms are a schematic distillation or structural reduction of social forces, which they express and represent in a symbolic medium. This, then, is a social psychology of the reader as a consumer of texts. The success of these forms in their circulation as commodities in the print market of publishers and readers, sellers and consumers, is measured in terms of the loyalty, size, and reach of a reading public. A form's success hinges on its fit with or adequacy to the specific problems raised by social relationships in a market area in a given period. Here we need to distinguish between three different levels of sociality. Literary forms are symbolic representations of social relations. But as commodities, they belong to the social intercourse of print market relations. Finally, these markets are embedded in a larger set of social relations with their specific problems. The survival of a literary form depends on the congruence between these different levels of sociality. Moretti calls this congruence "artistic usefulness," a term borrowed from Viktor Shklovsky. It designates literature's functionality or utility for social subjects who take pleasure in a work because its forms and devices resolve at an imaginary level a fundamental contradiction structural to the social dynamics that organize their existence.[36] In Moretti's words, "literary genres are problem-solving devices, which address a contradiction of their environment, offering an imaginary resolution by means of their formal organization. The pleasure provided by that formal organization is therefore more than just pleasure—it is the vehicle through which a larger symbolic statement is shaped and assimilated. . . . The structure provided [by the devices] . . . makes [readers] feel that the world is fully understandable."[37]

But this means that literature's force—a literary form's capacity to survive, its conatus, if you will—is entirely derivative. Literary form has no force of its own. As a symbolic expression of social relations, it is merely a relay of social forces, a medium for refracting them. Moreover, a representation's effectiveness in arousing pleasure depends on its fit with the social context of the reading public. Hence, the primary ground of literature's force is the play of social forces at work in the constitution of readers or, more precisely, the contradictions of their social environment and the existential problems they generate. Literary form is merely a tool or instrument for expressing social relations, which are its deeper kernel or inner truth. These relations explain why a form survives, and the survival of a form in turn confirms the primacy of social forces. Moretti's emphasis on literature's symbolic function is significant here. The natural motivation between the symbol and what it represents supports the view that literary forms are mere tools for the imaginary resolution of social contradictions.

What then of the agency of the reader's imagination or interpretive powers? It turns out that the reader is no better off than literary form. Both the literary text and the reader are simply dummies through which social forces are ventriloquized. Since the reader's pleasure in literature is that of a consumer, it is merely a social pleasure and desire. Because readers-consumers are merely ciphers for the transmission of social forces, their desire is reactive in the Nietzschean sense.[38]

Hence, although Moretti posits a direct causal link between literature and the world of social forces, as in Casanova's account, world literature also has no transformative agency in the world. A work of world literature merely acts by reflecting and refracting the stronger primary social forces operative within it and to which its form corresponds via a natural symbolic relation. This is why in his polemical disagreement with Damrosch, Moretti favors distant reading and explanation over close reading and interpretation. The former approach is governed by the premise of the derivative character of literary representations and explores how their reception and consumption is determined by social forces. In contradistinction, the latter approach requires attention to literature's force of signification, how it moves readers in singular experiences of reading that point to the opening of other worlds.

Perhaps all sociological accounts of world literature necessarily attenuate the worldly force of literature by reducing its worldliness to social forces as exemplified by market processes. Where a sociological approach is combined with the Marxist position that social forces and their economic basis constitute the most fundamental infrastructure of human existence, the reactive character of literature becomes even more pronounced. In this regard, it is important to note that critical Marxist geographers influenced by Henri Lefebvre's understanding of representational space (space lived through images and symbols) have suggested that literary forms have a more active causal power in the world than Moretti allows because of the role of images and the imagination in social intercourse, not only in maintaining and facilitating existing modes of sociality, but in instituting emergent forms of social experience through revolution.[39] Indeed, as I will show when I turn to the materialist account of the world in chapter 3, Marx did not identify the world as such with the world market. He pointed instead to a higher, nonalienated sociality beyond the commodity relations of bourgeois civil society, namely, a world different from the capitalist world of space-time compression.

We can say in summary that recent accounts of world literature have failed to attend to two related issues: first, the question "What is a world?" or, more precisely, whether the world is a normative or merely descriptive category, and second, literature's causality in relation to the world. Indeed, these accounts show the most stubborn resistance to thinking through these problems. Moretti explicitly dismisses normative approaches to world literature on the grounds that they "are more concerned with value judgments than with actual knowledge."[40] Yet world literature can only be a very weak causal force in the world unless its normative dimension is broached. As I have shown, its causality is variously the force of circulation that moves literature around the world, thereby generating new meanings (Damrosch), the struggles over criteria that govern the production and recognition of literary value as cultural capital (Casanova), or the social forces that determine a given genre's ability to elicit pleasure from and attract a reading public, that is, the power of a symbolic form over a reader-consumer's imagination (Moretti).

The neat conflation of the world with market processes of global extensiveness (the globe made by economic globalization) conveniently hides the need to address these issues because it makes the meaning of "world" self-evident. But does the market create a world and, if so, how exactly? If we assume that the freeing of trade beyond national borders creates a sense of membership in a world, then is the world merely a form of intercourse or sociality that exceeds the boundaries of the territorial state? Or does "world" have a normative meaning? Is market exchange the sole paradigm and privileged model of worldliness or is it only a specific type of worldliness? In what way is literature, whether we understand it as a mode of communication or a process of signification, related to the opening and making of a world?

These questions are crucial to any rethinking of world literature because unless they are broached, world literature is only *of* the world in a limited sense. It is affected by worldly forces but it cannot be a force in the ongoing cartography and creation of the world that negotiates with and contests the world brought into being by commercial intercourse, monetary transactions, and flows of global mass culture. A return to Goethe's thoughts on *Weltliteratur* is indeed timely because he addresses many of the questions that are foreclosed in the contemporary revival of the idea.

Goethe Revisited: The Normative Dimension of World Literature

For Goethe, the vocation of world literature consists in its ability to forge spiritual connections, so much so that we can understand world literature as a constitutive modality of cosmopolitanism. Goethe conceived of world literature as a dynamic process of literary exchange, intercourse, or traffic, as exemplified by the international character of his own relations with foreign authors and intellectuals and the beneficial revitalizing movement of mirroring (*Spiegelung*) brought about by the reception, translation, review, and criticism of literary works in other languages.[41] "There is being formed a universal world literature, in which an honorable role is reserved for us Germans. All the nations review our work; they praise, censure, accept, and reject, imitate and distort us, understand or misunderstand us, open or close their hearts to us. All this we must accept with equanimity, since this attitude, taken as a whole, is of great value [Werth] to us."[42] World literature is an active space of transaction and interrelation. What is important is the dynamic character of world literature and not the content of the ideas that are exchanged. What is of greatest worth is the ethos generated by the transaction. The world is only to be found and arises in these intervals or mediating processes. The world is constituted by and, indeed, is nothing but exchange and transaction.

The ethical end of this intercourse is not to produce uniformity between nations but mutual understanding and tolerance of each other by revealing the universal humanity across particular differences even as such differences are valued. "The idea is not that nations shall think alike, but that they shall learn how to understand each other [sondern sie sollen nur einander gewahr werden, sich begreifen], and, if they do not care to love one another, at least that they will learn to tolerate one another."[43] World literature is an ongoing work of negotiation among a range of particulars in order to arrive at the universal. The particular is not obliterated by subsumption under an a priori universal but is integrated as a member of a universal spiritual whole through gradual coordination. This negotiation is properly worldly because it creates the world.

Indeed, we can speak of the world itself as intercourse in which there is appreciation and tolerance of the particular. Goethe brings out the mediational character of world literature, the fact that the particular literary forms of different nations are bearers of universal human values, by comparing the reading of foreign literatures to translation between languages and the exchange of currency:

> It is obvious that the efforts of the best poets and aesthetic writers of all nations have now for some time been directed towards the universally human. In each particular field, whether in history, mythology, or fiction, . . . one sees that universal always more clearly reveal and illuminated through nationality and personality [wird man durch Nationalität und Persönlichkeit hindurch jenes Allgemeine immer murch durchleuchten und durchschimmern sehn].
>
> Though something of the same sort prevails now also in the practical course of life [Lebensgange], pervading all that is earthly, crude, wild, cruel, false, selfish, and treacherous, and striving to diffuse everywhere some gentleness, we cannot indeed hope that universal peace is being ushered in thereby, but only that inevitable strife will be gradually more restrained, war will become less cruel, and victory less insolent.
>
> Whatever in the poetry of any nation tends to this and contributes to it, the others should endeavor to appropriate. The particularities [Besonderheiten] of each nation must be learned, and allowance made for them, in order by these very means to hold intercourse with it; for the special characteristics [Eigenheiten] of a nation are like its language and its currency: they facilitate intercourse, nay they first make it completely possible.[44]

Like languages and currency forms, the particularities of national literatures must be respected because the respect for differences is the first step in literary intercourse, the function of which is to bring out the universal kernel. The work of translation best exemplifies the greater tolerance of the particularities of different peoples because translation does not remove but attempts to bridge differences. "A genuine universal tolerance is most surely attained, if we do not quarrel with the particular characteristics of individual men and peoples, but only hold fast to the conviction, that what is truly excellent is distinguished by its belonging to the whole of humanity. To such exchange [Vermittlung] and mutual recognition, the German people have long contributed."[45] As a means to further intercourse and mediation between peoples, the activity of translation enacts a certain dynamic universality that Goethe elucidates through metaphors of mercantile and evangelical activity.

Whoever understands and studies German finds himself in a market where all nations offer their wares; he plays the interpreter, while he enriches himself.

And thus every translator is to be regarded as a middleman [Vermittler] in this universal spiritual commerce [allgemein geistigen Handels], and as making it his business to promote/further this exchange [Wechseltausch]: for say what we may of the insufficiency of translation, yet the work is and will always be one of the weightiest and worthiest matters in the general concerns of the world.

The Koran says: "God has given to each people a prophet in its own tongue!" Thus each translator is a prophet to his people. Luther's translation of the Bible has produced the greatest results, though criticism gives it qualified praise, and picks faults in it, even to the present day. What indeed is the whole enormous business of the Bible Society, but the evangelization to all *people* in their own tongue?

Because the German language has historically functioned as a medium for the translation of other (presumably European) national literatures, Goethe likens German to a world market for the exchange of literary commodities. The translator is like a merchant who is able to profit and benefit from the fact that his activity gives others access to something. Although he neither produces nor owns the original object but only acts as a comprador who brings that object to another, this work of mediation is nevertheless inherently creative because without it, the universal human values expressed in the original would never have been shared by different peoples. Indeed, a translation can be said to possess greater universality than the original because translation universalizes the original by exposing it to a wider gaze. This is why translation is crucial to "universal spiritual commerce." In his second analogy, Goethe further likens the merchant-translator to a holy prophet who mediates between the divine and the mundane and spreads the word of God to his people through vernacularization. Like Luther, the translator conveys and makes visible to the masses what is eternally human in foreign literatures.

The analogy with the transmission of the sacred word clearly indicates that world literature has a normative dimension that cannot be reduced to the greater facility of global communications. "Increasing communication between nations" and "the increasing speed of intercourse" are undoubtedly means for bringing about world literature.[46] But world literature is a special form of mediation with the higher end of explicating humanity. Indeed, Goethe's sacralization of world literature suggests that the world transcends mere geography. In another text, he distinguishes between two different senses of "world": the world as an object of great physical-spatial extensiveness such as the expansion of the mundane or the diffusion of what is pleasing to the crowd (*Menge*), and the world as a normative phenomenon, a higher intellectual community that opens up a new universal horizon.

> The wide world, extensive as it is, is only an expanded fatherland, and will, if looked at correctly, be able to give us no more than what our home soil can endow us with also. What pleases the crowd spreads itself over a limitless field, and, as we already see, meets approval in all countries and regions. The serious and the intellectual meet with less success, but those who are devoted to higher and more productive things will learn to know each other more quickly and more intimately. For there are everywhere in the world such men, to whom the true progress of humanity are of interest and concern.[47]

Despite its extensiveness, the physical world remains as spiritually limited and particularistic as the nation. In contradistinction, the higher world of cultivated intellectuals who point to the spiritual unity of humanity has a temporal-historical dimension. This higher world will transcend the limitations of the spatio-temporal present and increase in power over time. But in the present, it can only maintain itself and coexist with the everyday world with difficulty. Its members are a vanguard so ahead of the times that they must hide from the light of day and withdraw from phenomenality. Yet this almost invisible community possesses a vital power with an enduring effectivity. It will unfold into full presence with human progress, which it will aid in stimulating.

> The serious-minded must therefore form a quiet, almost secret Church [eine stille, fast gedrückte Kirche bilden], since it would be futile to set themselves against the current of the day; rather must they manfully strive to maintain their position till the flood has passed. Their principal consolation, and indeed encouragement, such men must find in the fact that truth is useful. If they can discover this connection, and exhibit its meaning and influence in a vital way, they will not fail to produce a powerful effect [den Einfluß lebendig vorzeigen und aufweisen können, so wird es ihnen nicht fehlen kräftig einzuwirken], indeed one that will extend over a range of years.[48]

Today, Goethe's distinction between two different senses of the world is significant because it cautions us not to obscure the normative dimension of worldhood by conflating worldliness with globalization. The world in the higher sense is spiritual intercourse, transaction, and exchange aimed at bringing out universal humanity. It does not abolish national differences but takes place and is to be found in the intervals, mediations, passages, and crossings between national borders and boundaries. The world is thus a form of relating, belonging, or being-with. In contradistinction, the globe—the thing produced by processes of globalization—is a bounded object or entity in Mercatorian space. We commonly say "map of the world" when we really mean "map of the globe." It is assumed that the spatial diffusion and extensiveness achieved through global media and markets give rise to a sense of belonging to a shared world, when one might argue that such developments lead instead to greater polarization and division of nations and regions. The globe is not a world. This is a necessary premise if the cosmopolitan vocation of world literature can be meaningful today.

Following Goethe, I suggest that we should conceive of the world not only as a spatio-geographical entity but also as an ongoing dynamic process of becoming, something that possesses a historical-temporal dimension and hence is continually being made and remade. Several voices in contemporary philosophy and critical theory have also insisted on a related distinction between the world and the globe. In his work on global democracy, Habermas distinguished between economic globalization, which is driven by particularistic system-imperatives, and deliberative democratic procedures based on a world community of shared risks that can regulate the former.[49] In a different vein, the final Derrida distinguished *mondialisation*, the becoming-world of the world, from globalization by pointing to the former's deterritorializing, expropriating, and universalizing exigency. He coined the word *altermondialisation* to describe a worldwide-ization that is other to hegemonic globalization.[50] Goethe's spiritualist model of world literature makes a similar distinction. We should thus understand world literature as literature that is *of* the world, something that can play a fundamental role and be a force in the ongoing cartography and creation of the world instead of a body of timeless aesthetic objects.

At the same time, it is clearly no longer possible to uncritically resurrect the visions of humanity and world history that inspired Goethe and gave Auerbach solace and hope. This is especially the case from the perspective of literature from the postcolonial peripheries, where addressing the history of colonial oppression and economic exploitation in contemporary globalization makes it important to ask: "What kind of world does world literature let us imagine?" This will be the topic of the third part of this book. I merely note here that Goethe's vision of world literature needs to be heavily qualified because his view of the world is patently Eurocentric. The normative dimension of world poetry is epitomized by classical Greece. Literatures from places and from periods other than Greek antiquity have a merely historical and therefore particular status, whereas the archetypal beauty of humanity as an eternal presence is embodied in Greek archetypes. "We should not think that the truth is in Chinese or Serbian literature, in Calderon or the *Nibelungen*. Instead, in our need/search for models, we should always return to the Greeks of antiquity in whose works beautiful man is exhibited [dargestellt]. The rest we contemplate historically and appropriate from it what is good as far as we can."[51] Within this hierarchical framework, the tolerance of differences between peoples can only be repressive.

But more important, in the absence of a critique of capitalism, Goethe is blind to the imbrication of literary processes of world formation in power relations. Indeed, he uses commercial activity as a metaphor for understanding world literary intercourse without underscoring the self-interested, exploitative character of commercial mediation, even as he repeatedly notes that the translator profits as a middleman. It is, however, clear that world literature always involves relations of power and inequality: Goethe figures literary worth as power or force (*Kraft*) and thinks of it in analogy with the military strength of a cohesive nation. "As the military and physical power of a nation develops from its internal unity and cohesion, so must its ethical-aesthetic power grow gradually from a similar unanimity."[52] Hence, some nations (Germany, for example) will benefit more from world literary relations because they have accumulated more literary worth.

Perhaps it is Goethe's celebratory view of commerce as a metaphor for world literary intercourse that has led contemporary theorists of world literature to identify the world with global markets and to ignore world literature's normative dimension. The equation of worldliness with the power of market exchange to unify human existence also glosses over the inherently exploitative character of commerce and the basis of commodification in violence and coercion. Indeed, we can say that recent theorists of world literature unwittingly inherit and repeat the position of classical liberal thought on trade as a form of world-making activity. Adam Smith wrote that the free movement of commodities accords with "the common sense of mankind."[53] "Trade which, without force or constraint, is naturally and regularly carried on between any two places, is always advantageous."[54] Hence, "commerce . . . ought naturally to be, among nations, as among individuals, a bond of union and friendship."[55]

But it is Kant who articulates the most spectacular spiritualization of trade as world-making activity by postulating an intrinsic connection between the sphere of commerce and the sphere of culture and the arts as two different forms of sociability. For Goethe, universal peace was an impossible pipe dream. Kant, however, argues that a cosmopolitan world federation can lay the institutional foundation for perpetual peace. The spirit of commerce (*Handelsgeist*) is a fundamental mechanism for establishing such a federation because trade brings "peoples into a peaceable relation to each other and so into understanding, community [Gemeinschaft], and peaceable relations with one another, even with the most distant."[56] But more important, this community formed by the external ties of material self-interest is supplemented and reinforced at the internal level of subjectivity by processes of culture and the imagination. These processes instill and deepen the feeling of belonging to humanity in us because they encourage universal social communication and sympathy. The beautiful arts and the sciences (*Schöne Kunst und Wissenschaften*) play a crucial role in developing our humanity (*Menschheit*) because they involve "a universally communicable [allgemein mitteilen] pleasure."[57] The humanities (*humaniora*) cultivate our mental powers by heightening and developing in us "the universal *feeling of participation* [das allgemeine *Teilnehmungsgefühl*] and . . . the capacity for being able to *communicate* one's inmost self universally [sich innigst und allgemein *mitteilen*], which properties taken together constitute the sociability [Geselligkeit] that is appropriate to humankind [Menschheit], by means of which it distinguishes itself from the limitation of animals."[58]

As part of the beautiful arts and the humanities, world literature creates the world and cosmopolitan bonds in at least two ways. Through the powers of figuration, it enables us to imagine a world. But more important, through the pleasure it arouses in us and our desire to share this pleasure through universal communication, literature and its criticism enhance our sense of (being a part of) humanity. Indeed, literature performatively brings humanity into being by integrating individuals into a universal whole by means of the sociability it occasions. One should emphasize here that this causal power of aesthetic pleasure is not derived from preexisting social forces. In Kant's view, an aesthetic judgment expressing the feeling of pleasure implies a *sensus communis*, an appeal to the agreement of others. But this communal or common sense does not issue from or refer to an empirically existing community. Rather, it is an a priori principle of sociality.[59] This nonempirical, prepositive modality of being-and-having-in-common, of worldliness, facilitates our sociability, the empirical human inclination to society.

It is paramount that we analytically distinguish arguments about the sociality of trade from those about the sociality of aesthetic forms that are entangled in Goethe's and Kant's views of the world and the arts as types of world-making activity so that we can foreground the normative dimension of the world that recent theories of world literature have occluded. When Auerbach tries to revive the project of world literature, he also draws on philosophies of world history from the German idealist tradition. But spiritualist models of the world do not necessarily regard world history as a progression toward the peaceful unity of humanity, whether this takes the institutional form of a cosmopolitan federation or a multilateral amity between a plurality of peoples and their sovereign states. In the next chapter, I examine Hegel's conceptualization of the world as a spiritual process that always involves power, domination, and structural violence and the important role he gives to culture in world history. I will then turn to Marx's materialist inversion of spiritualist models of the world and the immense obstacles it poses to any normative conception of world literature.

CHAPTER 2

The World According to Hegel

Culture and Power in World History

It is now de rigueur to rail against Hegel's philosophy of world history for its developmentalist teleology and Eurocentrism and the racist remarks he undoubtedly made about many non-European nations. His account of world history is worth further consideration for at least three reasons. First, it is a spiritualist account of the world that foregrounds the reality of violence in history. Hegel explicitly rejects the Kantian ideal of perpetual peace achieved through a world federation. Second, insofar as Hegel gives an important role to culture in the justification of violence in relations between peoples in world history, he disagrees with Goethe's suggestion that world literary intercourse brings about tolerance and respect for differences that will soften the struggle for superiority in international relations. For Hegel, the world is also a forum for the recognition of the culture of other nations. But far from being a form of tolerance of others that leads to gentleness, the restraining of conflict, or the mitigation of the cruelty of war, recognition leads instead to the acceptance of one nation's domination over others in a given historical epoch. Hegel's philosophy of world history may be the most elaborate philosophical account of cultural capital. However, unlike Casanova's world republic of letters, the recognition of world-historical cultural significance is not merely a struggle over literary value with negligible impact on international political struggles. It directly justifies one nation's political victory and supremacy. Third, Marx's brief comments on world literature are part of a materialist conceptualization of the world that inverts Hegelian dialectics. Because Marx polemically targets Hegelian world history as an exemplary expression of a mystifying dialectics, an understanding of the latter is crucial to grasping the problems Marx's account of the world poses for world literature as a normative project.

The Optic of World History: Slaughter Bench and Theatrical Spectacle

My discussion of Hegel's account of the world focuses on the three main metaphors he uses to characterize world history: the slaughter bench, the theatrical spectacle and the judicial court. The gross political incorrectness of Hegel's views about world history has distracted the nonspecialist reader from the crucial point that he introduced the concept of the world to solve an important normative problem. Whereas the metaphorical template of Goethe's account of world literature is market exchange, Hegel's account of the world arises out of a political concern: the violent historical struggle for dominance among nations. In Hegel's system, world history is a phase of objective spirit that provides the transition to absolute spirit.[1] In the *Philosophy of Right*, world history is part of the state, the third phase of ethical life, insofar as it develops out of and bears on the state's external sovereignty and its relations to other states (international law).[2] But it is also a distinct realm into which sovereign states have to pass. The passage of states into this higher sphere is needed to solve the problem of the state's ineluctable finitude. As an objective shape of universal spirit, the state is infinite to its own citizens and, thus, appears as ideal (the state as the idea of freedom or freedom that has been actualized). But the absence of effective international laws means that a state remains a finite particular in its relations to other equally sovereign states. Hence, states exist in an international state of nature and their norms become infected by finitude. "Since states function as *particular* entities in their mutual relations, the broadest view of these relations will encompass the ceaseless turmoil not just of external contingency, but also of passions, interests, ends, talents and virtues, violence [Gewalt], wrongdoing, and vices in their inner particularity. In this *turmoil*, the ethical whole itself—the independence of the state—is exposed to contingency."[3] When we view the actions of states from the broader perspective of history, the spectacle of destruction can cause a corrosion of normativity of epidemic proportions and lead to despair and futility. As Hegel poignantly puts it,

> We grow weary of singularities [Einzelheiten] and ask ourselves to what end they all contribute. We cannot accept that their significance is exhausted in their own particular ends; everything must be part of a single enterprise. Surely some final end [Endzweck] must be promoted by this enormous expenditure of spiritual resources [geistigen Inhaltes]. We are compelled to ask whether, beneath the superficial din and clamour of history, there is

not perhaps a silent and secret inner process at work, whereby the power [Kraft] of all phenomena is conserved. What may perplex us, however, is the great variety and even inconsistency of the content of history. We see complete opposites venerated as equally sacred, capturing the attention of different ages and nations. We feel the need to find a justification [Recht-fertigung] in the realm of ideas for all this destruction.[4]

When we see the evil, the wickedness, and the downfall of the most flour-ishing empires the human spirit has created; and when we are moved to profound pity for the untold miseries of individual human beings—we can only end with a feeling of sadness at the transience of everything. And since all this destruction is not the work of mere nature but of the will of man, our sadness takes on a moral quality, for the good spirit in us . . . eventually revolts at such a spectacle [Schauspiel]. Without rhetorical exaggeration, we need only compile an accurate account of the misfortunes which have over-taken the finest manifestations of national and political life, and of personal virtues or innocence, to see a most terrifying painting [dem furchtbarsten Gemälde] take shape before our eyes. Its effect is to intensify our feelings to an extreme pitch of hopeless sorrow with no redeeming circumstances to counterbalance it. We can only harden ourselves against it or escape from it by telling ourselves that it was ordained by fate and could not have been otherwise. . . . Indeed, we retreat into that selfish complacency which stands on the calmer shore and, from a secure position, smugly looks on at the distant spectacle of confusion and wreckage. But even as we look upon history as the slaughtering bench [Schlactbank] on which the happiness of nations, the wisdom of states, and the virtue of individuals are sacrificed [zum Opfer gebracht worden], our thoughts inevitably impel us to ask: to whom, or to what final end [Endzweck] have these monstrous sacrifices been made?[5]

The spectacle (*Schauspiel*) that history stages for us is clearly not the edify-ing vision of human achievements that Auerbach had in mind in his explica-tion of world literature's vocation. It is a bloody slaughter bench. To avoid succumbing to passive despondency, Hegel argues, we must look beyond the violence and contingency of historical events. We must see this drama in a different light so that events form a progression toward "a final end in and of itself [einer Endzweck an und für sich]."[6] Since reason is the only thing that is a final end in and of itself, we need to believe that "the world is governed by reason [in der Welt herrschende Vernunft]."[7] The study of world history gives proof for this belief because it is "the image and enactment of reason [das Bild und die Tat der Vernunft]."[8]

World history is therefore an optic, a way of viewing and interpreting the drama of human events in the world such that they are seen as moving toward a final end prescribed by reason. As Hegel puts it, "this final end is that which is intended in the world [dieser Endzweck ist das, was in der Welt gewollt wird]."[9] This way of looking is a specular structure with two defining features. First, because the final end of the world is reason itself, the spectator is not passive but active. To the extent that the spectator views this play as being directed by reason, the play is a picture composed by reason. It is, therefore, also an action or doing of reason, a performance of reason. Moreover, reason gives this picture to itself. It makes itself into a drama so that it can see and become conscious of itself as the spirit of world history, spirit being reason that is conscious of itself. The self-recognition of reason occurs in the following manner: the spectator of the drama is a rational being who recognizes himself as the bearer of reason. In the act of recognition, he also understands that he plays an active role in the process of making the world qua spectacle. The spectator thereby affirms his own spiritual being and remakes himself anew as spirit. Hence, in the optic of world history, seeing and doing/making are moments of the same process in which reason finds and recognizes itself in and as the world that it has made and can continually remake. The process by which reason produces the world is thus simultaneously a process of auto-production. Second, the reason that actively governs the world organizes it into a restricted economy in which all individual events are part of a larger circular movement in which reason returns back to itself as the final end. The world of world history is a totality in the sense that it is completed or rounded off by being thoroughly permeated by reason. Better yet, the world is the rounding off of reason, the rounding off that *is* reason.

In Hegel's view, the world is not merely a matter of spatial extensiveness, the magnitude of the space within which an object circulates. Indeed, the world is not a natural object but a *spiritual process* with a complex temporal dimension. Compared to space, which is the category for understanding matter in its fixity as something given, time is the category for understanding change and transience. As such, "time entails the determination of the negative."[10] Time is our relation to nonexistence (*Nichtsein*). Its central principle, which is personified by Chronos's devouring of his children, is the destruction of what exists, namely, finite nature.[11] Because it annihilates everything, time is "an unhistorical power."[12]

As objective spirit, however, world history is a temporal process in which reason demonstrates its power to appropriate, control, and harness the dynamism of temporal change to introduce a degree of permanence for the end of its own production. As Hegel puts it in his Jena philosophy of spirit, spirit "is *time*, which is for itself, and [it is] the freedom of time as well—this pure subject that is free of its content but also *master* of it, unlike space and time which are selfless."[13] In world history, spirit recognizes itself in the largest possible external objective shape, namely, world events that progress toward a final end-in-and-for-itself. Hence, unlike the change that occurs in the realm of nature, annihilation in the spiritual realm of world history is in fact universal progress, where the destructiveness of time is sublated into a form of production. "Higher forms [Gestaltung] are produced through the transformation of earlier and less advanced ones. The latter accordingly cease to exist; and the fact that each new form is the transfiguration of its predecessor explains why the appearance of spiritual forms occurs within the medium of time [die Erscheinung der geistigen Gestaltungen in die Zeit fällt]. Thus, world history as a whole is the expression of the spirit in time just as nature is the expression of the Idea in space."[14] Because spirit recognizes the objective world as the product of a spiritual process, the world is no longer an inert spatial object. It is embedded in an ongoing dynamic activity that creates and destroys all existing forms, where the natural limitations of any given form are overcome so that spirit can develop further. Hegel's metaphorical use of the theatrical spectacle brings out spirit's restless activity.

Each of the creations in which it found temporary satisfaction presents itself in turn as a new material, challenging the spirit to develop it further still. The forms [Bildung] it produced become the material on which it labours to raise itself up to new forms. It manifests all its powers [Kräfte] in all aspects. We learn what powers it possesses from the multiplicity of forms it produces. In this sheer pleasure in activity, it is entirely absorbed in itself. Nature admittedly imposes internal and external limitations on it, and these not only resist it and place obstacles in its path but can even cause it to fail completely in its endeavours. But even when it is frustrated, it remains true to its vocation as a spiritual being [geistiges Wesen], a being whose end is not the finished work [das Werk], but instead its own activity [seine eigene Tätigkeit], so that it still affords the spectacle of having exhibited such activity.[15]

Justifying Violence and Domination:
The World as a Court of Judgment

But what precisely is the final end that the optic of world history gives us to see that solves the problem of the corrosion of the normativity of sovereign states? World history's normativity derives from its spiritual character. Because the spirit of world history is objective, it is not an inscrutable providence or the *nous* of ancient Greek philosophy. It is not an abstract indeterminate principle but a self-conscious reason with the power (*Macht*) or capability to actualize its own ends.[16] Indeed, as a self-producing object, the universal of world history is simultaneously concrete and eternal. It "is infinitely concrete, all-comprehending and omnipresent, for the spirit eternally remains at home with itself [ewig bei sich ist]; it has no past, and remains for ever the same in all its power [Kraft] and force [Gewalt]."[17] Although spirit transcends the particularistic ends of national interests, it necessarily becomes concrete and acquires determinate content only through nations. Thus, "in world history . . . we are concerned with individuals which are nations [Völker] and wholes which are states. We cannot, therefore, be content with this . . . trivial faith in providence, nor indeed with a merely abstract and indeterminate faith which conceives in general terms of a providence that rules the world but refuses to apply it to determinate reality. . . . The concrete events are the ways of providence, the means it uses, the phenomena in which it manifests itself in history."[18]

Historical events are thus amenable to the scrutiny of rational consciousness, which brings out their underlying reason. The impossibility of the existence of a world judicial institution to settle interstate disputes means that the actions of a given state can only be judged from the perspective of world history.

> The determinate national spirit . . . is in time and thereby has as its content essentially a particular principle on the lines of which it must go through a determinate development of its consciousness and its reality; it has a history of its own. As a limited spirit [beschränkter Geist], its independence is something secondary; it passes into *universal world-history*, the events of which exhibit the dialectic of particular national spirits—the court of the world [deren Begebenheiten die Dialektik der besonderen Völkergeister, die Weltgericht, darstellt].[19]

The principles of the *spirits of nations* [*Volksgeister*] are in general of a limited nature because of that particularity in which they have their objective actuality and self-consciousness as existent individuals, and their deeds and destinies in their mutual relations are the manifest [erscheinende] dialectic of the finitude of these spirits. It is through this dialectic that the *universal* spirit, *the spirit of the world* [*der Geist der Welt*], produces itself in its freedom from all limits [als unbeschränkt], and it is this spirit which exercises its right—which is the highest right of all—over finite spirits in *world history* as the *world's court of judgment*.[20]

World history is also a court of judgment. It exhibits the dialectic of particular national spirits in order to judge their rightfulness. World history is governed by the world spirit (*Weltgeist*), a higher power with greater universality than particular national spirits. This higher spirit moves behind the interactions of different national spirits and is the substance and underlying unity that subtends these particular shapes, the substrate in which they subsist as members of a whole. But although it transcends these contingent shapes, it has no separate existence of its own since as something existent, it has to take a particular shape and can only exist in the relations between particular national spirits.[21] There is a necessary link between the world spirit and national spirit, world and nation, because the world can only exist through relations between nations. Hence, in a given epoch, the world spirit is vested in one national spirit, whose actions will have universal normative force. We recognize a nation as the bearer of the world spirit if its political institutions and spiritual-cultural products are such that it has achieved the highest level of the actualization of freedom possible in that epoch. This indicates that its institutionalized norms coincide with the direction of world-historical progress. In other words, because it has made an eternal contribution to the development of freedom, that national spirit possesses the right to be recognized as the dominant nation in a given world-historical era. Even when it has gone into decline in subsequent epochs and no longer embodies the world spirit, its norms are irrevocable. They retain their universal validity even though they are modified in later stages of development.

The world of world history is thus a dynamic process and an objective structure. We conventionally think of a judicial forum as a space. But because world history is the specular structure for the self-conscious recognition and auto-production of spirit, its status as the court of the world involves a double genitive. On the one hand, world history is the forum in which the interactions of nations that are in and constitute the world are judged. Here, the world is an object that is judged in terms of a national spirit's rightful place in world history. But on the other hand, because the judgment involves the recognition that a national spirit is the bearer of the world spirit, it is also the world (qua the world spirit) that judges. When the philosopher of world history makes a judgment about it, he recognizes the spirit underlying world history and, at the same time, also recognizes himself as part of the world spirit. Hence, the judgment is made by the world spirit. This is the implicit meaning of common idiomatic remarks such as "(world) history will judge" or "the world watches and judges." The world is thus both the subject and object of judging. It judges itself, although the 'self' must be understood in two different senses. At the same time, because this judging affirms the final end of world history and reveals the true direction of universal progress, it also makes world history. The process of judging is, therefore, also an objective structure for and process of the production of the world. As Hegel puts it, "the goal of history" is "the spirit's development towards self-consciousness, or in its making the world conform to itself [die Welt sich gemäß mache] (for the two are identical). . . . The goal of world history, therefore is that spirit should attain knowledge of its own true nature, that it should objectivise [gegenständlich mache] this knowledge and actualize it into a real world [es zu einer vorhandenen Welt verwirkliche], and give itself an objective existence."[22]

As in Goethe's remarks on world literature, Hegel also distinguishes the world from a physico-geographical entity. We see the same bifurcation of a spatial object and a spiritual world with a temporal dimension and normative force (world history). However, Hegel breaks with Goethe's account of the world in three important respects. First, Goethe regarded the world as a series of intellectual exchanges between cultivated individual subjects—what Hegel calls merely subjective spirit—that explicate the key features of humanity underlying the multiplicity of cultures. Humanity is the universal ideal that enlightened subjects can attain by participating in world literary intercourse. In contradistinction, for Hegel, the world is simultaneously an objective shape and a spiritual process. World history is produced by the activity of an inner spirit that actualizes itself in an objective existence. It is "the realm of the [spirit] which is actually and actively present in the world [des in der Welt wirklichen und tätigen (Geistes) herausgekommen ist]."[23] It is both the object and expression of reason and reason's product, the field of its operation and the process of its performance. "World history is a rational process, the rational and necessary course of the world spirit. This spirit [is] the substance of history; its nature is always one and the same; and it makes explicit this nature in the existence of the world [Weltdasein]."[24]

Consequently, Hegel gives the world greater efficacy and normative power. World history is the dynamic movement of the world spirit, the sphere where the world is constitutively tethered to a teleological process in which the universal spirit exhibits itself and gains knowledge of itself as free by actualizing itself in the shape of a world spirit that transcends the actions of particular national spirits.[25] The world spirit is a deep unconscious power that operates and expresses itself in objective worldly existence through states, nations, and persons. These actors function according to their own principles and interests. Their dialectical relations produce world history as the arena or stage where they act. However, world history contains a deeper rationality that directs the actors, and they do not have conscious access to and cannot know the final end of this governing power. They are "at the same time the unconscious instruments [bewußtlose Werkzeuge] and organs [Glieder] of that inner activity in which the shapes which they themselves assume pass away, while the spirit in and for itself prepares and works its way towards the transition to its next and higher stage."[26] This deep unconscious power retroactively confers a higher right on the national spirit that embodies it.

Second, although the world is governed by a rational spirit, it is a domain constituted by relations of power, domination, and structural violence. The optic of world history opens up a special realm of visibility that reconciles reason with violence. World-historical nations "are the living expressions [Lebendigkeiten] of the substantial deed of the world spirit and are thus immediately identical with it."[27] But for that very reason, their vocation is invisible to them: "they cannot themselves perceive it and it is not their object and end [Zweck]."[28] Indeed, the visibility of world history is superior to and transcends the phenomenal regard of any transient temporal world. The vocation of world-historical nations, Hegel writes, will not be recognized by those who are part of their world or the public opinion of subsequent worlds: "They receive no *honour* or thanks on its account, either from their contemporaries [Mitwelt] or from the public opinion of subsequent generations [Nachwelt]."[29] But this lack of honor is offset by the "undying fame" they will receive, which elevates them into the permanent sphere of world history.

The rightfulness proper to world history is not that of morality, justice, or ethics. The universal judgment and recognition of the court of world history exceeds those spheres. It metes out eternal fame. The phenomenality of world history entails political hierarchy and domination. Nations that are obscured in its light do not count and have no rights in its court. Their obscurity is accompanied by the misery and suffering of being dominated by world-historical nations. Hence, unlike world-literary intercourse, world-historical judgment is neither tolerant nor benevolent. Because it is not concerned with the morality or justice of state actions in the sphere of conscious actuality, it legitimizes the violence suffered by nations that do not embody the world spirit as the consequence of universal progress. "In contrast with this absolute right [absolutes Recht] which it possesses as bearer [Träger] of the present stage of the world spirit's development, the spirits of other nations are without rights [rechtlos], and they, like those whose epoch has passed, no longer count in world history [zahlen nicht mehr in der Weltgeschichte]."[30] Here, the court is a sacrificial altar. Historical violence is absolved by a theodicy of spirit's teleological progress toward the actualization of freedom in the world. In Hegel's words,

> in order to justify the course of history, we must try to understand the role of evil in the light of the absolute power [Macht] of reason. . . . We cannot fail to notice how all that is finest and noblest in the history of the world is immolated upon its altar. Reason cannot stop to consider the injuries sustained by single individuals, for particular ends are submerged in the universal end. In the rise and fall of all things it discerns an enterprise that has arisen from the universal labor of the human species, an enterprise which is actual in the world to which we belong.[31]

International Recognition: The World Hierarchy of Cultural Forms

Third, for Hegel, cultural forms have a more powerful worldly function than in Goethe's project of world literature. They are of paramount importance in discerning which national spirit embodies the world spirit at a given stage of its universal progress. Each national spirit has a unique inner principle that distinguishes it from other national spirits. This principle is manifested in and determined by the powers (Mächte) by which a national spirit particularizes itself, such as religion, knowledge, and the arts and sciences. These cultural powers are the objective media or (self-)mediations through which a national spirit can recognize its own principle and appear to itself "as self-activating and self-determining [als sich betätigend]."[32] These powers are world-making in the sense that a national spirit creates a spiritual world, an environment or sum total of spiritual objects, for itself. Through this spiritual world, it expresses and externalizes its inner principle so that it can perceive and know itself as an existent world and have itself as its own object.[33] The national spirit's activity, Hegel writes,

> consists in making itself into a present world [einer vorhandenen Welt zu machen] which also exists in space. Its religion, ritual, ethics, customs, art, constitution, and political laws—indeed the whole range of its institutions, events, and deeds—all of this is its own creation, and it is this which makes the nation what it is. . . . Once the nation has created itself [Hat das Volk sich so zu seinem Werke gemacht], the dichotomy between its essence [Wesen] (or what it is in itself) and its actuality [Wirklichkeit] is sublated [aufgehoben], and it has attained satisfaction: it has created its own world out of its inner essence. The spirit now indulges itself in the world of its own making.[34]

Such cultural forms are a way of discerning a national spirit's contributions to world-historical progress and whether it embodies the world spirit in a given epoch because they indicate the extent to which its inner spiritual principle corresponds with the actualization of freedom. Cultural forms thus function to justify the violent hierarchy between nations that stuctures the world. Accordingly, the court of world history is also a forum for the comparative recognition of cultural forms. World history is the objective condition of possibility of art, religion, and philosophy, the three shapes of absolute spirit. We can only recognize these forms as expressions of absolute spirit *after* we understand how different national spirits are positioned within the chain of world-historical events. Hence, the study of art, religion, and philosophy is necessarily comparative and must range across different cultures and periods of world history.

The comparative study of cultural forms replicates the political hierarchy of obscurity and visibility that organizes world history. Hegel places the spiritual products of each people within a (Eurocentric) developmental hierarchy where the cultural forms of nations that dominated in earlier stages are judged as defective compared to those of now dominant Europe, because the former expresses an inner principle in which universal reason's consciousness of freedom is less developed compared to those of European national spirits.

> In all world-historical nations, we do indeed encounter poetry, plastic art, science, and even philosophy. But these differ not only in their tone, style, and general tendency, but even more so in their basic import; and this import involves the most important difference of all, that of rationality. . . .

For even if one ranks the Indian epics as highly as Homer's on account of numerous formal qualities of this kind—greatness of invention and imagination, vividness of imagery and sentiments, beauty of diction, etc.—they nevertheless remain infinitely different in their import and hence their very substance; and the latter involves the interest of reason, which is directly concerned with the consciousness of the concept of freedom and the way in which it expresses itself in individuals.[35]

World history's comparative optic consigns Africa to the eternal darkness of prehistory and hierarchically divides history into the four different developmental stages of the Oriental, Greek, Roman, and Christian (Germanic) worlds in analogy with the development of an individual from childhood to old age. It produces the Eurocentric characterizations of non-Western art that abound in Hegel's *Aesthetics*, for instance, the judgment that whereas classical beauty is achieved in the Greek world, the failure of the Egyptian, Indian, and Persian peoples to grasp the true nature of the absolute leads them to produce bizarre and grotesque objects whose phenomenal forms are forced to express a higher meaning inappropriate to their shape.[36] We can call this world history from the present of (nineteenth-century) European hegemony. It looks at the past in a way that affirms Europe as the teleological model by which to judge all other nations as wanting and elevates Europe into a developmental standard to which all other nations should aspire.

Despite its disturbing political and ethical implications, Hegel's spiritualist account of the world provides a more complex framework for reconceptualizing world literature than the theories discussed in chapter 1. First, Hegel anchors the world to an explicitly teleological understanding of time that overcomes temporal finitude by reconciling the passage of time with the ends of reason. The spirit behind world history organizes all actors and their actions into members and processes of an articulated totality. Second, it follows that every major event in the world is imbued with a deeper normative significance. Hence, the world is not a spatial container for the sum total of objects and subjects but a dynamic spiritual whole. Third, worldliness is not a mere ideal or ethic of tolerance that points to a hidden humanity, as it was for Goethe. As reason that actualizes itself in history, the world is an objective structure that is dynamically constituted by relations of violence and domination between nations. Finally, aesthetic and cultural forms contribute directly to the world's normative force. They are directly related to political struggles in the world and are a world-making power because they are fundamental to a world's objective structure and justify its political hierarchies and relations of domination.

My argument about Hegel's usefulness for understanding postcolonial world literature will undoubtedly face objections concerning the patent Eurocentrism of his philosophy of history. Indeed, recent postcolonial thought has forcefully argued that his emphasis on the role of violence in world history is morally egregious because it legitimizes colonialism. Ranajit Guha, the founding father of the Subaltern Studies collective of South Asian historians, has suggested that we need "to confront the philosophically certified 'higher morality' of World-history with its politics by asking some difficult questions about the morality of colonizers claiming to be the authorized historians of lands and peoples they have themselves put under a colonial yoke."[37]

However, Hegel's account of world history is valuable precisely because it foregrounds the role of violence and conflict in the world. His vision of the end of history is politically dubious because he used a teleology of progress that organized the different nations into a developmental hierarchy centered on Christian Europe to resolve worldly conflict. This hierarchy is reproduced in his Eurocentric comparison of aesthetic and cultural forms. The philosophical basis of Hegel's Eurocentrism is the teleology of the concept. As spirit, the concept develops itself by externalizing itself in the sphere of objective existence that is other to it. Spirit returns back to itself when it recognizes this other as nothing but itself, when it recognizes itself in this other, which is *its* other. By means of this movement of self-return where it becomes in-and-for-itself, spirit harnesses the dynamism of temporal alteration and overcomes the destructiveness of what Wordsworth called "the unimaginable touch of Time." This circular movement of self-return is identical to the movement of the world spirit's organization of the events of world history into a totality by rounding them off according to an overarching unifying principle of reason, namely, the final end that the world spirit posits to justify events by giving them a narrative meaning.

The examples of world literature from the postcolonial peripheries discussed in the third part of this book are indebted to Hegel's account of the world in two ways. They confront the irreducible reality of violence in the world-system, and they express the belief that literary forms are part of the world's objective structure. Literature does not merely reflect social forces. It is itself an important force in contesting existing hierarchies in the struggle to remake the unequal world created by capitalist globalization. The postcolonial novels that I examine suggest that the world is constituted by different histories and temporalities and articulate alternative teleologies so that peoples who have been left out of Eurocentric world history can emerge, be heard and recognized, achieve self-determination, and improve their place in the world. However, these texts also undermine Hegelianism by decoupling normative worldly force from teleology. They suggest that we must rethink world literature on the basis of a world that is not governed by a single unifying principle but is instead the effect of overlapping and frequently conflictual processes of world-making that issue from different local, national, and regional sites.

CHAPTER 3

The World as Market

The Materialist Inversion of Spiritualist Models of the World

The industrial capitalist is constantly faced with the world market; he compares and must compare his own cost prices not only with domestic market prices, but with those of the whole world.

—KARL MARX, *Capital*

Any account of world literature today needs to address Marx's immanent critique of spiritualist accounts of the world because it deprives world literature of its normative force. Simply put, Marx's materialist inversion of spiritualist conceptions of the world reembeds subjective and objective spiritual phenomena such as world literature and world history in the world market and its global mode of production. In the famous passage from the *Manifesto of the Communist Party* that theories of world literature fondly cite, Marx and Engels write:

> The need for a constantly expanding market for its products chases the bourgeoisie over the whole terrestrial globe. It must nestle everywhere, settle everywhere, establish connections everywhere.
>
> The bourgeoisie has through its exploitation of the world market given a cosmopolitan shape to production and consumption in every country. . . . All old-established national industries have been destroyed or are daily being destroyed. They are dislodged by new industries, whose introduction becomes a life and death question for all civilized nations, by industries that no longer work up indigenous raw material, but raw material drawn from the remotest zones; industries whose products are consumed, not only at home, but in every part of the world. In place of the old needs, satisfied by the productions of the country, we find new wants, requiring for their satisfaction the products of distant lands and climes. In place of the

old local and national seclusion and self-sufficiency, we have intercourse in every direction [allseitiger Verkehr], universal [allseitiger] interdependence of nations. And as in material, so also in spiritual production. The spiritual creations of individual nations become common goods. National one-sidedness and narrow-mindedness become more and more impossible, and from the numerous national and local literatures, a world literature is formed.

The bourgeoisie, by rapid improvement of all instruments of production, by the unendingly facilitated means of communication, draws all, even the most barbarian, nations into civilization. . . . It compels all nations, on pain of extinction, to adopt the bourgeois mode of production; it compels them to introduce what it calls civilization into their midst, i.e., to become bourgeois themselves. In one word, it creates a world after its own image.[1]

Similarly, Hegel's history of the world spirit is only an alienated shape of the actual history of the world as a concrete material totality.

In history up to the present it is certainly an empirical fact that separate individuals have, with the broadening of their activity into world-historical activity, become more and more enslaved by a power alien to them (a pressure which they have conceived of as a dirty trick on the part of the so-called world spirit, etc.), a power which has become more and more enormous and, in the last instance, turns out to be the world market.[2]

The transformation of history into world history is not indeed a merely abstract act on the part of "self-consciousness," the world spirit, or any other metaphysical spectre, but rather an entirely material, empirically verifiable act, an act the proof of which every individual furnishes as he comes and goes, eats, drinks and clothes himself.[3]

Since the actual ground of history is the sum of forces and relations of production, genuine world history only comes into being with the rise of the world market.[4] "[Big industry] produced world history for the first time, insofar as it made all civilized nations and every individual member of them dependent for the satisfaction of their needs on the whole world, thus destroying the former natural exclusiveness of individual nations."[5]

In this chapter, I argue that although the world market's centrality in Marx's analysis of capitalism appears to support the spatialization of the world in recent theories of world literature, his critique of capitalism is based on a temporal account of the world as the material product of human activity. Through our rational appropriation and control of the time of production, we create a world in which we can fully regulate our existence as finite beings and achieve the universal satisfaction of our material needs. Such a world is truly human because it is a world where our humanity is actualized. The materialist characterization of literature as a phantomatic superstructure, however, denies literature any normative force. I outline a materialist account of world literature that draws on critical theories of space to ameliorate literature's normative deficit and on world-systems theory to address Marx's reductive view of global capitalism as a homogenizing system.

The Spatialization of the World

The defining motif of the materialist inversion of spiritualist accounts of the world is spatialization. This follows from Marx's geographical determination of worldhood. For Marx, the world market brings nations together and unifies them as members of a system of needs because it makes nations throughout the globe dependent on each other for the fulfillment of needs. Simply put, a world is a global system for the satisfaction of material needs. In spiritualist accounts, the world is a normative category because it is a rationally projected temporal horizon that preserves the achievements of humanity from the corrosiveness of time. Marx's reduction of the world to the space of market exchange empties out this normative dimension. It is the original source of the normative deficit of contemporary accounts of world literature. Henceforth, world literature's normativity consists merely in the unquestioned assumption that the crossing of national boundaries and the erosion of territorial borders by the circulation of literary works is good because wider circulation attests to the strength of a literary genre or adds value and significance to a literary work.

But what exactly does Marx mean by *world*? We take this for granted whenever we describe Marxism as a cosmopolitanism. Marx sublates subjective and objective spiritualist understandings of world-making. Like Kant and Goethe, he uses *world* as an adjective to describe the transcendence of the particularistic limitations of local or national borders. *World* refers in the first instance to a universality achieved by enlarging spatial extension. It is synonymous with broadness, the many-sided, and therefore with generality or universality. It is variously opposed to the local, the immediate, the parochial and narrow-minded, and therefore the particular.

In the German tradition of *Bildung* that Marx inherited, this vocabulary of transcending and overcoming the particular carries a decidedly ethical charge. Kant noted that the education of the human being so that he can be worthy of humanity involves struggling against "the crudity of his nature."[6] Natural crudeness is exemplified by the limited, one-sided perspective of egoism, which can be overcome by cultivating pluralism, "the way of thinking in which one is not concerned with oneself as the whole world, but rather regards and conducts oneself as a mere citizen of the world [Weltbürger]."[7] Similarly, Hegel understood *Bildung* as "the imposition [aufgeprägt] of a universal quality upon a given content," a mental process of social cultivation that leads to the purification of selfish drives.[8] *Bildung* is the precondition of ethical action because it makes us renounce one-sidedness and particularity and see things from the multiple perspectives of others so that we can act in accordance with universal principles. Thus, "the cultured [gebildete] man recognises the different facets of objects; all of them are present to him, and his fully developed [gebildete] powers of reflection have invested them with the form of universality. . . . [He] takes in all the different aspects, and . . . is accustomed to act in the light of universal perspectives and ends."[9]

For Goethe and Hegel, world literature and world history are ways of transcending particularistic limitations at the level of nations. Marx provocatively suggests that such spiritual formations are merely the epiphenomena of *material* processes that operate in every aspect of concrete existence, namely, the development of productive forces by world trade and production. Thus, where Goethe uses commerce as a metaphor for understanding world literary relations, Marx's immanent critique of world literature as an ideological formation inverts the relation between the literal and the figural. He literalizes Goethe's metaphor by pointing out that the metaphor is in fact the real referent. The material world created by capitalist economic activity, which breaks down parochial barriers and national exclusiveness, is the concrete basis of world literary relations and the world spirit. The transcendence of particularity that world literature and world history promise is illusory because they are the autonomized products of alienation.

Marx's argument that the world market is the material basis of world literature is directly responsible for the confusion of global trading circuits with the world in theories of world literature. These theories have fixated on the spatial process of the breaking down of territorial limitations to commodity circulation.[10] Marx appears to support the conflation of world with globe.

First, he was fascinated by how a global market led to the revolutionizing of production, which he described as the endless breaching of restrictive limitations. The world market is the substrate in which modern capitalism first appears and thrives.

> The circulation of commodities is the starting-point of capital. The production of commodities and their circulation in its developed form, namely trade, form the historic presuppositions under which capital arises. World trade and the world market date from the sixteenth century, and from then on the modern life-history of capital starts to unfold.[11]
>
> [The revaluation and devaluation of capital and the release and binding of capital] assume for their full development the credit system and competition on the world market, the latter forming the very basis and living atmosphere of the capitalist mode of production.[12]

Moreover, the rise of capital occurs in a global theater of violent dispossession. It is coextensive with European expansion and the invasion and colonization of other parts of the globe.

> The discovery of gold and silver in America, the extirpation, enslavement and entombment in mines of the indigenous population of that continent, the beginnings of the conquest and plunder of India, the conversion of Africa into a preserve for the commercial hunting of black-skins, are all things which characterize the dawn of the era of capitalist production. These idyllic processes are the chief moments of primitive accumulation. On their heels treads the commercial war of the European nations, which has the globe as its theater [Schauplatz]. It begins with the revolt of the Netherlands from Spain, assumes gigantic dimensions in England's Anti-Jacobin War, and is still going on in the Opium Wars against China, etc.[13]

Second, Marx's definition of human activity in terms of material production leads to an inversion of spiritualist world history that grounds world history in the spatial phenomenon of the world market. Hegel understood world history as a normative process in which reason overcomes the contingency of time by appropriating the dynamism of temporal change for the end of spiritual production. The spiritual principles of world-historical nations transcend the geographical basis of their spatially bounded existence. In contradistinction, because material activity involves the manipulation and transformation of objects to fulfill our material needs as sensuous finite beings, human activity no longer transcends but only regulates our finitude. Consequently, normative activity becomes a power immanent to our spatial existence. The field of production spans the entire world because our capacity for production is boundless. The world market is merely the function and geographical expression of production under capitalism.

In fact, Marx oscillates between two different accounts of the world in a manner that is reminiscent of Goethe's distinction between the physico-geographical world and the world in a higher, normative sense. He initially defines the world in terms of spatial connections established across the globe's entire surface. Capitalist relations and intercourse make a world by bringing together disparate places around the globe. What is crucial to world-creation is the annihilation of spatial distance through advanced means of communication and instruments of production that create new products from materials sourced from throughout the globe and the need for these new products everywhere. The local and domestic is defamiliarized and opened up to the alien, and their ensuing integration enlarges the system of needs until it spans the globe.

However, closer examination shows that Marx complicates his spatial account of the world in two ways. First, what defines a world is not merely geographical extension but rational-purposive human relationality, the connections and intercourse that unite people and places for the determinate end of production to satisfy human needs. Material relations of production cannot be reduced to their physico-spatial dimension because they involve rational human ends. Second, Marx's definition of the world as a system for the universal satisfaction of needs leads to a distinction between true and alienated forms of human production. The world market is the function and field of the production of commodities for profitable exchange instead of production for the direct satisfaction of needs. Accordingly, the world market is not a true world. It is certainly not the only world that is possible, but merely an alienated world, *a* world that the bourgeoisie has made in its own image.

The Retemporalization of the World: The Upside-Down World of Commodities, the Appropriation of Time, and the Immanent Drive to Overcome Capital

Because theories of world literature are mesmerized by market exchange, they have repressed the fact that despite its universalizing tendency, the world market created by capital is the monstrous antithesis of genuine human community. It is an alienated world, a heteronomous totality imposed from the outside on the true agents of production, the workers. Marx's critique of this alienated world also applies to recent theories of world literature.

First, the world of commodities is an ironic inversion of the cosmopolitanism of true intersubjective relations and human sociality. Speaking of the expanded form of value, Marx acerbically notes that a commodity has a cosmopolitan existence because it is a member of a world of commodities: it "no longer stands in a social relation with merely one other kind of commodity, but with the whole world of commodities as well. As a commodity it is a citizen of this world."[14] With the general form of value, commodities appear to have an intrinsic value independent of their usefulness to human beings. Hence, an objective world arises where commodities have the anthropomorphic shape of agents that engage in intersubjective relations of recognition and consensual cooperation. "The general form of value . . . can only arise as the common work of the whole world of commodities. A commodity only acquires a general expression of its value if, at the same time, all other commodities express their values in the same equivalent; and every newly emergent commodity must follow suit. It thus becomes that because the objectivity of commodities as values is the purely 'social existence' of these things, it can only be expressed through the multiple sides of their social relations; consequently the form of their value must possess social validity."[15] Commodities have a twofold "worldliness." First, because the equivalent in which all commodities express their values is arrived at by common agreement, the form of value expresses social relations. The objectivity of value is a *social* objectivity. Second, the worldliness of commodities reflects a defective, alienated form of human sociality. This is a world in which human labor has been reduced to an undifferentiated mass because the infinite equivalence of all commodities is premised on the uniformity of labor that went into the making of each commodity. "All kinds of actual labour . . . [are reduced] to their common character of being human labor in general. . . . In this way it is made plain that within this world the general human character of labour forms its specific social character."[16]

For Marx, commodity fetishism occurs when social relations between producers, the social characteristics of human labor as an activity involving cooperation, are reflected as objective properties of products. The social relations presupposed by commodity exchange are thus already commodity relations whereby human producers view their labor not as part of a process of collective collaboration but in terms of the production of objects for exchange by private individuals. Their sociality is therefore not a genuine human sociality but that between objects. In other words, human sociality is already modeled after the market exchange of commodities—a relation between things. Consequently, social relations are not relations between human beings. They are directed toward things, which have interposed themselves as intermediaries between human beings: "They do not appear as immediate social relations between persons in their work, but rather as material [sachliche] relations between persons and social relations between things [Sachen]."[17] The sociality of market relations presupposes and is unwittingly reproduced by human subjects that are no longer concrete, the abstract human beings of quantifiable homogeneous labor.[18]

Second, the illusory and fantastical world of commodities is the product of reification (*Versachlichung*). Reification is the fusion of the technical-material aspects of the production process with the specific social forms that shape these technical processes in such a way that the social forms are regarded as natural.[19] Bourgeois economic life makes capitalist social relations appear natural because bourgeois economic processes obey autonomously functioning market mechanisms for the generation of value.[20] The reification of social relations culminates in the world market. There, market processes appear as a natural force with the greatest freedom from human activity. As Marx puts it, "in presenting the reification of the relations of production and the autonomy they acquire vis-à-vis the agents of production, we shall not go into the form and manner in which these connections appear to them as overwhelming natural laws, governing them irrespective of their will, in the form of the world market and its conjunctures, the movement of market prices, the cycles of industry and trade and the alternation of prosperity and crisis prevails on them as blind necessity."[21]

Marx's critique of the spatialized world, which he characterizes in the negative terms of inversion, alienation, mystification, and reification, points to a higher world that will be created by the *Aufhebung* of the world of commodities. This sublation is nothing other than the temporalization of the world. In the first place, the world market is always secondary to world production. For Marx, the global extensiveness of trade is only important as a condition for revolutionizing production. Although the world market initially "forms the basis for the capitalist mode of production," once the capitalist mode of production has been created, "the immanent necessity that this has to produce on an ever greater scale drives it to the constant expansion of the world market, so that *it is not trade that revolutionizes industry, but rather industry that constantly revolutionizes trade*. Moreover, commercial supremacy is now linked with the greater or lesser prevalence of the conditions for large-scale industry."[22] Consequently, "trade now becomes the servant of industrial production, for which the constant expansion of the market is a condition of life. An ever-increasing mass production swamps the existing market and thus works steadily towards its expansion, breaking through its barriers. What restricts [beschrankt] this mass production is not trade (in as much as this only expresses demand), but rather the scale of the capital functioning and the productivity of labour so far developed."[23]

This means that the limitations to be overcome are ultimately not the spatial territorial barriers to trade. The undermining of spatial barriers by the world market is only a function of the transcendence of barriers immanent to capitalist production. Marx's analysis of circulation clearly indicates that these immanent barriers are temporal. The augmentation of capital involves circulation in the general sense, namely, the endlessly repeatable process of M-C-M, where money is invested in production, commodities are made, and the product is realized as money. Here, circulation is an infinitely dynamic process of immanent becoming that constitutes capital.

> In the circulation of capital . . . [the capitalist] exchanges money for the conditions of production, produces, realizes [verwertet] the product, i.e. transforms it into money, and then begins the process anew. . . . The circulation of capital constantly ignites itself anew, divides itself into its different moments, and is a *perpetuum mobile*. . . . The circulation of capital is at the same time its becoming, its growth, its vital process [Lebensprozeß]. If anything was needed to be compared with the circulation of the blood, it was not the formal circulation of money, but the content-filled circulation of capital.[24]

By extending the spatial range of trade, the world market creates the need for greater production to meet greater demand. It increases the amount of profit and the quantity of profit put back into production and thus increases the quantity of circulating capital. However, this increase in spatial distance also increases the *circulation time* of capital because it increases the time of the realization of the product, that is, how long it takes to exchange commodities for money. As distinguished from the production process, the process of realization is circulation in the narrower or strict sense: the turnover (*Umlauf*) of commodities and money.[25] Marx calls this "circulation itself."[26]

Although Marx initially explains circulation in the strict sense in spatial terms, he immediately notes that spatial extension constitutes a *temporal* barrier that needs to be overcome because it slows down the *speed* of circulation. "The second moment is the space of time [Zeitraum] running from the completed transformation of capital into the product until when it becomes transformed into money. The frequency with which capital can repeat the production process, self-realization, in a given amount of time, evidently depends on the speed with which this space of time is run through, or on its duration."[27] With the expansion of the world market, a greater difficulty of exchange arises because of "the greater distance of the market in space and hence delayed return," and this slows down the speed and the frequency of the realization of capital.[28] "The longer time required by capital A to realize itself would be due here to the greater spatial distance it has to travel after the production process in order to exchange as C for M."[29] Costs for the means of transportation and communications have to be added to the entire process of capital's circulation. Hence, the spatial extension of the world market constitutes a drag on and devalues capital. The longer the time in which the commodity remains a commodity before it is converted into money, the longer its value is a mere potentiality that is yet to be actualized, and "this is pure loss."[30]

Because theories of world literature have relied on a very partial interpretation of Marx, they fail to see that global capitalism's power to make a world is temporal, namely, the ability to remove temporal barriers to capital's endless circulation and self-actualization. Capital's universalizing power is not merely the erosion of spatial barriers by the world market but a global mode of production that *destroys space with time*, where the time taken to traverse the space opened up by the world market's breaching of territorial barriers must be reduced to nothing. As the condition of the universal development of productive forces, capital's power to control and appropriate time is nothing other than the capacity to create a world and endlessly actualize itself in the world. This is capital's "normative force," so to speak. As Marx puts it,

> while capital must on one side strive to tear down every spatial barrier [örtliche Schranke] to intercourse, i.e. to exchange, and conquer the whole earth for its market, it strives on the other side to annihilate this space with time, i.e. to reduce to a minimum the time spent in motion from one place to another. The more developed the capital, therefore, the more extensive the market over which it circulates, which forms the spatial orbit of its circulation, the

more does it strive simultaneously for an even greater extension of the market and for greater annihilation of space by time. . . . There appears here the universalizing tendency of capital, which distinguishes it from all previous stages of production. Although limited by its very nature, it strives towards the universal development of the forces of production, and thus becomes the presupposition of a new mode of production, which is founded not on the development of the forces of production for the purpose of reproducing or at most expanding a given condition, but where free, unobstructed, progressive and universal development of the forces of production is itself the presupposition of society and hence of its reproduction; where advance beyond the point of departure is the only presupposition.[31]

Capital's normativity is its power to revolutionize the development of productive forces by destroying limits imposed by societal goals in specific periods. It liberates the production process from these social fetters and makes the development of production an end in itself. This liberation leads to the denudation of territorial barriers by the expansion of the world market. The persistent expansion of the sphere of circulation is a consequence of a force immanent to capital.

A precondition of production based on capital is therefore the production of a constantly widening sphere of circulation, whether the sphere itself is directly expanded or whether more points within it are created as points of production. . . . The tendency to create the world market is immediately given in the concept of capital itself. Every limit [Grenze] appears as a barrier [Schranke] to be overcome. Initially, to subjugate every moment of production itself to exchange and to suspend every moment of direct use values not entering into exchange, i.e. precisely to posit production based on capital in place of earlier modes of production, which appear natural from its standpoint.[32]

This liberation of production is also a process that demystifies the external world, and, thus, a process of humanization that transforms the whole world according to human ends at the same time that the human being is cultivated so that new needs and pleasures can be created to foster the consumption of new products. Marx emphasizes that the enhancement of the physical and spiritual capacities of humanity, the domination of nature and the creation of a borderless cosmopolitan world are moments in the same process of capital's liberation of production.

The discovery, creation and satisfaction of new needs arising from society itself; the cultivation [Kultur] of all the qualities of the social human being, production of the same in a form as rich as possible in needs, because rich in qualities and relations—production of this being as the most total and universal possible social product, for, in order to take gratification in a many-sided way, he must be capable of many pleasures, hence cultured [kultiviert] to a high degree—is likewise a condition of production founded on capital. . . . Thus capital creates the bourgeois society, and the universal appropriation of nature as well as of the social bond itself by the members of society. Hence the great civilizing influence of capital; its production of a stage of society in comparison to which all earlier ones appear as mere *local developments* of humanity and as *nature-idolatry*. For the first time, nature becomes purely an object for humankind, purely a matter of utility; ceases to be recognized as a power for itself. . . . In accord with this tendency, capital drives beyond national barriers and prejudices as much as beyond nature worship, as well as all traditionally limited, complacent, encrusted satisfactions of present needs, and reproductions of old ways of life. It is destructive towards all of this, and constantly revolutionizes it, tearing down all barriers which hem in the development of the forces of production, the expansion of needs, the manifoldedness of production, and the exploitation and exchange of natural and spiritual forces [Geisteskräfte].[33]

Capital is world-making at the subjective and objective level: it creates the cultivated cosmopolitan human being who is free from national prejudices and a material world that is united by trade and production.

However, capital also restricts the revolutionizing power it releases because it makes its self-valorization the end of the development of productive forces and measures value in terms of commodified abstract labor. The cosmopolitan humanity and the world it makes are an alienated subject and an inverted world mystified by the sheen of bourgeois ideology. The contradiction between the universalizing tendency that drives capital and the restrictive barriers it erects then becomes an immanent force that leads to the overcoming of capital. As Marx puts it,

The universality towards which it irresistibly strives encounters barriers in its own nature, which will, at a certain stage of its development, allow it to be recognized as being itself the greatest barrier to this tendency, and hence will drive towards its own sublation [Aufhebung].[34]

This tendency—which capital possesses, but which at the same time, since capital is a limited form of production, contradicts it and hence drives it towards dissolution—distinguishes capital from all earlier modes of production, and at the same time contains this element, that capital is posited as a mere point of transition [Übergangspunkt].[35]

The *true barrier* to capitalist production is *capital itself*. It is that capital and its self-valorization appear as the starting and finishing point, as the motive and end [Zweck] of production; production is production only for *capital*, and not the reverse, i.e. the means of production are not simply means for a steadily expanding configuration of vital processes for the *society* of producers. The barriers within which the maintenance and valorization of the capital-value has necessarily to move—and this in turn depends on the dispossession and impoverishment of the great mass of the producers—therefore come constantly into contradiction with the methods of production that capital must apply to its end and which set its course towards an unrestricted expansion of production, to production as an end itself [Selbstzweck], to unconditioned development of the social productive powers of labour. The means—the unconditioned development of the social productive powers—comes into persistent conflict with the restricted end, the valorization of the existing capital. If the capitalist mode of production is therefore a historical means for developing the material powers of production and for creating a corresponding world market, it is at the same time the constant contradiction between the historical task and the social relations of production corresponding to it.[36]

As with Hegel's account of world history, capital's world-making force is grounded in the human power to appropriate time. Its universalizing tendency is not merely the increasing of the range of spatial movement. As the power of breaking all barriers, it is the infinite capacity of unobstructed crossing. This is premised on the endless acceleration of speed, that is, the intensity rather than the extensiveness of movement. Locomotion within barriers is confined because one moves within space. When an activity breaks out of a barrier, it is still contained by a larger space. In contradistinction, the power to remove all barriers annuls the distinction between activity and space because the perpetual overcoming of barriers means that the activity is its own barrier. Or better yet, when I recognize that I can overcome my barriers because they are what I posit myself, then this is the same as not having any barriers. The movement is no longer just movement across and within space. It has become united with space such that the activity creates the space in which it moves by its movement. It creates its own space, gives itself being, and perpetually enhances and intensifies its own being. The movement is thus equally a return to a self that no longer has any barriers. Hence, the world is no longer an external object or power that stands against productive activity. The latter is no longer simply *in* a given or existing world as a spatial container, nor is the world an external object toward which it is directed. Instead, productive activity makes the world and, indeed, is the world, such that the world's becoming is our becoming. Nowhere is the trite phrase of contemporary globalization "We are the World" more true than when applied to the temporal force of world-making immanent to capitalist production. Compared to it, the world market is an alien natural power that rules over us by blind necessity.

This power to appropriate time and remove all barriers is teleological. Instead of moving within externally imposed barriers, unfettered activity is self-directed and sets its own ends. The return to self is therefore not merely a process of growing larger in space but the rational and free self-development of the society of producers. Marx describes this as a constantly developing configuration of vital processes. By interpreting circulation as spatial *mobility*, theories of world literature miss the point that for Marx, circulation is "normative" because its dynamism is temporal. It is not merely movement across borders but the circulation of blood throughout the entirety of the world qua body, the *motility* of the organism. Where the world (social relations) is no longer an external power that stands outside and restricts the production process but has become united with it, the world is no longer spatial. It becomes temporalized and alive. At the same time, the production process, which capitalism alienated from producers, no longer appears as something that stands outside the producers but is recognized as amenable to their control in the same way that external nature is demystified and appropriated in productive activity. The becoming-world of the production process is also the self-actualization of the society of producers in and as the world. Because the reappropriation of the production process involves the appropriation of time and not merely space, what takes place is precisely the temporalization of the world. I will later show how postcolonial world literature reinscribes Marx's emphasis on vital motility in embodied place into an injunction to make a vital world in which a people can emerge as self-determining.

From a subjective standpoint, the proletariat is the world historical agent who self-consciously bears the temporal force of world-making. Capital also paves the way at the level of subject-formation, because the factory as the site of industrial production brings workers together and fosters a mode of co-operation, thereby developing the immanent sociality of production and the conscious actuality of being part of a world with other workers.

The immanent sociality of production is a philosophical anthropological theme in all of Marx's writings. Production is a social, cooperative activity because the production of others is required to satisfy one's needs. As Marx puts it, "the production of life, both of one's own in labour and of fresh life in procreation, now appears as a double relationship: on the one hand as a natural, on the other as a social relationship. By social, we understand the co-operation of several individuals, no matter under what conditions, in what manner and to what end. It follows from this that a determinate mode of production, or industrial stage, is always combined with a determinate mode of co-operation [Zusammenwirkens], or social stage, and this mode of co-operation is itself a 'productive force.'"[37] Accordingly, production is also a socializing and potentially humanizing activity, the means for the self-actualization of the human being as social or human insofar as he can only attain his full human individuality in society. Alluding to Aristotle, Marx suggests that "the human being is in the most literal sense a ζῶου πολιτικον, not merely a social animal, but an animal which can individuate itself only in the midst of society. Production by an isolated individual outside society . . . is as much an absurdity as is the development of language without individuals living together and talking to each other."[38]

The human being's disposition toward sociality is a potentiality that cannot be reduced to positive forms of society. Indeed, throughout history, the immanent potential of sociality has existed in contradiction with existing forms of society, which have obstructed its actualization. This immanent sociality is the basis of the persistent critique of existing society until the contradiction is removed in communism. The contradiction is also one between an immanent worldliness and the alienated world created by capitalism. The immanent sociality of human life is a power that makes worlds because the maximum development of productive forces requires the integration of the entire world into the system of production. The universal intercourse of all men should optimally lead to the remaking of the world according to universal human ends. For Marx, human reality and belonging to a world presuppose each other. It is tautologous to say that human beings should be cosmopolitan because human reality is necessarily social and social intercourse transcends the borders of nation and state.

The capitalist mode of production develops the immanent sociality of production at the level of subject-formation by bringing workers together to form a social power. Large-scale production and the imposition of a social character on the instruments and process of labor that is required to lower the value of the means of production in proportion to the goods produced created a social force (*gesellschaftlichen Kraftpotenz*) that is greater than the sum of its parts. As Marx puts it, "not only do we have here an increase in the productive power of the individual, by means of co-operation, but the creation of a new productive power, which is a mass power [Massenkraft] in and for itself."[39] This new power is generated from the fusion of many forces into a total force (*Gesamtkraft*). Capitalist techniques of organization thus actualize the immanent sociality of production. These connections constitute a totality, where different individual acts form "a total operation" (*Gesamtverrichtung*), and the new total force created by combination and coordination is stronger than the aggregate of different component forces.[40] "The special productive power of the combined working day is, under all circumstances, the social productive power of labour, or the productive power of social labour. This power arises from co-operation itself. In planned co-operation with others, the worker strips off the barriers of his individual being, and develops the capabilities of his species [Gattungsvermögen]."[41] Just as the liberation of the production process involves a temporal force that imparts vital becoming to the world, Marx compares the direction and coordination of social labor to the vitality of a productive organic totality (*produktiven Gesamtkörpers*).[42] However, because the unity of the workers is imposed on them by capital for its self-valorization, it is not the complete reciprocity between member-organs and whole found in a living organism. Their cooperation is not under the workers' rational control but comes from a despotic alien form that subjugates them.[43] Their social power arises under conditions where it is expropriated from them and absorbed by capital.

The important point is that Marx gives collective human action a paramount role in transforming the world. The various modalities of universality created by capitalism have a merely natural form because the production process is separated from its human producers. One must therefore distinguish between the globe as a spatio-geographical entity, the alienated world created by the restrictive teleological time of the capitalist mode of production, and a world with genuine universality created by the teleological time of socialist revolution. The world can be changed precisely because it is an ongoing process created by material activity. Contra Hegelian world history, the world is not the expression of a deep structure impervious to the actions of human actors but is instead an ongoing material process of creation. The deficient capitalist world contains the seeds of its own destruction because it creates universal forms of interconnectedness that unite all workers and universal conditions of exploitation that are unbearable, thereby making the actualization of another world inevitable.

> This development of productive forces (which itself implies the actual [vorhandene] empirical existence of men in their world-historical, instead of local, being) is an absolutely necessary practical premise because without it *want* is merely made general, and with destitution the struggle for necessities and the entire old shit [die ganze alte Scheiße] would necessarily be reproduced; and furthermore, because only with the universal development of productive forces is a universal intercourse between men established, which produces in all nations simultaneously the phenomenon of the "propertyless" mass (universal competition), makes each nation dependent on the revolutions of the others, and finally has put world-historical, empirically universal individuals in place of local ones.[44]

Our degraded world can be transformed if the fully developed productive forces are self-consciously reappropriated by a world society of producers. The society of producers is the temporal force of world-making embodied in a self-conscious collective subject: the proletariat as subject of world history (double genitive), a subject produced by even as it actively produces the history of the world.

> All-round dependence, this natural form of the world-historical cooperation of individuals, will be transformed by the communist revolution into the control and conscious mastery of those powers.[45]

> The proletariat can thus only exist world-historically, just as communism, its activity [Aktion], can only have a "world-historical" existence. World-historical existence of individuals means, existence of individuals which is immediately linked up with world history.[46]

For Marx, world history is an empirical universality. It is composed of concrete individuals who are universally connected in a material sense through the productive activity by which they actualize themselves. The proletariat is world-historical in two senses. Its formation and the communist revolution are grounded in material world history. But, more important, the proletariat is world-historical because it can directly make world history. "Communism," Marx emphasizes, "is for us not a *state of affairs* which should be established, an ideal to which actuality [Wirklichkeit] [will] have to adjust itself. We call communism the actual [wirkliche] movement which sublates [aufhebt] the present state of things."[47] Communism does not merely project a utopian ideal world. Rather, it is a movement stirring in the current world, and its actuality comes directly from the proletariat's effectivity as a material agent.

Toward a Materialist World Literature: Zonal Inequality and the Plasticity of Social Space

If we simply convert Marx's descriptions of the world market into a methodological framework for studying world literature that privileges global circulation, we ignore what is innovative about his materialist account of the world: the teleological temporal dimension that constitutes the normative force of world-making and its identification with our productive activity. This is why recent theories of world literature suffer from a normative deficit. Marx situates world literary relations in a field of forces that include productive forces and direct struggles against exploitation. This is important today because contemporary world literature is bound to a globalized culture industry that makes it vulnerable to the negative consequences of what David Harvey calls postmodern space-time compression: the manipulative constitution of taste and desire by global commodity circuits of image production to promote sanitized cultural plurality for mass consumption. "The general implication," Harvey writes, "is that through the experience of everything from food, to culinary habits, music, television, entertainment, and cinema, it is now possible to experience the world's geography vicariously, as simulacrum. The interweaving of simulacra in daily life brings together different worlds (of commodities) in the same space and time. But it does so in such a way as to conceal almost perfectly any trace of origin, of the labour processes that produced them, or of the social relations implicated in their production."[48] Postindustrial techniques of marketing, advertising, and value-adjudication form a seamless web in the production, reception, interpretation, and criticism of world literature, and these techniques in turn shape its form and ideational content and the kind of world it enables us to imagine. We need to attend to how this undermines world literature's normative vocation.

The pertinence of Marx's immanent critique of world literature becomes clear if we return briefly to Casanova's theory of world literature. Casanova remains caught by Goethe's sleight of hand: like Goethe, she argues for the autonomy of the world republic of letters by borrowing metaphors of exchange, trade, and struggle from the sphere of global political economy. But because these are merely metaphors, world literature has no force in relation to this material sphere. Indeed, if the global unity created today is one of mass cultural homogenization through sign systems and chains of images that are not of literature, then why is the study of literature still relevant in an age of global mass culture? If literature still possesses normative force, we would have to speak of the end of literature in the same way that Hegel spoke of the end of art: a sensuous form of absolute spirit that is no longer connected to our daily lives because it does not move us in its sensuous immediacy but only appeals to the intellect. More and more books of world literature are being published today. But what hold do they have on most people? The problem is not going away by insisting that global literary processes are distinct from and unaffected by economic processes. This is to repeat the ideological formation of world literature Marx diagnosed in Goethe—the autonomy of the literary as a symptom of autonomization under global capital.

However, the materialist understanding of the world also poses a serious obstacle to world literature for two reasons. First, although Marx gives human activity an unprecedented normative power because he equates the temporal force of world-making with our control and appropriation of time in production, he denies literature any world-making capacity because he sees it as an ideological reflection of economic forces without worldly efficacy. Second, Marx's view that global capitalism is a homogenizing power that simplifies inequality to that between two global classes, the proletariat and the capitalist, needs to be revised in light of the structural inequality between different parts of the world. These problems can be addressed with the help of Immanuel Wallerstein's analysis of polarization in the capitalist world economy and critical theories of space, which connect the temporal force of world-making to aesthetic practices.

Recent theories of world literature are cognizant of the world economy's uneven character and have relied on the center-periphery vocabulary of Wallerstein's theory of the capitalist world-system as a theoretical resource. The starting point of world-systems theory is that the basic unit for social-scientific analysis should be the world social system instead of the nation-state. The modern world-system is a capitalist "world-economy." Global capitalist economic activity with its single division of labor thrives best in the absence of a correspondingly global unified political structure (a world-empire) because the maximization of profits requires "the development of variegated methods of labor control for different products and different zones of the world-economy."[49] This is best achieved by territorialized political entities. Because some areas of the world-economy benefit more at the expense of other areas, the different social groups, political structures, and the areas they control form zones that exist in a systematic power relationship of hierarchy and dependency. The world-economy is thus internally differentiated into core, semiperiphery, and periphery, where each zone has specific economic roles. Groups in core zones profit more from the world market because they have more power than those in the other zones.[50]

Prima facie, world-systems theory conceives of the world in spatio-geographical terms. Wallerstein defines the world-system as a system whose size exceeds the boundaries of sovereign territorial states: "it is a 'world' system, not because it encompasses the whole world, but because it is *larger* than any juridically-defined political unit."[51] The spatial expansiveness that characterizes a world-system is driven by the calculative logic of capitalist accumulation, whose key principle is to reap greater and greater profits from production to fulfill material needs. The essential feature of a capitalist world-economy, Wallerstein notes, is "production for sale in a market in which the object is to realize the maximum profit. In such a system production is constantly expanded as long as further production is profitable, and men constantly innovate new ways of producing things that will expand the profit margin."[52] Accordingly, the extension of the world(-system) is measured by quantitative economic and social growth.[53] Indeed, Wallerstein distinguishes between earlier phases of the modern world-system, where the world-system is merely regional or continental, where it is "still only a European world-system," and the later phase, from 1733 to 1817, where a world-system with truly global extension comes into being by incorporating zones outside the European world-system, such as the Indian subcontinent and West Africa, through colonial expansion.[54] "These incorporations took place in the second half of the eighteenth and the first half of the nineteenth centuries. The pace, as we know, then accelerated and, eventually by the end of the nineteenth century and the beginning of the twentieth, *the entire globe, even those regions that had never been part even of the external arena of the capitalist world-economy, were pulled inside.*"[55]

Wallerstein's emphasis on the fact that these processes of incorporation always involve violence, domination, and struggle is crucial to any materialist conception of the world. The incorporation of external areas was never consensual but was imposed by the dictates of capitalist accumulation. An area that is integrated into the commodity chains of the capitalist world-economy is subordinated and deprived of economic freedom. As Wallerstein puts it, incorporation "involves 'hooking' the zone into the orbit of the world-economy in such a way that it virtually can no longer escape."[56] Imperialism and colonization brought about the loss of political freedom and the destruction of cultural traditions. Hence, "the geographic expansion of the European world-economy meant the elimination of other world-systems as well as the absorption of the remaining minisystems."[57] The peripheries produced by incorporation are the self-consolidating other of the capitalist world-system. An external arena consists of worlds that are outside the calculative logic of the European capitalist world-system. Despite trading with Europe, these worlds remained autonomous world-economies because the objects of trade were not daily necessities central to either the functioning of their own economies or the European economy. In contradistinction, the peripheries are a former outside that have been organically integrated as a subordinate part of the system. Thereafter, a periphery develops its economic activities "more consciously within the framework of the needs of the European world-economy."[58] The culture of core countries can be used to reinforce the economic and political subordination of the peripheries.[59]

As I showed in chapter 1, Casanova uses Wallerstein's center-periphery vocabulary to analyze the influence of (Western) "international" modern aesthetic standards on the formation of literary value even as she insists that literary relations are relatively autonomous from political-economic dependencies. This analytical schema implies the possibility of a cultural "delinking" in the struggle for literary recognition. Alternatively, when the movement of circulation is privileged in the study of world literature, it is argued that the circulation of literary works can subvert the hierarchy between core and periphery (Damrosch) or that flows of literary influence and the spread of literary genres do not necessarily move from the Western center to the non-Western peripheries (Moretti). Such arguments are valuable because they emphasize the effects of an uneven world for literary processes. Where they are lacking is that they see literature as only having a weak normative force in changing the world.

In contrast, the examples of world literature studied in the third part of this book are concerned with the pressures of global cultural hegemony on the production of postcolonial literature and the negative impact of globalization in exacerbating inequality and suffering in the postcolonial world. To understand how postcolonial world literature challenges the world created by globalization, we need to go beyond a spatial account of the world. Wallerstein's theory of the world-system is useful precisely because, following Marx, he contrasts the current world-system with an alternative world. The spatial extensiveness of the capitalist world-system alone is not enough to constitute a genuine world, what Wallerstein calls a substantive rationality. "A socialist world government in which the principles governing the economy would not be the market but rather the optimum utilization and distribution of resources in the light of a collectively arrived-at notion of substantive rationality."[60] The formation of a world through collective action is a temporal process—the teleological time of humanity's self-actualization.

In summary, the Marxist distinction between the world market and the world society of producers as the natural and self-conscious forms of world-historical cooperation is the materialist inversion of Goethe's distinction between the world as spatial extension and the higher spiritual realm conjured up by literary exchange and of Hegel's distinction between geography and world history. It takes into account the role of material economic forces, especially that of exploitation, in the making of the world. However, for Marx, literature can have no part here. Only labor in its various historical forms has the power of remaking the world, because the world as it *really is* is the material world of production. Because spiritual products are the alienated reflections of labor as living effectivity and self-activity, ideational forms cannot be a positive force in relation to reality. They can only represent reality faithfully as science or function as ideology to mystify the existing world.

The question of literature's worldly causality touches on issues central to Marxist aesthetic theory. Although a systematic engagement with Marxist aesthetics lies beyond this book's scope, I can say in schematic summary that Marxist theory affirms the revolutionary-normative vocation of the aesthetic in two ways. It can attribute a highly qualified positive power to art in terms of its pedagogical function in reconstructing the human personality within the complex web of social relations as the teleological subject of history with the aim of cultivating a revolutionary consciousness. This approach is exemplified by Lukács's celebration of realism.[61] As he puts it, "the central aesthetic problem of realism is the adequate presentation of the complete human personality."[62]

> Respect for the classical heritage of humanity in aesthetics means that the great Marxists look for the true highroad of history, the true direction of its development. . . . For the sphere of aesthetics this classical heritage consists in the great arts which depict man as a whole in the whole of society. . . . The Marxist philosophy of history analyses man as a whole, and contemplates the history of human evolution as a whole, together with

the partial achievement, or non-achievement of completeness in its various periods of development. It strives to unearth the hidden laws governing all human relationships. Thus the object of proletarian humanism is to reconstruct the complete human personality and free it from the distortion and dismemberment to which it has been subjected in class society.... The ancient Greeks, Dante, Shakespeare, Goethe, Balzac, Tolstoy all give adequate pictures of great periods of human development and at the same time serve as signposts in the ideological battle fought for the restoration of the unbroken personality.[63]

Lukács can only affirm world literature's normative vocation by resorting to a spiritualist conception of world history that is almost identical to the universal history of the human spirit celebrated in Auerbach's vision of world literature. World literature would be an adequate form of presentation of the world as it was and is. But, more important, world literature would also project an image of the world as it ought to be, in a future where humanity can be restored to its full, nonvitiated, and nonalienated vitality.

Alternatively, when there is critical skepticism about the teleological progress of history, the autonomy of the aesthetic can be affirmed, as in the writings of the Frankfurt School, as the ability of art to negate the existing world and its ideology. As Herbert Marcuse puts it, "art contains the rationality of negation. In its advanced positions, it is the Great Refusal—the protest against that which is."[64] One finds similar formulations in Adorno's writings: "Art becomes social by its opposition to society, and it occupies this position only as autonomous art.... Art's asociality is the determinate negation of a determinate society."[65] The vocation of the aesthetic is essentially the power of the critical imagination. The formative imagination either portrays the complexity of present reality by embedding it in the history of its making, or it negates and points beyond this reality by generating a picture that perpetually contradicts reality. Literature's relation to the world is derivative or negative. It represents and expresses reality or opposes it.

While these approaches have the virtue of connecting literature to the temporal-normative dimension of the world, they merely circumvent the dilemma that Marxist materialism poses for the positive causality of literature by resorting to a spiritualist account of world history or by attributing to literature the power of negating the present material world. Critical theories of space are important to a materialist understanding of literature's worldly force because they connect literature to the temporal force of world-making through a dynamic account of space that (1) reconciles space with time, and (2) gives cultural and aesthetic forms an important role in the production of space.

Henri Lefebvre's influential theory of space begins with a critique of Hegel's philosophy of history. Following Marx, Lefebvre argues that Hegelian world history leads to a static understanding of space. In Hegel's account of modernity, the national spirit is embodied in the ideal state, which rules over space as an absolute power through its institutions. Lefebvre suggests that the resulting ossification of time in the space of the state has two consequences. First, space becomes static when it is statized or saturated by the rationality of the state. Second, time is also emptied of meaning because the state is the exclusive bearer of reason. "According to Hegelianism, historical time gives birth to that space which the state occupies and rules over. . . . Time is thus solidified and fixed within the rationality immanent to space. . . . What disappears [in the Hegelian end of history] is history, which is transformed from action to memory, from production to contemplation. As for time, dominated by repetition and circularity, overwhelmed by the establishment of an immobile space which is the locus and environment of realized Reason, it loses all meaning."[66] Because the critique of Hegelianism has focused on revitalizing time, space itself has been left untheorized. It is regarded as inert and static, and even as the site of reification.[67]

Questioning the separation of space and time is politically important, because this separation enables the intensified exercise of state bureaucratic power over society. The dissociation of space from time gives rise to nuanced theories of time and a theory of abstract space that cannot account for the complexity of lived space. The exercise of capitalist power presupposes the conceptualization of space as abstract. Abstract space is completely amenable to instrumental manipulation by bureaucratic authority because it presupposes an impersonal subject that conceals state power.[68] In a move that resonates with my discussion of Marx's rejection of a spatial conception of the world as market, Lefebvre points out that the world market is the expansion of abstract space. Abstract space is the space of commodity circulation because exchangeability presupposes substitutability and, therefore, homogeneity.

> Upon this historical basis industrial capitalism was founded—a great leap forward for the commodity, putting it on course for the conquest of the world—i.e. the conquest of space. Ever since, the world market has done nothing but expand. . . . The actualization of the worldwide dimension,

as a concrete abstraction, is under way. "Everything"—the totality—is bought and sold. . . . Chains of commodities (networks of exchange) are constituted and articulated on a world scale: transportation networks, buying- and selling-networks (the circulation of money, transfers of capital). Linking commodities together in virtually infinite numbers, the commodity world brings in its wake certain attitudes towards space, certain actions upon space, even a certain concept of space. Indeed, all the commodity chains, circulatory systems and networks, connected in high by Gold, the god of exchange, do have a distinct homogeneity.[69]

Spatial analysis aims to disrupt the abstract space of the world market and foster conditions for revolution. It retemporalizes space by bringing out its dynamic character. It demystifies abstract space by showing that it is devoid of lived experience and that it is not something eternally given but can be contested and transformed because it is produced by the processes of capitalist accumulation.

Exchange necessarily occurs in concrete places. Each moment of the exchange process and each point of the commodity chain has to be localized, because exchange is undertaken by concrete subjects for the purpose of consumption in order to satisfy specific needs. Lefebvre argues that social space has three components. The concrete places where use and consumption occur are the sites of spatial practices. Here, space is produced by *actions* concerned with production and reproduction that take place in perceived space. Perceived space is conditioned and shaped by two other kinds of space: representations of space and representational space.[70] Representations of space are conceived space, where knowledge, signs, and codes order social relations. Conceived space is a form of practical knowledge with physical effects in the world because here, ideas are actualized in the ordering and shaping of the texture of physical space. As Lefebvre puts it, representations of space "intervene in and modify spatial *textures* which are informed by effective knowledge and ideology."[71] "Their intervention occurs by way of construction—in other words, by way of architecture, conceived . . . as a project embedded in spatial context and a texture which call for 'representations' that will not vanish into the symbolic or imaginary realms."[72] In contradistinction, representational space is space directly lived and experienced through symbols, images, and meanings.

There is a tension between conceived and meaningfully lived space because the former presents itself as static and unchanging, whereas the latter is dynamic and constantly mutates because of changes of meaning in our daily lived experiences. Conceived space is drained of time and obscures its active role in constructing space. For example, abstract space appears as the permanent frame for the exchange of commodities when it is a type of conceived space historically specific to capitalism. In contrast, the lived space of daily human existence is temporalized space. In Lefebvre's words, it "is alive: it speaks. It has an affective kernel or center: Ego, bed, bedroom, dwelling, house; or square, church, graveyard. It embraces the loci of passion, of action and of lived situations, and thus immediately implies time. Consequently it may be qualified in various ways: it may be directional, situational or relational, because it is essentially qualitative, fluid and dynamic."[73] Spatial analysis lays bare the dialectical contradiction between concrete places where things are meaningfully used in daily life and the abstract space of commodity exchange. It shows how the space we perceive is created by this contradiction.[74]

What is significant for us is that Lefebvre gives art an important role in the temporalization of space. Representational space is epitomized by art and the imagination. It is "space as directly lived through its associated images and symbols, and hence the space of 'inhabitants' and 'users,' but also of some artists and perhaps of those, such as a few writers and philosophers, who *describe* and aspire to do no more than describe. This is the dominated—and hence passively experienced—space which the imagination seeks to change and appropriate. It overlays physical space, making symbolic use of its objects. Thus representational spaces may be said . . . to tend towards more or less coherent systems of non-verbal symbols and signs."[75] Representational space is constructed by signification. Unlike conceptualization, which works through thematic construction, that is, the shaping and construction of physical reality by ideas, signification changes the *meaning* of physical reality to prepare for the changing of reality itself. Lefebvre associates signification with the vitality of life, because meanings are persistently revalued in living experience. Life is the constant appropriation of reality whereby we give it new meaning according to changes in our lives. The power of aesthetic forms to change the world by constructive shaping derives from the plasticity of social space as a historical artefact of human creation. Aesthetic forms shape representational space. Representational space influences the spatial practices of individual subjects when they become aware that they do not merely inhabit social space as passive subjects but can actively participate in making it.

The role of literature in subject-formation is an important topos in literary studies. Lefebvre's account of social space gives a concrete empirical grounding to literature's worldly efficacy by specifying how it works in the quotidian social space inhabited by corporeal subjects. First, the meaningful lived experience of physical objects is shaped by historically inherited images and symbols. These images and symbols influence *how* we inhabit or live in space and *how* we act. Moreover, these inherited images and symbols can also be revalued and resignified. Second, when we are aware that we can change the meanings of images and symbols, we view social space critically. Otherwise, existing social space will constrain and impede transformative social practices. A critique of ideology is therefore immanent to representational space. Its ultimate aim is to produce a new alternative space that is conducive to and, indeed, coextensive with radical social activity. Whereas "representations of space are shot through with a knowledge [savoir]—i.e. a mixture of understanding [connaissance] and ideology," representational space involves the appropriative transformation of objects in physical space. It imbues objects with a layer of symbolic meaning that is critical of the ideological elements at work in the making of physical space by conceived space.[76] Indeed, for Lefebvre, signs and images are privileged instruments for ideological mystification and its critique. Because they mediate between the conceived and the perceived, they can either articulate or obscure the causal connection between the different components of social space and spatial practices. In contemporary capitalism, the world of signs and images is a fraudulent world that hides the constructed character of the world market, and our ability to change it through spatial practices.[77]

Third, Lefebvre generalizes aesthetic creation into the paradigm for the making of space. Although he observes that representational space can only generate works with a transient power, he nevertheless models the revolutionary production of space after aesthetic production.[78] The imagination, he notes, has a revolutionary potential because it can aid the revolution in producing a space that is revolutionary in itself.

> On the horizon, then, at the furthest edge of the possible, it is a matter of producing the space of the human species—the collective (generic) work of the species—on the model of what used to be called "art"; indeed, it is still so called, but art no longer has any meaning at the level of an "object" isolated by and for the individual.[79]

> A revolution that does not produce a new space has not realized its full potential; indeed it has failed in that it has not changed life itself, but has merely changed ideological superstructures, institutions or political apparatuses. A social transformation, to be truly revolutionary in character,

must manifest a creative capacity in its effects on daily life, on language and on space.[80]

"Change life! Change society!" These precepts mean nothing without the production of an appropriate space. A lesson to be learned from the Soviet constructivists of 1920–30, and from their failure, is that new social relationships call for a new space, and vice versa. . . . The injunction to change life originated with the poets and philosophers, in the context of a negative utopianism, but it has recently fallen into the public (i.e., the political) domain. In the process it has degenerated into political slogans—"Live better!," "Live differently!"[81]

In Lefebvre's injunctions to create space following the model of artistic practices, we see the critical negation of existing reality espoused by the classical Frankfurt School. The crucial difference, however, is that for Lefebvre, the negation of reality is also a worldly causality because representations are forces immanent to the real world. They are directly part of social space understood as the dialectical connection of spatial practices, representations of space, and representational space.[82]

But a materialist project of world literature needs to explain literature's causality in the uneven theater of global capitalism. David Harvey's work is helpful here because he fuses an account of the uneven geographical development of global capitalism with a critical theory of space. In so doing, he offers a more dynamic picture of global inequality than the center-periphery topography of world-systems theory and opens up more possibilities for challenging the capitalist world-system. In his famous account of the spatial fix of capitalist accumulation, Harvey had argued that the instantaneous mobility of various kinds of capital (money, commodities, etc.) throughout the globe required spatially located institutional arrangements provided by the state, such as credit systems and transportation networks. The necessity of fixing capital engenders new territorial barriers that impede capital's mobility. These barriers contradict the drive toward universality immanent to capital because they create a geographically differentiated and unequal world.

The drive to create a credit system as free as possible from material spatial constraints . . . rests, paradoxically, upon territorial differentiations, which can prevent the movement of money under certain conditions. . . . [Similarly,] the spatial mobility of commodities depends upon the creation of a transport network that is immobile in space. In both cases, spatial barriers are overcome only through the creation of particular spatial structures. When the latter become the barriers . . . they must become, then we can see more clearly how it is that "the universality towards which it [capital] irresistibly strives encounters barriers in its own nature."[83]

At times of crisis, credit moneys are forced to relate back to a monetary basis that is geographically differentiated. Each nation-state strives to protect its monetary basis if the viability of the credit system is to be assured. This means enhancing value and surplus value production within its borders or appropriating values produced elsewhere (through colonial or imperialist ventures). Interstate competition with respect to flows of capital . . . automatically follows. Each nation-state may then find it necessary to protect its monetary basis by restricting the movement of capital (through protective tariffs, production subsidies, foreign exchange controls, etc.). The movement of labour power may also be controlled. But the whole logic now collapses back on to itself. In order to protect the monetary basis that forms the foundation for credit money—the most mobile form of capital—it may become necessary to restrict the spatial mobility of capital in general.[84]

Harvey's subsequent work elaborates and deepens this argument by drawing on Lefebvre's analysis of space. Because space is an active component of social processes, capital accumulation requires the creation of different spatial forms on a global scale. In these geographical spaces, social relations are "materially embedded" by different social groups "into the web of life understood as an evolving socio-ecological system."[85] Hence, the structural inequalities between center and periphery are concretely expressed in and sustained by uneven geographical development in center and peripheral societies. This means that social groups have agency in creating and changing geographical spaces. Their actions have a direct impact on whether and how the unequal center-periphery dynamic is materialized in concrete situations.

Repeating Marx's thesis of the thorough fetishization of commodity relations in daily life and the reification of consciousness as elaborated by Lukács, Harvey argues that we fail to recognize our social agency because the thorough pervasiveness of capital circulation in our daily lives has led us to mistake it for an alien power beyond our control. "We construe the abstractions and fictions of capitalism's logic as the property of some mystical external force—'capital'—outside of the 'web of life' and immune to materialist influences when they should be characterized, rather, as the product of a perverse and limiting logic arising out of the institutional arrangements constructed at the behest of a disparate group of people called capitalists."[86] Following Gramsci, Harvey calls our reified consciousness "common sense."[87] The different structures of common sense are mediatic devices that restrict social action. A critique of common sense is needed to change the web of life that determines social action so that we can contest the production of spaces of uneven geographical development.

Drawing on Lefebvre's theory of space, Harvey argues that aesthetic practices have an important role in the changing of common sense. "The oceanographer / physicist swimming among the waves may experience them differently from the poet enamored of Walt Whitman or the pianist who loves Debussy. . . . The spaces and times of representation that envelop and surround us as we go about our daily lives likewise affect both our direct experiences and the way we interpret and understand representations."[88] Attending to the dialectical relationship between different types of space and spatial practices helps us identify "alternative political possibilities" because it makes us aware that "we physically shape our environment and the ways in which we both represent and get to live in it."[89] Indeed, Marxism has narrowed its vision of transformative politics because it has failed to engage in spatial analysis. "If, for example, socialist realist art fails to capture the imagination and if the monumentality achieved under past communist regimes was so lacking in inspiration, if planned communities and communist cities often seem so dead to the world, then one way to engage critically with this problem would be to look at the modes of thinking about space and space-time and the unnecessarily limiting and constricting roles they may have played in socialist planning practices." Aesthetic practices, Harvey suggests, have the power of letting us see an alternative world because of their role in creating social space. They enable us to grasp the dynamism immanent to the web of life and to recognize that we do not have to be constrained by specific representations of space and time because as spatially embodied consciousnesses, we can change the web of life.

Harvey's framework is helpful for understanding how literary works map the production of space of the societies they portray to illuminate their position in the existing world order. The usefulness of such an account for a materialist articulation of world literature is twofold. First, these literary cartographies of social space are themselves active transactions and negotiations with representational space that can critique, challenge, and contest existing material space. Their agency operates at the level of individual and collective consciousness. As representational space, they also lead to the transformative remaking of the concrete spaces that actualize and sustain the existing world order. To use Harvey's Gramscian phrase, they remake the world by constituting a good sense that challenges the common sense of reified everyday consciousness.

Second, the examples of world literature discussed in the third part of this book are concerned with societies negatively impacted by uneven development. Their cartographies of the places of postcolonial societies in the capitalist world hierarchy are critical windows onto the social dynamics of uneven development. They show readers how social relations of capitalist accumulation are materially embedded in the web of everyday life through institutions and organizational forms and their corresponding forms of consciousness and how this maintains the existing hierarchy of world zones. But they also indicate sites of struggle in concrete social space and stimulate a revolutionary consciousness so that the world can be changed.

A materialist account of world literature from the postcolonial peripheries informed by critical theories of space is situated at the productive intersection between social scientific studies of postcolonial societies and literary studies. At the level of literary analysis, we are concerned with the interface between the empirical content of the themes of the work in question, its referential and mimetic functions, and the concrete context of the work's setting and the work's formal features as an aesthetic process engaged in representational and signifying activity that gives new meanings to the social space that is represented. In Lefebvre's vocabulary, representations of space tend "towards a system of verbal (and therefore intellectually worked out) signs," whereas representational spaces "tend towards more or less coherent systems of non-verbal symbols and signs."[90] A literary work is a representation of space insofar as it is a linguistic text with a thematic component (a form of cognition and knowledge). It is a representational space because it also has an aesthetic, significative dimension that exceeds the thematic content and semantic meaning of verbal signs. Its participation in the production of space involves a dialectical tension between these two dimensions.

I have argued that Marx locates the temporal force of world-making in the human ability to appropriate time. This means that in spiritualist and materialist accounts, the world is a product of human rational appropriation and obeys the march of teleological time. The difference between them is merely that in materialism, the power of transcending finitude is now immanent to human material activity and is a power of regulation. The world is nothing other than the immanent process of human self-transcendence in its productive activity. Critical theories of space reinscribe the vital human capacity to create the world as the material causality of aesthetic forms. But does not Marx's determination of the temporal force of world-making as the material activity of production remain a spatialization of the world? It is important to recall here that the temporal dimension of the circulation of capital, which Marx calls the space of time (*Zeitraum*), is already a spatialization. Time is measured quantitatively as how long it takes a commodity to traverse space. The annihilation of space by time in capitalism is actually the auto-annihilation of space. In part II, I will look at phenomenological and deconstructive accounts that approach worldliness from the standpoint of more radical theories of time. What they bring to the study of world literature is the thought of literature as a force of worlding.

worlding and unworlding

worldliness, narrative, and "literature" in phenomenology and deconstruction

CHAPTER 4

Worling

The Phenomenological Concept of Worldliness

and the Loss of World in Modernity

Elucidation of the world-concept is one of the most central tasks of philosophy. The concept of world, or the phenomenon thus designated, is what has hitherto not yet been recognized in philosophy.

—MARTIN HEIDEGGER, *Basic Problems of Phenomenology*

The force (or lack of it) attributed to literature by spiritualist and materialist accounts of the world presupposes the concept of causality. But what if the concepts of force and causality prevent us from seeing the world because they already take it for granted, overlook and skip over worldliness insofar as they focus on relations among subjects and objects that are already in a world such as those between humans and nature and the spiritual or material intercourse between human subjects? As Heidegger puts it, "*vulgar understanding cannot see the world for beings*, the world in which it must constantly maintain itself simply to be able to be what it itself is."[1] We are fixated with objects and, indeed, can only grasp the world as the sum of objects when we ought to ask instead: "What is this mystery, the world, and above all, *how is* it [*Wie ist* sie]? If the world is not identical with nature and the totality of beings [Seienden], and if also it is not their result, then in what way *is* it [wie *ist* sie dann]? Is it a mere fiction, a hypothesis?"[2]

The phenomenological account of worldliness rejects the common view of the world as the sum of all objects. Since an object (*Gegenstand*) is that which stands against a human subject, Heidegger also rejects as inadequate the principle of intersubjectivity that underwrites spiritualist accounts of the world and the materialist view that the world is created by the cooperative activity of production.

The three chapters in part II discuss Heidegger's account of the world and Hannah Arendt's and Jacques Derrida's responses to it. Deconstruction is here viewed as a radical form of postphenomenological thought. Heidegger's account of worldliness, which arises out of an ontological inquiry about being, has fundamental practical implications. First, the reduction of all beings to objective presence leads to unworlding (*Entweltlichung*), the deprivation of world. In the later Heidegger's analysis of modernity, this has the dire existential consequences of worldlessness (*Weltlosigkeit*) and homelessness. Second, a world holds all beings together in a way that is prior to and makes possible human activity because it gives us access to other beings. Heidegger's grounding of the world in temporality means that the world is a "force" of opening or entry. This force is the ground of resolute authentic action in relations with others that can help us overcome the worldlessness of modernity.

It is widely accepted that Arendt broke with Heidegger's fundamental ontology on the grounds that he disdains politics, privileges solipsistic contemplation, and subordinates action to thought. Hence, whereas for Heidegger the world cannot be an object of human creation, Arendt suggests that the world is made by the practical activities of work, speech, and action that define the human subject. We can understand Arendt as critically developing Heidegger's conception of the world in a way that overcomes its limitations or as shrinking back from his grounding of the world in temporality by reintroducing elements from an anthropologistic philosophy of the subject that are incompatible with his thought. In contradistinction, Jacques Derrida takes Heidegger's thought to its most radical end by suggesting that the temporalization that opens up a world presupposes the gift of time as a pure event that comes from the inhuman other. The gift constitutes time even as it disjoins it. Hence, worldliness is first and foremost a disjunctive being with the inhuman other that interrupts even as it makes our existence possible.

The two common threads that run through phenomenological and deconstructive accounts of the world are first, the understanding of modernity and its contemporary manifestation, globalization, as world-impoverishing and world-alienating because of their instrumental and calculative reduction of existence, and second, the special connection between world-making and world-opening and structures that we can call "literary": the disclosure of meaningfulness (Heidegger), storytelling (Arendt), and the secret of literature and textuality (Derrida). In the current conjuncture, where capitalist globalization has cast doubt on the feasibility of grand teleologies of universal human progress toward freedom, the phenomenological idea of worlding is a more powerful way of understanding world literature's normative force than the idea of teleological time underwriting spiritualist and materialist accounts of the world. It suggests that temporalization is a power of worlding that cannot be destroyed by attempts of calculative reason to reduce the world to quantifiable space that can be regulated for oppressive economic and political ends. Because the unification of the world as a meaningful whole is associated with practices of collective existence, a principle of real hope persists and is structurally inscribed in the very processes of global modernity that repeatedly threaten the world with annihilation. "Literature" discloses and enacts this unerasable promise of the opening of other worlds.

Heidegger develops his understanding of the world and its ontological connection to temporality and transcendence in three stages. First, he explores our experience of the surrounding world (*Umwelt*) in our everyday relations with useful things. Second, he argues that the totality of useful things and their disposability for us is grounded in a total context of meaningful connections in which we exist with others. This meaningful whole is "a world." Finally, he suggests that the world is held together by temporality, which belongs to our existence as Dasein.[3] I will first consider Heidegger's rejection of the widely accepted understandings of the world as objective presence and as something that subjects create in their intercourse with each other through the imparting of value and how this leads to a critique of both the world as a cartographically delineatable spatial object and the spiritualist and materialist teleological conceptions of the world of Goethe, Hegel, and Marx. I will then discuss Heidegger's argument that radically finite temporality is a "force" of worlding, a process that, in giving rise to existence, worlds a world. Following this, I will consider the ethicopolitical consequences of the loss of world in modernity and Heidegger's solution for overcoming worldlessness. Finally, I will examine the important role that Heidegger gives to poetry and art in uncovering and maintaining worldliness.

The Primary Sense of the World: The Violence of Objective Reality and the Critique of the World as a Realm of Value

We conventionally regard the world as a container for the totality of objectively present (*vorhanden*) beings and identify it with nature.[4] In a section of his Marburg lecture course, *History of the Concept of Time: Prolegomena* (summer 1925), "The traditional passing-over of worldhood [Weltlichkeit]," Heidegger characterizes the ascendancy of this view of the world as a violent fall from an original condition of dwelling with other beings in nonthematic relations of care (*Sorge*) into one in which we are subjects who stand opposed to objective things. In the relations of taking-care (*Besorgen*) that constitute our everyday existence, we encounter beings nearest to us in terms of their usefulness.[5] These relations point to an environing world (*Umwelt*) that has the characteristic of aroundness. Heidegger calls the *Umwelt* "the primary and original space [ursprünglichen Raum] of the world" and "the primary sense of world."[6]

Worldliness is the constitutive ontological structure of our existence. It refers to our original openness to other beings, our transportability toward other beings, or their accessibility (*Zugänglichkeit*) to us. The world is not something separate from us in the initial instance, what we subsequently add on to ourselves by going beyond our initial selves when we create a larger habitat through productive activity or extend the range of our lives through sociability. Hence, the world is not, as is commonly understood, a spatial container in which our existence takes place. Indeed, it cannot be understood in terms of spatial extension, that is, as nature and objectivity, because these have extension and lie outside the human subject. The world's primary reality is that of nonobjectivity (*Ungegenständlichkeit*).[7] But as I will show later, it is also nonsubjective. As the condition that enables subjects to encounter objects, the world is prior to subject and object.

When we regard beings as subjects and objects, we obscure and even efface the world. "This kind of knowledge," Heidegger observes, "has the character of a certain 'de-worlding' [Entweltlichung] of the world" (BT, 61; 65). Its way of looking is literally an amputation that does violence to the objectified being and the world: it cuts inner-worldly beings away from the web of relations that allows them to appear as objects. The world that is their enabling support is taken away from them just as the world is excluded from the realm of presence. As Heidegger notes, "[the] bodily presence [of perceived objects] has its basis in a specific '*unworlding*' *of the environing world, a deprivation of its worldhood* [*Entweltlichung der Umwelt*]. Nature as object of natural science is in general *discovered* only in such an '*unworlding*'" (HCT, 196; 266, emphasis in the original). The exemplary culprit for this degradation of being is the Cartesian determination of being as substance. Because Descartes conceives of the substance of *res corporea* through the primary attribute of extension, Euclidean geometrical space is privileged as the a priori framework for understanding the world's being.[8] This determination of the world as spatial extension is the founding principle of recent theories of world literature.

To truly understand what the world primarily is, Heidegger emphasizes, "metric space must first be put out of play" (HCT, 171; 230). Instead of explaining the world on the basis of space, spatiality has to be explained in terms of worldliness. Our spatiality is worldly because our being is such that we exist in a world. This worldliness is first revealed in our taking-care of things immediately around us. In our relations with things closest to us, we experience the worldliness of space in terms of an *Umwelt*, that which is around us (*das Umhafte*).[9] From this immediate sense of worldliness, two other dimensions of the world come into presence: the world of useful handy things near us (*Zuhandenheit*) and the world of extant things on hand (*Vorhandenheit*) that lies beyond the sphere of handy things.[10]

An analysis of our practical relations to useful things as exemplified by the craftsman's relation to his tools reveals the world's nonobjective reality. A tool has a reference because it is used for the purpose of producing a work. The craftsman does not experience it as an object but in terms of the end of its use such that it is completely absorbed in the reference. Indeed, the true reality of a tool is encountered when it is not perceived as a mere thing at hand, but precisely by looking away from it as an object.[11] A work thus implies a world in three ways. First, because its production is the basis and end of the referential totality of the craft, the work is a work-world (*Werkwelt*). Second, the usability of a produced work brings into presence the world of users and consumers, thereby opening up an individual's *Umwelt* to a public world.[12] Third, because the usability of a work and the tools used to make it depend on the materials they are made of, a work also refers to "the worldly as already extant [Vorhandenes]," the world of nature (HCT, 193; 262).

The world disclosed in a work is not an objective presence. It and the beings we encounter in it are not given by theoretical apprehension but are made present through practical behavior. Echoing Aristotle's hierarchical distinction of *praxis* from *poeisis* (fabricating, making), Heidegger notes that the world is experienced through *pragmata*, "that with which one has to do in taking care of things in association (*praxis*)" (BT, 64; 68). Looking after things is a form of *praxis* and not the causal action of a subject on an object. In contrast, the subjective action of making is founded on objective presence because the target and ground of action is theoretically determined as objectivity in the first instance. For Heidegger, the world is not an object of human making. It is not the sum total of handy things but the ground of handiness. For beings to be handy, I must have encountered them in such a way that they are amenable to my use. Hence, the practical reality of the work-world is grounded in the inherent disposability of beings for us. The world is the "how" of our encounter with beings that enables us to dispose them. It grounds our apprehension and is more original and prior to the presence of objects. When we focus on what is handy and make it a matter of thematic consciousness, it appears as a mere object and is no longer handy. Our looking at it as something useful destroys its worldliness. As Heidegger puts it, "when the world appears in the modes of taking care . . . what is handy becomes deprived of its worldliness [eine Entweltlichung des Zuhandenen] so that it appears as something merely objectively present [Nur-vorhandensein]" (BT, 70; 75).

Worldliness is a capability of my being. It enables me to encounter other beings as part of a world, to have this possibility at my disposal.[13] But it is a fragile power. If I fail to grasp my original worldliness, I lose access to the world and can only encounter other beings in an impoverished way, as objects and things. The world's fragility lies in the fact that it can disappear with as little as a glance: it is no longer there when we look at beings through our theoretical gaze. The world can vanish in various ways. First, the world of handy beings is maintained only on the condition of nonknowledge, when we do not seek to know it, because knowledge makes what is handy emerge from its inconspicuousness (BT, 70; 75). Second, the world's withdrawal is hastened when we see the world of extant things as an objective presence, that is, when we reduce looking after to a "mere looking at the world" (HCT, 195; 265). Because it spatializes the world, "looking at" blocks off the full possibility of encountering the world. It extracts us from our ontological condition of being in the world through spatial separation, when it is precisely our being in the world that makes it possible for us to look after things and place them at our disposition.

Heidegger's critique of the world as objective presence reveals the poverty of the geometrical-spatial understanding of world and the inadequacy of geographical concepts that inform current theories of world literature. Our worldliness is a capacity for disposing and placing beings in the world. The active assignation of the place of handy things (placement) is neither the contiguity of spatial apposition nor the locomotion of things in geometrical space. Handy beings around us are not thrown together randomly but belong to a "where," because relations of taking-care hold them together in specific ways. Placement indicates direction and presupposes a web of meaningful relations, namely, a world, in which each being has a proper place and can be placed in relation to other beings. However, when this power of placement is interpreted as a matter of spacing (*Abstand*), what ensues is the violent expropriation of world, because the meaningful relations between oneself and other beings are reduced to quantified spatial location. These beings become "unworlded" (*entweltlich*) because they are only related by meaningless quantitatively measured distance between geometric points.[14]

Heidegger argues that geographical concepts are similarly inadequate for understanding world regions. These are first discovered on the basis of the oriented character of being-in-the-world and its meaningful relations. When these meaningful relations are interpreted in terms of a geometric-mathematical system of points or geographical coordinates, the world is transformed into the pure homogeneous space of geometry, and its "aroundness" is destroyed. As a result, the meaningful orientation of worldly processes we experience daily are emptied of significance. They are understood only by calculations of changes of location within objectified nature across time.[15]

The critique of objective presence clearly undermines the spatialized understanding of world in recent theories of world literature. But Heidegger also distinguishes the world as a meaningful whole from a spiritual realm, a constructed realm of human values, and the totality of cultural artifacts. Spirit, value, and culture remain derived from objective nature because they are defined as its opposite. The world remains obscured if we view it as a higher spiritual realm that is opposed to and transcends the merely given world of corporeal nature because spirit as *res cogitans* is defined in a negative way against the spatiality of *res extensa*: "Spirit, person, the authentic being of man, is some sort of an aura which is not in space and can have nothing to do with space, because we associate space primarily with corporeality" (HCT, 224; 307). By the same token, understanding worldliness in terms of values that adhere to a material thing of nature is based on a determination of the world as objective nature. Although the world is now seen as the sum total of things that are conferred with value by human beings through the prescription of ends, the worldly thing remains "a thing of nature with the fundamental stratum of materiality, but at the same time laden with predicates of value" (HCT, 183; 247).

Heidegger's argument is nothing less than a critique of constructionism and its complicity with dogmatic anthropologism and naturalism. A value-laden thing is composed of a natural thing and the qualities of value generated by human construction. This view impoverishes the world's being because it takes for granted the primary status of the thing's natural character, its character as a value, and the status of the anthropos as a rational animal capable of creating values.[16] Indeed, Heidegger's account of the handiness of tools explicitly rejects a teleological understanding of the human technical manipulation of objective nature. The handiness of usable things is not an ideal quality or end that a practical subject imposes on and actualizes in objects. Handiness, Heidegger stresses, "must not be understood as a mere characteristic of interpretation, as if such 'aspects' were discursively forced upon 'beings' we initially encounter, as if initially objectively present world-stuff were 'subjectively colored' in this way" (BT, 67; 71). This would ground the world in the human capacity to instrumentalize objects. Instead, handiness refers to the ontological character of beings that we encounter, how they are accessible to us as useful.

What is at stake in the mode of our encounter with things such that we can dispose them is a notion of meaning that is not derived from a rational subject's ends, values, and norms. We experience disposable beings as references because they "serve to" or are "useful for." Each reference is constituted by being part of a referential totality (*Verweisungsganzheit*). For example, a tool refers to the relations that are part of its making, the products it is used to make, the world of consumers and users, and the world of extant materials that go into its making. Or a pair of scissors is used for cutting, cutting has to do with making a blanket, and this has to do with providing warmth to a person's body. Each reference gradually leads us to a referential whole, an entire network of relations with other beings. This whole is no longer a being that is in relation to other beings but is instead relationality itself. For Heidegger, the world is this referential network of meaningfulness that precedes the rational subject and brings all beings into relation (BT, 70; 75). Because this referential whole cannot be another handy being in the world, it is nothing other than the world itself as the condition of possibility of being with and relating to other beings.[17] The world is what lets us be together with other beings and frees them for us to encounter.

Because the world is not an extant object, that to which it becomes present is not a subject but a being who is structurally being-in-the-world. Put another way, the being that accompanies the world's mode of presence is one for whom worldliness is constitutive. This being is not separate from but co-belongs with the world. For Heidegger, we, or more precisely, the Dasein in us, are such beings because our capacity for looking-after means that we have access to beings. Moreover, we understand our own worldliness because we are signifying beings that have an understanding of being. As he puts it, "worldhood is the specific presence [Anwesenheit] and encounter for an understanding looking-after [ein verstehendes Besorges]" (*HCT*, 209; 286). Understanding is not a faculty that produces knowledge and information, that is, thematic content about objects. Meaningfulness is not generated by attributing ideational content through interpretations or ideal projections of reason, the ascription of values and norms to a material objective world by a rational subject that stands apart from the world. Understanding is merely the ability to disclose the world's inherent meaningfulness as the totality of referential connections that enables us to discover other beings. Our ability to signify does not create the world but merely expresses that there is a totality of meaningful connections without which we could not signify at all.

Thus far, Heidegger's critiques of existing conceptions of the world have two implications for a normative theory of world literature. His trenchant critique of the spatialized objective world shows the limits of the emphasis on global circulation in recent theories of world literature. The suggestion that newer meanings are generated from the global locomotion of literary texts across territorial borders is especially ironic in light of Heidegger's argument that spacing destroys the world's meaningfulness and is expropriative because it deprives us of our proper worldliness. Circulation may lead to a proliferation of interpretations. But the quantitative increase in the meaning of mobile literary works does not have a normative horizon. More important, how readers can have access to texts and what enables them to generate new meanings is left ontologically unexplained. At the same time, Heidegger's account of the world also contains a critique of teleological accounts of the world that have a normative dimension. Teleology takes for granted how we are able to have access to other beings before we apprehend them as objects and form values and norms that we seek to actualize in the objective world. In short, what is left unexplained is how a world brings us into relation and how the world's meaningful unity comes about. I will now consider Heidegger's critique of the basic axiom of spiritualist and materialist teleologies of the world: the view that the world is constituted through intersubjective relations.

Being-with-Others: Heidegger's Critique of the World as Intersubjective Intercourse

For Heidegger, the world is also not a human community or society formed by material or spiritual intercourse. It is not the sum of all human subjects who exist with each other in the sense of "'the wide world,' of a woman or man 'of the world' [von 'der großen Welt,' von 'Weltdame' oder 'Mann von Welt']"

(*MFL*, 180; 232). When worldliness is equated with intercourse, we view ourselves as subjects that are originally separated from and relate to each other through contiguous contact. This reduces us to objectively present beings who reach out to one another across spatial distance. Heidegger thus emphatically rejects a foundational axiom of idealism and Marxist materialism—the thesis of intersubjectivity, where a discursive intersubjective relation constitutes the self-consciousness of individual subjects and furnishes the basis of a subject's social relations and relations to an objective world. Heidegger calls this the vulgar concept of the world, a naïve understanding of the world as something we create by adding up extant intraworldly human beings. Seeing the world as something created by communication or discursive exchange presupposes that Dasein is a subject that reaches out to another subject through language in order to form a world. The vulgar concept underwrites the normative theories of the world that I discussed in part I. This concept is also central to non-normative theories of world literature that privilege literary circulation and translation. For example, translation takes place between subjects who are either individual or collective, insofar as cultures and languages are viewed as subjects writ large. But this begs the question of how we can communicate with each other across the plurality of languages, that is, the access of one language to another and the porosity between languages. Without this accessibility and porosity, new meanings and interpretations could not be generated with the translation of literature. The vulgar concept of the world is inadequate because it begins from the premise that we are initially solipsistic and worldless individual selves and, therefore, obscures the fact that our being-in-the-world is always already being-with others. As I will show, worldliness as a power of worlding is always already collective in its structure but in a manner that is prior to and cannot be reduced to cosmopolitanism, and literary works are important in disclosing this power.

We can schematize Heidegger's argument as follows. Heidegger had already pointed out that our encounter with useful things opens up a public world because we also encounter others who will use the products of our work and for whom the handy things we experience are also handy. These others are not merely handy beings we find in the world, because as Dasein like us, they also have a world in which they encounter beings as useful. Hence they share the world with us, and we encounter them *with* it. "The world of Da-sein thus frees beings which are not only completely different from tools and things, but which themselves in accordance with their kind of being as *Da-sein* are themselves 'in' the world as being-in-the-world where they are at the same time encountered as inner-worldly. These beings are neither objectively present nor handy, but they *are like* the very Da-sein which frees them—*they are there, too, and there with it* [*mit da*]." (*BT*, 111; 118). Hence, being-in-the-world and having a world is also sharing a world with other Dasein. This being with others is an openness that is original to Dasein and not a consequence of a willed decision to engage in intercourse with other human subjects. As Heidegger puts it, "the others" are

> those from whom one mostly does *not* distinguish oneself, those among whom one is, too. This being-there-too [Auch-da-sein] with them does not have the ontological character of being objectively present "with" them *within a world* [eines "Mit"-Vorhandenseins *innerhalb einer Welt*]. The "with" is of the character of Da-sein, the "also" means the sameness of being as circumspect, heedful [besorgendes] being-in-the-world. . . . On the basis of this *with-adhering* [*mithaften*] being-in-the-world, the world is always already one that I share with the others. The world of Da-sein is a *with-world* [*Mitwelt*]. Being-in is *being-with* others [Das In-Sein ist *Mitsein mit* Anderen]. The innerworldly being-in-itself of others is Mitda-sein. (*BT*, 111–12; 118, translation modified)

Conversely, the world is the basic condition of my encounter with others and my accessibility as an other to other Dasein. "'Thou,'" he notes, "means 'you who are with me in a world'" (*BPP*, 298; 422).

The world is thus an irreducible openness where we cannot avoid being-with others. Being-with others has four important traits. First, like the referential connections of the *Umwelt*, the world where I am with others is inconspicuous. Even when I do not perceive other Dasein as on hand, they always accompany me as co-Dasein (*Mitda-sein*) in my daily absorption in the world that is looked after. Second, being-with others precedes and is independent of the objective presence of positive others. Solitude is a mere deficiency of being-with, a modification by virtue of the other's absence. Accordingly, being-with-another (*Miteinandersein*) is not a matter of adding the occurrence of multiple others, that is, a matter of counting or aggregative quantification.

Third, the fact that the other always accompanies me is an ontological mutual dependency that is based on and in turn supports our shared world (*HCT*, 240; 331). This mutual dependency is presupposed in all daily activities and cannot be avoided. I can only ignore another because I am already with that other in the same world. Avoiding and ignoring are acts that modify our mutual dependency. As Heidegger puts it, "it is only insofar as Dasein as being-in-the-world has the basic constitution of being-with that there is a *being-for* and–*against* and–*without-one-another* [*Für-* und *Wider-* und *Ohne-einander-sein*] right to the indifferent walking-alongside-one-another" (HCT, 241; 351–52). Fourth, the reference to the self in being-with is not the location of an objective presence in space who then joins up with another objectively present being. The self is not objectively locatable because in its being, it is always originally directed and transported outside itself toward the world and others. "In the 'here' Da-sein . . . speaks away from itself, in circumspection, to the 'over there' of something handy and means, however, *itself* in its existential spatiality" (BT, 112; 120).

We can understand being-with others as an ontological community that grounds all positive forms of human community. The original community of our worldliness is being-with-Dasein (*Mitda-sein*), where being-with (*Mit-sein*) is also being with other Dasein. It is meaningless to speak of a worldless, isolated Dasein who exists alone by itself before it is with other beings and other Dasein in the world.[18] Hence, we are not and cannot be solitary and solipsistic beings in the primary instance. This original community is prior to and exceeds the combative relation between subjects implied by the philosophy of intersubjectivity. Moreover, because being-with another is not the sociality of ontic human subjects, it leads to a critique of the idea that a subject who is initially isolated in its interior life relates to another alien psychic life through feeling and empathy. Dasein's relations to other Dasein in being-with are those of concern (*Fürsorge*). By showing that others also look after handy things, concern reveals the Dasein in them. It refers to others and is for the sake of others. Here, the world is a web of meaningful connections in which we encounter others as beings with whom we share the world because like us, they care for things (BT, 116; 123). Our worldly being-with-one-another, however, is often obscured because it usually occurs in deficient modes such as empathy. When empathy is regarded as being-with, we confuse an ontic phenomenon with the ontological ground it should disclose. We mistakenly view others not as those with whom we are originally in a world but as numerically quantified subjects we reckon (*rechnet*) with and add to ourselves to extend the circle of subjects whom we misrecognize as the world. Reckoning with others obscures the co-dependency with others that holds us together as a world because it is a deficient mode of being-with that looks at others through calculation and quantification. "Encountering a number of 'subjects' itself is possible only by treating the others encountered in their *Mitda-sein* merely as 'numerals.' This number is discovered only by a determinate being-with and being toward another. 'Inconsiderate' being-with 'reckons [rechnet]' with others without seriously 'counting on them' or even wishing 'to have anything to do' with them" (*BT*, 118; 125).

Abandoned to a World We Cannot Master: Radical Finitude
and Temporal Ecstasis as the Ground of Worldliness

Heidegger's critique of the inadequacy of concepts derived from geometrical space or quantified spatial extensiveness for understanding our existence leads him to suggest that our existential spatiality is based on temporal processes. I will now consider how he grounds the world's meaningfulness in temporalization.

Although we are the center of the web of meaningful relations that holds Dasein and other beings together as a world, we have a fundamentally ambivalent relation to the world. On the one hand, our self-understanding is an understanding of our worldliness. In referring to itself, Dasein opens out onto the world, and in referring to the world, Dasein returns to itself, such that we can say that Dasein is that opening that is world. *"In its familiarity with meaningfulness Da-sein is the ontic condition of possibility of the disclosure of beings encountered in the mode of being of relevance (handiness) in a world that can thus make themselves known in their in-itself. As such, Da-sein always means that a context of handy things is already essentially discovered with its being. In that it is, Da-sein has always already referred itself to an encounter with a 'world.' This dependency of being referred belongs essentially to its being"* (*BT*, 81; 87, translation modified). On the other hand, however, Dasein's self-referentiality is also marked by passivity: it is "the dependency of being referred." Dasein oscillates between active freedom (the power of placing, opening, and having access) and passive dependency. This passivity arises from the fact that there is no *reason* why beings are held together by a totality of referential connections. Because we are not connected with other beings by the reason of a higher being, the meaningfulness of the world—the fact that a world holds us and other beings together—is utterly contingent. And yet we are held together. Worldliness is structural to Dasein because it is thrown amid other beings. However, the passivity of being-thrown modulates into an active relation to the world when Dasein grasps its own thrown-ness as a power of projection that originates from its temporal character. Its "freedom" is not that of *making* the world through productive causal relations to objects but of maintaining the openness that is world.

If the world does not consist of calculable and measurable relations among subjects and objects, then how is Dasein held together with other beings as a common world? Heidegger's most important idea for world literature is his understanding of the world as transcendence and temporalization as a power of worlding. "The ontological concept of world," he notes, "indicates ontologically the metaphysical essence of Dasein as such with respect to its basic metaphysical constitution, i.e., transcendence" (MFL, 180; 232). In an obvious but fundamental sense, there is a world only because we exist and there is time. We are worldly only because we are beings with a finite temporal existence. In European philosophy, the finitude of human existence is derived from an absolute infinite being outside time who creates the temporal world and all worldly beings. This view combines the Greek philosophical idea of an absolute self-sufficient Being who contains the ground of its own existence and is free from contingency and the Christian idea of God as creator. In the case of human beings, the finite/infinite distinction is usually conflated with the mortality/immortality distinction. A finite existence is a mortal existence governed by life and death. During the limited term of life, we are part of a temporal world from which we depart when we die. Death releases us from this world. It is optimally a process of transcendence where we attain an eternal state of being, variously figured as the immortal soul, the kingdom of heaven, and so on. Because reason is the trace of the infinite in humanity, living a virtuous life according to reason's laws enables us to transcend finitude.

For Heidegger, this entire way of conceptualizing the world is wanting because it fetishizes the world as an objective presence and views the temporal world as a deficient condition to be transcended. In an illuminating discussion of this tradition, he charts the gradual shift from the pre-Socratic understanding of the world as a process to the vulgar concept of world of modern ontology, namely, the world as the sum of extant natural things or the community of human beings.[19] For Parmenides and Heraclitus, *cosmos* did not refer to extant beings but to a determinate condition or mode of being that is whole, the total condition (*Gesamtzustand*) in which beings are. More important, this condition is a process of worlding (*welten*), of being originally opened up to, included in and part of a whole such that partitioning or dividing occurs on the basis of world. Being in a world means "what worlds as a whole in a determinate manner, what has a definite basic condition and context [was als ganzes in einer bestimmten Weise weltet, einen bestimmten Grundzustand und Zusammenhang hat]" (MFL, 171; 220). In its fundamental ontological meaning, a world is a temporal process that brings all beings into relation or holds them together as a whole. "World means the totality [Gan-zheit], the unification and possible dispersal of beings," and "world has a con-nection with movement, change and time" (MFL, 172; 221).

Christian thought's decisive contribution to the thinking of world is its characterization of the world as a distinctively *human* mode of being that turns away from God. World refers to the "how" or manner and not the "what" of being.[20] For Paul, *cosmos* "means this condition and this situation of human beings, this manner [Art] and way of their Dasein, indeed the way they act towards virtues and works, towards nature and everything, their way of evaluating goods" (MFL, 173; 322). It "is the world, in the sense of human-ity, the community and society of humans in their attitude of forsaking God [gottabgekehrten], i.e., in their basic stance toward themselves and all beings. 'Worldly' then becomes the expression for a basic manner of human existence" (MFL, 173; 222). For Augustine, *mundus* likewise refers to those who inhabit the world and their ways of behaving towards other beings, for example, *dilectores mundi* (enjoyers of the world) or the just, who live with God in their hearts in their carnal worldly existence (MFL, 173–74; 223). Similarly, for Thomas Aquinas, world refers to the *saeculum*, the children of the world. "*Mundanus* [*worldly*] is equivalent to *saecularis* [*secular*], worldly in attitude, in contradistinction to *spiritualis* [*spiritual*]," where having a worldly attitude connotes cleverness or slyness (MFL, 174; 223).

The Greek idea of cosmos and its subsequent Christian iterations have the virtue of foregrounding Dasein's meaningful connections to other beings, "God-forsaken man in his association [Zusammenhang] with earth, stars, ani-mals, and plants" (BPP, 297; 422). In contradistinction, the modern or vulgar concept of world reduces the world to objective presence because it is only con-cerned with beings and not their mode of being. Baumgarten defines *mundus* as the totality of beings, the series of finite existing things. "In this contrived definition," Heidegger scathingly notes, "all determinate features are confused and lumped together in the superficial sense of summation. World is simply the sum of the actually extant. Thus the discriminations that were possessed by antiquity are here completely lost" (MFL, 174; 224).[21]

However, Christian and modern ontology also regard the world as a finite state of existence that should be surpassed. The theological interpretation of the world as a region of secular existence removed from its divine creator nec-essarily implies that it is a corporeal substance that needs to be transcended through higher spiritual activities that return human beings to God. In an-cient metaphysics, transcendence is the stepping-over that transports us to the unconditioned or the Absolute that exceeds the contingent sphere of finite human existence (MFL, 161; 206). Christian metaphysics substitutes the notion of a creator God for the transcendent, such that the unconditioned is identified with the divine (MFL, 162; 207). The modern epistemological concept of transcendence is continuous with the theological concept. It contrasts the transcendent, as that which lies outside consciousness and the soul, with the immanent. Cognition is a movement of transcendence where the subject breaks through the barriers that limit and restrict it to maintain a passage between the inside and the outside. In the final instance, what is transcendent to the subject is an absolute being who towers above everything as the cause of all and lies beyond experience (MFL, 162; 207). Consequently, modern philosophical conceptions of the world, secular or otherwise, regard the world as something in need of transcendence. The spiritualist and materialist theories of the world that I discussed in part I are organized around the transcendence of finitude. The spiritual world is a higher realm constructed through rational-moral activity, a refuge in which our highest human goods are preserved from the erosion of time. Here, the transcendence of finitude is a rejection of the contingency of the material world. In materialist accounts, transcendence refers to the overcoming of the realm of necessity through the rational regulation of the material world so that the mode of production can be organized according to the universal fulfillment of human needs.

Heidegger breaks with this entire tradition. He unmoors worldly existence from its erstwhile anchor in an infinite being. Instead of deriving the temporal world from an atemporal being as its ground and end, he argues that the world is grounded in radically finite temporality.[22] As an original process, temporality is not a condition to be transcended but the movement of transcendence itself. Because it is generated by the *process* of temporalization, the world *is* transcendence, the opening that puts us into relation with all other beings as a whole.

But what is radically finite temporality? How does it ground a world? Why are we worldly beings? Because radically finite temporality is not derived from an infinite atemporal being who gives existence, the unity of past, present, and future can only come from the movement of temporalization, which opens them up to one another. Hence, temporality is ecstatic or an opening-out-onto. In Heidegger's words, it is "the *ekstatikon par excellence. Temporality is the original 'outside of itself'* [*das ursprünglich 'Außer-sich'*] *in and for itself.* Thus we call the phenomena of future, having-been, and present, the *ecstasies* of temporality. Temporality is not, prior to this, a being that first emerges from *itself*; its essence is temporalizing [Zeitigung] in the unity of the *ecstasies*" (*BT*, 302; 329, translation modified).

Temporalization opens a world because the temporal ecstasies of past, present, and future are the basis of the three fundamental characteristics of our worldly existence: for-the-sake-of-itself, being-thrown, and in-order-to. First, as radically finite, we do not exist for the sake of an absolute infinite being but for the sake of our own power to be (*Seinkönnen*). Second, we find ourselves thrown into a world. "We are" always means "we have been thrown." Third, as factical beings, we are thrown amid other beings whom we need to exist factically. This precipitation forms an actual world. However, because the question of whether other beings in the world are created by an absolute infinite being is left undecided, their in-order-to is not some higher rational end but the human being's for-the-sake-of-itself. These characteristics are fundamentally temporal. They correspond to the three ecstasies of future, having-been (past), and present. Hence, what holds together the characteristics of our existence and maintains them as a whole can only be the original unity of time. By joining together the temporal ecstasies, the unifying movement of temporalization also unifies the characteristics of worldly existence. Our present (existence amid other beings) is generated from the unity of our future (our power to be) and our having-been (our thrownness). Temporalization discloses a world as that which co-belongs with our existence. Temporalization simultaneously maintains our existence and connects it to a world.[23] We exist with and in a world because our existence and the world are both grounded in the movement of temporalization.

Because temporality is a fundamental structure of our existence, we have an original power in relation to the world. Indeed, for Heidegger, only human Dasein is capable of posing the meaning of the concept of world—*how* we exist with other beings as a whole. "Since the Dasein is being-in-the-world and the basic constitution of the Dasein lies in temporality, *commerce with intraworldly beings is grounded in a determinate temporality [Zeitlichkeit] of being-in-the-world*" (*BPP*, 291; 413, emphasis in the original, translation modified).[24] Because Dasein is the process of temporalization, to say that temporality holds the world together also means that Dasein always accompanies and supports a world. As Heidegger puts it, "insofar as Da-sein temporalizes itself, a world *is* too. Temporalizing itself with regard to its being as temporality, Dasein *is* essentially 'in a world' on the basis of the ecstatic and horizontal constitution of that temporality. The world is neither objectively present nor at hand, but temporalizes itself in temporality [zeitigt sich in der Zeitlichkeit]. It 'is' 'there' together with the outside-itself [dem Außer-sich] of the ecstasies. If no Dasein exists, no world is 'there' either" (BT, 334; 365).[25] In line with Heidegger's trenchant critique of values and norms, the constitution of the world by temporalization is not the human power to create a spiritual world through the imposition of rational form and ends on the objective world. The teleological actualization of human ends in the world is modeled after the absolute capacities of an infinite being. Teleology thus obscures the power of temporalization as the source of the unity of the world and its meaningfulness by identifying this unity with human reason. Teleology seeks to regulate and appropriate temporality by representing it in the image of rational activity. In contradistinction, Dasein's worldly power is merely our involvement with our own finite temporality and our awareness that this temporality constitutes the world. The centering of other beings in the world on Dasein is emphatically not the teleological view that nature exists for human ends. Dasein as for-the-sake-of-which is not an ideal end of reason that the human subject recognizes as actualized in other beings, because we are the only beings with the capacity to set ends. Although we are accompanied by a world and encounter inner-worldly beings in our factical existence, we cannot rationally control the beings we find ourselves amid. "Only *what*, in *which* direction, *to what extent, and how* it [Dasein] actually discovers and discloses is a matter of freedom, although always within the limits of its thrownness" (BT, 334; 366). Hence, the meaningful relations of the world are "not a network of forms that is imposed upon some material by a worldless subject" (BT, 334; 366). Instead, the world is meaningful because it is held together by the temporalization that Dasein is.

Heidegger poignantly figures Dasein's radical finitude as our abandonment to a world we cannot control. We are thrown into a strange world because without an absolute creator, there is no absolutely rational basis for why we exist in the world and can have access to other beings. But there is some ground for consolatory resolve. We have a familiarity with this strange world because a certain strangeness is structural to our being, namely, the opening onto the outside that is our temporalization. Even if we cannot rationally explain why a world is there, we can find our way in it because the temporality on which our existence is based is also the power that gathers and holds the world together. Hence, Dasein can "understand itself in its abandonment [Überlassenheit] to a 'world' of which it never becomes master. . . . Factically existing Da-sein in a way always already knows its way around, even in a strange 'world'" (BT, 326; 356).

The World as Transcendence and the Force of Worlding

In my view, despite his rejection of the conception of the world as a domain that is constructed by human values, norms, and ends and organized according to teleological time, Heidegger regards the world as a "normative force" in his account of the world as temporal transcendence. Here, we have to understand "normative" in the qualified sense of the ontological ground of normativity and "force" as a power of opening that is suspended between the active and the passive and that precedes what we commonly conceive as "causal force."

Transcendence is worldly because it does not leave the world behind but *is* precisely worldliness, our constitutive opening up to inner-worldly beings and other Dasein. However, transcendence is not merely the movement of our being factically thrown amid other beings. In our thrownness, we relate and have access to other beings such that we understand their being and disclose our being to ourselves. "Dasein is thrown, factical, thoroughly amidst nature through its corporeality, and transcendence lies in the fact that these beings, among which Dasein is and to which Dasein belongs, are surpassed by Dasein. . . . As transcending, i.e., as free, Dasein is something alien to nature" (MFL, 166; 212). Our transcendence of nature refers to our separation from the factical beings we encounter as objectively present such that we reveal ourselves as constituted differently from them. However, this is not a rejection of the temporal world for a supersensible atemporal realm, a higher eternal world that insulates us from the ravages of time because it has greater permanence than the contingent finite world. Dasein transcends objectively present nature. But the temporal world cannot be reduced to the sum of objectively present beings. That toward which Dasein transcends is precisely the world as the condition of possibility of our relations to nature. Transcendence is the opening of a world, the openness of being that is world. As Heidegger puts it in "Letter on 'Humanism,'"

> in the name of "being-in-the-world," "world" does not in any way imply earthly as opposed to heavenly being, nor the "worldly" as opposed to the "spiritual." For us "world" does not at all signify beings or any realm of beings but the openness [Offenheit] of being. The human being is, and is human, insofar as he is the ek-sisting one.
>
> He stands out into the openness of being. Being itself, which as the throw has projected the essence of the human being into "care," is as this

openness. Thrown in such fashion, the human being stands "in" the openness of being. "World" is the clearing [Lichtung] of being into which the human being stands out on the basis of his thrown essence.[26]

Worldly transcendence can only be considered a kind of causality or force by catachresis, because these categories pertain to subjects and objects. The world's reality is nonobjective and nonsubjective because it is the ontological condition that precedes and exceeds relations between a subject and an object. The world is not of the order of the subject because it arises from the sheer movement of temporalization. Nor is it an objective being or thing. It is "already 'further outside' than any object could ever be" (BT, 335; 366). The world is nothing because it is not an objectively present thing in the same way that "time 'is' not, but rather temporalizes itself [Zeit 'ist' nicht, sondern zeitigt sich]" (MFL, 204; 264). As Heidegger puts it, "'nothing' means: not a being in the sense of something extant; also 'nothing' in the sense of no-thing, not one of the beings Dasein itself transcends. . . . The world: a nothing, no being [kein Seiendes]—and yet something: nothing of beings—but being [nichts Seiendes—aber Sein]" (MFL, 195; 252).

This nothing is not the simple negation of something. As the ineffable condition for the appearance of beings, the world is more objective than any possible object.[27] "The world is nothing in the sense that it is nothing that is. It is nothing that is yet something that 'is there' [es gibt]. The 'there is' which is this not-a-being is itself not being, but is the self-temporalizing temporality [Das 'es,' das da dieses Nicht-Seiende gibt, ist selbst nicht seiend, sondern ist die sich zeitigende Zeitlichkeit]. And what the latter, as ecstatic unity, temporalizes is the unity of its horizon, the world. World is the nothing which temporalizes itself originally, that which simply arises in and with temporalization. We therefore call it the *nihil originarium*" (MFL, 210; 272). This nothing at the origin is the power that originates objective reality. Worldly transcendence thus bears directly on our agency in relation to the objective world. Our abandonment to a strange world is not a condition of inadequacy, loss, or despairing helplessness but a strength or capability. Although Dasein does not make the world or constitute it through intersubjective relations, a world nevertheless cannot exist without Dasein because any world is grounded in our temporalization. Hence, our ability to understand the temporal process that opens a world is a power of freedom. Indeed, because we are not held together with other beings by the grace of an absolute creator but by the sheer existence of our being-in-the-world, we share a world with other Dasein, and we world the world and support it by this process of sharing. Heidegger elaborates on the power to world (*welten*) as a "force" through the concepts of world-entry (*Welteingang*) and world-formation (*Weltbildung*).

World-entry refers to how beings enter a world and become inner-worldly beings who are not yet objects by virtue of Dasein's existence. As the ground of my factical existence amid other beings, the movement of transcendence allows beings entry into the world and enables them to be revealed to me. Temporalization allows a being to be, gives a being its being, by giving it time. Temporalization is thus a worlding, the propulsion of Dasein toward beings that allows them to factically enter into a world. Just as there is no world without Dasein, worlding only takes place with Dasein's self-temporalization. Without Dasein, beings could never enter a world and be encountered because they are incapable of transcendence. Hence, world-entry has the status of a historical occurrence. "Entry into world is not a process of extant things, in the sense that beings undergo a change thereby and through this change break into the world. The extant's entry into world is 'something' that happens to it. World-entry has the characteristic of happening [das Geschehens], of history. World-entry happens when transcendence happens, i.e., when historical Dasein exists" (MFL, 194; 250–51).

What is important for present purposes is that for Heidegger, transcendence is freedom. "Beings of Dasein's essence must have opened themselves as freedom, i.e., world must be held out in the upswing, a being must be constituted as being-in-the-world, as transcending, if that being itself and beings in general are to become manifest [offenbar] as such. Thus Dasein . . . is therefore, as factically existent, nothing other than the existent possibility for beings to gain *entry to world*. When, in the universe of beings, a being attains more being in the existence of Dasein, i.e., when temporality temporalizes itself, only then do beings have the hour and day to enter the world" (MFL, 193; 249, translation modified). As a being that understands its own power to be (its temporal structure), Dasein is free because it discloses its full possibility or capability to be to itself. We are always thrown amid factical beings that restrict the fullness of our possibility to be. Grasping our possibility to be is at the heart of freedom, because this grasping projects a world as the clearing in which Dasein's power to be is no longer hampered. Worlding is the surpassing of actual beings that limit our full possibilization.

Unlike Heidegger's earlier existential approach, the idea of world formation elaborates on worlding by comparing the fact that Dasein has a world to the stone's and animal's relations to a world.[28] Dasein's power of world-formation, he suggests, distinguishes it from the stone's worldlessness (*Weltlosigkeit*) and the animal's poverty in world (*Weltarmut*). Heidegger's existential analyses employed terms such as *weltlos* and *ein bloßes Subjekt ohne Welt* (a mere subject without world) to describe what Dasein, which is always with-world, is not. Regarding Dasein as an initially worldless subject leads to a deprivation of world (*Entweltlichung*). The comparative approach goes further by suggesting that worldlessness and poverty of world are constitutive of the essence of other beings.

What is world-formation and how does it co-belong with human beings? How can it be an activity if the world is not an object that human beings produce through their causal activity? Reiterating his earlier argument that the world is not a rational form that consciousness imposes on material reality, Heidegger notes that the wholeness of the world is not a frame we prescribe onto other beings to make them manifest to us. World does not mean "subjective form and the formal constitution of the human conception of beings in themselves" (FCM, 285; 413). Forms presuppose a human subject who actualizes them as an objective world by the practical causality of fabrication or action. In contradistinction, world-formation refers to the process where Dasein's sheer existence gives rise to a world. The world, understood as "the manifestness [Offenbarkeit] of beings as such as a whole," forms itself. But because manifestness belongs to Dasein's worldly being, this is identical to saying that Dasein is world-forming (FCM, 349; 507).

Heidegger elaborates on world-formation as follows:

> It is not the case that man first exists and then also one day decides amongst other things to form a world. Rather world-formation is something that occurs, and only on this ground can a human being exist in the first place. Man as man is world-forming. This does not mean that the human being running around in the street as it were is world-forming, but that the Dasein in man is world-forming. . . . The Dasein in man forms world: (1) it brings it forth [es stellt sie her], (2) it gives an image [Bild] or view [Anblick] of the world, it sets it forth; (3) it constitutes the world, contains and embraces it. (FCM, 285; 413–14)

The setting forth of the world through the giving of an image is a sly allusion to the German tradition of *Bildung* and the idealist topos of *Darstellung*. *Bildung* is the spiritual work of cultivating a moral personality when a subject remakes itself in the image of collective ideals that it prescribes to itself through the interiorization of moral norms from the ethical world. *Darstellung* is the power of presentation that gives actuality to a concept by exhibiting it in intuition. These are powers of a subject. World-formation, however, is prior to and constitutes the powers of a subject because it is a fundamental ontological process grounded in the force of temporalization. What forms a world is not a subject but Dasein. Here, *Bildung* is not a subject's activity but the ecstatic temporalization of Dasein's sheer existence that brings and sets forth an image of the manifestness of beings as a whole. Accordingly, world-formation is a fundamental occurrence that happens in Dasein in the same way that the world-entry of other beings is an occurrence.

There is, however, one important difference. World-entry happens *to* other beings that are worldless or poor in world. It brings them into a world. In contradistinction, world-formation is an occurrence *in* Dasein. It does not befall Dasein from outside its own essence. Because the world is grounded in the temporalization of our existence, as Dasein, we hold the world together and embrace it. But at the same time, because the world is our opening to other beings as a whole, the world also holds us together with other beings and embraces all beings. The world gathers and binds together.

This is the closest Heidegger comes to calling the world a force. In "On the Essence of Ground" (1928), Heidegger had already reinscribed "world" as a verb, *welten*, that is associated with the process of prevailing (*walten*): "*Freedom alone can let a world prevail and let it world for Dasein [kann dem Dasein eine Welt walten und welten lassen]. World never is, but worlds [Welt ist nie, sondern weltet].*"[29] Here, he develops the motif of prevailing by arguing that the world's essence is to prevail on us from within us. Colloquially, forces (*Gewalt*) are what prevail, such that we often speak of the prevalence of natural forces (*Naturgewalt*) or divine forces (*Gottesgewalt*). In philosophical discourse, force can refer either to the physical efficient force (*Kraft*) of nature as mechanism, the vital force (*vis vitalis*) of living beings, or to the normative force of laws or moral reason as a ground of obligation (*Verbindlichkeit*) in a Kantian formulation. Force in both senses is characterized by the necessitation of law, whether it is that of natural causal laws or those of practical reason. The "force" of worlding and letting a world prevail is neither the necessitation of nature nor the imperativity of moral willing and action but the sheer propulsion that opens a world. It is prior to subjects and objects and hence is suspended between the passive and the active.

For us to enter into the fundamental occurrence of world-formation and for the world to prevail, we must let the world's essence unfold. This means that although the "force" of the world is originally related to the Dasein in us, it is not *our* "force," a power that we can actively deploy. It implies a certain passivity of receptive awaiting, letting be, and preparation. The prevailing of the world presses upon us, but this pressing is not the impact of an object on our faculties of observation or cognition, because these attitudes obscure the world. "All observation of whatever kind must remain eternally distant from what world is, insofar as its essence resides in what we call the prevailing of world [das Walten der Welt], a prevailing that is more originary than all those beings that press themselves upon us" (FCM, 351; 510). Nor can the world's essence as prevailing be unfolded by discursive knowledge, by "the power of the concept and of comprehension [Begreifens]" (FCM, 351; 510). Instead, one can only wait for the force of the world to happen. We can only "*prepare our entering into the occurrence of the prevailing of world*" (FCM, 351; 510).

Yet this preparation is also the action (*Handeln*) of thought. Our entering into the "force" of world takes place through a thinking that is neither conceptual nor the power of setting rational ends.

> Awakening is a matter for each individual human being, not a matter of his or her good will or even skillfulness, but of his or her destiny, whatever falls or does not fall to him or her. Everything that contingently falls upon us, however, only falls and falls due to us if we have waited for it and are able to wait. Only whoever honors a mystery gains the strength to wait. Honouring in the metaphysical sense means action that engages in the whole that in each case prevails through us. Only in this way do we enter the possibility that this "as a whole" and world will *explicitly* prevail through us. (FCM, 351; 510)

Although it is not the causal activity of making, our access to the world is active in three senses. First, it involves the action of engaging with the prevalence of the whole through an honoring of the world. Second, this thinking is a praxis. When the world prevails, its "force" transforms us by bringing out and returning us to the Dasein in us. At the same time, however, one does not effect a transformation in the world but only prepares for the world to prevail. Unlike Marx's eleventh thesis on Feuerbach, the imperative here is not to change the world but to "transform the humanity of us human beings into the Da-sein in ourselves," to "take upon ourselves the effort to transform man, and thereby traditional metaphysics, into a more originary Da-sein [being-there], so as to let the ancient fundamental questions spring forth anew from this" (FCM, 350; 508–9). Inquiry into the problem of the world thus lets the "force" of the world prevail through us.

Third, the fundamental structure of the world's prevalence is projection. "World prevails in and for a letting-prevail that has the character of projecting" (FCM, 362; 527). In temporal projection, we are thrown in anticipation onto the possibilities presented by other beings we live with that are otherwise hidden. The world is the whole of these anticipated possibilities. Hence, the world is neither merely what is possible or actual. It is not the already possible or the already actual but the "space" of possibility that enables something to be possible and to be subsequently actualized. The world is sheer possibilization or making-possible (*Ermöglichung*). Because projection opens the "space" that makes possibility and actuality possible, it is prior to the distinction between act and potentiality. The world's projecting "force" is not action in any sense derived from Aristotle's concept of *energeia*, namely that which makes actual the matter that is merely potential (*dynamis*) through a process of formation. It is instead an original action before actualization. It does not make anything actual but is the irruptive releasing of the power of possibilization into actuality. As Heidegger puts it, "in the occurrence of projection world is formed, i.e., in projecting something erupts and irrupts toward possibilities, thereby irrupting into what is actual as such, so as to experience itself as having irrupted as an actual being in the midst of what can now be manifested as beings" (FCM, 365; 531). The world's actuality is the actuality of making-possible. When the world is disclosed to us, we experience the power of making-possible as actual being.

Worlding is the origin of normativity in two respects. First, as I have shown, worldly transcendence is ontological freedom. For Heidegger, it is also the original source of obligation. Transcendence opens and binds a world. Without these binding ties, we could not be subjects who freely choose in rational spontaneity to act in accordance with obligations. As Heidegger puts it, "freedom simultaneously unveils itself as making possible something binding, indeed obligation in general [die Ermöglichung von Bindung und Verbindlichkeit überhaupt]."[30]

Second, the world is nothing other than the source of meaningfulness from which human values and norms are derived. The world held together by time is neither a higher spiritual realm nor a material whole created by the causality of human self-regulation by a society of associated producers who remake the world in its image. Instead, the world as temporalization is "below" or "before" beings. It is the condition of possibility of spiritual transcendence and material activity. It forms a total context of meaningfulness that enables us to encounter the beings we have been thrown amid, and without this access, we could not prescribe ends onto objects and engage in intersubjective intercourse that creates values and norms.

There is thus a quiet obligation to safeguard the ontological source of obligation. Worlding is not a normative end that human subjects rationally prescribe because it is universally good. But it is nevertheless marked by necessitation. The sheer fact of temporalization as the ground of existence gives rise to an imperative to exist in its fullest possibilities. Hence, although worldliness is not a value that can be used to compare humans with beings of different kinds of being, there is an implied imperative to have a world and to let it prevail: unless we prepare for this, we will be unworlded, leveled into a homogeneous kind of worldless being, and will mistake our being for that of animals or stones.

The Loss of the Proper: Unworlding and the Homelessness of Modern Humanity

The "force" of worlding is prior to and remains after every objective and intersubjective world as the (re)opening of the world and, therefore, of worlds other than the present one. It is a real promise of a future that is structural to any present world. This "force" is proper to us because Dasein's existence is grounded in temporality. However, this promise is fragile because worldliness is easily obscured. Because worldliness is being-open and being-transported to what is outside, we can easily lapse into a derived, inauthentic mode of outside-ness that carries Dasein away from or transports it beyond itself without return, insofar as we fail to recognize the structural openness to the outside that is proper to our being. This is the root of all unworlding. Unworlding can happen at the level of philosophical discourse, for example, when the world is determined as homogeneous geometrical space. More important, in our daily life, we are absorbed by the objects we care for and the mass subjects we interact with. In the latter case, our being-with others is obscured when we identify with an indeterminate other or anonymous collective subject, the they (Das Man), a key feature of bureaucratically administered mass society and its manufactured public opinion. Whereas our original being-with propels us outside ourselves and gives rise to authentic community with others, the interpretation of our relations to others as a relation of geometrical distance (Abständigkeit) to the they perverts our authentic relations to others and turns them into a passive belonging to an average neutral subject. We unwittingly submit to its domination because we have ceded our responsibility to it.

In his later writings, Heidegger views unworlding as a historical development of the space-time compression of globalized modernity. In "The Age of the World Picture" (1938) he argues that modernity's essence is the reduction of the world to a picture, a type of representing (*vorstellen*, literally, a fore-setting—*vor-stellen*) that places beings before us as objects in a way that maps out a set place for each and every being in an interconnected system, much as each figure in a painting has a specific place in its frame. The world as picture unworlds because it reduces the being of beings we encounter to their representedness as objects and our being to that of representing subjects who can dispose of objects according to our ends and values. In modernity, being consists in "being brought before man as the objective," "in being placed in the realm of man's information and disposal so that in this way alone, it is in being."[31] Because the representing subject puts all other beings into the picture, the anthropos is elevated into the referential center and measure of all beings. It thereby usurps the ground of being, namely, the holding and gathering together of the world by temporalization.

The interminable innovation and control of nature that typifies modernity is based on the ability of humankind as the source of all standards to constitute all other beings, "the realm of human capacity as the domain of measuring and execution for the purpose of the mastery [Bewältigung] of beings as a whole" ("AWP," 69; 92). The modern conquest of the world is epitomized by the space-time compression of globalization: the emergence of the gigantic, the "destruction of great distances by the airplane," "the representations of foreign and remote worlds in their everydayness produced at will by the flick of a switch" ("AWP," 71; 95). In *Gelassenheit* (1955), modern mass media is said to render us homeless. Films carry us into "realms of representation [Vorstellungsbezirke], and give the illusion of a world that is no world."[32] The reduction of beings to objects of representation leads to a loss of being (*Seins verlustig*) ("AWP," 77; 101). The world is no longer a meaningful whole but merely what we create through subjective representation. We compensate for the loss of being by attributing value to the constructed being (*ausgelegten Sein*) of objects. But these values have no ground or substance other than ourselves and merely objectify our needs as the highest ends to be achieved in the self-establishment of the human subject as the ground of being. Values, Heidegger poignantly notes, are "the powerless and threadbare mask of the objectification of beings, an objectification that has become flat and devoid of background. No one dies for mere values" ("AWP," 77; 102).

In "Letter on 'Humanism'" (1946) the modern denudation of the world leads to homelessness. Because the human subject has usurped being as the ground of the world, we have lost our worldliness and are no longer at home in the world. This usurpation was possible because being has already abandoned the world we live in. Being's abandonment of the world must be distinguished from our ontological condition of being abandoned to a strange world. The latter entails a certain freedom in our ability to understand the transcending character or structural openness of our existence. We reveal our worldliness by posing the question of being and not confusing being with extant beings. In contrast, "the abandonment of beings by being [Seinsverlassenheit]" is "the oblivion of being" ("LH," 258; 339). Because we have turned away from the question of being, we have been abandoned by being and have obscured and lost the world. The homelessness of modernity is a symptom of our forgetting of being. Indeed, for Heidegger, Marx's topos of human alienation is merely a derived interpretation of the modern destiny of homelessness ("LH," 258; 339).

Heidegger's Critique of Cosmopolitanism

Heidegger's elaboration of the problematic of unworlding from a historical and practical perspective indicates that far from being a utopian ideal, the world is the real ground of possible practical projects for a future beyond the impoverished and abandoned world of modernity exemplified by capitalist globalization. Here, we need to distinguish the project of worlding from modern cosmopolitanism, which sees active membership in a community of human beings that stretches across the globe as the solution to the moral and political problems of global modernity. Heidegger's critique of intersubjectivity implies a critique of modern and contemporary cosmopolitanisms. In "Letter on 'Humanism'" Heidegger is more explicit. Poetry, he suggests, "herald[s] the destiny of the world." "The world-historical thinking" of Hölderlin's poetry is superior to "the mere cosmopolitanism of Goethe" because it is "essentially more primordial and thus more futural [zukünftiger]" ("LH," 258; 339, translation modified).

Cosmopolitanism is informed by a vulgar concept of world in two respects. First, it presupposes membership in a world based on universal characteristics of human subjects. These characteristics are the constitutive features of humanity, defined variously in terms of feeling, reason, dignity, or sociality. The world is as much created as it is affirmed through the recognition of being human and the universal pursuit of the highest ends of humanity. Second, cosmopolitanism involves a projection outside an individual subject's spatio-geographical location, for example, one's family, village, nation, and so on. Through this projection, the subject steps out into a wider world and in that process becomes a larger self, a member of a collective subject of increasing range. Cosmopolitanism therefore understands the world as something constructed from intersubjective relations, especially communication or linguistic intercourse. The upward projection or ascending movement from a given location is often understood as a dialectic between a bounded locality and a world that overcomes borders and boundaries.

Cosmopolitanism obscures worldliness because the world refers to the being-with of all peoples, groups and individuals, and other beings. It is the original openness that gives us accessibility to others so that we can be together. Gradually expanding intersubjective relations so that the geographical boundaries of human community are extended transnationally does not create a world but instead obscures it by reducing worldliness to spatial extension. More important, Heidegger notes that mere communication, which includes the circulation of discourse through translation celebrated by recent theories of world literature, cannot build a world because it already presupposes a world.[33] Sharing a world with others is what enables us to reach out and communicate in the first place. We do not become part of a world, that is, cosmopolitan, by communicating with others. That a meaningful world is original to my being is what enables me to understand the other in general, including those others from a foreign world or a past world separated by the passage of time. In such situations, I am always already with the other and share a world with him or her even when we are not of the same culture or linguistic "world" and even when the other cannot be objectively present.[34] Being-with others is an original "cosmic" condition where Dasein is already with all possible others, including those from other cultures and historical eras. Cosmopolitan feeling and belonging is derived from this original worldliness. But because cosmopolitanism's starting point is a parochial subject who becomes cosmopolitan, it also obscures the force of temporalization that holds the world together.

Here, one should note that Heidegger's critique of modernity proceeds from different grounds from those of Marxist cosmopolitanism, despite an apparent similarity in vocabulary. His critique of the homogenizing violence of spacing differs in several respects from the critique of abstract space in Marxist geography. Abstract space is the homogeneous space of commodity circulation that the world market has extended across the globe. This homogenized space is a consequence of the fact that labor and its products have lost all qualitative distinction, because the living activity of creative labor has been reduced to commodified abstract labor and alienated from the worker. Alienation is the sundering of an object from its producer. It leads to the depletion of self because the producers can no longer recognize themselves in their products and affirm their essential being as human in the object as their self-actualization. For Marx, labor is living, the source of life, because human life is the survival of a biological and social subject through the material processes of production. In contradistinction, what Heidegger repeatedly calls "the authentic vitality [eigentliche Lebendigkeit] of being-in-the-world" (HCT, 231; 371) refers to Dasein's co-belonging with the force of temporalization. For Heidegger, homogeneous space is the consequence of determining being as objective presence. Although the alienation of labor is an important historical symptom of this, the loss of world is not reducible to Marxist alienation. From a Heideggerian perspective, the concept of living labor is underwritten by an ontology of objective presence. Labor is an activity by which a human subject remakes objective nature according to his or her needs. Both subject and objective nature inhabit geometrical space, and labor takes place within spatialized time. The material causality of production is thus an instance of calculative thinking that effaces Dasein's worldliness.

The fact that progressive normative discourses of world-making such as Marxism and cosmopolitanism are informed by ontologies that promote inauthentic existence and obscure worldliness does not mean that the concept of worlding is incompatible with these other accounts of the world. Heidegger emphasizes that inauthenticity is a possible consequence that necessarily accompanies being-in-the-world. Our structural openness makes it possible for us to lose ourselves by being absorbed in the world, and we mostly understand ourselves inauthentically in everyday life. But because the world is grounded in the force of temporalization, it always persists and can be disclosed again by living authentically. Heidegger's solution to the unworlding of the world is governed by a powerful discourse of the proper (*eigen*) that draws on the rich etymological links between authenticity (*Eigentlichkeit*), own-ness or being one's own (*Sich-zueigen-sein*), self-belonging, being in possession of and having oneself, what is appropriate (*eigentlich*) to oneself, and self-proximity. These "values" of the proper are opposed to inauthenticity, the forgetting and loss of the proper of Dasein. Heidegger figures the achievement of authentic existence as Dasein's return to its own proper self so that we exist according to our capacity to be proper to ourselves such that "we at the ground are *able* to be own to ourselves [zu eigen sein *können*]" (*BPP*, 160; 228). We can regain the world by understanding that having a world is proper to our being.

Heidegger is often criticized for privileging the contemplative activity of solitary Dasein over practical action in concert with others as the optimal way of disclosing authentic existence. For example, he suggests that the being-with others of our everyday collective life generally leads to an inauthentic they-self, whereas the fullest disclosure of authentic existence takes place in my solitary anticipation of my own death. I will address these criticisms in my discussion of Arendt's conception of the world in the next chapter. For the moment, it bears emphasizing that although Heidegger does not elaborate on authentic modes of being-with others, Dasein's authentic self-relation is not a withdrawal from the world. The resoluteness of authentic existence involves actual commitments in the world and acting with concrete others to "actualize" the original ontological community structural to Dasein's self-hood. In Heidegger's words, "as *authentic being a self* [*eigentliches Selbstsein*], resoluteness does not detach Da-sein from its world, nor does it isolate it so that it becomes a free-floating ego. How could it, if resoluteness as authentic disclosedness is, after all, nothing other than *authentically being-in-the-world*? Resoluteness brings the self right into its being together with handy things, actually taking care of them, and pushes it toward concerned being-with the others" (*BT*, 274; 298).

The relation between the normative force of worlding and Marxist and other cosmopolitanist forms of world-making is aporetic. World-making obscures worlding, and an understanding of worlding undermines the ontological basis of specific projects of world-making and shows their limits. However, the openness to other beings is the original ground of cosmopolitanism, understood as intercourse among subjects and belonging to a world community even if this openness cannot be reduced to cosmopolitanism. Moreover, however much it is obscured, worlding is always an immanent possibility. As the indestructible possibility of opening up other worlds, it is a valuable supplement to Marxism and cosmopolitanism in situations where the calculations and imperatives of capitalist accumulation appear to have saturated the entire globe. Capitalist globalization can destroy human life and create alienated and reified subjects in its image. But because the process of accumulation needs time and capitalism cannot destroy time, temporalization persists as the opening of new worlds that cannot be effaced. It is the persistent regrounding of cosmopolitan projects.

Poetry and the Uncovering of Worldliness

The phenomenological concept of worlding offers a radically new perspective on literature's relation to the world based on the affinity between the realities of literature and the world. Because worlding is grounded in temporalization, the world eludes and confounds received philosophical understandings of reality. It is nonobjective and nonsubjective. It is nothing, but it nevertheless is, and its "force" is suspended between the active and passive. It is the "site" of a complex interplay between possibility and actuality. The world is lost when our possibilities of being are leveled by its reduction to objective presence. We regain the world when we grasp it as the force of making-possible that enables possibility and actuality.

The causal power that spiritualist and materialist accounts of the world attribute to literature is based on a view of the world as an objective presence that needs to be transcended or remade and regulated through a subject's rational formative activity. In contradistinction, Heidegger privileges a specific type of literature, poetry, as the intimation of the world's peculiar reality. Poetry is neither a subject's spiritual product nor a material cause in the objective world. It is instead the power of joining-together. It has an ontological affinity with the world's complex reality because this power is the essence of the logos.

In his earlier writings, Heidegger suggests that poetry makes worldliness visible because it has an ontological status similar to that of world. The world is the total context of meaningfulness that holds us together with other beings at the same time that it is held together by the force of temporalization. Poetry reveals this holding-together because as an expression of the logos, it is itself a meaningful whole. Commenting on Rilke's *Aufzeichnungen des Malte Laurids Brigge*, Heidegger argues that "poetry [Dichtung], is nothing but the elementary coming into words [Zum-Wort-kommen], the becoming-uncovered, of existence as being-in-the-world. For the others who before it were blind, the world first becomes visible by what is thus spoken" (BPP, 171–72; 244, translation modified). Rilke's words show us "the original world" that sustains our encounter with things, the complex connections and multiple meanings that are obscured when we regard things merely as objects of theoretical observation and knowledge. Being-in-the-world is the philosophical content of the concept of life. The meaning expressed in Rilke's poetic description is not creatively projected onto the described thing by a subject's cognitive powers but arises from the very real connections that enable us to encounter things in the first place. "What Rilke reads . . . from the exposed wall is not imagined into the wall, but, quite to the contrary, the description is possible only as an interpretation and elucidation of what is 'actually' in this wall, which leaps forth from it in our natural comportmental relationship to it" (BPP, 173; 246).

The world's meaningfulness can only be expressed in nonthematic discourse. Poetry has an ontological affinity with the world because it exemplifies nonthematic discourse. Commenting on Aristotle's characterization of man as *zoon logon echon*, Heidegger interprets logos as the faculty of being able to speak or talk discursively. Aristotle's phrase means "that living being that essentially possesses the possibility of discourse [Rede]" (FCM, 305; 442). When *ratio* was used to translate *logos* and when man was described as a living being with reason (*animal rationale*), we lost this definition of the human being in terms of discourse and language. Our intrinsic connection to the world comes from the fact that language and discourse are proper to man. Because discourse gives something to be understood and elicits understanding, it involves the comportment and activity of human beings among one another. Discourse brings human beings together.

The meaning of discourse also has this dimension of bringing-together. Unlike an animal cry that responds to a physiological stimulus, a word does not arise from physical connections because it is a meaningful utterance. The former only generates noise, meaningless vocal utterances that cannot be understood. In contradistinction, discourse is grounded in meaning and the possibility of understanding. This means that "meaning does not accrue to sounds, but the reverse: the sound is first formed from meanings that are forming and already formed" (FCM, 307; 445). The formative stamping or impressing (*Prägung*) of sound by already-formed meanings means that language is a symbolic whole. It is a joining of one thing to another in at least two senses: the meaningful word joins a meaning and a sound, and the fact of discourse joins the speaker and the addressee together in a circle of understandability as parts of a whole that necessarily belong to each other. Hence, "discourse and word are to be found only in the occurrence of the symbol, whenever and to the extent that an agreement and a holding together [Zusammenhalten] occur" (FCM, 308; 446).

Discourse is essentially nonthematic. It does not originate in isolated concepts that are attached to sounds and posited via propositional statements as the truth of individual objects. Instead, discourse arises from and expresses the holding-together that makes individual meanings and meaning in general possible. The logos is a whole of connections that gathers and holds every being together such that the parts belong to each other. This holding-together is the condition of possibility of meaning. The symbolic dimension of discourse is nothing other than the world as a total context of meaningful connections that enable the human being to have access to and understand other beings, that is, the world as transcendence. "In accordance with his essence, man holds himself together with something else, insofar as he holds himself in a comportment toward other beings, and on the basis of this comportment toward other beings is able to refer to these other beings as such. . . . Sounds which emerge out of and for this *fundamental relation of letting something come into agreement and holding it together are words*" (FCM, 308; 446–47).

For Heidegger, poetry exemplifies nonthematic discourse. It expresses the world's meaningfulness as such and exceeds the functioning of grammar and phonemics. Hence, the true study of poetry is driven by "a passion for the logos."

> When a poem [Gedicht] is made the object of philological interpretation, the resources of grammar find themselves at a loss, and precisely with respect to the greatest creations of language. . . . This task is also that of laying the foundations of philology in the broader sense. And by this we understand neither the unearthing of grammatical rules and sound-shifts, nor gossiping about literature after the manner of the literati, but rather a passion for the λογος; for it is in the λογος that man expresses what is most essential to him, so as in this very expression to place himself into the clarity, depth, and need pertaining to the essential possibilities of his action, of his existence. (FCM, 303; 438–39)

Heidegger's later writings make an even stronger connection between the force of worlding and works of art in general.[35] The work of art is constituted by a perpetual breach (*Riss*) between world and earth. The earth is the ground that provides a shelter for human dwelling. But as the self-sustaining support for human existence, an inexhaustible "resource" that we cannot use up, the earth conceals itself from the penetration of human cognition and calculation. Developing his earlier account, world is both the domain into which we are thrown as existing beings by temporalization *and* the site of our openness to beings, where we can take up the full possibilities of existence. "World is that always nonobjectual [Ungegendständliche] to which we are subject as long as the paths of birth and death, blessing and curse, keep us transported into being. Wherever the essential decisions of our history are made, wherever we take them over or abandon them . . . there the world worlds [weltet die

Welt]."³⁶ World designates a "force" of opening that necessarily rests on the earth. It raises up the earth and brings it into the open as that which hides itself so that it can be repeatedly drawn on. The earth is not atemporal. It is the movement of self-secluding, and it "unfolds . . . into an inexhaustible richness of simple modes and shapes" ("owa," 25; 34). What is important for present purposes is that by virtue of its being a process of coming-into-being, the work of art is ontologically the same as the process of worlding. It is worlding to a second degree. It exemplifies worlding by making worlding its structure. It "make[s] free the free of the open [freigeben das Freie des Offenen] and install[s] [einrichten] this free place in its structure. . . . As a work, the work holds open the open of a world [stellt . . . eine Welt auf]" ("owa," 23; 31). To use the early Heidegger's vocabulary, which is echoed here, the work of art exemplifies world-entry—it brings the earth into the opening that is world and maintains this opening. Thus, a work of art is a privileged way of maintaining the force of the world's prevailing: "Rising-up-within-itself the work opens up a *world* and keeps it abidingly in force [im waltenden Verbleib]. To be a work [Werksein] means: to set up a world [eine Welt aufstellen]" ("owa," 22; 30).

If we take the liberty of extending what Heidegger says about poetry and art to literature in general, the phenomenological idea of worlding is important to rethinking world literature's normative force in two respects. First, the world is grounded in a nonanthropologistic force of temporalization that is prior to and makes possible all the powers of the rational subject and the entire domain of objects we produce, including the activity of (re)making the world as spatialized objective presence. Worlding exceeds and remains "after" any world made by human subjects. It is a power of possibilization that is proper to us when we are confronted with the leveling of possibilities in a given factical present in the course of history. In view of the objectification and degradation of the world by the socioeconomic processes and political projects of global capitalist modernity, this force is a real promise of a future "beyond" the present, a "to-be" that is projected from the full manifold of possibilities inherent to sheer existence. Second, worldliness is fundamental to literature and even part of its structure. Literature cannot cause or make anything, because its reality is neither spiritual nor material, subjective nor objective. But as the expression of the total meaningfulness of the logos or the setting up of a world, literature uncovers the world and opens up other possible worlds, thereby giving us resolve to respond to modernity's worldlessness and to remake the world according to newly disclosed possibilities.

In the next two chapters I will examine how Hannah Arendt and Jacques Derrida challenge Heidegger's conception of the world by questioning whether he restricts and closes off the opening of world by attributing it to temporalization and the contemplation of being and by defining temporalization as proper to human Dasein. I will also discuss the accounts of literature's worldly force that result from their respective critiques.

CHAPTER 5

The In-Between World

Anthropologizing the Force of Worlding

World alienation, not self-alienation as Marx thought,
has been the hallmark of the modern age.
—HANNAH ARENDT, *The Human Condition*

The provocation of Arendt's revision of Heidegger's conception of world lies
in her attempt to fuse a theory of (inter)action drawn from the philosophy
of the subject with a phenomenological understanding of the world as a
whole of relations that hold together human beings. Instead of developing
the implications of grounding the world in radically finite temporality, she
revives fundamental motifs in Greek philosophy and Christian thought that
characterize human beings as finite mortal creatures who are placed on an
unfamiliar earth by a divine creator. The world is a durable dwelling we make
to protect ourselves from our perishability. Worldly things give our lives
permanence because they outlive individual existence.

This chapter is concerned with the differences between Heidegger's and
Arendt's conceptions of the world and her views on literature's worldliness.
My discussion of Arendt follows three threads: first, what did she find inadequate about Heidegger's understanding of the world? Second, I will examine
whether the two components of Arendt's account of the world—the objective world of *homo faber* and the intersubjective world of speech and acts,
and the concept of natality that underwrites them—overcome the alleged
shortcomings of Heidegger's conception of world. Here, Arendt's critique of
Marxist materialism and the central role she gives to storytelling in the maintenance of the world bear directly on literature's worldly force. Finally, I will
assess the solutions she proposes to modern world alienation.

Departures: Arendt's Heidegger-Critique

Arendt expresses her departure from Heidegger's concept of world with the backhanded compliment that it may be useful for political thinking even though he aborted its potentially valuable insights.

> It is almost impossible to render a clear account of Heidegger's thoughts that may be of political relevance without an elaborate report on his concept and analysis of "world." This is all the more difficult because Heidegger himself has never articulated the implications of his philosophy in this regard, and in some instances has even used terms with connotations that are quite apt to mislead the reader into believing he is dealing with the old prejudice of the philosopher against politics as such, or with the modern rashness of escaping from philosophy into politics. . . . For our purposes what is much more important . . . is Heidegger's definition of human being as being-in-the-world.[1]

Although Arendt never provided the "elaborate report" of Heidegger's account of the world she deemed necessary, she nevertheless proceeded to criticize its shortcomings for a genuine understanding of the political world.

Arendt details four inadequacies, which she discusses with varying degrees of emphasis in different periods of her thought. First, Heidegger privileges contemplative thought over praxis and action, which leads him to show contempt for and dismiss the worldly realm of political affairs. His disdain is indicated by his hostility toward the public political sphere as a form of inauthentic collective existence. "Thus we find the old hostility of the philosopher toward the *polis* in Heidegger's analyses of average everyday life in terms of *das Man* (the 'they' or the rule of public opinion, as opposed to the 'self') in which the public realm has the function of hiding reality and preventing even the appearance of truth" ("CP," 432–33). Heidegger reductively conflates inauthentic public everyday life with "the whole of public life . . . [including] the public realm outside of *das Man*, outside of society and public opinion" ("CP," 433). The resoluteness he privileges as the stance of authentic existence is an unworldly state of being without an object because it is not a mode of worldly action but a withdrawal from the world.[2] Finally, Heidegger's concept of historicity, which defines thought as an event, deliberately turns away from "the center of politics—man as an acting being" ("CP," 433).

Second, Arendt argues that Heidegger views human existence as solipsistic, individualistic, and egoistic and willfully ignores the fundamental plurality of human life.[3] His analysis of Dasein primarily focuses on solitary Dasein's relations to itself—its instrumental relations to the *Umwelt* in everyday life and the various modes for the disclosure of authentic existence such as anxiety, guilt, being-toward-death, and resoluteness. This view is all the more deplorable because in failing to recognize human plurality it reduces individuals to atomistic selves and effectively destroys their humanity. "The concept of Self . . . leaves the individual existing independent of humanity and representative of no one but himself. . . . The experience of guilty nothingness insists on . . . the destruction in every individual of the presence of all humanity. . . . Being-a-Self has taken the place of being human."[4]

For Arendt, human beings always live and act with each other. "Existence itself is, by its very nature, never isolated. It exists only in communication and in awareness of others' existence. Our fellow men are not (as in Heidegger) an element of existence that is structurally necessary but at the same time an impediment to the Being of Self. Just the contrary: Existence can develop only in the shared life of human beings inhabiting a given world common to them all" ("WEP," 186).

Arendt's remarks make light of Heidegger's elaboration of being-in-the-world as being-with others. In "Concern with Politics," she anticipates the issue of whether Heidegger's thought allows for plurality in another backhanded compliment. Philosophy, which only conceives of man in the singular and in solitude, fails to comprehend political life, which is premised on our plural existence ("CP," 443). Heidegger's concept of world seems to promise a solution to this quandary because he defines human existence as being-in-the-world and because his existential analyses focus on our being together with others. His later work appears to emphasize the plurality of human existence by using "mortals" instead of "man." However, "it may be presumptuous to read too much significance into his use of the plural," because its implications are never developed ("CP," 443).

Third, following her criticism of the solipsism of his thought, Arendt rejects Heidegger's grounding of human existence in the experience of mortality. The privilege he gives to being-toward-death as a mode for disclosing authentic existence is structurally isolating because it affirms Dasein's authenticity by tearing it away from the world of human relations. Because we live most authentically when we withdraw from the world into our innermost possibility of being, we become fundamentally worldless beings that "free [ourselves] . . . once and for all from the world that entangles [us]" ("WEP," 181). In contradistinction, natality as an alternative principle for human existence transports us into the midst of relations with plural others.

Finally, Arendt argues that the shortcomings of Heidegger's concept of world close off access to the public political world and obstruct any genuine engagement with worldly affairs. This withdrawal led to his later involvement with National Socialist politics because he needed the mythologizing concepts of "folk" and "earth" to provide a shared ground for isolated selves.

Existing scholarship on Heidegger and Arendt has largely sided with her. However, Arendt's critique is not based on a careful analysis of Heidegger's account of worlding. It is a description that positions his ideas within larger trends in the history of Western philosophy that obstruct an adequate understanding of the political dimension of human existence. Similarly, in comparison to their detailed explication of Arendt's writings, most of the scholarship on Heidegger and Arendt exhibits a relatively cursory knowledge of Heidegger's account of worldliness.[5] They also regard Heidegger's association with National Socialism as a direct consequence of the shortcomings of his concept of the world. This suggests that the negative assessment of Heidegger's concept of the world is in part prejudicially predetermined by a justified abhorrence of his subsequent political affiliation and, more generally, by a sociological-historical deterministic view of philosophy.[6] Such deterministic arguments are largely speculative and should not substitute for a critical evaluation of Heidegger's thought that does justice to his insight that worldly human action is grounded in temporalization. What I will call "the Arendtian critique" turns away from the argument that temporalization is a force of worlding. It leads to several distortions that need to be corrected. I drily enumerate.

First, there is a tendency to conflate the transcendental concept of the world with the work-world opened up by our use of tools, sometimes to the point of characterizing Dasein's relations to handy things as instrumental means-ends relations or in teleological terms.[7] However, Heidegger is, as I have shown, critical of teleological and instrumentalist interpretations of our encounter with handy things. What is at issue is not that we use things as means or prescribe ends to the objects we make but *how* we are able to have access to and encounter beings, *how* they become disposable by us. This *how* reveals the world as a whole of meaningful connections grounded in temporality. A teleological interpretation of the work-world leads to our absorption by objects and the confusion of their being with ours.

Second, the charge of solipsism overstresses Heidegger's arguments about the inauthenticity of the everyday world and his privileging of the anticipatory experience of death as the mode of disclosing authentic existence. It ignores his explicit critique of the solipsistic human subject and tendentiously avoids his explorations of *Mitsein* and being-with-others, the original I-thou relation and the ontological community structural to selfhood, and the sphere of understandability that Dasein inhabits by virtue of its status as a discursive being that is constitutively linked to the logos. These aspects of Heidegger's thought suggest the possibility of authentic modes of collective existence with others. As he notes, when common existence is accompanied by authentic awareness of the force of temporalization, Dasein is "pushe[d] . . . toward concerned being-with the others."[8]

Third, these criticisms show an unequivocal preference for the anthropologistic concept of world that Heidegger found ontologically inadequate. The philosophical reasons for reverting to this anthropologistic concept are unclear, aside from our subjective need for the consolatory belief that we can change the world because it is made by our activity. To say that the being of Dasein is its existence means that there is an ontological and a factical (ontic) dimension to our existence. Heidegger argued that Dasein possesses an understanding of the difference between these two dimensions because it is the only factical being capable of posing the question of being. Hence, Dasein is able to disclose that the world is held together by temporalization. In contrast, the Arendtian position is exclusively devoted to the ontic dimension of worldly existence and views the world as something constituted through the human subject's ability to make objects and its relations with other subjects. For Arendt, the question of temporality obfuscates politics. When Heidegger says that "temporality is the meaning of Being," she writes, he gives a "provisional and inherently unintelligible answer" to the question of being because he "implies . . . that the meaning of Being is nothingness" ("WEP," 176). The hallmark of the Arendtian position is an impatient leap from ontology to the ontic dimension of human existence. Arendt "anthropologizes" worlding. She turns ontological processes into ontic human activities.

The fundamental question we should ask of Heidegger's concept of the world is how the temporal force of worlding as this is revealed in authentic existence "translates" into factical action. Heidegger does not shed much light on this question. His emphasis on the patient preparation for the prevailing of world and his dismissive characterization of the ontic dimension as being informed by vulgar concepts of time and the world that lead to inauthenticity suggest that he regards the ontic as inferior to the ontological dimension. But we cannot address these shortcomings by willfully ignoring the ontological issue of temporality and leaping impatiently into the domain of ontic relations. Heidegger's prioritizing of temporality as the ontological ground of being-in-the-world and his failure to specify forms of authentically aware action in everyday life do not preclude the possibility of worldly action and interaction with others. Authentic existence entails acting in concert with others because we necessarily live in the world with them. The task is to examine the possibility of types of factical action or politics that draw on the temporal force of worlding. What, in other words, are forms of authentic worldly action?

If it is reconciled with an awareness of the temporal force of worlding, Arendt's theory of the world can strengthen Heidegger's concept of the world with a rich understanding of worldly action. It makes two important contributions to reconceiving world literature. First, she challenges Marx's materialist understanding of the world's objective reality by distinguishing work as the activity that produces the objective world from labor and by insisting that the higher world produced by speech and action has a nonobjective reality that is infrastructural to the material reality of economic production. Second, because Arendt gives storytelling a fundamental role in the making of a world, she elucidates what I will call the "literary" structure of the world.

Of Being-Born: Natality and the Immanent Relation to the Absolute

Plurality is central to Arendt's account of the world. "The world and the people who inhabit it are not the same," she succinctly observes. "The world lies between people."[9] The world is existence with plural others. Indeed, no human being in the singular exists. There are only human beings: "The whole political sphere of human life exists only because of the plurality of men, because of the fact that one man would not be human at all" ("CP," 447). Closer examination shows, however, that worldliness is grounded in natality because we have to enter into worldly existence through birth before we can be amid others.

The opening chapter of *The Human Condition* states that human life is shaped by three basic conditions: life, worldliness, and plurality. We respond to them through the activities of labor, work, and action. Labor is required by biological necessity. The finitude of merely biological life means that we constantly confront the threat of being extinguished. We arrest the inevitability of death by laboring to keep the human organism alive. Worldliness is the desire to create an artificial environment in which we can dwell or live with greater security in an uncertain natural world. The world's permanence gives us additional shelter from our biological finitude. Through work, we transcend our finitude by fabricating durable objects that have continuity between generations. Finally, action is a response to plurality, the fact that we exist and achieve our full individuality in an intersubjective world with others who are human like us but are also necessarily different from us because each individual life is unique. We need to act "because we are all the same, that is, human, in such a way that nobody is ever the same as anyone else who ever lived, lives, or will live."[10]

These basic conditions are grounded in the most general condition of human existence: the possibility and facticity of birth and death, natality and mortality, the two poles of the term of life. Arendt emphasizes that although some of our activities appear to be shaped by mortality because they seek permanence, all human activities are rooted in natality because they involve an element of beginning, the emergence of something new. Hence, natality is the *arche*, the originating ground of the existence of human beings qua political beings.

> Labor and work, as well as action, are also rooted in natality in so far as they have the task to provide and preserve the world for, to foresee and reckon with, the constant influx of newcomers who are born into the world as strangers. However, of the three, action has the closest connection with the human condition of natality; the new beginning inherent in birth can make itself felt in the world only because the newcomer possesses the capacity of beginning something anew, that is, of acting. In this sense of initiative, an element of action, and therefore of natality, is inherent in all human activities. Moreover, since action is the political activity par excellence, natality, and not mortality, may be the central category of political, as distinguished from metaphysical, thought. (HC, 9)

"The Concept of History" affirms the priority of natality. "Human action, like all strictly political phenomena, is bound up with human plurality, which is one of the fundamental conditions of human life insofar as *it rests on the fact of natality*, through which the human world is constantly invaded by strangers, newcomers whose actions and reactions cannot be foreseen by those who are already there and are going to leave in a short while."[11] Although Heidegger is never named in *The Human Condition*, we see Arendt's move away from radical finitude in her centering of human existence in beginning and its repetitions and the recalling of past birth rather than ending and the anticipation of future death. Arendt suggests that we experience natality as the force of initiation in everyday life. Although action is closest to natality because it is initiation in its purest form, all activities contain an element of initiation.

Labor brings something new into the world, if only for it to be immediately consumed and extinguished by the biological life process. Work creates new objects that endure and change the objective world to which they are added. All human activities are relays of natality. They introduce three types of newness into the world and the unpredictability that accompanies the emergence of the new. First, the birth of any human being is the beginning of something new in the existing world that disrupts deterministic causal chains. Second, the introduction of new objects into the fabricated world is metaphorically likened to birth. These objects become another factor that conditions human life. Third, the fact of plurality means that other new subjects will be born into the world. Each entry changes the world and gives rise to actions on the part of existing subjects that also change the world. The persistent coming of new others intensifies the unpredictability of actions and their outcomes, leading to greater variability in the human-made conditions that shape our lives.

Human existence is thus a dynamic and constantly changing web of relations and connections constituted through our activities. Contra Heidegger, we do not primarily assume an attitude of contemplative awareness in response to our thrownness into a world of others. Instead, there is an endless influx or invasion of the world by others, and we respond to their repeated coming through our activities. Hence, the world is always disrupted, punctured, and opened up by the continual emergence of something new, and our activities enrich and "dynamize" the world. The world is thus a set of changing conditions generated from the interplay between natural processes and human activities that in turn shapes and conditions our activities. As Arendt puts it,

> the world in which *vita activa* spends itself consists of things produced by human activities. . . . In addition to the conditions under which life is given to man on earth, and partly out of them, men constantly create their own, self-made conditions, which, their human origin and variability notwithstanding, possess the same conditioning power as natural things. . . . Whatever enters the human world of its own accord or is drawn into it by human effort becomes part of the human condition. The impact of the world's reality upon human existence is felt and received as a conditioning force. The objectivity of the world—its object- or thing-character—and the human condition supplement each other; because human existence is conditioned existence, it would be impossible without things, and things would be a heap of unrelated articles, a non-world, if they were not conditioners of human existence. (HC, 9)

Because human existence is conditioned and finite, we need to make a durable world. But since what we make also conditions us, our existence involves a degree of self-conditioning. For Arendt, the world is not unified by temporalization. It is assembled and held together by the ongoing activity of human subjects. Accordingly, she transposes the different modalities of presence that characterize our relations with handy and extant beings and our understanding of the world's meaningfulness into the practical activities of labor, work, and action. Heidegger's focus on temporalization is a withdrawal from the world, the opposite of *amor mundi*, caring for the world. Work and action are daily eruptive processes by which we constitute and change the everyday public world instead of being absorbed by the world of common objects and the they.

But Arendt's infusion of the world with the dynamism of anthropologistic agency entails some serious costs. It reduces the force of temporalization to the human condition of natality, and worlding to the making of the world through human activities that remember natality. This is what I have called "anthropologization." Although natality is a coming-into-being that is not within human control because, as finite beings, we cannot initiate our own existence, the human being as a political subject is always defined by the anthropologistic category of action. Hence, although Arendt repeatedly stresses that the human subject is not sovereign because its actions have radically unpredictable outcomes, the fact that its existence is primarily conditioned by processes that are proper to it, namely, action, necessarily implies the sovereignty of human self-determination. The concept of natality is an anthropologistic reduction of existence. It shrinks back from radically finite temporality and encrypts an immanent relation to an absolute divine being in the facticity of human existence by drawing on Neoplatonic and Christian metaphysical influences.

Natality is the sheer fact of our coming into presence as beings who are born. It is simply "the naked fact of our original physical appearance" (HC, 176–77), "the fact that human beings are *born* into the world."[12] This fact has a decidedly redemptive meaning. The birth of human beings introduces something new into the world, "the beginning which came into the world when we were born" (HC, 177). Hence we "are *initium*, newcomers and beginners by virtue of birth" (HC, 177). Our coming into the world thus renews and saves it from inevitable ruin: "This world is constantly renewed through birth. . . . Ruin . . . except for renewal, except for the coming of the new and young, would be inevitable."[13]

The anchor of birth's redemptive power can only be an absolute creator. Arendt's interest in natality dates back to her dissertation on Augustine. She repeatedly returns to the same phrases from Augustine's *City of God* to argue that natality is the ontological condition of freedom.

> [*Initium*] *ut esset, creatus est homo, ante quern nemo fuit* ("that there be a beginning, man was created before whom there was nobody").... This beginning is not the same as the beginning of the world; it is not the beginning of something but of somebody, who is a beginner himself. With the creation of man, the principle of beginning came into the world itself, which, of course, is only another way of saying that the principle of freedom was created when man was created but not before. (*HC*, 177)[14]

> Man does not possess freedom so much as he, or better his coming into the world, is equated with the appearance of freedom in the universe; man is free because he is a beginning and was so created after the universe had already come into existence: [*Initium*] *ut esset, creatus est homo, ante quern nemo fuit.* In the birth of each man this initial beginning is reaffirmed, because in each instance something new comes into an already existing world which will continue to exist after each individual's death. Because he is a beginning, man can begin; to be human and to be free are one and the same. God created man in order to introduce into the world the faculty of beginning: freedom.[15]

Three things stand out in Arendt's glosses of Augustine's phrase. First, human beings are created by an absolute creator. Second, the fabrication of man is characterized by a different degree of being than the fabrication of the world, which was created prior to man. With man, a "who" or "somebody" is made, not a "what" or "something." Moreover, man is brought into being to bring newness into the world. Third, because the end of man's existence is newness, the *telos* is also an *arche*. Unlike other created beings, the human creature's power of initiation recalls God. God's creation of newness in creating man is the first beginning. It is affirmed in two repetitions: the birth of each human being and our actions. These repetitions are also beginnings that introduce newness into the world.

The miracle of creation, then, is the ontological basis of human freedom. For Arendt, the very fact of earthly existence—that there is something instead of nothing—and the genesis of different forms of existence, such as life from inorganic matter and human consciousness from animal life, are infinitely improbable events. They are unanticipatable and radically inexplicable in their interruption of preceding causal processes. We represent this "startling unexpectedness" as a miraculous force in quotidian reality (HC, 178). Newness "breaks into the world" and "constitutes the texture of everything we call real," such that "our whole existence rests . . . on a chain of miracles" and our experience of events as inexplicable miracles is "most natural and, indeed, in ordinary life almost commonplace."[16] This means, Arendt suggests in her *Nachlaß*, that an irreducible relation to the absolute is structural to factical existence. Quotidian miracles are a form of transcendence immanent to reality: "The demonstrably real transcendence of each beginning corresponds to the religious transcendence of believing in miracles."[17]

The miracle of existence is not exhausted in the moment of the world's creation and the emergence of different forms of being. It continues in the human capacity for action. Action is also a miracle. It begins something new and interrupts the determinism of preceding processes. We therefore play an active role in constituting the dynamic web of ongoing miracles that is reality.

What we call real [wirklich] is already a web which is woven of earthly, organic, and human realities [Realität], but which has come into existence through the addition of infinite improbabilities. . . . The crucial difference between the infinite improbabilities on which earthly human life is based and miraculous events in the arena of human affairs lies, of course, in the fact that in the latter case there is a miracle worker [Wundertäter]—that is, that man himself evidently has a most amazing and mysterious talent for working miracles. The normal, hackneyed word our language provides for this talent is "action." . . . The miracle of freedom is inherent in this ability for beginning, which itself is inherent in the fact that every human being, simply by coming into a world through birth, a world that was there before him and will be there after him, is himself a new beginning.[18]

Three senses of newness are concentrated in natality. First, the sheer miracle of birth is the force of the coming of the new, of novel-ization. But, more important, it brings into presence a being that is new *in relation* to the *old* world that existed before. Third, this new being is in turn a force of newness whose actions will change the existing world. Thus, action is literally the actualization of natality as potentiality according to the Aristotelian concepts of *dynamis* and *energeia*: it makes actual a merely potential condition, unfolding and bringing it into the light of day. Action translates the sheer potency of natality into actuality. It affirmatively actualizes to the fullest extent the force of natality and strengthens it through infinite distribution. As Arendt puts it, "because each man is unique . . . with each birth something uniquely new comes into the world. With respect to this somebody who is unique it can truly be said that nobody was there before. . . . Action as beginning corresponds to the fact of birth. . . . It is the actualization of the human condition of natality" (HC, 178). Human action constantly renews, recreates, and dynamizes the world because it disseminates and suffuses every facet of human life with the power of the absolute creator of the world. Arendt calls it a right: the right of initiation and spontaneity. "What stands in opposition to all possible predetermination and knowledge of the future is the fact that the world is daily renewed through birth and is constantly dragged into what is unpredictably new by the spontaneity of each new arrival. Only if we rob the newborn of their spontaneity, their right to begin something new, can the course of the world be defined deterministically and predicted."[19]

Arendt thus substitutes a quasi-theistic metaphysics of creation for Heidegger's ontology of radical finitude. Natality repeats an absolute being's creative power. Human action can hold together and renew the world because it is a relay of natality. Arendt's break from Heidegger is already signaled in her dissertation by her divergence from his interpretation of Augustine's concept of *mundus*. In a footnote discussing "On the Essence of Ground," she observes that although Heidegger "distinguishes between two Augustinian meanings of *mundus*," namely, as *ens creatum* and as being as a whole and *how* human existence relates to being, he restricts his explication of the world to the latter.[20] Arendt wishes to "make this twofold approach understood." As I have already noted, Heidegger defined the God-forsaken condition of worldliness as the "how" of Dasein's existence and the accessibility of other beings to Dasein. Arendt, by contrast, places greater emphasis on the world as a "what," a created being that originates from a divine creator. The *ens creatum* "coincides with the divine fabric." It is "God's creation (heaven and earth), which antedates all love of the world" (LSA, 66). "The divine fabric" is an ontic whole, something extant that precedes human existence. We make an artificial world through our activities so that we can be at home in the preexisting world. Our fabricating activities remember the origin of heaven and earth and our capacities in an absolute creator, because these activities are relays of the creation of the divine fabric. Hence, our ability to make a world enables us to transcend our mortal worldly existence.

It is from the divine fabric (*fabrica Dei*), from pre-existing creation, that man makes the world and makes himself part of the world. . . . What happens by our will is guided by love of the world (*dilectio mundi*), which for the first time turns the world, the divine fabric, into the self-evident home of man. When living man finds his place in the pre-existing creation he is born into, he turns the fabric of creation into the world.

Love for the world, which makes it "worldly," rests on being "of the world." Just as God's creation is not worldly as such, neither is man who is of the world already worldly. . . . Man has the chance of not wanting to be at home in the world and thus keeping himself constantly in a position to refer back to the Creator. (*LSA*, 66)

The concept of natality, which Arendt introduces here for the first time, expresses the human relation to our divine creator. It fuses the Greek philosophical idea of an absolute, self-sufficient primal being and the Christian notion of a divine creator in order to give us consolation and hope in the face of mortality. "The decisive fact determining man as a conscious, remembering being is birth or 'natality,' that is, the fact that we have entered the world through birth. . . . Gratitude for life having been given at all is the spring of remembrance, for a life is cherished even in misery. . . . What ultimately stills the fear of death is not hope or desire, but remembrance and gratitude. . . . This will to be under all circumstances is the hallmark of man's attachment to the transmundane source of his existence" (*LSA*, 51–52). Consciousness and memory are analogous to and derive from the fact of our creation by a divine being. They are the means by which we express gratitude for the gift of life. This link to the absolute elevates us beyond our finite existence. By creating the world, we compensate for our deficient finite being through the analogical remembrance of our own creation by an infinite being.

Arendt's dissertation departs from Heidegger's concept of worlding in two respects. First, the idea that the human world recalls a divine fabric foreshadows her subsequent impatient replacement of an ontological concept of the world with an ontic concept of the world as a fabrication of *homo faber*. Second, she explicitly contrasts the memory of natality and gratitude for the gift of life with Heidegger's privileging of the anticipation of death. Memory's temporal structure is past-oriented. Hence, the past and not the future gives existence its unity.

The fact that the past is not forever lost and that remembrance can bring it back into the present is what gives memory its great power (*vis*). Since our expectations and desires are prompted by what we remember and guided by a previous knowledge, it is memory and not expectation (for instance, the expectation of death as in Heidegger's approach) that gives unity and wholeness to human existence. In making and holding present both past and future, that is, memory and the expectation derived from it, it is the present in which they coincide that determines human existence. This human possibility gives the man his share in being "immutable"; the remotest past and the most distant future are not only, objectively speaking, the single twofold "before" of human life, but can be actualized as such while man is still alive. . . . Since he can concentrate through remembrance and anticipation his entire life into the present, man can participate in eternity and thus be "happy" even in this life. . . . The presentation of past and future in which both coincide annihilates time and man's subjection to it. (LSA, 56–57)

Temporality becomes the faculty of memory by means of an anthropologistic reduction. Memory's ability to hold the past and the future together in the present enables us to participate in eternity during our mortal existence. Its temporal unity is an immortalizing power that frees us from our subjection to time. Nothing could be further from radically finite temporality. Arendt always views time as an endless cycle of meaningless, purposeless destruction. It is not a creative force because only an infinite being has creative power. Natality places us in time but also gives us the power to undo time's corrosiveness. This distinguishes us from other created beings. In her words, "the beginning that was created with man prevented time and the created universe as a whole from turning eternally in cycles about itself in a purposeless way and without anything new ever happening. Hence, it was for the sake of *novitas*, in a sense, that man was created" (LSA, 55).

What is important about Arendt's anthropologization of the force of temporalization is the fundamental role of repetition. Memory is the power to remember and repeat the fact of natality. Hence, human activity, which issues from the faculty of memory, has the structural form of repeating an original event, relating and narrating a story about the very first beginning, that of humankind. Human activity is always the performance of a story: "Since man can know, be conscious of, and remember his 'beginning' or his origin, he is able to act as a beginning and enact the story of mankind" (LSA, 55). Arendt's importance to rethinking world literature lies in the centrality of storytelling to world-making. I will now examine her account of the world's objective reality and its "narrative" structure.

The Objective In-Between: Work, the Enduring World of Objects, and Culture as Outliving

In my discussion of Marx's account of the world and sociological theories of world literature influenced by Marxist theories of social force, I observed that literature has an extremely limited causal power in Marxist discourse. According to Marx's materialist ontology of creative labor, spiritual objects have the same ontological status as the commodity fetish, an inhuman thing that possesses magical powers that in fact come from social relations. Marxism, however, commits another fetishism. Its fundamental premise that the material activity of labor, from which sociality is generated, is self-originating, the essence of human species-being, and the primary ground of the real world fetishizes social forces and labor. Arendt's account of the world begins with a critique of Marxism's fetishization of material activity.

In Arendt's view, Marx misunderstood the true character of worldliness because he confused *homo faber* with *animal laborans* and defined material labor as the essential activity of human beings. For Marx, the world is the totality of objects produced by material activity for the ends of human use and consumption and the community that regulates the social relations organizing production, distribution, and consumption. Arendt contends, however, that this is the opposite of a world. What Marx calls the world is merely the realm of natural necessity, where everything becomes extinguished in the endless cycle of consumption and the satisfaction of biological needs. The prolongation of human life through the universal fulfillment of needs is a capitulation to nature, where human beings succumb to the relentless biological life-process that levels everything to the life-cycle and deprives us of any meaningful distinction beyond the quality of mere living. The only viable response to finitude, she suggests, is to attain a degree of immortality. This alone can shield us from the corrosive life-process.

Accordingly, *world* refers in the first instance to a web of relations among human beings that has durability and permanence because it arises in the presence of products of work. In its first and most basic aspect, a world is a stable environment of objective being created by human artifice. *Homo faber* is "the fabricator of the world," and his ideals are "permanence, stability, and durability" (HC, 126). The objectivating character of work, the fact that it produces durable objects, is crucial. Whereas labor only produces temporary objects that disappear by being consumed, products of work are things that endure, because they are meant for repeated use. They constitute a permanent framework necessary for consumption and production. "The products of work," Arendt writes, "guarantee the permanence and durability without which a world would not be possible at all" (HC, 94). First, the repeated use of these objects establishes stable relations that connect subjects to objects and intersubjective relations concerning the use of objects. Pointing to the double meaning of use as utility and habitual intimacy, Arendt suggests that as we use such objects, "we become used and accustomed. As such, they give rise to the familiarity of the world, its customs and habits of intercourse between men and things as well as between men and men" (HC, 94). Second, this web of relations precedes and exceeds the lives of individual subjects.

The world of useful things is an objective in-between we place between nature and ourselves to shield ourselves from the vicissitudes of the life-process. It is a house that shelters and protects us. "The work of our hands, as distinguished from the labor of our bodies, fabricates the sheer unending variety of things whose sum total constitutes the human artifice, the world we live in. They are not consumer goods but use-objects, and their proper use does not cause them to disappear. They give the world the stability and solidity without which it could not be relied upon to house the unstable and mortal creature that is man."[21] More important, the world of useful things is the condition of possibility of subjectivity and objectivity. Individual subjects achieve a stable identity by finding it in the sameness established by the daily use of objects amid the contingent flux of mortal existence. These activities also generate objective nature.

> The things of the world have the function of stabilizing human life, and their objectivity lies in the fact that men, their everchanging nature notwithstanding, can retrieve their identity by being related to the enduring sameness of objects, the same chair today and tomorrow, the same house formerly from birth to death. Against the subjectivity of men stands the objectivity of man-made artifice, not the indifference of nature. Only because we have erected a world of objects from what nature gives us and have built this artificial environment into nature, thus protecting us from her, can we look upon nature as something "objective." Without a world between men and nature, there would be eternal movement, but no objectivity.[22]

The objective world carves out the profile of each human life. Because its durability underscores our mortality, it marks the limited term of individual lives and gives each life the distinction of being this or that particular life. The world further enables us to measure our mortal life span in terms of what we have managed to achieve because it is a sphere in which we can leave something behind that will outlast our lives. These achievements are what we call culture, which is a power of outliving. The objective world is culture's condition of possibility. For our achievements to survive beyond their originating human subjects, they require an objective world as the substrate in which they can be reified and gain an objective existence. As Arendt puts it, the world of objects

> derives from a desire to erect a dam against one's own mortality, to place something between the perishability of man and the imperishability of nature that serves as the yardstick for mortals to measure their mortality. What occupies this place is the man-made world that is not immortal but nevertheless considerably more durable and lasting than the life of human beings. All of culture begins with this kind of world-making, which in Aristotelian terms is already ... a making-immortal. ... The earthly home becomes a world only when objects as a whole are produced and organized in such a way that they may withstand the consumptive life-process of human beings living among them—and may outlive human beings who are mortal. We speak of culture only when this outliving is assured.[23]

The Subjective In-Between: The "Literary" Structure of the World as a Web of Authorless Stories

The telling of stories is central to world-making because of the limited permanence of the world of *homo faber*. First, following the privileging of *praxis* over *poiesis* in Greek philosophy, Arendt argues that fabrication is an inferior mode of activity. Objects are worn out by use and destroyed with the passage of time. More important, the public social world that arises from market exchange suffers from a normative deficiency. *Homo faber's* instrumental attitude to the objective world leads to the confusion of utility with meaningfulness such that usefulness becomes the meaning of all things. The infinite conversion of ends to means—the fact that all products of work can be degraded into means for pursuing other ends—and the contingent and arbitrary character of usefulness—the fact that these objects have no intrinsic worth because their utility is subject to the changing circumstances and fickle whims of individual subjects—render the objective world utterly devoid of intrinsic meaning. "*Homo faber*, in so far as he is nothing but a fabricator and thinks in no terms but those of means and ends," Arendt observes, "is ... incapable of understanding meaning" (HC, 155). The standards of the objective world are those of mere value, and this "universal relativity" undermines the articulation of universal standards and rules that give the world greatest permanence (HC, 166). This aspect of Arendt's argument resonates with my earlier point that defining literature's worldliness in terms of circulation in a global market deprives it of normative force.

The web of intersubjective relations created by speech and action, Arendt argues, has greater permanence than the objective world. They constitute the second, higher dimension of worldliness. Fabrication cannot take place without establishing relations among subjects. This requires the disclosure of human actors to each other through words and deeds. In addition to referring to things, words and deeds serve the more fundamental purpose of disclosing subjects. They thereby form a *meaningful* intersubjective world that is more fundamental than the world of things.

Speech always accompanies action because action is a response to the human condition of plurality. Because we are born into a preexisting world among plural others and many others will come into our world, action necessarily has a structure of intersubjective interlocution. Action is connected to speech in two ways. First, when I distinguish or individuate myself from the others with whom I exist by acting, I must first mark the distinctiveness of these actions by claiming them as *my own*, as the actions of a unique subject. The disclosure of my unique identity as the agent to whom those actions belong requires me to indirectly answer the implicit question "Who are you?" by revealing their animating intentions. Speech enables us to own (up to) and appropriate our actions. We reveal our distinctiveness to ourselves and claim our identity in front of others by thematically expressing our intentions.

> Without the accompaniment of speech . . . action would not only lose its revelatory character, but and by the same token, it would lose its subject, as it were; not acting men but performing robots would achieve what, humanly speaking, would remain incomprehensible. Speechless action would no longer be action because there would no longer be an actor, and the actor, the doer of deeds, is possible only if he is at the same time the speaker of words. The action he begins is humanly disclosed by the word, and though his deed can be perceived in its brute physical appearance without verbal accompaniment, it becomes relevant only through the spoken word in which he identifies himself as the actor, announcing what he does, has done, and intends to do. (HC, 178–79)

As the expressive medium for the intentional self-constitution of the acting subject's unique identity, speech is the original source of the world's meaningfulness. Although an action's meaning is not exhausted by its actor's intentions but changes depending on how it is received and its unpredictable outcomes, without the disclosure of an intentional subject behind it, the action would not be intelligible because it would have no animating meaning.

Second, speech is also connected to action because individuation requires the support of plurality. Action and speech are evanescent phenomena that disappear with the exhaustion of their process. Because their existence depends on preserving the moment of their initial presence, they need to be marked in perceptual experience, representation, memory, or intellectual cognition. This requires the presence of others, who receive, experience, interpret, and remember them as the actions and speech of a unique agent. Indeed, Arendt suggests that the subject's disclosed identity is generally hidden from him and only "appears . . . clearly and unmistakably to others" (HC, 179). Plurality thus reinforces the distinctiveness of our individual selves and our actions.

Because speech and action are the fundamental conditions of human practical activity, the meaningful world they create is more infrastructural, to use Marx's term, than the material world created by production and exchange.

> [Objective worldly] interests constitute, in the word's most literal significance, something which *inter-est*, which lies between people and therefore can relate and bind them together. Most action and speech is concerned with this in-between. . . . Since this disclosure of the subject [as a speaking and acting agent] is an integral part of all, even the most "objective" intercourse, the physical, worldly in-between along with its interests is overlaid and, as it were, overgrown with an altogether different in-between which consists of deeds and words and owes its origin exclusively to men's acting and speaking directly *to* one another. This second, subjective in-between is not tangible, since there are no tangible objects into which it could solidify; the process of acting and speaking can leave behind no such results and end products. But for all its intangibility, this in-between is no less real than the world of things we visibly have in common. We call this reality the "web" of human relationships, indicating by the metaphor its somewhat intangible quality. (HC, 182–83)

Economic activity presupposes the prior disclosure of subjects in a world of speech and action because it requires a subject who acts in relation to others.

The central shortcoming of Marxist materialism is that it dismisses the effectivity of these intangible processes by characterizing them as superstructural when they have a fundamental reality of their own that is constitutive of the material world of production. "To be sure, this web is no less bound to the objective world of things than speech is to the existence of a living body, but the relationship is not like that of a façade or, in Marxian terminology, of an essentially superfluous superstructure affixed to the useful structure of the building itself. The basic error of all materialism in politics . . . is to overlook the inevitability with which men disclose themselves as subjects, as distinct and unique persons, even when they wholly concentrate upon reaching an altogether worldly, material object" (HC, 182–83). Arendt's hierarchization of objective and intersubjective worlds follows the division of the world into a spatial-geographical category and a temporal-normative category in the philosophies I discussed in previous chapters. The objective world marks the term of a particular finite life by the quantitative measurement of its temporal length but cannot impart any meaning to the lives it delimits. For a human life to be remembered by posterity for its achievements, the individual's coming and departing need to be given significance as a unique birth and death, a beginning and ending of a life that is meaningful to others. As the source of meaning, speech elevates the objective world into a genuinely human world. It enables us to transcend our finitude and escape the indistinction of merely biological life. "Life in its non-biological sense" is a linear movement that unfolds against the backdrop of the destructive cycles of natural biological life (HC, 173). "The chief characteristic of this specifically human life," Arendt writes, "whose appearance and disappearance constitute worldly events, is that it is itself always full of events which ultimately *can be told as a story, establish a biography*; it is of this life, *bios* as distinguished from mere *zōē*, that Aristotle said that it 'somehow is a kind of *praxis*'" (HC, 97, emphasis added).

What is important is Arendt's heuristic use of the narrative form of the story to elucidate the world's temporal structure. Although she is not interested in stories as a literary form, her exploration of their world-making power sheds light on literature's worldly force.[24] Because speech and action are evanescent, they require their recipients to testify about the "who" that is disclosed. This testimony takes the paradigmatic form of a story. Arendt distinguishes between three different levels of narrative in the making of a world: stories, narration, and history. Actions set off a new process of events that have reverberations in the existing web of human relations. Observers give meaning to events after they are over by interpreting them in light of their consequences, thereby organizing them into a chain of meaningfully connected events, namely, a story. What is important here is the generation of meaning by remembrance of the past and its narrative repetition. An act's meaning only becomes clear when it is over and it has "become a story susceptible to narration."[25] Similarly, a person's life is best understood through its recounting because its full significance can only be determined after the person's death. Hence, the storyteller has a more fundamental role in illuminating the world than the actor. "Action reveals itself fully only to the storyteller, that is, to the backward glance of the historian, who indeed always knows better what it was all about than the participants. All accounts told by the actors themselves . . . can never match his story in significance and truthfulness. . . . Even though stories are the inevitable results of action, it is not the actor but the storyteller who perceives and "makes" the story" (HC, 192).

Narration is a recounting that connects different stories into a larger whole in which "the unique life story of the newcomer" affects "uniquely the life stories of all those with whom he comes into contact" (HC, 184). This whole is the world. When narration is concerned with the past, it establishes history, the story of the past. Narration enables events to enter into history because it gives them meaningful permanence. History is "the great story without beginning and end," "the storybook of mankind, with many actors and speakers and yet without any tangible authors" (HC, 184). It is an open-ended whole made up of individual human life stories that we "master," in the sense that we make sense of them by recounting and reinterpreting them anew in subsequent narrations.[26]

The world therefore has a diegetic structure. Stories and narratives, Arendt argues, have a world-constituting power that is lacking in science because they are the source of meaningfulness that illuminates human existence (HC, 324). Although historians and poets specialize in the skills of narration and creating history, we are all capable of the power of narration. We exercise it in our daily lives in our "need to recall the significant events in our own lives by relating them to ourselves and others."[27] As a type of repetition, telling a story is isomorphic with how action remembers and discloses the infinite power of natality that brings us into the world. A story is repetition and remembrance to the second degree: it expresses a subject's newness by meaningfully recounting the chains of events his actions catalyze. The larger narratives of historians and poets are third-degree repetitions. They are composed of smaller stories that they "immortalize" as part of history. Together, these three forms of repetition create and maintain a human world that simultaneously has permanent significance and is fluid and open-ended because it arises from "the living flux of acting and speaking" (HC, 187). The world is both the synchronic whole of human existence (the world of speech, action, and stories) and a diachronic whole (the history of humankind).

I have discussed Heidegger's privileging of poetry as a form of nonthematic discourse in the disclosure of worldliness and the work of art as being itself the process of the opening of a world. In contradistinction, because Arendt is concerned with how the meaning of human actions can be disclosed instead of the worlding force of temporalization, she views drama as the artistic reification with the greatest revelatory power (HC, 187). An elaboration of the implications of her thought for rethinking literature's worldliness is, however, better served by focusing on narrative because of its centrality to her conception of the world.

Literature is fundamentally connected to the world's dynamism in three ways. First, the world has structural features we commonly associate with a type of literary narrative, the story, that has no author. An agent is disclosed when he becomes the protagonist in the unique life-story told about him. The world is a plot made up of many stories. Every actor is like a character with a story, and he contributes to the larger plot through his actions. The actor's relation to his story is, however, that of a protagonist without sovereignty. No actor can ever be the sovereign author of his own story because we exist in the condition of plurality, which contradicts "the ideal of uncompromising self-sufficiency and mastership" (HC, 234). The dynamic web of worldly relations consists of many life stories. Someone's insertion into this web will change it by affecting the stories of others. Moreover, because we cannot control what will happen when we act, no actor can foretell the outcome of his actions and control the direction of his own story. His position is not that of an author but that of either a mere character or a rather hapless first person narrator-cum-protagonist without omniscience. In Arendt's words, "although everybody started his life by inserting himself into the human world through action and speech, nobody is the author or producer of his own life story. . . . Somebody began it and is its subject in the twofold sense of the word, namely its actor and sufferer, but nobody is its author" (HC, 184).

The world is more precisely an open-ended web of authorless stories. We can productively contrast this with the Hegelian-Marxist teleological conception of the world as a closed totality with an overarching end. In narrative terms, the latter is similar to a bildungsroman, where spirit or the proletariat is the omniscient author-cum-protagonist. For Arendt, however, the world is constituted by narratives in which protagonists—actors who initiate chains of events—can never be the authors of the eventual outcomes of their stories. Indeed, there cannot be a god-like author who stands above human history, the ongoing storyline of the world, pulling the strings and directing characters toward intended outcomes. Hence, the world is a dynamic and open whole. It is "the real story in which we are engaged as long as we live," and all of us can actively participate in its making (HC, 186). Here, literature's world-making power is not the power of imaginative aesthetic forms (literature in the strict sense) to construct a world. Rather, the world has what can be called a "literary structure." "Literature" in this general sense is not derived from or subsidiary to a material reality that it represents. Instead, it is infrastructural to reality, and its workings help us to understand worldly processes.

Second, although Arendt distinguishes a real story from a fictional story on the grounds that the fictional story has an author-maker, literature in the narrow sense is a privileged means of access to the world's literary structure because it foregrounds by enacting in its form of address how human actors emerge in and change an existing world through narratives. As an experience, literature opens a world for its reader. The transaction between writer and reader is an imaginative staging or exhibition (*Darstellung*) of the experience of how new subjects come into and change the existing world. Through reading, we experience the entry of characters into the world the literary work portrays and how their coming changes the lives of other characters.

Third, as a type of reification, a literary work transforms the real stories of human existence (literature in the general sense) into tangible objects that survive the finite lives of individual subjects. Because of their futility and fleetingness, real stories "need the help of *homo faber* in his highest capacity, that is, the help of the artist, of poets and historiographers, of monument builders or writers," to survive (HC, 173). Works of art give the world of stories the greatest permanence. They impart historical depth to the world and point to an infinite future because as fabricated objects that are divorced from the context of ordinary usage and have no utility or purpose, they have the highest durability.[28] As long as a literary work continues to be read, its objective form gives permanent existence to the world it discloses. This world can influence the remaking of the existing world and even open new worlds.

Indeed, Arendt suggests that a person's emergence in the world is "poetry" in a general sense. Literary production is an analogical repetition of poetry. It is the eruption of newness *within* a person that leads to the creation of something new in the world.

We are constantly preparing the way for "poetry," in the broadest sense, as a human potentiality; we are, so to speak, constantly expecting it to erupt in some human being. When this happens, the telling-over of what took place comes to a halt for the time being and a formed narrative, one more item, is added to the world's stock. In reification by the poet or the historian, the narration of history has achieved permanence and persistence. Thus the narrative has been given its place in the world, where it will survive us. There it can live on—one story among many. There is no meaning to these stories that is entirely separable from them—and this, too, we know from our own, non-poetic experience. No philosophy, no analysis, no aphorism, be it ever so profound, can compare in intensity and richness of meaning with a properly narrated story.[29]

Just as a human actor exists with others, a reified story is also part of a plurality of stories. A reified story is superior to a real life-story in one respect: it outlives or survives the person. Thus, a narrated story's intensity and richness of meaning exceeds its thematic dimension. It comes from the act of narration, which is a relation in a double sense: repeating and relaying something to another by addressing him and establishing connections with others through the structure of address. Narrative is the repetition that enables real and fictional stories to live on. It constitutes a story's worldly life because it arises from and repeats the force of worldly life itself, that is, natality.

We can sum up Arendt's understanding of literature as a power of world-making as follows. First, the story form is the metaphorical template for understanding the meaningful world of speech and action. Second, because the literary work of art is a model of eternally meaningful objectivity, literary production imparts imperishable significance to the world. Third, compared to Arendt's position, the recent theorizing of world literature as a statistical matter of circulation detaches literature from the web of normative intersubjective relations. These accounts of world literature efface its world-making power as a structure of address that announces a subject and a process that imparts permanent meaning because they reduce worldliness to global processes of marketing, circulation, and distribution. There is a fourth implication that is important for the study of world literature if we understand the world as the in-between of collective cultural subjects. In this case, fictional stories can play an important part in the disclosure of postcolonial peoples as they announce their emergence and tell their real stories in the geopolitical world. In part III, I will flesh out this argument.

The Absolute Guarantee of Newness: Arendt's Utopian Solution to World Alienation

Arendt can be read as radically revising Heidegger's account of the world to make room for a detailed elaboration of authentic being-with others as practical action. For Heidegger, the world is neither made by human fabrication nor constituted by intersubjective relations. Worlding is instead their condition of possibility. Accordingly, the world cannot be reduced to the sum of handy objects, and the world's meaningfulness is the condition of human speech. Arendt reverses the world's *a priori* relation to human activity. For her, the world is a human fabrication and consists of useful things. It is then given meaningful permanence by speech and action. She reformulates being-with others as intersubjective relations "where people are *with* others and neither for nor against them—that is, in sheer human togetherness" (*HC*, 180). "Without being talked about by men and without housing them," she notes, "the world would not be a human artifice but a heap of unrelated things" (*HC*, 204). Arendt thus revives elements of the spiritualist view of the world. In assessing whether her account of the world has greater explanatory power than Heidegger's, the abiding question should be whether it is a more cogent and effective solution to the worldlessness of modernity they both diagnose. I will contend that natality is a utopian principle of salvation in the face of capitalist globalization's destruction of worldliness.

The basic principle of Heidegger's account of modern worldlessness is unworlding (*Entweltlichung*). It is a consequence of the obscuring of the temporal force of worlding proper to human beings. Hence, although unworlding leads to inauthentic existence and makes us worldless, the world cannot be alienated from us because it is not an object we produce. The world is there where Dasein exists. Arendt's reformulation of worlding as the human subject's activities of world-making leads to a quasi-spiritualist understanding of worldlessness as world alienation (*Weltentfremdung*), a term with a distinct provenance in a Hegelian-Marxist philosophy of the subject.

Arendt argues that modernity is the age of world alienation because it undermines the stability of the world we have created to transcend our finitude.[30] The two decisive events that are relevant for us are the conquest of the world and its reduction to a globe by the scientific development of human capacities of surveying and the rise of the principle of inner-worldly asceticism in the Reformation. They touch directly on the distinction between world and globe that is crucial to any normative conception of world.

The development of our powers of surveying compresses the vastness of the inhabited earth and reduces it to a globe, a representable object with quantifiable dimensions. Once it is geometrically delimited and bounded, this whole can be measured by the quantified time needed to circumscribe and conquer it. This is the origin of space-time compression. As Arendt puts it, in modernity "man has taken full possession of his mortal dwelling place and gathered the infinite horizons, which were temptingly and forbiddingly open to all previous ages, into a globe whose majestic outlines and detailed surface he knows as he knows the lines in the palm of his hand" (*HC*, 250). These developments alienate us from the earth by shrinking it into a tangible ball that we can observe from a distance, as epitomized by the model globe (*HC*, 251). The normative-temporal dimension of the world is destroyed with its reduction to a geo-metrico/graphical entity.

The Christian Reformation alienates the world from the opposite direction. Inner-worldly asceticism throws us back from the world onto ourselves because it prescribes that mundane human activity should no longer be concerned with the world but with our pursuit of salvation beyond it via worrying and caring for ourselves (*HC*, 254). Capitalist expropriation is the epitome of our separation from the world. Ownership of property roots us to and gives us a place in the world. Expropriation alienates us from the world by destroying our stable stake in it and exposes us to the exigencies of naked biological life (*HC*, 254–55). Prior to modernity, expropriation did not bring about total world alienation because it always led to the creation of new property and therefore, new worldly relations. However, modern capitalist expropriation, which is set off by the liberation of labor power as a natural process, completely alienates us from the world because it destroys the durability of things on which belonging to a common world is based. Modern capitalist accumulation does not create new property but relentlessly transforms wealth into capital so that any wealth that expropriation generates is "fed back into the process to generate further expropriations, greater productivity, and more appropriation" (*HC*, 255). "The process [of capitalist accumulation] can continue only provided that no worldly durability and stability is permitted to interfere, only as long as all worldly things . . . are fed back into it at an ever-increasing speed. . . . [It] is possible only if the world and the very worldliness of men are sacrificed" (*HC*, 256).

The radicality of Arendt's critique of natural law theories of human rights becomes clearer in light of her account of worldliness. Modern world alienation is the historical condition of the plight of refugees and stateless persons in the post–World War II world. In *The Origins of Totalitarianism*, Arendt argued that such persons challenged the eighteenth-century natural law understanding of human rights because the difficulty of asserting their rights indicated that the deprivation of human rights is a consequence of the loss of a world.[31] Her more radical critique is that the institutionalized discourse of natural human rights unwittingly violates humanity. By deriving universal rights from the natural fact of being human, the human rights instruments of her time reduce humanity to a biological species, to "the abstract nakedness of being human and nothing but human."[32] Hence, the very gesture of endowing the human being with naturally given, inalienable rights ironically deprives him of his humanity and worldliness, the human capacities for action and speech that create a meaningful world.[33]

The homeless refugee is Arendt's historical transposition of Heidegger's mere subject without a world into a merely biological human being, a worldless isolated individual in nature. But the similarity in their analyses of modern worldlessness—for example, the figures of nakedness and homelessness and the critique of geometrical spatialization—is misleading. World alienation presupposes that the world is an objective and intersubjective whole produced by human activity that is subsequently alienated. Arendt takes human activity for granted and shies away from inquiring into *vita activa*'s ontological basis in temporalization. Instead, she refigures temporalization as natality. Natality is the ontological ground of action and the principle that saves us from ruin and futility.

> If left to themselves, human affairs can only follow the law of mortality. . . . The life span of man running toward death would inevitably carry everything human to ruin and destruction if it were not for the faculty of interrupting it and beginning something new, a faculty which is inherent in action like an ever-present reminder that men, though they must die, are not born in order to die but in order to begin. . . . The miracle that saves the world, the realm of human affairs, from its normal, "natural" ruin is ultimately the fact of natality, in which the faculty of action is ontologically rooted. It is, in other words, the birth of new men and the new beginning, the action they are capable of by virtue of being born. (*HC*, 246–47)

Although natality brings us into the world, it is not immanent to the world. It is something from beyond that is added on to human affairs so that they are not merely left alone to fulfill their immanent tendency toward ruin and destruction. Natality opens up the world to a transcendent eternal source from which human life springs and that gives human existence the end of newness. It encrypts the transcendent within human existence as humanity's proper end to battle the principle of mortality internal to the world. As the memory of natality and its repetition within the world, action is the movement of immanent transcendence that repeatedly connects the world to what transcends finite existence.

However, grounding worldliness in natality is problematic for two reasons. First, it dogmatically presupposes the idea of an absolute creator as a principle of hope and salvation. Although Arendt occults the creator by recasting it as the human condition of natality and our power to begin something new through action, some recourse to the absolute is needed to explain why finite human beings possess the power to make worlds. Arendt's argument that the world of *homo faber* is of inferior permanence in comparison to the world of speech and action presupposes a more fundamental comparison between the deficiency of human fabrication and an absolute being's power of creation. What humans make will not last because we are finite, but we can be redeemed because an absolute creator has left its trace in our natality and the higher activity of action. This reference to an absolute being gives the lie to Arendt's critique of the idea of an author-creator behind the world such as Providence, Adam Smith's invisible hand, world history, and so on (HC, 185). The identification of the freedom of action with the repeated miracles of the coming of new beings into the world necessarily raises the question of what brings us into the world. Even if we are not concerned with who made us or the "how" of our making, we are nevertheless only free beings because we are *made* to bring newness into the world. The open-ended end of newness distinguishes us from other beings. But unless we presuppose an absolute creator who makes us with this end, there is no guarantee that our births and actions will bring newness into the world. Positing in advance the end of newness also undermines Arendt's argument about the world's structural openness or the impossibility of asserting sovereignty over it. This openness is premised on the reality that there are events that cannot be anticipated. However, a purely unexpected event is one about which we would not be able to say in advance whether it will bring newness or merely the same as what came before. Positing the end of newness closes off the world's openness through a totalizing reference to a sovereign creator.

Second, Arendt's implied faith in a transcendent sovereignty arises out of desperation. For her, the obscuring of action by *homo faber*'s ascendancy, its confusion with making, and the subsequent displacement of work by labor that completes the process of world alienation are part of the inexorable movement toward death that is immanent to human existence. Her later prognosis of the state of the world, which takes into account the annihilation of total nuclear war, is even more pessimistic. Although she emphasizes that "the inherent vocation" of the "authentic human realm . . . is not to come to an end by force," the human world—unlike the objective world, which can be rebuilt after its destruction—is not easily reconstructed if it is annihilated by catastrophe or war.[34] What is left behind is a desert, a space devoid of legal and political organization where the boundlessness of human action becomes an exponentially growing world-destroying force. "The world of relationships that arises out of action—man's authentic political activity—is considerably more difficult to destroy than the manufactured world of things. . . . But once this world of relationships [Bezugswelt] is destroyed, then the laws of political action . . . are replaced by the law of the desert, which, as a wasteland between men, unleashes devastating processes that bear with them the same lack of moderation inherent in those free human actions that establish relations. . . . [Such processes] drag a whole world with its entire wealth of relationships to its doom."[35] The desert is the absence of world. Its spread is a metaphor for "the modern growth of worldlessness, the withering away of everything *between* us."[36] Arendt can only counter such desolation by arguing that the source of human life is an absolute principle transcendent to finite existence. Only in this way can world alienation be understood as the result of a deficient mode of human activity that perverts our authentic existence, a foreign contamination that befalls human life from outside its original and proper source and causes it to deviate from its proper end.

Arendt's reliance on a minimalized sovereign creator to save the world from ruin appears especially utopian in contemporary globalization. Although Heidegger does not attend to the question of collective action, his idea of worlding is precisely an account of the world that has no absolute creator behind the scenes. There is a world instead of nothing because of the absolute chance of radically finite temporality. This is an ontological principle of real hope. The unpredictable and incalculable force of temporalization is the condition of possibility of the instrumental imperatives of modern capitalist accumulation and contemporary globalization that appropriate, erode, and undermine the world. For instrumental activity to take place, there must already be time. Although worlds can be destroyed, we cannot destroy time. Because temporalization is immanent to and exceeds instrumentality, it is a persistent force of (re)world-ing, a genuine principle of hope for maintaining the openness of the world that globalization closes off. In the next chapter I will elaborate on this principle of worldly hope and its connections to literary narrative with the help of Derrida's work.

CHAPTER 6

The Arriving World

The Inhuman Otherness of Time as Real Messianic Hope

Within this abyss of the without-world, this abyss without support, indeed on the condition of this absence of support, of bottom, ground, or foundation, it is as if one *bore* the other, as if I felt, without support and without hypothesis, *borne* by the other and *borne* toward the other, as if, as Celan says, *Die Welt ist fort, ich muss dich tragen*: the world goes away; the world disappears; I must bear you, there where the world would no longer or would not yet be, where the world would distance itself, get lost in the distance, or be still to come.

—JACQUES DERRIDA, *Rogues: Two Essays on Reason*

Deconstruction is a philosophical engagement with the question of time that takes Heidegger's thought as one of its key references.[1] The question of time bears directly on the question of the world, which only exists if there is time. Derrida only addressed the question of the world in the final phase of his writings where he engaged with the ethicopolitical problems posed by globalization, the failure of Marxist internationalism, and the possibility of cosmopolitan democracy. This chapter is a critical reconstruction of Derrida's sketchy outlines of a deconstructive account of worldliness that argues for its pertinence to understanding literature as a worldly force.

Unlike Arendt, who backed away from rethinking the world on the basis of radically finite temporalization, deconstruction radicalizes Heidegger's account of temporality to its extreme by suggesting that time is not proper to human Dasein but comes from the absolutely or nonhuman other. Derrida's argument that the coming of the other opens a world leads to a conception of the world as the text in general, a nontotalizable whole constituted by a movement of overflowing. The imperative to act to change the world is a response to the advent of the other, which puts time out of joint even as it gives and renews time. Derrida suggests that literature, in particular, narratives that are concerned with their own narrative status, give us a special insight into the opening of worlds.

Time as the Gift of the Nonhuman Other

Derrida's deconstruction of the metaphysics of presence is a radicalization of the question of time. This deconstruction also applies to Heidegger's fundamental ontology because, despite his critique of objective presence, he privileges the value of presence, especially in his account of authentic existence.[2] When Dasein anticipates its being-toward-death in resoluteness, it is fully present to itself because it grasps that temporalization is proper to it. Dasein can thus give itself time in the qualified sense of freely assuming its mortal end. The deconstruction of presence is also a critique of the proper as a form of presence. In questioning the residual anthropologism in Heidegger's characterization of the human being as the proper, as that being that is proper to itself because it is its own proper end, deconstruction raises the issue of whether temporalization is proper to human existence.

Heidegger elucidates Dasein's self-giving of time by contrasting authentic temporality with the reduction of the world to spatialized time in the idea of world time (*Weltzeit*). What is at issue here is the mistaking of time itself for an objective presence in the world. World time is our everyday understanding of time as an inner-worldly objective presence, something within the world that we take care of.[3] We experience, measure, and date time as part of the world because we reckon (*rechnen*) with time when we take care of beings in the world we are thrown amid. For example, we allow for time when we calculate, plan ahead, and prepare for something or prevent it from occurring. In these reckonings, we determine time as a container for things that are objectively present. We view it as a "now" and use it as a means to date things by marking their being as present *in* a "now." This is the condition of possibility of using instruments such as the clock to determine time.

The determination of time as a punctual now by dating things is in itself not a vulgar concept of time. Properly interpreted, datability points to Dasein's ability to allow and give itself time. "Da-sein, thrown into the world, temporalizing, and giving itself time [zeitigend sich Zeit gebende], takes account [Rechnung] of its regular recurring passage" (*BT*, 379; 413). When Dasein exists authentically, "it never loses time and 'always has time'" because it is aware of itself as the power of temporalization and consciously thematizes its ability to give itself time (*BT*, 377; 410). However, when Dasein exists inauthentically and is absorbed by the things it takes care of, it forgets that it is the power of temporalization and obscures the time it gives to itself. Instead of relating the temporal structure of care to the ecstatic temporality that opens up and connects the present to the past and the future, it closes this opening. Time becomes reified and confused with the objective presence of extant things and is viewed as something that can be quantified by the clock. In the vulgar interpretation of time, the origins of which Heidegger attributes to Aristotle, time becomes a meaningless succession of nows and is devoid of "transcendence" (*BT*, 386; 421 and 416n30; 432–33n14). "The ecstatic-horizontal constitution of temporality, in which the datability and meaningfulness of the now are grounded, is *levelled down*. . . . The nows are cut off from these relations . . . and . . . they simply range themselves along after one another so as to constitute the succession. . . . The vulgar interpretation of world time as now-time does not have the horizon available at all by which such things as world, meaningfulness, and datability can be made more accessible" (*BT*, 387; 422–23, translation modified).

In his deconstruction, Derrida points out that Heidegger tendentiously elides the fact that Aristotle already anticipates his critique by emphasizing the difficulties of understanding time as presence. In his *Physics*, Aristotle points out that it is problematic to think of time as composed of parts (nows) because, by definition, a current or present now cannot coexist with another now and still be present. It can only exist by itself, as an absolute unity or oneness, because its presence is fleeting. A now cannot simultaneously be with other nows as parts of a whole because any present now has to be destroyed by the next now just as it destroyed the previous now. The essence of a now qua presence is that it cannot coexist with an other that is the same as itself. Yet conceiving time as the mere succession of nows fails to explain the internal connection between nows, how the now stays the same and can be identified as a now even as it changes. Time is aporetic: it involves a certain coexistence of nows that is impossible because according to the essence of a now, coexistence with other nows would render it impossible.

We do, however, experience the impossibility of coexistence of nows as possible, Derrida argues, because to speak of another now that cannot coexist with this now already presupposes that they are all nows, that the present now and another now are the same. We presuppose the sameness of nows in our experience of time, and this allows us to preidentify this and other nows as nows. Sameness lets us experience the impossible coexistence of nows by synthesizing the self and the other and implicating the other in the self. "The impossibility of coexistence can be posited as such only on the basis of a certain coexistence, of a certain *simultaneity* of the nonsimultaneous, in which the alterity and identity of the now are maintained together in the differentiated element of a certain same."[4] As the connected flow of nows, time "is a name for this impossible possibility."[5] Better yet, time *is* its own impossibility.

The fundamental point Derrida draws from Aristotle's reflections on time is that time as presence is maintained by the aporetic play of otherness in the same. Aristotle's problematization of time is more radical than Heidegger's because the play of otherness in the same constitutes not only the now but also *any* determination of time as presence, including the superior form of presence Heidegger calls original time or authentic temporality. Heidegger explains the maintaining of the sameness of the now by referring to the superior concept of time as the moment (*Augenblick*). The moment's unity is not a mere succession of objectively present things but instead the holding or gathering together of the present, the future, and the past in a more powerful present (*Gegenwart*) (BT, 311; 338). Derrida contends, however, that the past, present, and future can only be unified in ecstatic temporality if they are already the same, that is, if they are all forms of the present. Hence, the genetic play of alterity, in constituting sameness, also produces ecstatic temporality.

Derrida's famous essay "Différance" makes the same point by recasting Saussure's account of the diacritical character of the linguistic sign—the constitution of a sign's meaning through differential relations—in temporal terms. As a form of presence, meaning is constituted by the play of alterity, which is described in this context by *trace* and *interval*.

> The movement of signification is possible only if each so-called "present" element . . . is related to something other than itself, thereby keeping within itself the mark of the past element, and already letting itself be vitiated by the mark of its relation to the future element, this trace being related no less to what is called the future than to what is called the past, and constituting what is called the present by means of this very relation to what it is not: what it absolutely is not, not even a past or a future as a modified present. An interval must separate the present from what it is not in order for the present to be itself, but this interval that constitutes it as present must, by the same token, divide the present in and of itself, thereby also dividing, along with the present, everything that is thought on the basis of the present, that is, in our metaphysical language, every being, and singularly substance or the subject.[6]

The scope of Derrida's deconstruction of presence has unfortunately been limited by a reductive interpretation of constitutive difference as the free play of literary signification. Read as an argument about the temporal constitution of presence, his point is that presence is always riven by the force of a radical alterity in its generation and maintenance. The differential relations that constitute the present by connecting past and future to the present as the same (i.e., as forms of the present) are simultaneously an interval that separates the present from what it is not (past and future). In producing the present, the interval both relates and separates the present to and from what is other. It separates by relating and relates through separation. Hence, the interval is a constitutive division within the present, a difference internal to and at the origin of presence. The play of alterity that constitutes presence does not belong to the order of time or being because these have always been understood on the basis of presence. It is neither spatial nor temporal but is the genetic play that generates space and time and "produces" being. As Derrida puts it, the coexistence of the same and the other in temporalization indicates "the complicity, the common origin of space and time, appearing together as the condition of all appearing of Being."[7] This complicity of other and same points to an absolute alterity that is not temporal and not of the order of presence but that produces the presence of time and being.[8]

I can now offer a precise articulation of Derrida's hyperradicalization of finite temporality. Although Heidegger repeatedly emphasizes that time "'is' not a *being* at all . . . but rather *temporalizes* itself," time still belongs to the order of presence because, first, it is the ground of being, and second, *self*-temporalization implies a form of presence—the presence to self in temporalization—that is superior to the presence of merely objective beings (BT, 302; 328). But if temporalization refers to a radical alterity that is not temporal and not of the order of being, then temporality cannot be grounded in the unity of self-temporalization proper to human beings. Derrida suggests that time is given by what is entirely other to being. The other is not temporal, not in the sense that it is an absolute being that transcends time, but rather because it is not a form of presence and exceeds the order of being. I emphasize in passing that Derrida's position is not merely a facile argument about the centrality of death to life and the need for living beings to affirm death and desire and value their mortal lives because human mortality is irreducible and not derived from immortality. This simplistic argument ignores the fact that time and being exceed human existence and even life as such because there is nonliving being. Radically finite temporality encompasses more than the phenomenon of mortal life.[9] This is precisely why Derrida insists that finite temporality cannot be proper to the mortal being called human. It refers to an otherness that cannot be reduced to being and presence.

Because alterity both constitutes time and presence and exceeds and renders them impossible, it is simultaneously their condition of possibility and impossibility. It grounds and also disrupts the economy of presence, subjecting presence to a law of radical contamination that makes it drift without return. Derrida's subsequent reflections on the gift elaborate on the aporetic relation of otherness to presence by arguing that time as the pure event should be understood through the figure of a gift that comes from the entirely other. The event is a privileged example of finite temporality because we experience it as an absolute alterity that is effaced when it becomes present. An event cannot be one if it is anticipated in advance, if we can tell when and from where it is or will be coming. Hence, an event can only come from or, better yet, is the entirely other. It comes from beyond the order of presence and is experienced as an unexpected irruption in and interruption of presence. However, when it becomes an empirical phenomenon, it is no longer an event because its alterity has become annulled by its appearance. The gift is an apposite heuristic figure for understanding the pure event because its peculiar phenomenality indicates that it is structured by a similar aporia between alterity and presence. A gift is truly one only if it does not appear and is not recognized as a gift. Once it enters into the circuit of exchange and reciprocity, it is no longer a genuine gift because its mere recognition by the donor or the donee will lead to indebtedness, the expectation of repayment, or self-gratification, praise, or self-congratulation on the part of the donor for generosity. A gift can therefore only be preserved if it is not recognized at all and not identified as such. This means that a gift can only appear or be present by being violated, destroyed, or annulled.[10] Its appearance takes place at the cost of its contamination by what it is not because it can only be present in and as what it is not.

The gift shares three traits with the pure event. First, just as the giving of time cannot be referred back to an infinite being who lies beyond and gives time, the gift cannot have an identifiable donor. Second, contra Heidegger, the giving of time is not a modality of self-temporalization. Temporalization annuls the alterity of the event because it reduces the event's otherness to a future presence through "anticipatory expectation or apprehension that grasps or comprehends in advance" (GT, 14). In the same way, the expectation of repayment that follows from the identification of the gift destroys the gift. Third, although the other from which the event comes is outside time and being, it is not an occulted ineffable presence that is thinkable although it cannot appear. The other does not conserve itself as an absent presence but gives itself to be violated when the event is experienced as a phenomenon. The gift similarly lets itself be contaminated when it appears. In Derrida's words, "The gift, like the event, as event, must *remain* unforeseeable, but remain so without keeping itself. It must let itself be structured by the aleatory; it must *appear* chancy or in any case lived as such, apprehended as the intentional correlate of a perception that is absolutely surprised by the encounter with what it perceives, beyond its horizon of anticipation. . . . The event and the gift, the event as gift, the gift as event must be irruptive, unmotivated. . . . [They] obey nothing, except perhaps principles of disorder" (GT, 122–23). Our experience of and being in time thus presuppose an otherness that exceeds the order of being and tears the flow of temporality. It puts time out of joint. But because it is the coming of the event and the giving of time, it also makes possible and renews the flow of temporal presents. Alterity's relation to presence is that of an outside that cannot be determined and delimited, because it is not a *simple* outside that is present(able). As that which constitutes presence, this indeterminable outside contaminates presence from its very inside, affecting presence without touching it.

The World as the Text in General and the Imperative to Act as a Response to the Other's Coming

In the deconstructive formulation of radical finitude, the world is opened up by the coming of the radically other. In *Speech and Phenomena*, Derrida had already played Heidegger against Husserl by arguing that time cannot be appropriated by the transcendental subject because temporalization relates the inside to the outside and thus implies a constitutive worldliness, the subject's irreducible openness to the outside.

> "Time" cannot be an "absolute subjectivity" precisely because it cannot be conceived on the basis of a present and the self-presence of a present being. . . . Like all that is excluded by the most rigorous transcendental reduction, the "world" is primordially implied in the movement of temporalization. As a relation between an inside and an outside in general . . . temporalization is at once the very power and limit of phenomenological reduction. Hearing oneself speak is not the inwardness of an inside that is closed in upon itself; it is the irreducible openness in the inside; it is the eye and the world within speech.[11]

He now goes a step further and argues that worlding entails a relation to radical alterity that contaminates the demarcation of any proper sphere. We can call this constitutive impropriety: a radical improperness marks out the proper boundaries of any present being, including the borders of intraworldly beings and even the world itself. This force also undermines these very boundaries by an overflowing that opens up beings and being itself to what is outside them.

The deconstructive critique of the proper has three methodological consequences for understanding the world. First, whereas Heidegger defined the world as a meaningful totality of referential relations centered on Dasein's power of temporalization, Derrida suggests that the world is a limitless weave or textile of forces, what he calls the text in general. The world is constituted by the systematic play of différance, a generative movement of referral that is without beginning and finality, *arche* and *telos*. This play produces the web of determinate differences from which the positive identities of present beings are generated. "What is written as *différance*, then, will be the playing movement that 'produces'—by means of something that is not simply an activity—these differences, these effects of difference. This does not mean that the *différance* that produces differences is somehow before them, in a simple and unmodified—in-different—present. *Différance* is the non-full, non-simple, structured and differentiating origin of differences. Thus, the name 'origin' no longer suits it."[12] The play of différance is not limited to language, especially literary language in the narrow sense. Phenomena and all forms of being and presence are generated by the play of differences. As Derrida puts it, "we will designate as *différance* the movement according to which . . . any system of referral in general, is constituted 'historically' as a weave of differences."[13]

Différance is a kind of "causality" that produces determinate differences. These differences produce identity-effects that cannot be referred back to a superior cause outside the play of differences. Hence, to say that the world is generated by différance signifies the impossibility of enclosing beings and regions of being in the world as a structured whole. Although Heidegger had defined the world as Dasein's opening up to other Dasein and to beings that are not Dasein, the world remains a closed whole that refers back to Dasein as its proper ground. For Derrida, however, the world cannot be rounded off as a totality. The constitution of the self-present identity of any system or whole by the play of difference means that the world is structurally open in its very constitution. Accordingly, the different regions of being in the world that are the objects of ontic knowledges such as anthropology, sociology, psychology, biology, and so on cannot be clearly demarcated from each other as autonomous spheres.[14] They bleed and flow into each other without return. The overflowing of their proper boundaries inscribes them as part of a text in general, "a weave of differences of forces without any present center of reference (everything—'history,' 'politics,' 'economy,' 'sexuality,' etc.—said not to be written in books)."[15] "*There* is such a general text," Derrida observes, "everywhere that . . . the discourse [of presence] and its order (essence, sense, truth, meaning, consciousness, ideality, etc.) are *overflowed*."[16]

Second, this overflowing also occurs at the borders between the ontological and ontic existence. The hierarchical difference between the ontological and the ontic organizes Heidegger's thought. Because the power of temporalization is proper to human Dasein, we are capable of world-formation and understanding being. Our existence is thus superior to that of other beings that are merely objectively present. Commenting on the centrality of the proper in the later Heidegger's characterization of being as appropriation (*Ereignis*), Derrida observes that a deconstruction of the proper should transform "the relation between general or fundamental ontology and whatever ontology masters or makes subordinate under the rubric of a regional or particular science."[17]

This has important consequences for the phenomenological account of the world. Heidegger advocated a patient waiting for the world to prevail instead of exploring the kinds of factical collective action authentic resoluteness might lead to because he regarded the force of temporalization as proper to Dasein. Arendt's impatience with Heidegger led to a cruder anthropologism— the reduction of temporalization to human action. She salvages a normative principle of worldly transformation by uncritically deriving action from the quasi-theological idea of natality. She thus represses Heidegger's insight that temporalization is a force of worlding and that a *real* principle of worldly transformation cannot come from an infinite creator but already inheres in temporalization. By arguing that temporalization entails the constitutive contamination of presence by alterity, Derrida retains Heidegger's insight that temporalization is transcendence. But, unlike Arendt, Derrida solves the problem of the transposition of the force of temporalization into factical action without privileging the human subject's rational will as the mediating bridge. Instead, he turns Heidegger's critiques of anthropologism and presence against his privileging of Dasein as the proper bearer of temporality. Because the temporal constitution of presence points to the coming of the wholly other, the translation of Dasein's authentic self-temporalization into worldly action is a necessity that arises from the overflowing of the border between being and ontic existence.

The constitutive contamination of the proper realm of ontology is manifested in and is nothing other than the precipitation into worldly action.

Derrida's later writings elaborate on this leap into action by arguing that the normative force of worldly ethical and political action originates in a *response* to absolute alterity. The wholly other is unconditional because it gives time. But as it is inscribed within and gives rise to presence through temporalization, it is *experienced* within presence as the condition of possibility and impossibility of presence. This quasi-transcendental operation opens up the order of presence to the unconditional, for example, when the circle of political economy is interrupted and renewed by the chance of the gift or when incalculable justice suspends the calculations of the law.

The other's unconditionality is not the unconditionality conventionally associated with human freedom, understood as self-present reason's ability to transcend externally imposed or particularistic conditions. Because processes of reason are types of presence and are constitutively exposed to alterity, what is truly unconditional is reason's sheer vulnerability to the interruption of temporality by the coming of an unforeseeable, incalculable other. Derrida elucidates this exposure to alterity through the pathological metaphor of autoimmunity. The other both gives and can take time away. Reason must be open to alterity to live on. But to avoid destruction, reason must also protect itself from the other. However, when reason immunizes itself against the other, it immunizes itself from its own powers of immunity, because the other also constitutes and maintains reason by giving time. Hence, the irreducible possibility of destruction haunts reason. As Derrida puts it,

> if an event worthy of this name is to arrive or happen, it must, beyond all mastery, affect a passivity. It must touch an exposed vulnerability, one without absolute immunity, without indemnity; it must touch this vulnerability in its finitude and in a non-horizontal fashion, there where it is not yet or is already no longer possible to face or face up to the unforeseeability of the other. In this regard, autoimmunity is not an absolute ill or evil. It enables an exposure to the other, to *what* and to *who* comes—which means that it must remain incalculable. Without autoimmunity, with absolute immunity, nothing would ever happen or arrive; we would no longer wait, await, or expect, no longer expect one another, or expect any event.[18]

The unconditional other is the impossible. But the impossible has a nonnegative relation to the realm of presence and possibility. Instead of paralyzing us into inaction or leading to quietism, the impossible is characterized by a structure of precipitation and urgency. In Derrida's words, "[the im-possible] announces itself; it precedes me, swoops down upon and seizes me *here and now* in a nonvirtualizable way, in actuality and not potentiality. . . . Such an urgency cannot be *idealized* any more than the other as other can. This im-possible is thus not a (regulative) *idea* or *ideal*. It is what is most undeniably *real*. And sensible. Like the other. Like the irreducible and nonappropriable différance of the other."[19] This structure of precipitation is how the unconditional gives itself to be inscribed within factical conditions. It is the origin of imperativity, responsibility, and ethics. The unconditional other demands that we respond and be responsible in the present, even if our response violates the other. This precipitation gives rise to the interruptive decision and to practical reason as the responsible accounting for any decision.

Because the force that impels rational action issues from the unconditional other, the imperativity to act cannot be reduced to a rational subject's sovereign autonomy. It is instead a decision that is passively endured because the decision comes from the alterity of reason (double genitive), the otherness that intimately inhabits reason.[20] Our exposure to the event's otherness is freedom in the most radical sense: freedom from the regularity of temporalization, whether we understand temporality as a succession of nows or as the anticipation of a future present. Following Kant, we commonly understand freedom as the self-determination of reason. But strictly speaking, freedom from being determined must also be freedom from self-determination, that is, freedom from the sovereignty of being determined by one's own reason, including being determined by the anticipatory power of consciousness. By setting off temporalization, the event frees or releases presence. But at the same time, the freedom of the event is also a freeing from temporalization and presence. Freedom is here no longer the subject's autonomy but involves the passivity of drifting toward or being delivered over to the other. But since the other is not another presence and this drifting constitutes the self, this passive delivery is not a form of subjection to another power, whether divine (as in the idea of providential fate) or secular (as in domination by someone else). As Derrida puts it, "what must be thought here, then, is this inconceivable and unknowable thing, a freedom that would no longer be the power of a subject, a freedom without autonomy, a heteronomy without servitude, in short, something like a passive decision. We would thus have to rethink the philosophemes of decision, of that foundational couple activity and passivity, as well as potentiality and actuality."[21] The passive decision is the structure of imperativity impelling factical worldly action that inheres in the gift of time.

Derrida's grounding of worldly action in the pure event should be distinguished from Arendt's account of action in three respects. Arendt defined the world as the in-between of subjects that is endlessly renewed by human action. For Derrida, however, the world is not a *present* field of relations between subjects. It is what is always arriving, or better yet, the force of arriving. Because the event comes from what is absolutely other to being, the other is never present but is that which is always yet to come. Hence, when the world is thought on the basis of the event, it has the structure of a to-come (*l'à-venir*), an opening onto a future that is not a future present. Derrida indicates this nonpresent futurity by spacing out the future (*avenir*) qua horizon that is calculatively determined in advance into the infinitive form, to come (*à venir*).

Second, because of its radical unpredictability and incalculability, the force of the other's coming that opens a world and prompts action should be distinguished from the figure of the newcomer that Arendt uses to elucidate the quasi-teleological relation between natality and action. Natality is the utopian guarantee of the coming of newness. This coming is incarnated in and personified by the newcomer, someone who is present and has come or others who will be present and whose repeated coming will continually change the world. Hence, although the newness that action brings is unpredictable in its outcome, the coming of newness into the world is a dead certainty. The ability of human beings who are worthy of being called newcomers to initiate something and change the world is also a dead certainty, because this is the end for which human beings are brought into the world by natality and the absolute power it implies. In contradistinction, because of its radical alterity, the to-come is not a newcomer, the inevitable coming of newness. As Derrida puts it, "birth itself, which is similar to what I am trying to describe, is perhaps unequal to this absolute 'arrivance.' Families prepare for a birth; it is scheduled, forenamed, caught up in a symbolic space that dulls the arrivance. Nevertheless, in spite of these anticipations and prenominations, the uncertainty will not let itself be reduced: the child that arrives remains unpredictable; it speaks of itself as from the origin of another world, or from an-other origin of this world."[22] The to-come is an openness that promises nothing certain because it does not posit a determinate end of any kind. What comes may be very good for humanity, but it can also be the worst evil. The to-come is instead the sheer structure of promise devoid of determinate promises, what Derrida sometimes describes as the messianic without messianism.

Third, the other that prompts the passive decision is not another newcoming human subject who addresses me, someone who resembles or is the same as me and to whom I relate intersubjectively and with whom I act in concert. The other that is to come is simply the absolute *arrivant*—that which is non-identifiable and arrives, that which is always arriving and yet to arrive and hence that which cannot be determined as a foreigner, a refugee, an immigrant, and so on, as "someone or something that arrives, a subject, a person, an individual, or a living thing."[23] It is an incalculable inhuman force that propels me amid determinate others and "demands" that I act responsibly toward them in the present because they are present with me.

Accordingly, the undoing of sovereignty by the passive decision should be distinguished from Arendt's account of the nonsovereign character of human action. Although Arendt sunders the conventional association of freedom with sovereignty by insisting on "the simultaneous presence of freedom and non-sovereignty," this nonsovereignty is limited to what follows from the fact that we are not "able to control or even foretell [the] consequences" of our actions because we act among a plurality of actors (*HC*, 235). Arendt conserves the actor's sovereign intention to initiate the new even if it is impossible for him to be a sovereign in actualizing his intentions. The intentional component of action remains sovereign, even if its operationalization cannot be.[24] In contradistinction, the passive decision indicates an original undoing of the practical subject's sovereignty, insofar as the assertion of sovereignty in action is a nonsovereign response to a decision of the other. Indeed, humanity's sovereignty is put into question because the other who makes me decide is nonhuman and cannot respond to the question "Who are you?" Whereas Arendt effaces the eventness of the event by appropriating it into an original human potentiality and giving it the anthropological shape of the newcomer, Derrida argues that rational human action is a response to our radical openness to the inappropriable nonhuman other.

The World to Come: The Deconstructive Account of Worldliness

In *Of Grammatology*, Derrida alluded to a radical idea of play (*jeu*) that would exceed Husserl's phenomenological problematic of the transcendental origin of the world and Heidegger's problematic of the world-ness (*mondanité*) of the world because it thinks *"the game of the world [jeu du monde] . . . before attempting to understand all the forms of play in the world [jeu dans le monde]."*[25] But he only returned to the deconstructive idea of world in some brief reflections in his later writings, where he suggests that the radical openness to the inappropriable other is an unerasable principle of transformability inherent to the world. I will call this principle "real messianic hope."²⁶ As with all the philosophical conceptualizations of the world I have discussed in previous chapters, a distinction between the globe as a spatio-geographical term and the world as a temporal term is central to the deconstructive rethinking of worldliness.

For Derrida, the world/globe distinction arises out of an urgent need to maintain the "normative" universalizing exigency of world in the face of the worldlessness caused by contemporary globalization, as exemplified by the predatory expropriating character of global capitalist accumulation and the decline of Marxist internationalism in the late twentieth and early twenty-first centuries. In a posthumous article in *Le Monde Diplomatique*, Derrida criticizes the misuse of the French word *mondialisation*, literally, the becoming-world of the world, to refer to the integrating processes of globalization.²⁷ Whereas *mondialisation* is a process of openness that alludes to worlding in the Heideggerian sense, *globalization* refers to antiworldly processes of inclusionary capture by global market exchange. Derrida describes social movements against neoliberal capitalist globalization, such as those that make up the World Social Forum and offer alternatives to the vision of the world of the G8, the Washington Consensus, the World Bank, the International Monetary Fund, and the Organization of Economic Cooperation and Development, as other-worlding (*altermondialistes*) movements. They are an-other worlding (*altermondialisation*) that worlds otherwise: "The growing and ceaseless pressure of the other-worlding mass movements and public opinion will weaken them [the superpowers represented by the IMF, the OECD] and will not fail to oblige them . . . to reform themselves."²⁸

Referring to the legacy of Heidegger's critique of the vulgar concept of the world, Derrida carefully discriminates between five different concepts of the totality of being: the terrestrial globe or the spherically bounded geographical entity that globalization seeks to remake; the Greek idea of *cosmos*; its Christianization in its Pauline interpretation as *mundus*, a universal fraternal *human* community, from which the modern French, German, and English terms *monde*, *Welt*, and *world* are derived; Heidegger's transcendental concept of world; and finally, the deconstructive sense of world that is open to the coming of the other and that points beyond the European filiation of the Christian concept.

If I maintain the distinction between these concepts [of world (*monde*) and *mondialisation*] and the concepts of *globalization* or *Globalisierung* . . . it is because the concept of world gestures towards a history, it has a memory that distinguishes it from that of the globe, of the universe, of Earth, of the *cosmos* even (at least of the cosmos in its pre-Christian meaning, which Saint Paul then Christianized precisely to make it say *world* as *fraternal* community of human beings, of fellow creatures, brothers, sons of God and neighbors to one another). For the world begins by designating, and tends to remain, in an Abrahamic tradition (Judeo-Christian-Islamic but predominantly Christian) a particular space-time, a certain oriented history of human brotherhood, of what in a Pauline language ... one calls *citizens of the world* (*sympolitai*, fellow citizens [concitoyens] of the saints in the house of God), brothers, fellow men, neighbors, insofar as they are creatures and sons of God.[29]

The concept of world is no less obscure, in its European, Greek, Jewish, Christian, Islamic history, between science, philosophy, and faith, whether the world is wrongly identified with the earth, with the humans on earth here below, or with the heavenly world above, the cosmos, the universe, and so forth. Successful or not, Heidegger's project beginning with *Sein und Zeit*, will have sought to remove the concept of world and of being-in-the-world from these Greek and Christian presuppositions. ... Unlike "globalization" or *Globalisierung, mondialisation* marks a reference to this notion of world that is charged with a great deal of semantic history, notably a Christian history: the world ... is neither the universe, nor the earth, nor the terrestrial globe, nor the *cosmos*.[30]

All interpretations of the totality of being prior to Heidegger can be considered worlding in a narrow sense. But the worlds that they make obscure worldliness in the phenomenological sense.

The differences between *cosmos*, world, the phenomenological idea of world, and the deconstructive inscription of world are differences between "normative" conceptions. The Abrahamic notion of world, which Derrida hastily narrows down to the Christian version, is distinguished from *cosmos* in at least three ways. First, whereas the *cosmos* is an eternal or timeless whole, the world is a finite or *temporal* whole made by an absolute creator. It has an origin or beginning and therefore a memory and a history of creation that is predominantly Christian. Second, whereas *cosmos* is an inherently meaningful and purposive whole that connects human and nonhuman beings, the Pauline definition of world is anthropologistic. It refers to a universal human community of brothers or compeers, other fellow humans who are like me. Third, because it is made, the world is the end of creative work, and its origin is situated at the completion of work.

Despite its name, modern cosmopolitanism, which is often expressed and embodied by concepts and institutions of international law such as human rights and crimes against humanity, is derived from the Christian notion of world and not the *cosmos*. Cosmopolitanism worlds the world in the image of humanity and posits the world as a universal fraternal community of human beings. It is identical with humanization: "The concept of man, of what is proper to man, of human rights, of crimes against the humanity of man, organizes . . . such a *mondialisation* or worldwide-ization. This *mondialisation* wishes to be a humanization."[31] Cosmopolitan concepts and institutions are thus part of a project of human self-making, where humanity actualizes itself by making the world in its image in a self-returning process. The figure of an enclosing circle is common to *cosmos*, world, and globe, whether this is the natural roundness of the globe, the immediately meaningful teleological whole of the *cosmos*, or the rational totality of a completely humanized world achieved through a historical teleology. The modern idea of cosmopolitan democracy, Derrida notes, indicates the complicity between the Pauline concept of world and the concept of globe because the universalization of democratic institutions is understood in terms of their dissemination across the spherical expanse of the globe in order to systematically integrate all peoples into a democratic whole.[32] Despite Heidegger's critique of the world as an object made by human activity and a community formed by intersubjective relations, the figure of the self-returning circle persists in his argument that the world is constituted by Dasein's self-temporalization.

The deconstructive inscription of world is distinguished from these earlier ideas by its figuration of the world as a deformation, effraction, and even puncturing of the enclosing circle. Because the inappropriable other that opens a world is the condition of (im)possibility of presence, the deconstructive inscription is concerned with the world at its point of disappearance, with "a spacing from 'before' the world, the cosmos, or the globe, from 'before' any chronophenomenology, any revelation, any 'as such' and any 'as if,' any anthropotheological dogmatism or historicity."[33] Unlike the dogmatic messianism of Arendtian natality, the world's disappearance is a principle of real messianic hope, because the inappropriable other that comes with every disappearance of the world is simultaneously the force of opening that lets a world be present. Simply put, the openness to the other is the zone of the world's appearance, its persistent facticity in the face of its destruction.

In a comment immediately preceding the quote from *Rogues* that I used as this chapter's epigraph, Derrida follows Heidegger and Arendt by arguing that globalization destroys the world that supports us. It creates massive inequalities in the distribution of natural resources, wealth, and scientific-technological capabilities and makes us worldless. Yet a world nevertheless persists. In this globalization "that is more inegalitarian and violent than ever, a globalization that is, therefore, only simply alleged and actually less global or worldwide than ever . . . *the* world, therefore is not even there, and . . . we who are worldless, *weltlos, form* a world only against the backdrop of a nonworld where there is neither world nor even the poorness-in-world that Heidegger attributes to animals."[34] Where the world has disappeared, we form a world through our relations with the other. It is "as if one *bore* the other, as if I felt . . . *borne* by the other and *borne* toward the other." Indeed, the absence of the world as support is "the condition" for my bearing and being borne by the other.

Derrida interprets the last line of Paul Celan's poem *Grosse, glühende Wölbung* (Vast, Glowing Vault)—"Die Welt ist fort, ich muß dich tragen [The world is gone, I must carry you]"—as suggesting that the world's disappearance is the source of an imperative or obligation for the self to bear the other. Because the other bears the self and supports it in the absence of the world as support, my support of the other heralds the opening of a world to come: "The world disappears; I must bear you there where the world would no longer or would not yet be, where the world would distance itself, get lost in the distance, or be still to come."

In an extended treatment of the same line, Derrida elaborates on how Celan deconstructs the phenomenological conception of world.[35] Derrida suggests that our relation to the death of determinate others is a phenomenological figure for the persistent opening of a world where the world has been destroyed. Because each life is singular and unique, the world as it is at any given time comes to an end with the death of each and every other. Because it is impossible for me to die at the same time as the other, my life (and each and every life) is always structured by survival and mourning. Hence, in my very existence, I survive beyond the other.[36] I am alone and worldless because the world has disappeared with the other's passing. However, in mourning the other, I carry the other and the world that has disappeared with him in me. Hence, although that world is gone, mourning opens a world in which I am and where I need to be in order to mourn the other.[37] The present world where I am is therefore supported by a remembered world where I am with the other, a world that has disappeared but nevertheless persists in its constitutive encryption in the world where I currently exist. Against Heidegger's argument that Dasein's anticipation of its own death discloses its authentic existence, Derrida suggests that we experience the fullest awareness of temporality in an a priori "sociality"—the death of the other—that is more fundamental than my relation to my own proper death. This is authentic being-with others, if you will.

Simply put, Derrida's argument is that time is only radically finite if it comes from an absolutely other that cannot be appropriated as a form of presence. A world always persists because its temporalization refers us to the inappropriable other as its abyssal ground. The processes that cause the world's disappearance take place in time. Hence, they necessarily entail the other's coming. Since the other is also the condition of possibility of the world's initial appearing and subsequent reappearing, its coming opens and gives rise to another world. Put another way, the world can never be destroyed because, being grounded in a relation to the inappropriable other, it is never fully present and is always still to come. Derrida suggests that the world's disappearing (*Fort-sein*, being-gone or being-away) exceeds and cannot be captured by Heidegger's metaphysical categories of being deprived of world, poor in world, and world-forming. These categories, which are premised on a conception of the world as meaningful presence, are insufficient for understanding the world's disappearance. The world's disappearing comes from "a wholly other place" that is not related to the order of presence in a simple negative or positive way, because the other interrupts and undoes presence *and* constitutes and maintains it.[38] The disappearing is neither a loss nor lack of world. It is the opening that enables the (present) world to persist and promises an arriving world.

Derrida specifies two concrete implications of the deconstructive concept of world. First, the deconstruction of world necessitates an analysis of the concept's genealogical ties to Europe and the Abrahamic religions, especially Christianity, even as we must uproot and deterritorialize this European heritage and displace it beyond European borders because the concept's "universalizing exigency" leads to its auto-deconstruction.[39] Such universalizing would divide and "split, or expropriate the Euro-Christian heritage" in the movement of sharing.[40] In other words, the concept's European legacy must be critically filtered so that what is valuable can be universalized beyond Europe, even if the universalization of these values, Derrida points out, can imply neocolonial and neoimperial violence and forms of global domination that exceed the nation-state. There must be another worlding (Derrida calls it a new "world contract") that will take us beyond the inequality and unevenness of the modern world-system. This expropriative legacy is an aporetic type of universal world history, a world history under erasure that empties it of eschatology and teleology. The contributions of different cultures or peoples would undergo a universalizing dissemination without return to a telos and without coming to an end (*eschaton*).

Second, Derrida suggests that the universalization of the concepts and institutions of international law is paramount. This leads to a cosmopolitanism and world citizenship that presuppose the sovereignty of the state. But it also leads to "another, democratic International beyond the nation-state, even beyond citizenship," that Derrida elaborates under the idea of democracy to come.[41] The New International, he specifies, "is an untimely link, without status, without title, and without name . . . without contract, 'out of joint', without coordination, without party, without country, without national community (International before, across, and beyond any national determination), without co-citizenship, without common belonging to a class."[42] As an alliance among undetermined anyones that is unconditionally open to any and every other, the New International is a political figure for the openness to the radically other.[43] It is a specifically political modality of worlding that sets to work the openness to the inappropriable other within the temporality of the political. As Derrida puts it, democracy to come is based on "another thought and another putting into practice of the concept of the 'political' and the concept 'world.'" It "would be more in line with what lets singular beings (anyone) 'live together,' there where they are not yet defined by citizenship, that is, by their condition as lawful 'subjects' in a state or legitimate members of a nation-state or even of a confederation or world state."[44]

What is most important about the deconstructive account of world, however, is not the specific political shapes it takes in Derrida's writings but the aporetic relation between the world's unerasable openness and capitalist globalization. Here, we should rigorously distinguish the destruction of the world in globalization from the structural disappearance of the world that accompanies the inappropriable other's coming. The opening and contamination of the world by alterity certainly makes the world vulnerable to destruction. The worldlessness caused by globalization does not befall us from the outside. It is an inherent possibility of worlding as the force of overflowing that undermines all proper boundaries. However, globalization is a specific contamination of the world. It destroys the world by leveling the world's opening to the other, because its fundamental imperative is the mastery of finitude through the management and appropriation of time. Its temporality is intentionally atemporal. Because it seeks to control time through calculation, it destroys the world's to-come. But because processes of capitalist accumulation necessarily take place in time and are based on temporal regulation, they too are necessarily contaminated and disrupted by radical alterity, which enables the world to persist and other worlds to come. In other words, there is something other that is structural to reality that radically resists human calculation and cannot be appropriated by the instrumental imperatives of globalization. The world to come is a real ongoing movement of messianic hope, because as the condition of experience, the inappropriable other is what is most real. As Derrida puts it,

> the affirmation of the impossible [is] always put forward *in the name of the real*, of the irreducible reality of the real—not of the real as the attribute of the objective, present, perceptible or intelligible *thing* (*res*), but of the real as the coming or event of the other, where the other resists all appropriation. . . . The real is this non-negative impossible, this impossible coming or invention of the event the thinking of which is . . . a thinking of the event (singularity of the other, in its unanticipatable coming, *hic et nunc*) that resists reappropriation by an ontology or phenomenology of presence as such. . . . Nothing is more "realist," in this sense, than a deconstruction. It is (what-/who-)ever happens [(ce) qui arrive].[45]

The deconstructive rethinking of world on the basis of the to-come demands that we analyze how globalization unworlds us. At the same time, it points to the interruption and subversion of these unworlding processes by an-other immanent force of worlding. Any given world, any world that we have received and has been historically changed and that we self-consciously seek to transform progressively through spiritual intercourse, labor, or action is riven by the force of a delivery over to the nonhuman other whose coming allows a world to appear or lets us receive a world. At the subjective level, this force animates and gives urgency to the desire, action, and decision to remake the world.[46]

Another Relation of Literature to the World

Literature is intimately related to the opening of another world by virtue of its peculiar ontological status. As something that is structurally detached from its putative source and that permits and even solicits an infinite number of hypotheses about its meaning even when there may not be one, literature exemplifies the undecidability that opens a world. There is a surfeit of scholarly discussion in literary theory about the deconstructive powers of literariness and the radical undecidability, self-referentiality, and free play of literary signification. But these debates rarely address the connection between literature and Derrida's radicalization of finite temporality and have never touched on literature's relation to the world to come.

Derrida is willfully imprecise about what he means by literature, because what literature puts at stake is precisely intentional meaning, the intention or meaning to say (*vouloir dire*).[47] He sometimes uses literature as an equivalent term for literary forms such as fiction, narrative, or the poem. Literature is also one item in a chain of deconstructive terms such as *writing* in the general sense, *mark*, *trace*, and so on. The two defining traits of "literature" are, first, the sundering of any verbal utterance or written text from authorial intention and its original context, and second, the structural impossibility of determining the meaning of the utterance or text that follows from this setting adrift.

Authorial meaning is the presence of a rational consciousness to itself in the ideality of the meaningful signs it produces. This meaning is the sign's reference. It is conventionally represented as a secret that proper decipherment will reveal. The sundering of texts from their authorially intended meaning is part of their phenomenological structure as ideal objects, because their legibility and intelligibility depends on their repeatability or iterability in their author's absence. There is something testamentary about these objects, something that links them to legacy and inheritance, because the full presence of their meaning can only be achieved if they are delivered over to the other in general. However, this drifting from and radical absence of authorial intention also renders a text illegible, makes its meaning undecidable and suspends its reference. This means that we will never be able to unlock the secret inner meaning a text encrypts, that it ultimately makes no sense to ask what a text means. Indeed, signification in general may be a secret without a secret, the appearance of a secret that may not be one at all.[48]

Of all the different kinds of text, literature is the best example of the structural loss of authorial meaning that characterizes signification because it is a type of signification about which it is meaningless to determine the author's final intentions with regard to the narrative voice, the characters, or even the meanings of a given line of poetry or fiction. Consequently, literature is characterized by a radical undecidability of meaning, the possibility of always meaning otherwise. This implies a fundamental superficiality or lack of meaningful depth that can be revealed. As Derrida puts it,

> there is . . . in the *exemplary* secret of literature, a chance of saying everything without touching upon the secret. When all hypotheses are permitted,

groundless and ad infinitum, about the meaning of a text, or the final intentions of an author, whose person is no more represented than nonrep-
resented by a character or by a narrator, by a poetic or fictional sentence,
which detaches itself from its presumed source and thus remains *locked
away [au secret]*, when there is no longer even any sense in making decisions about some secret behind the surface of a textual manifestation
(and it is this situation which I would call text or trace), when it is the call
[appel] of this secret, however, which points back to the other or to something else, when it is this itself which keeps our passion aroused, and holds
us to the other, then the secret impassions us.[49]

This structural setting-adrift of meaningfulness from the presence of authorial intention affects not merely texts in the narrow sense but all marks, including those of experience. "This structural possibility of being severed from
its referent or signified," Derrida emphasizes, "seems to me to make of every
mark, even if oral, a grapheme in general, that is . . . the nonpresent *remaining*
of a differential mark cut off from its alleged 'production' or origin. And I will
extend this law even to all 'experience' in general, if it is granted that there is
no experience of *pure* presence, but only chains of differential marks."[50] This
ontological dimension of Derrida's interest in literature, about which deconstructive literary criticism has been relatively silent, illuminates literature's
worldly force.[51]

The temporalization that opens up phenomenality and lets a world appear
is an iterability that constitutively infects presence with alterity. This contamination points to the inappropriable other that gives time and being and opens
a world. There is a world, although we cannot know or explain why or how
this is so, because it comes from the other. Literature's ability to always mean
otherwise than what the author intended exemplifies the disruption of presence by the coming of the inappropriable other and the accompanying undecidability of meaning and knowledge. "Literature," Derrida writes, "is only
exemplary of what happens everywhere, each time there is some trace (or
grace, i.e., each time that there is something rather than nothing, each time
that *there is (es gibt)*, and each time that it gives [ça donne] without return,
without reason, freely, and if *there is* what there is then."[52]

Literature's role in the coming of a world hinges on an isomorphism between
the literary critical concept of authorial intention and the phenomenological
concept of the intentionality of consciousness. The latter refers to the fact that
consciousness is directed at something, whether it is a real or imaginary ob-

ject. An object's intentional structure refers to the transcendental conditions that enable it to appear to consciousness as *its* object. For Derrida, literature's superficiality or "flatness" as an undecipherable open secret, a secret that may be devoid of meaningful interiority, suggests a certain phenomenal nonphe-nomenality, an exteriority or otherness that appears but is resistant to and cannot be appropriated by the interiorizing power of intentional conscious-ness. What is at stake is a reality that cannot be determined by consciousness and is not given by intuition to the determinative power of judgment, that is, a reality that, being devoid of the mastery of a subject, undoes the subject.

Because literature is entirely devoid of intentionality and is inaccessible to the subject, it is the privileged locus of the inviolable secret as a figure for the force of otherness that cannot be appropriated by any kind of transcenden-tal, rational, material, or phenomenological subject (*GT*, 153). First, there is no point to wondering about the true intentional meaning or wanting-to-say (*vouloir dire*) in a character's or narrator's consciousness because they have no depth beyond their sheer "appearance" in the world evoked or portrayed by the literary text. As Derrida puts it, "as these fictional characters have no consis-tency, no depth beyond their literary phenomenon, the absolute inviolability of the secret they carry depends first of all on the essential superficiality of their phenomenality, on the *too-obvious* of that which they present to view" (*GT*, 153). Second, echoing Wimsatt's critique of the intentional fallacy and Barthes's argument about the death of the author, Derrida points out that an author's in-tentions are irrelevant to a consideration of a literary text's meaning and effects. Because of its radical undecidability of meaning, literature, like the inappropri-able other, exhibits a resistance to determinative judgment.

Literature is the radical possibility of nontruth. Its functioning depends on "the altogether bare device of being-two-to-speak [l'être-deux-à-parler]" (*GT*, 153). Hence, its very existence points to its condition of possibility in some-thing that is inaccessible to intellectual insight and cannot be reduced to the structure of an intentional subject. The secret, Derrida writes, "is constituted by the possibility of the literary institution and revealed by that institution in its possibility of secret only to the extent to which it [the secret] loses all interiority, all thickness, all depth. It is kept absolutely unbreakable, inviolate only to the extent to which it is formed by a non-psychological structure. This structure is not subjective or subjectible, even though it is responsible for the most radical effects of subjectivity or of subjectivation. It is superficial, without substance, infinitely private because public through and through" (*GT*, 170). Accordingly, the reader's relation to literature is identical to the fundamental passivity and defenselessness that characterizes the subject's relation to the other's coming. The reader is not a hermeneut who probes the text to reveal an inner truth or secret meaning through exegesis. Instead, he is "prey to literature, vulnerable to the question that torments every literary corpus and corporation. Not only 'what is literature?' 'what is the function of literature?' but what relation can obtain between literature and sense?"[53]

What Derrida calls "literature" is a generalization of the structural features of literature in the strict sense into a force that exceeds the power of rational determination. Literature in the general sense happens, or a literary object comes into being, whenever a text is delivered over to the other in the process of its constitution as a meaningful presence: "Every text that is consigned to public space, that is relatively legible or intelligible, but whose content, sense, referent, signatory, and addressee are not fully determinable *realities—*realities that are at the same time *non-fictive* or *immune from all fiction*, realities that are delivered as such, by some intuition, to a determinate judgment—can become a *literary* object."[54] Put another way, the constitution of presence through a relation to radical alterity is nothing other than the process of genesis of "literary" reality, the becoming-literature of reality.[55]

Narrative in particular is the best intimation of the other's coming because it enacts the aporias of the gift of time in the constitution of presence. The relation between narrative and the gift is not merely one in which the gift is thematized in narrative discourse, such as an "accounting, archive, memoirs, narrative, or poem" (GT, 43). Instead, Derrida notes that the gift is connected to the internal necessity "of a certain poetics of narrative" (GT, 41). "The given of the gift arrives, if it arrives, only in narrative," such that "the gift would always be the gift of a writing, a memory, a poem, or a narrative, in any case, the legacy of a text" (GT, 41, 43–44).[56] "Narrative" in this sense is not derived from and opposed to reality. It neither presents nor represents the world but is a catachresis for the fabulous process of the opening of a world by the gift of time.

Derrida cautions that he is not endorsing an account of narrative as presentation where "the narrative is the very event that it recounts, the thing presenting itself and the text presenting itself—presenting *itself*—by producing what it says."[57] He is concerned with how narrative is a "non-presentation of the event, its presence*less* presence, as it takes place place*lessly*."[58] The gift of time as event is not of the order of presence because it is the coming of the world, "the origin of visibility, the origin of origin, the birth of what . . . 'sees the light of day' [voit le jour, is born] when the present leads to presence, presentation or representation."[59] This is why the gift can only be rendered in narrative. But despite its "narrative" structure, a gift also renders narrative impossible because it cannot be narrated. Narrative presupposes the gift of time as its origin: a narrative requires the passage of time because it recounts something that has taken place and the act of narration itself takes time. Hence, "the gift, if there is any," Derrida notes, "requires and at the same time excludes the possibility of narrative. The gift is on condition of the narrative, but simultaneously on the condition of possibility and impossibility of the narrative" (GT, 103). Narrative that reflects on its own status as narrative necessarily broaches its own impossibility because it comes up against its origins in the gift of time. This makes narrative exemplary of the gift.

For Derrida, literature in this general sense opens a world and is the immanent principle of the world's transformability because it points to an alterity that cannot be appropriated by the subject. This means that the relation between literature and world is not originally a process of construction. Literature is not merely a causal force that makes social space through symbols, images, and meanings as envisaged by critical theories of space. However, where Heidegger saw poetry as an expression of the world's meaningfulness and the holding-together of world by time, for Derrida, what literature intimates is the disjoining of time by the other's coming.[60]

The contrast between Derrida's and Arendt's views on literature is even more instructive. For both, narrative is fundamental to world-opening. For Arendt, narrative is a world-making power because it responds to radical finitude through the human appropriation of time. Through the activities of speech, action, memory, and the reification of real stories, we create and maintain a subjective in-between that gives our existence permanence and durability. In contradistinction, deconstruction is concerned with how the condition of possibility of narrative points to the opening of a world. The coming of the other is the condition of possibility of narration because narrating involves repetition and presupposes temporalization. However, the other's nonappropriability means that it cannot be narrated. Hence, the condition of possibility of narration blocks narrative sequentiality.[61] However, this impossibility of advancing the narrative opens up something new. By tearing the succession of time and interrupting the continuity of past, present, and future, the coming of the other breaks open teleologies of the world and opens a world to come. Where Arendt sees the world as an authorless web of real stories that is constructed by many actors and storytellers, for Derrida, the subject's sheer defenselessness in the experience of literature and narration lets us receive a world and makes us act in response.

We must here understand literature not merely as a product of the *human* faculty of the imagination—the faculty of a subject, whether psychological or transcendental, who can respond to the question "Who are you?"—that represents or duplicates material reality, but as the force of a passage, an *experience*, of the gift of time through which we are given any determinable reality. Literature enacts receptibility as such, namely, the structure of opening through which one receives a world and another world can appear. This structure is prior to and subtends all social forms of mediation, as well as any sense of public space (*Öffentlichkeit*). It is nothing other than the force of giving and receiving a world. It is a "perhaps" or "otherwise" that cannot be erased, because this equivocation constitutes reality.

Arendt's and Derrida's critical transformations of the phenomenological conception of worlding can be reconciled as follows. Deconstruction reaffirms the world's grounding in temporalization in a way that directly addresses the problem of how worlding is related to world-making activity. Time can never be completely appropriated by and made proper to human existence because it is given by an inappropriable other whose coming tears and suspends temporalization. Consequently, the world is always to come. It can never be destroyed or completely unworlded by human design. Indeed, the world's disappearance is the abyssal background for the emergence of an-other world. At the same time, the other's coming is the original force that impels us to worldly action. It makes us into responsible practical subjects who respond to the other and participate in the world's ongoing (re)worlding through activities of world-making.

————————————

Literature, I suggest, can play an active role in the world's ongoing creation because in its very existence, it enacts the opening of a world by the coming of the other, and it makes the world by disclosing and constituting actors. Moreover, literature in the strict sense is a spiritual and material process that fashions or constructs a human world by imparting values, norms, and meaning to the given world through imagination, representation, signification, and interpretation. As part of the process that generates determinable reality, literature in the general sense both opens up the existing world to politically committed literature that seeks to change the world and throws into question the meaningful ends such literary representations posit for the world. Understood in this way, literature is not merely superstructural. It is instead an inexhaustible resource for reworlding and remaking the degraded world given to us by commercial intercourse, monetary transactions, and the space-time compression of the global culture industry. In part III, I elaborate a normative theory of world literature from various elements of the philosophies of world discussed earlier and use this theory to analyze postcolonial world literature as an alternative reworlding of the world.

# of other worlds to come

CHAPTER 7

Postcolonial Openings

How Postcolonial Literature Becomes World Literature

World Literature as Literature of the World

In parts II and III, I examined philosophical conceptions of the world to address questions about literature's worldly causality and normative force that have been marginalized by recent theories of world literature. Whereas these theories reduced the world to the globe, an object of spatio-geographical extension, I proposed that a more rigorous normative account of the world should focus on its temporal dimension. The philosophies of the world that I have discussed fall into two categories. The first views the world as being governed by teleological time. Here, temporal progression assumes the image of human reason and harmonizes with our universal ends. Worldly events proceed according to a narrative of universal historical progress toward the realization of freedom, where the normative activity of realization is either spiritual or material. The phenomenological concept of worlding suggests that temporalization is a force that gives rise to a world. Accordingly, there is a "normative force" immanent to the world that cannot be reduced to the ends prescribed by human reason. This force is prior to and grounds normative activity.

Although they take issue with each other, these different philosophical conceptions of the world do not cancel out each other. Whereas Hegelian world-history improves on Goethe's project of world literature by alerting us to the role of violence in the creation of a spiritual world by the arts, the materialist concept of world emphasizes the centrality of material-economic forces in making a world. Heidegger's idea of worlding stresses the primacy of temporalization as a power of world-formation. Arendt insists on the importance of human practical action as a world-making power, whereas Derrida suggests that the world has the structure of real messianic hope because time is a gift from the inhuman other. These theories of the world seek to disclose a more fundamental ground from which the world is generated. By supplementing and improving on each other, they contribute to a richer and more complex sense of the world that can help us rethink world literature.

If we heed their lessons, the first step in reenvisioning world literature's vocation is to see the world as a dynamic process with a normative practical dimension instead of reducing worldliness to circulatory flows within a spatio-geographical whole. Flows of market exchange and their geographical mapping are certainly important material conditions of a world. But as phenomenological and deconstructive accounts of worldliness remind us, they are modes of world-making that ultimately make us worldless. Goethe's distinction between the world as spatial extension and the higher spiritual realm conjured up by literary exchange; Marx's distinction between the world market and the world society of producers as the natural and self-conscious forms of world-historical cooperation; and Arendt's distinction between the objective and subjective in-between and so on are variants of the fundamental distinction between a spatio-geographical entity and the world as an ongoing work.

This distinction is especially important because it directly concerns the second central theme of any understanding of world: inclusion/exclusion. I have not mentioned this theme so far but have chosen to focus on the reality of the world as a temporal category in order to enable a better understanding of literature's worldly causality. Inclusion/exclusion is an important preoccupation of recent theories of world literature. They have sought to remedy the Eurocentrism of the Goethean project as it has been institutionalized in publishing, literary criticism, and university curricula by alerting us to intercultural exchanges and the circulation of literature across the East-West and North-South divides and across different media. But these theories have in fact exacerbated the problem of worldlessness. Because they understand inclusion as the expansion of the size of the spatial container for human activities, they propose that the market circulation of literature in the age of globalization can cure literary parochialism and nationalism. However, what is at stake is not merely the inclusion of the greatest possible number of human beings and the maximal increase of the range of circulation of peoples and products so that it spans the entire globe but the manner of inclusion and the kind of whole that is created. As the greatest possible whole of existence, a world must be structurally open. Better yet, it must be the endless process of opening itself.

This brings us back to the world's temporal dimension because time is the original opening, the first and ongoing relation to exteriority. Capitalist globalization seeks to include as many members of humanity and parts of the globe as possible. But this inclusion is only the spatial expansion of capitalist accumulation, the incorporation and integration of what is external into a hierarchical world-system under conditions of structural inequality. As Immanuel Wallerstein observes, the modern western Europe–centered world-system is "the first unity of the world," and its expansion from the sixteenth century onward involved the gradual incorporation of other civilizations that were external arenas as *its* peripheries through imperial expansion and violent colonial dispossession.[1] External arenas maintain their integrity. They are the location of other worlds that exist outside the logic of the European world. The incorporation of external arenas into the world-system as peripheries destroys these worlds because they are subordinated within a uniform system governed by the homogenizing logic of capitalist accumulation. Peripheralization, which closes off the opening to the outside, is the most cogent example of unworlding through the total control and appropriation of time. Rethinking world literature solely in terms of global circulation intensifies globalization's unworlding of the world. Circulation is celebrated for its own sake as an inherently liberating process, when it merely retraces the closed sphericity of the globe.

Much of the problem arises from the fact that recent theories of world literature are reactive responses to the world-system and globalization. Instead of studying world literature as a process in the capitalist worlding of the world and, conversely, the role that it can play in a counter-worlding, these recent theories have reflected on the implications of world-systems theory for understanding literary production. Yet Wallerstein suggests that literature can have a stronger role in the world-system, albeit only at the level of ideological hegemony, when he points to the importance of cultural power. Once an external arena has been transformed into a periphery, he observes, "the economically more powerful group is able to reinforce its position by cultural domination as well."[2] In turn, the cultural domination of core countries can be resisted by reassertions of indigenous culture, because "cultures are precisely arenas where resistance to hegemony occurs, where appeals are made to the historical values of established 'civilizations' against the temporary superiorities of the market."[3]

The Temporality of Decolonization

If world literature is rethought in the more robust sense of literature that worlds and makes a world, then the fundamental question that needs to be addressed is what kind of world does world literature open and make. Is it a world that remains open to the coming of other worlds? The literature of the postcolonial South has a special connection to the normative project of world literature for two reasons. First, decolonization is precisely an attempt to open up a world that is different from the colonial world. Second, the reworlding of the world remains a continuing project in light of the inequalities created by capitalist globalization and their tragic consequences for peoples and social groups in postcolonial space.

We commonly explain decolonization in terms of the urgent need to satisfy the basic biological needs of colonized peoples so that they can survive. In fact, the wave of decolonizations after World War II and the Non-Aligned Movement as a third way beyond the polarity of the two Cold War blocs are animated by the wish to subvert European colonial worlding and open other worlds where new collective subjects can emerge and change the world-political stage. As Hannah Arendt notes, the foundation of revolutions is not the necessity of biological life, such as the desire to eliminate poverty and starvation, but freedom, defined as the power of originating something new and the meaningful life it leads to.[4] The fact that decolonization is a temporal project of emergence becomes especially clear once we grasp that cultural genocide is a consequence of colonial domination. Modifying her account in *The Human Condition*, Arendt suggests that genocide destroys the human world because a plurality of peoples within the human species is necessary to the constitution of humanity and the world.

> The world comes into being only if there are perspectives; it exists as the order of worldly things only if it is viewed, now this way, now that, at any given time. If a people or state [Staat], or even just some determinate human group, which offers a unique view of the world arising from its particular position in the world—a position that . . . cannot readily be duplicated—is annihilated, it is not merely that a people or a state or a given number of human beings perishes, but rather that a part of our common world is destroyed, an aspect of the world that has revealed itself to us until now but can never reveal itself again. . . . Human beings in the authentic [eigentlichen] sense of the term can exist only where there is a world, and there can be a world in the proper sense of the term only where the plurality of the human race is more than a simple multiplication of copies of a species.[5]

Because worldliness is a fundamental condition of human life and a world requires perceptions from multiple perspectives, the destruction of a people's culture depletes the world and vitiates humanity. Arendt thus fuses Goethe's idea of spiritual intercourse across the diversity of national cultures with humanity's emergence through plurality.

One of the aims of revolutionary decolonization is the struggle against cultural genocide. It ushers a new temporality that reworlds and opens another world for a people in the face of colonial violence, even though we usually interpret this temporal structure as biological survival. We see this two-step at the conclusion of Frantz Fanon's *Black Skin, White Masks*.

> The problem considered here is located in temporality. Disalienation will be for those Whites and Blacks who have refused to let themselves be locked in the substantialized "tower of the past." For many other black men, disalienation will come from refusing to consider their reality as definitive.
>
> I am a man, and I have to rework the world's past from the very beginning. . . . In no way does my basic vocation have to be drawn from the past of peoples of color.
>
> In no way do I have to dedicate myself to reviving a black civilization unjustly ignored. I will not make myself the man of any past. I do not want to sing the past to the detriment of my present and my future.
>
> It is not because the Indo-Chinese discovered a culture of their own that they revolted. Quite simply this was because it became impossible for them to breathe, in more than one sense of the word.
>
> When we recall how the old colonial hands in 1938 described Indochina as the land of piastres and rickshaws, of houseboys and cheap women, we understand only too well the fury of the Vietminh's struggle.[6]

In decolonization struggles, the openness of worlding is figured as an opening of the existing world to colonized peoples by the inauguration of a new temporality. They can emerge as new subjects and make a new world in which they will flourish if they project a future through revolutionary struggle instead of being imprisoned by a fossilized civilizational culture from the precolonial past. Fanon figures the temporal project of decolonization as the creation of a world in which one can "breathe" in a metaphorical sense. But one can very easily conflate this with the literal breathing of air as a basic necessity of animal life for two reasons. First, temporalization, which is the ground of human existence, is generally apprehended as biological life because our loss of life and loss of time coincide. As individuals, we run out of time when we die. Second, there is an entire Western philosophical tradition that uses the vitality of organic life as a metaphorical template for understanding freedom.[7]

This oscillation between the temporality of freedom and the rhythms of biological life, or better yet, between life in two senses, runs through Fanon's writings such that freedom is constantly fused with the satisfaction of needs. Commenting on the colonized subject's struggle for survival, Fanon notes that "for the Antillean working in the sugarcane plantations in Le Robert, to fight is the only solution. And he will undertake and carry out this struggle not as the result of a Marxist or idealistic analysis but because quite simply he cannot conceive his life otherwise than as a kind of combat against exploitation, misery, and hunger."[8] In *The Wretched of the Earth*, he similarly suggests that the imperative behind anticolonial revolution is the dignity of sheer corporeal life. "For a colonized people, the most essential value, because it is the most meaningful, is first and foremost the land: the land, which must provide bread and, naturally, dignity. But this dignity has nothing to do with 'human' dignity. The colonized subject has never heard of such an ideal. All he has ever seen on his land is that he can be arrested, beaten, and starved with impunity; and no sermonizer on morals, no priest has ever stepped in to bear the blows in his place or share his bread."[9]

The temporality of anticolonial nationalist revolution is clearly teleological. The motif of corporeal survival recalls Marx's eschatological argument that the proletarian revolution is imperative not only for individuals "to achieve self-activity [Selbstbetätigung], but, also, merely to safeguard their very existence."[10] Fanon characterizes the spontaneity of the Mau Mau uprising as a dialectical process of the nation's self-actualization as a sovereign subject. Individuals become articulated as a vital self-determining whole through revolutionary action. "Every colonized subject in arms represents a piece of the nation on the move. . . . [The revolts] are governed by a simple doctrine: The nation must be made to exist. . . . The national cause advances and becomes the cause of each and everyone. . . . Everywhere, one encounters a national authority. The action of each and everyone substantiates the nation and undertakes to ensure its triumph locally."[11]

Culture can be an important part of revolutionary teleology. By instilling hope and animating a people to action, culture temporalizes their lives and projects a future. Fanon notes that "when the colonized intellectual writing for his people uses the past he must do so with the intention of opening up the future, of spurring them into action and fostering hope."[12] What is significant here is that the form and content of national culture are entirely determined by revolutionary action. The content of revolutionary national culture is political solidarity. Its expression of this content in turn strengthens national consciousness by interpellating individuals. This means that literature is part of the process of anticolonial struggle. It is "combat literature" because "it calls upon a whole people to join in the struggle for the existence of the nation" and "informs the national consciousness, gives it shape and contours, and opens up new, unlimited horizons."[13] For Fanon, traditional literary forms can be effective in interpellating new members if they are radically reinvented so that instead of having an unchanging precolonial past as their content, they open a future.

Activist thinkers participating in decolonization movements were attracted to the materialist dialectical variety of teleological time as a schema for making sense of anticolonial resistance and revolution because it emphasized the material character of colonial exploitation and oppression, explained revolutionary struggle against the colonial state as the force of negation, and saw the emergence of an independent people and its battle against neocolonialism as an ongoing process of dialectical sublation. As C. L. R. James observed, Nkrumah, the father of Ghanaian independence and Ghana's first prime minister and president, "fulfills and completes the strivings of the Ghanaian people to become a free and independent part of a new world. . . . [He] has most fully embodied in action an independent current of Western thought, the ideas of Marx, Lenin, and other revolutionaries worked out chiefly by peoples of African descent in Western Europe and America, to be used for the emancipation of the people of Africa."[14]

Some versions of the teleological time of decolonization regard the revitalization of precolonial traditions as crucial to the fashioning of a new collective personality. Accordingly, the retelling of precolonial histories that contests the version found in official colonial archives and the revival of traditional culture and customs have a more important role than in Fanon's account of revolution. Nkrumah's philosophy of consciencism is the best example of this variation. "In the new African renaissance," he writes, "we place great emphasis on the presentation of history. Our history needs to be written as the history of our society. . . . European contact needs to be assessed and judged from the point of view of the principles animating African society, and from the point of view of the harmony and progress of this society. When history is presented in this way . . . it can become a map of the growing tragedy and the final triumph of our society. In this way, African history can come to guide and direct African action . . . and . . . become a pointer at the ideology which should guide and direct African reconstruction."[15] The ideology that forms the African personality should also include "the original humanist principles" underlying African society, namely, the "traditional African egalitarian view of man and society" that furnishes the basis of African communalism and undermines the formation of hierarchies of socioeconomic class.[16]

A colonized people's emergence also requires a supporting institutional framework. This framework can be national, for example, a mass-based political party, or regional, for example, the continental unity of pan-Africanism.[17] The Bandung Conference of 1955 attempted to expand this institutional framework internationally by establishing international cooperation to further the entry of Asian and African peoples as equal members into the world community. As expressed in its founding injunction—"Let a New Asia and a New Africa be born!"—the spirit of Bandung clearly resonates with Arendt's concept of natality. Nehru, the Indian prime minister, described Bandung as "a final symbol of the emergence of Asia after 200 years of domination by Western countries."[18] President Sukarno of Indonesia emphasized that liberated peoples are peoples who possess the powers of speech and political decision-making and action. Asian and African nations "are no longer the tools of others and the playthings of forces they cannot influence" but "peoples of a different stature and standing in the world."[19] They are no longer "the voiceless ones in the world," "the unregarded, the peoples for whom decisions were made by others whose interests were paramount, the peoples who lived in poverty and humiliation."[20] Maintaining the momentum of this teleological time required economic cooperation, cultural cooperation, respect for universal human rights, and the establishment of a framework for the promotion of world peace and cooperation.[21] As Nkrumah put it, international peace and security according to the terms of the UN Charter "will enable us to assert our own African personality and to develop according to our own ways of life, our own customs, traditions and cultures."[22]

Alternative Modernities and Other Times:
A Critique of Heterotemporality

The teleological time of decolonization remains tragically uncompleted. The betrayal of the egalitarian ideals of anticolonial revolution and the rapid onset of neocolonialism have cast grave doubt on the continuing viability of the teleological time of decolonization. The devastating impact of capitalist globalization for the lower strata of postcolonial societies indicates the urgent need for opening another world today. According to a teleological conception, the opening of another world in the present situation requires the negation of the existing capitalist world-system by a more powerful, nonalienating rational activity, for example, the formation of a higher world through spiritual transcendence, the rational regulation of material production, the checking of instrumental reason by critical reason, or, in the case of decolonization, the emergence of a liberated collective personality through anticolonial struggle. These forms of negation are examples of the plasticity of reason, its endless ability to remake the external world in its image and refashion itself according to its own projected ideal images and norms. Reason's plasticity is essentially the human ability to appropriate time in the pursuit of universal ends. This power's progressive use has, however, been severely undermined by capitalist globalization, which also relies on techniques for the regulation and appropriation of time, but for the particularistic ends of accumulation. In postcolonial globalization, the complete negation of the existing capitalist world-system increasingly appears impossible. Here, it is not only the question of the arrestation of the teleological time of decolonization. Even more worrying, the pervasive web of ideological instruments and biopolitical technologies that sustain the global capitalist system has so thoroughly penetrated human existence at the level of consciousness and corporeality that instrumentality has become indistinguishable from the self-determining plasticity of human existence. These technologies no longer seek to subjugate or destroy human powers. Instead, they feed into, enhance, and draw on our liberating human capacities of world- and self-making as the most fundamental resources of their sustenance. The paramount role accorded to *human* capital in the discourse of postcolonial economic development clearly illustrates this. Many postcolonial peoples live under conditions of inequality, oppression, and exploitation as a result of global economic (under)development.

In this scenario, the teleological time of anticolonial revolution has been replaced by more modest theories of heterotemporality that affirm precolonial temporalities and imaginaries, either as resources for the cultivation of a people but without the nationalist search for a state or by completely rejecting the impulse to fashion these temporalities into a people or nation. I will critically discuss the solution of alternative temporalities as part of my argument that in postcolonial globalization we need to insist on the inhuman dimension of the opening of a world by the inappropriable other that gives time.

Theories of heterotemporality arise in the context of the contemporary critical rethinking of modernity from perspectives that come from various sites outside the North Atlantic that have either been excluded and marginalized by the relentless universal historical march of Euro-American modernity in the cultural, political, and economic spheres or incorporated through the subordinating sign of belatedness or backwardness. The common aim of writings ranging from Enrique Dussel's or Walter Mignolo's Latin American–based accounts of colonial modernity to that of the Subaltern Studies historians of South Asia is to contest a homogeneous universalistic modernity by showing its structural connections to colonial violence. Because colonial modernity forcibly suppresses and eradicates other cultures and traditions, it logically follows that modernity itself needs to be pluralized or multiplied. The different experiences of modernity in these contact zones lead to novel transformations and transpositions of modernity.

Although these critical accounts of modernity clearly have a spatio-geographical dimension, they are at heart an argument about the nature of time. By its very name, modernity is a time-consciousness, a consciousness obsessed with the time of the "now." Because the present cannot be arrested and is always vanishing, it is a precious resource that has to be maximized in its fleeting duration. In Habermas's words, such a consciousness experiences "time as a scarce resource for mastering the problems that the future hurls at the present. This headlong rush of challenges is perceived as 'the pressure of time.'"[23] As Heidegger and Arendt noted, the ability to manage and appropriate time generates modernity's linear understanding of universal progress with its temporality of infinite succession in which time becomes a perpetually self-renewing resource.

This time-consciousness gained a spatial dimension because the human capability to make time self-renewing or, which is the same thing, to make ourselves anew in every successive instant of time—and the social structures, institutions, and technological innovations associated with this ability—were tethered to western European civilization, which became a prototype or model that marked the spread of modernity to other places. In this way, modernity became a necessary element of colonial discourse. According to a quasi-Hegelian schema, different time-consciousnesses were spatialized, apportioned to different geographical spaces, which were hierarchically ordered in a grand teleological narrative of universal progress in which deficient "nonmodern" or "traditional" time-consciousnesses were to be eradicated, corrected, or reformed through education and civilization. This narrative persists in the contemporary political economic discourse of modernization and development.

In the humanities, the critique of this scheme logically took the form of the argument that we have to see the world as consisting of multiple temporalities that overlap and that should not be hierarchized by means of a teleological progression from "earlier" and "outmoded" to "later" and "new," from the "not yet there" to a universal end that is actualized in the present. The coextensiveness of the teleological understanding of modernity with European colonialism and colonialism's role in the global expansion of the capitalist mode of production has endowed arguments about multiple temporalities with the tenor of anti-Eurocentric resistance. However, these anti-Eurocentric arguments do not necessarily lead to a grand teleological narrative with a non-Western nation or civilization as protagonist. I have already discussed the teleology of decolonization. Today, the triumphalist teleology of non-Western civilizations is best exemplified by the argument about East Asian modernity that takes its bearings from the East Asian economic miracle to suggest that the rapidly developing and postindustrial nation-states of East Asia are embodiments of a superior non-Western ideal of capitalist development capable of reconciling modernization with Asian ideals of community. This position, loosely based on a repackaged Confucianism that reverses Max Weber's thesis about the Protestant ethic, is a displaced repetition of the chauvinism of Eurocentric modernity, an East Asianized version of Hegel's end of history.[24] The suggestion that we should replace Western ideas of cosmopolitanism with the Chinese concept of *tianxia* (天下, all that is under heaven) is a milder variation of this argument.[25] In sharp contrast, theories of heterotemporality arise from a critique of these grand teleologies. They are accounts of alternative modernity "from below," subaltern modernities that are critical of the modernization paradigm taken up by the indigenous bourgeoisie from the early stirrings of anticolonial nationalist movements to the formation of the postcolonial nation-state.

The idea of heterotemporality was implicit in Partha Chatterjee's disagreement with Benedict Anderson over the nature of Asian and African anticolonial nationalisms. These nationalisms, he argued, did not simply passively consume models borrowed from European and American modernity but imaginatively fabricated a modern national culture that was different from Western modernity. "The most powerful as well as the most creative results of the nationalist imagination in Asia and Africa are posited . . . on a *difference* with the 'modular' forms of the national society propagated by the modern West. . . . Nationalism declares the domain of the spiritual its sovereign territory and refuses to allow the colonial power to intervene in that domain. . . . Here nationalism launches its most powerful, creative, and historically significant project: *to fashion a 'modern' national culture that is nevertheless not*

Western."[26] National culture is the first alternative modernity that arises in resistance to Western colonial modernity. But the opposition between the two modernities turns out to be false, because bourgeois national modernity uses similar ideological ruses of legitimation to co-opt subaltern forces in the colonial period. In the postcolonial era, the bourgeois national project of modernity relies on modern state and civil society institutions inherited from the colonial regime to exclude, silence, and exploit the subaltern sectors of the population. Hence, "below" the bourgeois nation's alternative modernity are other marginalized alternative modernities and political communities that cannot be represented through the nation-state because they appear to be antimodern within the discourse of modernization—the untouchables, women, peasants, and so on.[27] Although they are not thorough solutions to postcolonial malaise, these subaltern modernities are at least ways of coping or forms of resistance.

What is of interest to us is the effectiveness of these other temporalities, given the pervasiveness of global capitalist time as an overarching frame, that is to say, quantified labor time as this develops into a totalizing global organizational grid emblematized by Greenwich Mean Time. Do these theories of non-Western modernities retain the same understanding of time as spatial presence, insofar as these different temporalities coexist and are copresent—coeval, as the anthropologist Johannes Fabian would say? I address these questions by critically examining the two influential accounts of heterotemporality or multitemporality elaborated in Dipesh Chakrabarty's *Provincializing Europe* and Nestor Garcia Canclini's *Hybrid Cultures: Strategies for Entering and Leaving Modernity*.

Provincializing Europe elaborates on the temporal dimension of subaltern communities. In Chakrabarty's view, the primary mechanism of marginalization and exclusion is the *historicism* that underwrites modern European political discourse, which has in turn influenced institutional forms in South Asia. Chakrabarty uses historicism loosely, as shorthand for the teleological narrative of universal progress.

> Historicism enabled European domination of the world in the nineteenth century. Crudely, one might say that it was one important form that the ideology of progress or "development" took from the nineteenth century on. Historicism is what made modernity or capitalism look not simply global but rather as something that became global over time, by originating in one place (Europe) and then spreading outside it. This "first in Europe, then elsewhere" structure of global historical time was historicist; different

non-Western nationalisms would later produce local versions of the same narrative, replacing "Europe" by some locally constructed center. . . . Historicism thus posited historical time as a measure of the cultural distance (at least in institutional development) that was assumed to exist between the West and the non-West. In the colonies, it legitimated the idea of civilization. In Europe itself, it made possible completely internalist histories of Europe in which Europe was described as the site of the first occurrence of capitalism, modernity, or Enlightenment. . . . The inhabitants of the colonies, on the other hand, were assigned a place "elsewhere" in the "first in Europe and then elsewhere" structure of time.[28]

Drawing on Ranajit Guha's work, Chakrabarty argues that historicism distorts the active political role of various types of subalterns in South Asian history because it imposes a restricted idea of the rational human subject who acts within "single, homogeneous and secular historical time." "Modern politics," he writes, "is often justified as a story of human sovereignty acted out in the context of a ceaseless unfolding of unitary historical time."[29] Within this frame, the role of the peasant or subaltern in modern Indian politics cannot appear as a type of political action, because "this peasant-but-modern political sphere was not bereft of the agency of gods, spirits, and other supernatural beings" and "did not follow the logic of secular-rational calculations inherent [sic] the modern conception of the political."[30] Accordingly, an adequate understanding of political modernity in South Asia must be based on two axioms of coevalness. First, we must acknowledge the existential coevalness of gods and spirits with humans found in deistic understandings of temporality. Second, deistic temporalities must be recognized as coeval with and equal in value to secular temporality. This means that historical time is not integral but irreducibly split. Instead of "the useful but empty and homogeneous chronology of historicism," we must see history as admitting "heterotemporality."[31]

We have to understand the subalternist pluralization of modernity as a matter of cultural difference or, more precisely, a matter of cultural interruption, the interruption that cultural difference introduces into the continuum of historicist time, which is also the time horizon of capital and the abstract commodified labor that sustains it.[32] Without this interruption, subaltern action can only be misrecognized as lack and inadequacy, as that which needs to be eradicated in the transition to a modern India. In Chakrabarty's words, "the subaltern fractures from within the very signs that tell of the emergence of abstract labor; the subaltern is that which constantly, from within the narrative of capital, reminds us of other ways of being human than as bearers of the capacity to labor. It is what is gathered under 'real labor' in Marx's critique of capital, the figure of difference that governmentality (that is, in Foucault's terms, the pursuit of the goals of modern governments) all over the world has to subjugate and civilise."[33] This view of subalternity's exteriority to capital, however, is perilously close to nostalgia for a pure past that could moreover be a cultural relativist and utopian disavowal of the pervasive reality of capitalist modernization at the socioeconomic level. Habermas has noted in another context that once Asian societies participate in a globalized system of market relations, "the question is whether the traditional forms of political and societal integration can be reasserted against—or must instead be adapted to—the hard-to-resist imperatives of an economic modernization that has won approval on the whole."[34] Insofar as the approval of economic modernization is a matter of state policy, it can be argued that subalternity refers to unruly forces that exceed the realm of state politics, one of whose aims is to govern and manage them. Chakrabarty suggests this, albeit with the qualification that subaltern excess is not a simple outside that comes before or after capital but instead "straddles a border zone of temporality, that conforms to the temporal code within which capital comes into being even as it violates that code, something we are able to see only because we can think/theorize capital, but that also always reminds us that other temporalities, other forms of worlding, coexist and are possible. . . . The resistance . . . is something that can happen only within the time horizon of capital, and yet has to be thought of as something that disrupts the unity of that time."[35]

This characterization of subalternity is, however, highly problematic. It tries to reconcile the Marxist critique of the homogeneous empty time of capital and the deconstructive critique of time as presence by conflating the temporal horizon of socialism and the constitutive interruption of presence by the absolute alterity of the pure event. But, as I have shown, the Marxist and deconstructive understandings of time are discontinuous. The former is uncomfortably close to homogeneous empty time. Both understand time as a form of presence. Marx's idea of actual labor, which Chakrabarty links to subalternity, is qualitative labor that creates use-value, as distinguished from abstract labor measured in units of time. Creative labor is self-renewing because it produces the means of subsistence and therefore creates the conditions of life. As I have argued in chapter 3 and elsewhere, the temporality of creative labor is teleological.[36] It is the course of a self-returning end, a self that returns to itself in a higher, more concrete form after a process of externalization, because this higher self was an end that was implicit at the origin and needed to be actualized or made explicit. The homogeneous empty time of capital is generated by the blockage of this teleological course, where the movement of self-externalization is perverted and becomes an alienating process.

Chakrabarty's association of actual labor with heterotemporality means that subaltern modernity follows a Hegelian-Marxist dynamic. This is best seen in his unwitting repeated reliance on the Hegelian motif of recognition in his exhortations that we recognize the contributions of subalterns to history and give due recognition to a nonsecular temporality where human beings coexist with gods and spirits. This is precisely Hegel's definition of spirit: the ability of reason to be at home with itself in the other, to coexist with the other and bear otherness as a contradiction. Hence, although heterotemporality interrupts homogeneous empty time, it remains a temporality of presence. The tension between historicist secular time and the other kinds of time that it obscures is only a quarrel between the secular enlightenment and the religious consciousnesses that the enlightenment tried to vanquish or contain. A world in which "the question of being human involves the question of being with gods and spirits" is as much a world of presence as a secular world where the human being is fully present to herself in her reason as the capacity of her self-grounding and self-determination precisely because it is a world of *being*. The alternative modernities thesis is thus a matter of the coevalness of different temporalities and ontologies of presence, of different rational sovereignties—the sovereign power of other rationalities. It juxtaposes the rationality of the modern human being in a disenchanted world with the nonmodern rationality of the human being who inhabits a world with gods and spirits. As different forms of rational sovereignty, humans, gods, and spirits are relays of each other. As Horkheimer and Adorno pointed out, this is why enlightenment itself becomes myth and religion. Chakrabarty envisions another twist in this dialectic—myth and religion becoming part of a more inclusive heterotemporal modernity. Accordingly, despite Chakrabarty's profession that Heidegger is a major inspiration, his account of heterotemporality never broaches Heidegger's fundamental question of how presence is constituted and Heidegger's thought of radically finite temporality, where instead of understanding time on the basis of presence, it is the movement of temporalization that creates presence. Indeed, Chakrabarty views temporality in anthropologistic terms as a collective cultural subject's experience of time and the determination of time-consciousness by a religious or secular worldview. This is why the acknowledgment of cultural difference leads to the pluralization of temporality.

Chakrabarty's account of subaltern modernity as another possible world of presence is problematic for another reason. It assumes that the desire for capitalist modernization is that of modern socioeconomic elites and state policy and that this desire is imposed on the subaltern through discipline and civilization. However, a more careful engagement with the operations of biopower that does not confuse technologies of government with those of discipline would show how the government of the population constitutes time as the rhythm of biological life itself, crafting the bodily capacities and needs that constitute the very time of actual labor before it becomes reduced to quantified labor time. Here, the creation of the subaltern desire for modernization is crucial. In contemporary globalization, there may no longer be a remainder of resistant subalternity. Such resistance may be the mere expression of the thwarted desire for modernization, especially its promise of an adequate level of consumption and standard of living.[37] To insist otherwise is to espouse a utopianism that forecloses the extent to which the contemporary world has been made at every material level by global capitalist processes and biopolitical technologies. Indeed, the fact that subaltern desire can be penetrated by governmental technologies confirms my point that subaltern and secular modern temporalities are both forms of presence. Otherwise, they could not coexist.

In the final analysis, subaltern modernity is a mode of the human appropriation of time. Canclini's account of alternative modernities clearly illustrates that heterotemporality is always premised on the human ability to appropriate time. Canclini is more attuned to the implications of contemporary globalization and argues that it offers important resources for undoing the linear time of modernization discourse. His main concern is how one can understand the temporally anomalous character of Latin American societies in which a loss of faith in economic and political modernization based on import-substitution-oriented industrialization and the strengthening of independent nation-states coexists with traditional/premodern forms of production, beliefs and goods, and cultural modernism and avant-garde experimentation. Heterotemporality is not only found in the inmixing of spirits, gods, and humans in ritualistic practice. It thoroughly permeates the production and consumption of cultural objects: "How can we understand the presence of indigenous crafts and vanguard art catalogs on the same coffee table? What are painters looking for when, in the same painting, they cite pre-Columbian and colonial images along with those of the culture industry, and then reelaborate them using computers and lasers?"[38]

The conventional explanation fixes on the belatedness of Latin American modernity as a symptom of the region's structural dependency and backwardness in relation to the modular countries at the center of the world-system.[39] Canclini argues, however, that these contradictions express the multiple temporalities of Latin American modernity. At the level of culture, Latin American countries are created from "the sedimentation, juxtaposition, and interweaving of indigenous traditions (above all in the Mesoamerican and Andean areas), of Catholic colonial hispanism, and of modern political, educational and communicational actions."[40] The multiple meanings and values of modernity in Latin American societies are thus determined by various sociocultural hybrids that mix tradition and modernity. These actors from various sectors participate in the modernizing project as a way of "taking responsibility for the multitemporal heterogeneity of each nation."[41] Hence, modernity is not a foreign force that eradicates the indigenous and traditional but an intensification of the multitemporal heterogeneity of Latin American societies.

Globalization facilitates this intensification. By increasing the flows of money, commodities, and cultural forms, it accentuates modern crosscultural contact and generates new mixtures in an unprecedented way. Such hybridization, Canclini suggests, further develops the multiple temporalities of development in a manner that opens up new possibilities for democratization. It can even generate a form of globalization that challenges "the homogenizing dictatorship of the world market."[42] Multitemporality is not the interruption of the homogeneous empty time of capital by another, nonsecular temporality. It is instead the intensification of an already existing heterogeneity by the forces of hybridization generated by global capital flows. In turn, these multitemporalities challenge capital's homogenizing tendencies. Their temporality is one of becoming and not that of being or presence. Indeed, Canclini emphasizes that what is important is not merely the actualization of what is potential, but an intensification of the process of becoming so that it never freezes into a state or subject. Because hybridization can never be presented as "a stable order of subjectivation," it is threatening to all real existing historical movements, hegemonic or subaltern. They "tend to exorcise that vertigo by instituting . . . essentializations of a particular state of hybridization."[43]

As an analytical strategy for understanding Latin American modernity, hybridization leads to a Bartleby-like "I would prefer not to choose" between modernity and tradition that enables the social subject and the critic to both enter and exit modernity. "The problem lies not in our countries having badly and belatedly fulfilled a model of modernization that was impeccably achieved in Europe; nor does it consist in reactively seeking how to invent some alternative and independent paradigm with traditions that have already been transformed by the worldwide expansion of capitalism. Especially in the most recent period, when the transnationalization of the economy and culture makes us 'contemporaries of all people' (Paz), and nevertheless does not eliminate national traditions, choosing exclusively between dependency and nationalism, between modernization or local traditionalism, is an untenable simplification."[44] Canclini's account of heterotemporality is superior to Chakrabarty's in two respects. First, it does not merely multiply different coeval temporalities of presence and privilege subaltern space as the repository of an alternative nonsecular modernity. He focuses instead on the force of hybridization that intensifies the coevalness of multiple temporalities already present in all sectors of Latin American societies. This force is not a type of being but an interval of becoming, a persistent crossing of categories and strata. Second, instead of being a resistant presence that capital tries to suppress, the disruption of homogeneous empty time is a direct consequence of the globalization of capital. However, despite all his efforts at extracting multitemporality from a metaphysics of presence, Canclini also ends up reducing it to a mode of the human appropriation and control of time when he argues that hybrid intensification can be a strategy of a social subject or critical intellectual. A strategy is precisely an instrument of human self-presence, a consciousness that is present to itself in its strategic capability. Yet, according to Canclini's terms, hybridization resists being stabilized into an "order of subjectivation."

The aporia encountered by theories of heterotemporality is as follows: they conceive of the disruption of a given order of time by positing as a final horizon a more inclusive form of presence that holds together multiple temporalities. The outside to the dominant order of time is itself another presence because it is another temporality, the time-consciousness of a collective cultural subject. But because theories of alternative modernities still understand temporality on the basis of presence (the presence of a non-Western cultural subject, religious or otherwise) and the temporalities they seek to retrieve remain within the order of presence, they necessarily beg the question of how presence can generate something within itself that tears the continuity of time apart and brings about the pluralization of temporalities. Marxism illustrates that this aporia is not merely scholastic. For Marx, the problem is how (the homogeneous empty time of) capital can generate its own negation or outside. Marx thought that he resolved the aporia by positing a more powerful teleological temporality. The time of capital is an alienated reflection of this time and would be negated, reappropriated, and returned to its living source in due teleological time. He defined creative labor as the material substrate and condition of possibility of capital and suggested that the proletarian revolution was creative labor's self-return at the level of world history. But the global pervasiveness of capitalist modernization and the unfeasibility of transcending it today means that we must ask how the direction of modernization's forward march can be pluralized from within without these forces of change being incorporated into capital by calculative appropriation or being reduced to its detritus. In other words, how can the world's plurality be affirmed without the celebratory commodification of difference or its denigration as that which is anachronistic?

The problem here is not merely what Gayatri Spivak has called the epistemic violence of the culture of imperialism in forming the minds of the indigenous elite, especially by colonial education.[45] The institutionalization of the imperatives of global capitalist modernity is more pervasive. It occurs through the exercise of biopolitical, ideological, and repressive technologies. At the level of subject-constitution, these technologies operate in countries outside the North Atlantic to inculcate the desire for global capitalist modernization at every level of social life. In his recent turn away from the Subaltern Studies project of retrieving a nonmodern peasant consciousness, Partha Chatterjee makes a similar claim when he observes that "what should be of greater interest to political theory are the ways in which actual practices in the field of government and politics cope with the realities of power in a world in which no society has the option of entirely escaping the tentacles of modern economic, political, and cultural institutions."[46] The central question then is how subjects can be animated to change the world made by capitalist globalization and to create other worlds. What force can destabilize and disrupt the time of capital, which has become hardwired at the level of subjective consciousness and the rhythms of material life, and create an opening for multiplying different temporalities of presence?

Here the deconstructive development of worlding is crucial, because it points to a force that can never be appropriated by human reason as the only remaining ground for the ushering of different temporalities: the "perhaps" or "otherwise" of the nonhuman gift of time. The inappropriable other from which time comes always eludes being appropriated and reduced by calculative technologies into another form of presence. Because the other's coming disrupts and renews presence, it makes possible the homogeneous empty time of capital but also renders it impossible, thereby opening up other worlds and other temporalities. I emphasize here that I am not rejecting the importance of reconceiving the world according to non-European cultural and religious traditions or dismissing the possibility that the modern capitalist world-system can be ethically transformed for the better according to the image of alternative non-Western modernities and the rhythms of different cultural temporalities. I am suggesting instead that the possibility and political effectivity of heterotemporality and alternative modernities must first be situated in the thinking of the inhuman other that is not a divine presence, in a thinking of difference that is not reducible to cultural difference. As ineffable forms of presence, gods and spirits are the effects of the play of radical alterity.

Narrating Emergence in Postcolonial Globalization: Some Working Hypotheses for Interpreting Postcolonial World Literature

The ontological equivocation that sets off the worlding force of temporalization is structural to the experience of literature. Hence, literature can play an important role in announcing the advent of new collective subjects and giving public phenomenality to their ongoing attempts to remake the world. I am proposing here a normative conception of world literature as the literature of the world (double genitive). This refers to imaginings and stories of what it means to be part of a world that tracks and accounts for contemporary globalization and earlier historical narratives of worldhood. Such imaginings are often informed by concepts of the world from non-Western traditions, both precolonial and postcolonial. Such a literature is also one that seeks to be disseminated, read, and received around the world so as to change it and the lives of peoples within it. More important, because it points to the opening of other worlds, such a literature is also a real and ongoing process *of* the world, a principle of change immanent to the world.

Here, I outline four criteria for rethinking world literature, synthesized from the philosophies of the world discussed earlier. These criteria will guide my study of literary texts in the chapters that follow. First, to track the processes of globalization that make the world and to contest this world by pointing to the temporality of another world, the literature in question must take the existing world created by globalization as one of its main themes in order to cognitively map (in Fredric Jameson's sense) how a given society is situated in the world-system. The Marxist understanding of global capitalism and the critical mapping of social space elaborated by critical geography will undoubtedly enrich our critical interpretation of these thematic representations of global flows and their impact on the postcolonial societies.

Second, we must also ask what world a given piece of world literature lets us imagine. Contemporary theories of cosmopolitanism largely ignore experiences of globalization in the postcolonial South because their mesmerizing focus is the North Atlantic, sometimes reconfigured to accommodate multicultural migrancy. If we take these experiences into account, the relation of nationalism to cosmopolitanism must be reconsidered beyond one of antagonistic opposition. As Goethe emphasizes, the world exists in the intercourse and relations between nations. Hence, a world literature does not necessarily mark the decline of the national, understood in the sense of a popular nation as distinguished from the national ideology or official nationalism of the state. Indeed, one can argue that since the nation is continually reproduced in contemporary globalization, the world that comes into being from contesting the world made by globalization is in some way mediated through the nation. This means that we can count as world literature in the robust sense activist literature that is about the nation as part of a world. In Arendt's vocabulary, it is a matter of disclosing and announcing through stories the experiences of a given people as a collective actor that is part of a shared world being destroyed by globalization. At the same time, this disclosure must also account for the problematic character of national collectivity in relation to disadvantaged minority groups and how the nation is interminably dislocated and reconstituted by various global flows.

Third, the sanctioned ignorance of the experiences of peoples in the postcolonial South in the full complexity of their religions, sociocultural norms, and geopolitical locations is underwritten by a hierarchical Eurocentric teleology of the world that leads to developmentalism. A more dynamic conception of the world would regard it as the effect of dynamic contestations from different national and regional sites instead of as a whole that is governed and closed up by an overarching telos of universal progress. In short, we should reinvent the dynamic aspect of worldhood in Goethe, Hegel, and Marx without its teleology. This would mean understanding the world as what Derrida calls the text in general, a limitless field of conflicting forces that are brought into relation and that overlap and flow into each other without return because each force, as part of a world, is necessarily opened up to what lies outside.

Fourth, at the same time that it cognitively maps the world through representation, world literature must also exemplify the process of worlding, or in the current argot, performatively enact a world. Better yet, world literature must work toward receiving a world or letting it come. Taking the world created by globalization and alternatives to it as themes is not restrictive if this thematization also points to the possibility of opening onto another world. Because the world is openness itself, world literature's world-making power is not merely the spiritual activity of depicting an ideal world as a transcendent norm from which to criticize the existing world. It is also a process that keeps alive the force that opens another world. Whether this force is conceived in terms of an intentional power of initiation by which a newcomer is inserted into an existing web of relations that recalls the force of natality (Arendt) or in terms of a radical openness to the to-come of the pure event (Derrida), what is indicated is a principle of radical transformation that cannot be erased because it is immanent to the present world. In the latter case, it is not a matter of utopian hope or the striving toward a rational ideal but the urgent precipitation of a "perhaps" or "otherwise" that sets temporalization in motion. This force is immanent to the existing world because existing reality necessarily refers to the impossible other in its persistence.

The chapters that follow explore the normative vocation of postcolonial world literature. Here, we encounter the intertwined issues of negotiating with capitalist modernity and opening up homogeneous empty time to heterotemporality as the formal problem of narration and, more specifically, as the crisis of narrating the postcolonial nation in contemporary globalization. Postcolonial literary studies have primarily understood this problem in terms of the authority or reliability of narration, the distortions of representation, or even its crisis in the nationalist novel. This debate was in large part inspired by Benedict Anderson's argument that the novel form is congenitally linked to the modern imagined community of the nation because both are examples of homogeneous empty time. Anderson's account of the rise of the nation provocatively suggested that capitalist accumulation in the form of print capitalism could give rise to a kinder, gentler, more communal face that was even redemptive. The imagined community of the nation gave meaning to an otherwise disenchanted modern world, and at its inception, this imagining of community was nourished by the realist novel, primarily through its role in the formation of vernacular reading publics.[47] In this way, the formal problem of narration became connected to the question of how to ameliorate the entropic effects of modern capitalism on the continuing viability of earlier communities and the formation of new ones. Indeed, in many formerly colonized countries, the novel became an important symbolic expression of cultural modernization. In particular, the bildungsroman was a favored genre because the *Bildung* of the protagonist from a naïve youth with utopian ideals to a mature and socially responsible ethical personality could be made to personify the teleological time of the nation's progressive development from anticolonial revolution to postcolonial stability.[48] But narrating the nation became more and more difficult with the betrayal of the egalitarian principles of decolonization and the frustration of national modernization projects. In contemporary globalization, this difficulty has been exacerbated for postcolonial countries that have been unsuccessful at developing their economies by attracting inflows of transnational capital.

In Salman Rushdie's view, the crisis in narrating the nation led to the rise of magical realism in the Third World. Commenting on Gabriel Garcia Marquez, he observes that "magical realism, at least as practised by Marquez, is a development out of Surrealism that expresses a genuinely 'Third World' consciousness. It deals with what Naipaul has called 'half-made' societies, in which the impossibly old struggles against the appallingly new, in which public corruptions and private anguishes are somehow more garish and extreme than they ever get in the so-called 'North' where centuries of wealth and power have formed thick layers over the surface of what's really going on."[49] What Rushdie calls "magic" refers to the actualization of the impossible and grotesque in situations of the extreme poverty of economically underdeveloped societies with repressive political regimes. Magical realism is a form of representation that reveals the grotesque truth that these societies are based in old and new forms of exploitation that are hidden in wealthy First World societies by consumerism. It attempts to solve the crisis of narrating the nation by staging a heterotemporality that interrupts the modern nation's linear temporality. "Magic" also refers to older "premodern traditions" that can offer resources to ameliorate the vicissitudes of capitalist modernity and resuscitate the ideals of independence betrayed by the postcolonial state. As Saleem Sinai, the narrator-protagonist of *Midnight's Children*, puts it, the magical children who personify the multitudinous traditions of India are "the grotesque aberrational monsters of independence, for whom the modern nation-state could neither have time nor compassion."[50] Saleem's elaboration of the lives and adventures of the magical children of midnight leads him to repeatedly interrupt the linear diegetic impetus and "tick-tock" of the novel's teleological time (which he calls "what-happens-next-ism") with dizzying digressions.

The chapters that follow are studies of postcolonial narrative fiction that has become world literature by virtue of its participation in worlding processes. The novels under consideration are an exemplary modality of world literature because they explore the negotiations between humane social development (or lack thereof) and global inflows of money and capital in different parts of the postcolonial South in order to craft new stories of world-belonging for postcolonial peoples. As part of their ethicopolitical vocation, they provide cognitive mappings of the position of the societies they portray in the global capitalist system and attempt to stage the heterotemporality of alternative modernities. They locate the opening of heterotemporality in the persistent presence of precolonial, non-European traditions that exert a powerful hold on the consciousness of key characters. The novels thus critically revive non-Western concepts of the world for progressive use in the present and future. They depict and enact two different modalities of heterotemporality: the persistence of revolutionary time in neocolonial conditions and a worldly ethics or practices of inhabiting the world where the teleological time of revolution no longer seems feasible. For resources, these heterotemporalities draw on Asian and African traditions of thinking about worldliness, such as practices of giving and communal belonging and animistic ideas about relations between humans, animal life, and spirits. However, the pervasiveness of modern capitalist time and its web of calculations means that these novels inevitably encounter difficulties in narration that can only be resolved by pointing to an inhuman force that opens up the homogeneous empty time of the novel and the postcolonial nation and brings about its interruption by heterotemporality. But this inhuman force, which enables reworlding in the name of alternative modernities, also contaminates and undoes "smaller-case" heterotemporal teleologies.

I will pay special attention to three related processes of postcolonial literary reworlding. First, how do these novels create alternative cartographies that foster relations of solidarity and the building of a shared world in which a postcolonial people or collective group can achieve self-determination by the constructive interpretation and critical mimesis of the existing world? How do these mappings critically rewrite canonical European literature that was disseminated through colonial education or deploy other Western textual sources for progressive ends? Second, how do central characters undergo a radical transformation of consciousness that leads them to set aside their initial desire for upward mobility within the framework of global capitalist modernization in favor of revolutionary transformation or worldly ethics, practices of inhabiting a world when revolutionary solutions are no longer effective? How do formal mechanisms that disrupt and disorient the reading experience convey to the reader a character's transformation? Finally, how do narrative and storytelling make new worlds in these novels by reviving alternative cultural temporalities? How does a metafictional preoccupation with a novel's own status as narrative point to the gift of time that destabilizes the existing world, opens new worlds, and disrupts the teleological time of these other worlds?

The novels map the flows of sugar capital, international tourist money, humanitarian aid, wildlife preservation funding, and funding for economic development. I have arranged the chapters in the order of when the places portrayed historically entered into the modern world-system as a result of trading interests followed by formal colonization: the Jamaica of Michelle Cliff's Clare Savage novels (1509), the India of Amitav Ghosh's *The Hungry Tide* (1612), and the Somalia of Nuruddin Farah's *Gifts* (1839). The exception is the concluding chapter / epilogue, which is on the Philippines as portrayed by Ninotchka Rosca's *State of War* and Timothy Mo's novel. The Spanish first settled in the Philippines in 1565 on the island of Cebu. But I have placed my discussion of the novels set there at the end of the book for thematic reasons and because they give greater emphasis to the (neo)colonialism of the arriviste US empire.

CHAPTER 8

Projecting a Future World from the Memory
of Precolonial Time

It is slavery which has given value to the colonies, it is the colonies which have created world trade, and world trade is the necessary condition for large-scale machine industry.... Prior to the slave trade, the colonies sent very few products to the Old World, and did not noticeably change the face of the world. Slavery is therefore an economic category of paramount importance.... All that modern nations have achieved is to disguise slavery at home and import it openly into the New World.
—KARL MARX

Every poor country accepts tourism as an unavoidable degradation. None has gone so far as some of these West Indian islands, which, in the name of tourism, are selling themselves into a new slavery.
—V. S. NAIPAUL

The privileging of global circulation as a form of freedom in recent theories of world literature recalls bourgeois political economy's celebration of the liberalization of trade. However, as Marx points out, the framework for such circulation—the world market—was created by chattel slavery. The economic channels of the two seventeenth-century trade triangles, the first, transporting manufactured goods to Africa, African slaves to the Americas, and American tropical commodities to Europe, and the second, selling rum to Africa, bringing African slaves to the West Indies, and bringing molasses back to New England to make rum, created the New World, the most important segment of the world market at its moment of origin. Needless to say, these human commodities experienced circulation as the antithesis of freedom. The New World is worldless for those transported by colonial slavery and for indigenous people who survived genocide.

In the Caribbean, the worldless condition of slave plantation life under colonial sugar capital casts a long shadow. A similar worldlessness persists in the region today under a different regime of capital accumulation whereby the Caribbean is sold as a global tourist destination for leisure seekers from the North and its people are commodified as workers who happily cater to the whims of wealthy foreigners. The plight of Clare Savage, the female protagonist of *Abeng* and *No Telephone to Heaven*, the two novels by Michelle Cliff that I discuss in this chapter, exemplifies the Jamaican postcolonial subject's worldlessness. She circulates from Jamaica, her birthplace, to the United States, to England, and back to Jamaica, retracing in reverse fashion the seventeenth-century trade triangles, without fulfilling her desire to find a place she can call home.

The global circulation of literature—world literature narrowly conceived—plays an important role in perpetuating this worldlessness. As the most effective way of disseminating European literature to all corners of the colonized world, the colonial education system brought about the first geographically far-reaching institutionalization of the canonical literature of the European colonial masters as world literature. Just as slaves experienced circulation as servitude, colonized and postcolonial subjects experienced this world literature as an indoctrination into the colonial racist ideology that justifies colonial oppression in terms of the mother country's cultural and racial superiority. The racial prejudices of Sir Walter Scott's Britain are part of the younger Clare's education as a privileged light-skinned Creole: "She knew, that when the time came, should she choose a husband darker than herself, it would be just as if she were Ivanhoe choosing Rebecca rather than Rowena."[1]

The transposition of European world literature through the oppressive circuits of imperial power and the colonial world market can result in subversive interpretations, for example, postcolonial readings of Shakespeare's *The Tempest* or Cliff's own reinscriptions of Charlotte Brontë's *Jane Eyre* and Emily Brontë's *Wuthering Heights*. However, the more logical antidote to the ideological victimage of colonial world literature is the assertion of a colonized people's cultural self-determination. This often takes the form of an attempt to revive precolonial traditions or to invent new local cultural practices that can be resources for forging a progressive popular national culture that seeks to break with the colonial past. As Rex Nettleford notes, "in post-colonial societies like Jamaica and the rest of the Commonwealth Caribbean, the question of *cultural identity* logically gains high priority alongside political independence and economic self-sufficiency in the awesome process of decolonization, or as some would put it, in the arduous struggle against external domination."[2] There are many obstacles to cultural decolonization. The structural Eurocentrism of humanistic knowledge means that "Jamaicans and their Caribbean counterparts are still perceived by themselves and others as extensions of Europe, historically speaking. Their actions are seen as 'responses' or reactions to the initiatives of Europe."[3] In the creative arts, where European aesthetic standards dominate, "the centuries of psychological conditioning and the inescapable on-going cultural bombardment from the North Atlantic sometimes transforms . . . an object of national pride into a product of doubt, ridicule and low worth. That hierarchy of excellence, with Europe at the top and the indigenous at the base, asserts itself with imperial majesty in the colonial mentality that is too timid to be itself."[4]

In the context of colonial cultural domination, the normative vocation of world literature is not the transgression of national parochialism but the creation of a space-time in which a colonized people can achieve cultural self-determination and emerge as a subject in the world. In Nettleford's words, "a commitment to an indigenous cultural ethos is a vital necessity for building a nation or achieving national unity in Jamaica."[5] Although his emphasis on indigeneity will undoubtedly be tempered today by an openness to transcultural influences, the reappropriation of culture remains imperative for postcolonial peoples. As distinguished from the *mobility* of circulation, the movement of cultural self-return is the vital *motility* of a fulfilling existence in a place that can provide shelter and repose in the larger world. Indeed, there is nothing inherently liberating about mobility. The migrant's aspirational path from the (ex-)colony to the metropolis, an attempt to escape from economic stagnation and cultural stasis, has debilitating psychical, emotional, and social costs. The omniscient narrator of *No Telephone to Heaven* suggests that the sense of helplessness driving contemporary Jamaican emigration echoes the Middle Passage: "So lickle movement in this place. From this place. Then only back and forth, back and forth, over and again, over and again—for centuries."[6] In contradistinction, the process of self-return involves actions by which postcolonial subjects can emerge and transform the existing world. Postcolonial literature that is part of this process is a force of worlding and world literature in the normative sense.

My approach to postcolonial world literature should be distinguished from the geographical turn in postcolonial criticism. Subscribing to a spatial account of the world, the latter approach examines how the geography of colonialism and imperialism has fundamentally shaped canonical Western literature and aesthetic values. Its pioneer, Edward Said, rightly observed twenty years ago that

> most cultural historians, and certainly all literary scholars, have failed to remark the *geographical* notation, the theoretical mapping and charting of territory that underlies Western fiction, historical writing, and philosophical discourse of the time. There is first the authority of the European observer—traveller, merchant, scholar, historian, novelist. Then there is the hierarchy of spaces by which the metropolitan center and, gradually, the metropolitan economy are seen as dependent upon an overseas system of territorial control, economic exploitation, and a socio-cultural vision; without these stability and prosperity at home ... would not be possible. The perfect example of what I mean is to be found in Jane Austen's *Mansfield Park*, in which Thomas Bertram's slave plantation in Antigua is mysteriously necessary to the poise and beauty of Mansfield Park, a place described in moral and aesthetic terms well before the scramble for Africa, or before the age of empire officially began.... Austen ... in *Mansfield Park* sublimates the agonies of Caribbean existence to a mere half-dozen passing references to Antigua.[7]

For Said, a literary work's worldliness is its geographical infrastructure, its *spatial* situated-ness, the "historical affiliation" that connects cultural works from the imperial center to the colonial peripheries and the interdependencies that follow from these connections.[8] The greater the literary work, the more it is able to formalize and encode and, thus, push into the background experiences of geographical complementarity and interdependence. The cognitive mapping of canonical European literature's colonial geographical infrastructure is an important exercise. Cliff's novels undertake this mapping by foregrounding the suffering of slaves in the sugar plantations and the ideological complicity of canonical English literary works with colonialism. But this approach merely focuses on "what Europe was," its historical constitution by its relations to its colonized other.[9] What interests me more is the continuing legacy of colonial cartography for postcolonial peoples today. This requires an understanding of how colonialism creates a world that is simultaneously unworlded at its moment of inception by genocide and slavery. More important, to understand postcolonial literature as a reworlding of the world, we need to supplement the spatio-geographical concept of the world with temporal concepts. The colonial and postcolonial cartography of Jamaica is created by the calculative management of time by regimes of capital accumulation. Resisting these regimes requires undoing this temporality and the inauguration of a new time.

The first part of this chapter discusses how colonial and postcolonial Jamaica is shaped by calculations and technologies of time that engender the temporalities of sugar capital and the tourist industry. I then examine Cliff's attempt to initiate a new time for the Jamaican people by reviving precolonial history and its cultural traditions as a way of stimulating revolutionary consciousness. This celebration of precolonial traditions is an example of heterotemporality. Because Cliff regards the classical European bildungsroman as a literary mechanism for the perpetuation of colonial ideological mystification, the initiation of revolutionary time necessarily involves a subversive reinscription of this genre. At the beginning of the novelistic diptych, Clare, a daughter from a privileged Creole clan in Jamaica, is largely ignorant of how colonial cartography has determined her life. She gradually learns to question and reject the culture of imperialism that has benefited her after her experiences as an immigrant to the United States and as a university student in the mother country, Britain. Instead of interiorizing the values and norms of her social class, her *Bildung* involves a process of unlearning. This leads to the cultivation of a revolutionary patriotic consciousness and what I will call a postcolonial dialectics of place, political activity that seeks to transform Jamaica from a subordinate segment of the abstract space of the capitalist world-system into a world, a place of belonging that sustains the lives of the Jamaican people. But although Cliff's novels associate the initiation of a new time and the opening of another world with the promise of revolution, they also portray the impossibility of revolution in contemporary global capitalism. Clare's ambivalent fate at the end of the second novel suggests that in the original instance, new worlds are opened up by a force that is quite other to the memory of precolonial heterotemporalities.

(Post)colonial Calculations: The Temporalities of Sugar and Tourism Capital

Marx has taught us that the accumulation of capital requires the control and management of the time of production so that more value can be extracted in a given time period. Capital's "immanent drive" and "constant tendency towards increasing the productivity of labor" is a form of temporality.[10] It quantifies time so that it can be measured and calculated. As Éric Alliez notes, the temporality of capital, where the form of abstract homogeneous time is identical to the abstract form of the commodity and money, is based on the Aristotelian definition of time as the number of movement. "Time . . . is discoverable as an empty *form*, a pure order of time, quantitative and differential, measurable and coinable, which nothing can come to fill. The time without qualities of a future-oriented humanity that cuts time into segments of linear duration that are put to profit in order to realize investments and 'accumulation.'"[11]

European colonialism imposes the temporality of capital onto the West Indies at two levels. Macrologically, colonialism drags places that were previously not associated with the capitalist system into its world of commodity production, thereby subjecting non-European environments and communities to the temporality of capital accumulation. Western European expansion, a response to the need for sugar as a source of calories, a substitute for fat, and an ingredient in beverages, predated the seventeenth century.[12] British sugar capital's entry into the West Indies and its subsequent development is significant because of its sheer economic scale as an engine for the growth of global capitalism and an unparalleled source of imperial profit. As it reached new heights of economic growth, the metropolis literally consumed the colonies. As Sidney Mintz notes, "from 1650 onwards, sugar began to change from a luxury and a rarity into a commonplace and a necessity in many nations, England among them; . . . this increased consumption . . . accompanied the 'development' of the West," such that the colonial production of sugar for mass European consumption epitomizes "the productive thrust and emerging intent of world capitalism, which centered at first upon the Netherlands and England."[13] After 1655, the year of Jamaica's colonization, the importation of sugar from the Caribbean colonies for consumption in Britain and for sale to other European countries became an important source of profit.

Sugar capital created a world market by bringing the Caribbean into a Europe-centered world, or better yet, by destroying the temporalities of precolonial ways of life and opening a world in the Caribbean that runs according to the temporality of capitalist accumulation. In the *Wealth of Nations*, Adam Smith repeatedly refers to the British West Indies with imperial possessive pronouns that deny them any identity other than the subservient role they play in supplying the center with the desired commodity. They are "our sugar colonies" and "our sugar islands," just as the American colonies are "our tobacco colonies."[14] John Stuart Mill is blunter about colonialism's exploitative, expropriative, and oppressive character. Colonies are not countries that engage in commodity exchange with other countries. They are similar to outlying agricultural or manufacturing estates belonging to a larger community. Our West Indian colonies, for example, cannot be regarded as countries with a productive capital of their own . . . [They are instead] a place where England finds it convenient to carry on the production of sugar, coffee and other tropical commodities. All the capital employed here is English capital; almost all the industry is carried on for English uses; there is little production of anything except for staple commodities, and these are sent to England, not to be exchanged for things exported to the colony and consumed by inhabitants, but to be sold in England for the benefit of the proprietors there. The trade with the West Indies is hardly to be considered an external trade, but more resembles the traffic between town and country.[15]

Mill's comments ominously portend the destructive consequences of colonial worlding for the economic development of the peripheries, a pattern that continues after decolonization. At the concrete level of sugar production, the destructive imposition of capitalist temporality leads to the organization of the sugar plantation system through calculations of time aimed at maximizing productivity. This temporality dictates the rhythms of the daily lives of plantation slaves.

The use of slaves by sugar capital is not an archaic form of labor organization but involves industrial techniques of time management. As Sidney Mintz observes, the sugar plantation system is "time-conscious" because of its crop's perishable nature. "Sugar cane must be cut when it is ripe, and ground as soon as it is cut. These simple facts give a special character to any enterprise dedicated to the production of sugar."[16] The mill and the boiling house had to be run with the sensitivity to time characterizing a factory at the same time that their operations had to be coordinated with the cutting crews on the field. This required the organization of field labor both in terms of seasons and between sugar cane and subsistence crops. The coordination between land and mill and the synchronization of different forms of labor required the strict organization of labor according to time and skill. "The specialization by skill and jobs, and the division of labor by age, gender, and condition into crews, shifts, and 'gangs,' together with the stress upon punctuality and discipline, are features associated more with industry than with agriculture."[17] The capitalist-industrial time-consciousness of sugar production is not confined to sugar-related activities. It "permeated all phases of plantation life," such that "the strictness of scheduling . . . gave an industrial cast" to the lives of plantation slaves.[18]

Slaves experienced the temporality of the plantation world as worldless-ness in a double sense. First, because slaves have no agency in regulating and controlling the time of their daily lives, they cannot be actors in a world. Just as the colonial Caribbean is not a world with its own temporalities but an appendage of the Europe-centered world-system that is subject to the temporality of capital accumulation, slaves have no world of their own. Second, they cannot create a home in this location where they have been forcibly transported because, as the property of others, they cannot lay claim to their surroundings through appropriative activity. By indirectly shaping the chromatist hierarchy of postcolonial Jamaican society, the colonial plantation's calculations of time cast a long shadow after the emancipation of slaves in 1834 and Jamaican decolonization in 1962. The lighter-skinned descendants of house slaves who served the colonial masters loyally and were spared the toil of work in the cane-fields became the new bourgeois elite who exploited the Jamaican masses deemed inferior because of their darker skin. In postcolonial Jamaica, the habit of colonial servitude became useful for another form of capital: the tourist industry.

When Caribbean sugar lost its preferential treatment in the British market in the second half of the nineteenth century and the Jamaican sugar industry declined because of sugar's plunging value, tourism emerged as a logical alternative to the traditional plantation economy. In his historical study of the Jamaican tourist industry, Frank Fonda Taylor notes that "the long-standing reputation for hospitality that the island had acquired since the mid-seventeenth century was renovated and converted into something that the elite could cash in on."[19] The demand for trade and travel associated with the rise of the United States as the world's leading economic power by the end of the nineteenth century led Jamaicans to view the tourist industry as "an instrument of providence to advance the economic lot of the colony."[20] Hence, Jamaica was "offered as a paradise, not only for health seekers and winter tourists but for foreign capital as well."[21]

In *The Wretched of the Earth*, Fanon had denounced the establishment of a tourist economy in the Third World by the neocolonial indigenous bourgeoisie because it prostituted the local population to Western interests. "The national bourgeoisie establishes holiday resorts and playgrounds for entertaining the Western bourgeoisie. This sector goes by the name of tourism and becomes a national industry for this very purpose. . . . The casinos in Havana and Mexico City, the beaches of Rio, Copacabana, and Acapulco, the young Brazilian and Mexican girls, the thirteen-year-old mestizos, are the scars of this depravation of the national bourgeoisie. . . . The national bourgeoisie assumes the role of manager for the companies of the West and turns its country virtually into a bordello for Europe."[22] Since the late 1960s, the World Bank, the United Nations, and OECD countries have sanctioned tourism as a key driver of economic growth and modernization in developing countries. The Jamaican tourist economy is a new form of imperialism and/or a neocolonialism that subjects the nation and its citizens to a new kind of slavery.

First, the tourist industry repeats broader neocolonial patterns of economic dependency whereby the Jamaican economy is driven by foreign capital investment and the export of raw agricultural products. What is commodified for foreign consumption is the beauty of the Jamaican landscape as a tourist destination, a paradisiacal "pasture for pleasuring the leisured" from abroad.[23] This commodified image of Jamaica is representational space in Lefebvre's sense, a fantasy for tourists that is far removed from the daily lives of the Jamaican masses. Their labor makes this fantasy so real that Jamaica itself has become a fantasy, such that many Jamaicans cannot make the connections between the neocolonial economy and the colonial plantation economy. In explaining how she became a revolutionary, Clare wryly notes in *No Telephone to Heaven* that "there are no facts in Jamaica. Not one single fact. Nothing to join us to the real" (*NTTH*, 92). The current reinvention of the Jamaican tourist industry, which emphasizes "heritage tourism," has produced a fantasy that glorifies colonial culture. A recent academic volume from a conference at the University of the West Indies devoted to the assessment of tourism's long-term potential as a driver of economic growth "sells" the colonial past as a tourist attraction without any irony: "Seville and Port Royal are the outstanding properties with rich histories. . . . [Seville] is endowed with a wealth of archaeological material of the Spanish period of Jamaican history. Seville also is the site of middens of the original Taino people, slave quarters, the first governmental seat and one of the earliest English great houses. . . . Falmouth is now being actively prepared as a heritage site. Although not as rich in historically relevant material, Falmouth is ideally located near Montego Bay to showcase its Georgian architecture and historical features of interest in a tourism setting."[24] Colonial sugar capital was European-owned and –managed. United States and European neocolonial capital dominates the Jamaican tourist economy. Neocolonial capital flows into the Caribbean, controls and develops its resources, and extracts the greatest profits from tourism.[25]

Second, the tourist industry is characterized by a racialized social hierarchy in which the Jamaican masses are sold as workers who serve demanding foreigners. "Foreign interests . . . induce Caribbean tourist destinations to supply whatever their tourists want—fast food, air-conditioning, swimming pools, and imported food and beverages—under the threat of directing their clients elsewhere if these commodities and services are not provided."[26] The scenario of Afro-Caribbean people serving white visitors as waiters, hotel maids, taxi drivers, and so on recalls the colonial plantation system "in which black slaves attend to their white masters and overseers."[27] Indeed, Jamaican blacks are often made to feel like aliens in their own country because they are excluded as guests from hotel resorts and its environments.[28] Hence, tourism has been described as "a new plantocracy" in which the state serves as the overseer of the businesses of a white elite and excludes the black population from decision-making.[29] Neocolonial social relations are justified in the name of economic development. Neocolonial hierarchies are exacerbated by tourism's reliance on commodified images of brown and black men and women that are based on myths about their hypersexuality and tourism's link to sexual services for foreigners. As Kamala Kempadoo notes, "tourism in the Caribbean at the end of the twentieth century reproduces exoticizing tendencies present in the region since the sixteenth century, while new global hegemonies that rest on an increasing economic gap between the postindustrial metropole and peripheral areas that provide cheap labor, natural resources and playgrounds for the rich, extend its scope. . . . The labor, sexuality, and bodies of Caribbean women and men constitute primary resources that local governments and the global tourism industry exploit and commodify, to cater to . . . tourist desires and needs."[30]

The extraction of tourist revenue requires a different temporality from that of the sugar plantation economy. Because the produced commodity is not a physical consumer staple but an image of a leisurely paradise, the calculation of time is not aimed at increasing the productivity of labor through disciplinary practices. To the contrary, an image of Jamaica as a place without the pressures of daily toil, where people enjoy a surfeit of leisure as a matter of course, is created. As a place that is naturally free from the calculations of labor time, Jamaica can then be tethered to the industrialized and postindustrial work-world beyond it and function as a place of off-time and release where the Northern tourist can recover from the wear and tear of work-time.

This fantasy of a world free from the calculative quantification of work-time, however, can only be constructed by suppressing other local temporalities. Although genocide eradicated the temporality of Jamaica's indigenous inhabitants and imported slaves were subjected to the time of capital, other temporalities emerged that escaped the colonial plantation's calculations. Sidney Mintz argues that the Caribbean peasantry grew out of plantation society's crevices, "in places where the plantations failed, or in places where the plantations never came. Such crevices have been both historical and ecological: *time periods* when European control faltered or was relaxed, when the political future was clouded, or when runaways and squatters were able to establish themselves 'outside'; *geographical spaces* where the plantation could not work because of soil or slope or aridity or distance from the sea."[31] Cliff portrays these noncapitalist temporalities of rural Jamaican life as resources Clare can draw on to reworld Jamaica.

Contemporary global capital threatens the survival of such temporalities. First, mining, tourist developments, oil refining, real estate speculation, highways, and similar developments expropriate the local land.[32] More important for present purposes, tourist capital effaces the temporality of peasant subsistence activity by representing it as an atemporal state of stagnation. Because capital accumulation is the measure of value, only its time counts, while other forms of temporality are viewed as being outside time. The entirety of Jamaican life can then be marketed as a life free from the pressures of labor time, in comparison to the busy activity of tourists in their normal working lives even as the Jamaican masses are incorporated as commodified labor to serve the tourist industry. In a perceptive study of the cultural construction of the Caribbean as a tropical paradise, Ian Strachan describes the complex temporal structure of tourist capital: the Caribbean is "frozen in a paradisiacal timelessness in which nothing is done and there is nothing to do. . . . These travelers work excessively and imagine that Caribbeans do not. They tell themselves that Caribbeans have instead an accumulated leisure, excessive freedom from toil. The typical Western tourist, in contrast, has only subsistence leisure—just enough time away from work to live."[33] Jamaica is thus imagined as a perfect destination for tourists who desire to return to a nature unspoiled by human appropriative activity so that they can replenish themselves before they rejoin the time of accumulation.

In his Nobel lecture, Derek Walcott figures the tourist economy's construction of Jamaica as a disease that destroys the Caribbean peoples' regenerative memory. Awareness of historical pasts enables Caribbeans to know how they came to inhabit their world so that they can build a future. The mystification of this knowledge is an unworlding in which the time of modern capitalist progress suppresses these histories and subordinates the future of the islands to its North-centric linear trajectory.

In our tourist brochures the Caribbean is a blue pool into which the republic dangles the extended foot of Florida as inflated rubber islands bob and drinks with umbrellas float towards her on a raft. This is how the islands from the shame of necessity sell themselves. . . .

All of the Antilles, every island, is an effort of memory; every mind, every racial biography culminating in amnesia and fog. . . . Decimation from the Aruac downwards is the blasted root of Antillean history, and the benign blight that is tourism can infect all of those island nations, not gradually, but with imperceptible speed, until each rock is whitened by the guano of white-winged hotels, the arc and descent of progress.[34]

A New Teleological Time: Resurrecting the Precolonial Past

Cliff goes further than Walcott by suggesting that activist literature has the power to create a world: "I am spoken into being—as . . . Senghor said of the world. . . . I use this speech to craft fiction . . . which is self-consciously . . . political. I do believe in the word, that a new world may be spoken into being."[35] In a flashback near the end of *No Telephone to Heaven*, Clare explains her commitment to the guerilla movement in terms of the urgent need to invent an alternative time that will free Jamaica from subjugation to neocolonial capitalist time: "I returned to this island because there was nowhere else. . . . I could live no longer in borrowed countries, on borrowed time. . . . I am not a missionary nor a Peace Corps volunteer. I have not been sent from somewhere. I came here because I could not go elsewhere" (*NTTH*, 193, 195). The time of the (neo)-colonial world implies a dependent relation of perpetual indebtedness where the Creole subject's very existence is borrowed from the metropolis, much as human beings exist by divine grace. The narrator calls this "the logic of a creole." It leads Clare to move from America to London for her university education: "This was the mother-country. The country by whose grace her people existed in the first place. Her place could be here. . . . This was natural" (*NTTH*, 109).

Here, the temporal calculations of global capitalist accumulation take the form of the teleological *Bildung* of the middle-class Jamaican Creole subject who facilitates neocolonial exploitation. Cliff reinscribes the (neocolonial) bildungsroman and replaces its teleological time with that of revolutionary consciousness. The two novels form the arc of a revolutionary postcolonial bildungsroman that critically engages with canonical English novels such as

Great Expectations and *Jane Eyre*. As part of her colonial education, such novels are ideological mystifications that have made Clare identify with the European colonizer as the subject of progress. The undoing of Clare's *Bildung* as a Europe-identified Creole subject and the *Bildung* of her revolutionary consciousness begins during her unhappy sojourn in England, catalyzed by her recognition of her mystification. She disidentifies with Jane Eyre and painfully identifies with Bertha Mason, Rochester's insane Creole wife from the Caribbean. "The fiction had tricked her. Drawn her in so she became Jane. . . . With a sharpness of mind, reprimanded herself. No, she told herself. No, she could not be Jane. Small and pale. English. No, she paused. No, my girl, try Bertha. Wild-maned Bertha. . . . Yes, Bertha was closer the mark. Captive. Ragout. Mixture. Confused. Jamaican. Caliban. Carib. Cannibal. Cimarron. All Bertha. All Clare" (*NTTH*, 116).

Clare also identifies with figures of indigeneity and anticolonial rebellion: the Caribs native to the Antilles, Maroon slave rebels, and Shakespeare's Caliban. Her revolutionary *Bildung* is a teleological process in which elements from the historical past are revived and raised up as another world that revolutionary action will actualize in the future. Her *Bildung* is meant as an example to incite Jamaican readers to resist neocolonial capital and redeem their nation. Although the novels' omniscient narrator grasps the connections between precolonial and colonial pasts and the future endpoint as moments of a totality, throughout *Abeng* and for much of *No Telephone to Heaven*, Clare (and every other character except Harry/Harriet) remains ignorant of the past. In *Abeng*, this epistemological gap between narrator and characters is indicated by a refrain about the ignorance of contemporary black Jamaicans about the violence of colonial slavery.

> In school they were told that their ancestors had been pagan. They were given the impression that the whites who brought them here from the Gold Coast and the Slave Coast were only copying a West African custom. . . .
>
> The congregation *did not know* that African slaves in Africa had been primarily household servants. They were not seasoned. They were not worked in canefields. The system of labor was not industrialized. There was in fact no comparison between the two states of servitude: that practiced by the tribal societies of West Africa and that organized by the Royal African Company of London, chartered by the Crown. . . .
>
> No one had told the people in the Tabernacle that of all the slave societies in the New World, Jamaica was considered among the most brutal.

They did not know that the death rate of Africans in Jamaica under slavery exceeded the rate of birth, and that the growth of the slave population from 1,500 in 1655 to 311,070 in 1834, the year of freedom, was due *only* to the importation of more people, more slaves. *They did not know* that some slaves worked with their faces locked in masks of tin, so that they would not eat the sugar cane they cut. Or that there were few white women on the island during slavery, and so the grandmothers of these people sitting in a church on a Sunday during mango season, had been violated again and again by the very men who whipped them. (*A*, 18–19, emphasis added)

Colonial education cultivates ignorance and represses the violence of slavery into the Jamaican people's unconscious. But Jamaicans are equally ignorant about the precolonial African traditions their ancestors brought over and the history of slave resistance and anticolonial rebellion, which is personified by the mythical figure of Nanny. Their ignorance breeds a sense of worthlessness and helplessness. The novels seek to rectify this by a cognitive mapping of Jamaica's historical entry into the capitalist world-system and its contemporary place. The mapping follows Clare through her childhood in preindependence Jamaica, her teenage years in the United States, her time as a university student in England, and her return to contemporary Jamaica to fight as a revolutionary against her country's degradation as a destination for global tourism and an exotic location for the global film industry. Clare gradually gains knowledge of how the fundamental moments of her life have been determined by Jamaica's colonial past, and she almost manages to suture the gap of knowledge between herself and the omniscient narrator. The intended reader of the novels, however, attains greater knowledge than Clare. Unlike her, we can interpret the significance of her death because we have access to the entire frame of the novels.

The novels portray Jamaican history and events in the colonial period and in postcolonial modernization. *Abeng*'s narrative begins in 1958, four years before Jamaican independence. However, postcolonial Jamaica remains enslaved by the time of modern capitalist accumulation. It is, the narrator sarcastically notes, "independence-in-practically-name-only" (*A*, 5). Postcoloniality is a state of suspension between the long past of colonial slavery and the hopeless future of gradual decline in the long transition from British imperialism to US neocolonial economic hegemony. A scene in chapter 4 evokes the eerie continuity between the times of sugar and tourist capital. The Savages are direct descendants of plantation owners. The plantation has long been lost. When

Clare visits the property with her father, it has been subdivided for American vacation homes with the name of "Paradise Plantation." However, the developers have left the great house standing as an advertising gimmick, "a 'come on,' to convince prospective clients they could buy into the past. Capture history in their summer homes" (*A*, 24). Foreigners desire a grotesque fantasy that glorifies colonial heritage. Without any sense of irony, black Jamaicans are paid to perform the parts of their slave ancestors. They are literally degraded into the neoslavery of neocolonial wage labor. The great house

> was spruced up and made into a flagship for the Paradise Plantation. Fitted with period furniture imported from a factory in Massachusetts which made replicas of antiques. And white plaster dummies from a factory in New York City, which supplied several Fifth Avenue department stores, were dressed in nineteenth century costume, and placed on the verandah and through the rooms. One larger-than-life white dummy was dressed like an overseer, with a cat-o'-nine tails in one plaster fist, and a wide-brimmed straw hat on his head. He stood firmly, with legs apart, to the side of the great house, welcoming purchasers to the subdivision.
>
> A small patch of canefield was left by the developers. And Black Jamaicans, also in period costume—but alive, not replicas—were paid to stand around with machetes and hoes, and give directions to interested parties.
>
> The brochure stressed "atmosphere." (*A*, 37)

The young Clare cannot grasp the systemic truth of what she perceives. She sees the foundation stones of the slave cabins, the sugar mill and the boiling house, but does not know "the former life they represented." She sees the smoke from the burning of cane-fields to clear the land for vacation homes but does not grasp the neocolonial present of the US informal empire, a state of economic hopelessness that led middle-class Jamaicans to desert their country in the 1970s for the United States "because there was no economic future for them, because it's an underdeveloped country and because they were light-skinned enough to pass."[36]

The novels interfere with the smooth functioning of capital time in two ways. First, they interrupt the triumphant narrative of capitalist modernity as the product of enlightened reason by foregrounding the Enlightenment's connections to exploitation and colonial violence. *Abeng* delves into the dark legacy of slavery in the chromatist racism of contemporary Jamaican social life and emphasizes slavery's inseparable ties to European modernity. Slavery is indispensable to the calculations of colonial sugar capital: "Three hundred acres was the minimum expanse of land a sugar plantation could measure—in order to make a profit. One slave was required for every two acres. . . . This estimate takes into account the fact that the slaves would be worked twelve hours a day and six days a week. At least" (*A*, 27).[37] The unpaid time of this unending supply of slave labor is the "infrastructure" of modern universal progress. The living experiences of slaves are the hidden underside of the discursive intercourse that characterizes the (literary) public sphere of the European Enlightenment celebrated by Habermas as embodying the spirit of modernity.[38] Cliff figures the connection as a text-ile or weaving.

> But sugar was a necessity of western civilization—to the tea-drinkers of England and the coffee-drinkers on the Continent, those who used it to sweeten their beverage, or who laced these beverages with rum. Those who took these products at their leisure—to finish a meal, begin a day, to stimulate them, to keep them awake, as they considered fashion or poetry or politics or family, sitting around their cherrywood tables or relaxing in their wingback chairs. People who spent afternoons in the clubs of Mayfair or evenings in the cafés on the rue de la Paix. People holding forth in Parliament. The Rathaus. The Comedie Française. People who talked revolution or who worried about revolution. They took their coffee and tea, their sugar and rum, from trays held by others, as their cotton was milled by others, and their lands were kept by others. The fabric of their society, their civilization, their culture, was an intricate weave, at the heart of which was enforced labor of one kind or another. (*A*, 27–28)

Indeed, the narrator points out that the English abolition of slavery did not disturb the seamless temporality of capitalist accumulation. "There had been no cataclysm in Jamaica; no bloody Civil War to end involuntary servitude. The end of slavery was a decision on the part of Her Majesty's government, after decades of consideration and decades of guerrilla warfare. And, of course, the growing Victorian desire for West African palm oil. . . . The perfect Victorian marriage of economy and altruism" (*A*, 27). A main motivation of emancipation is the growing trade in West African palm oil to make soap, which became more profitable than the trade in slaves. At the same time, the freeing of slaves merely led to a legalized form of exploitation of "free" consensual wage labor. The former slaves remained part of the totality of the capitalist world-system, the cognitive mapping of which is required to cultivate a revolutionary consciousness.

It is important to take it all in, the disconnections and the connections, in order to understand the limits of the abolition of slavery. The enslavement of Black people . . . made other forms of employment in the upkeep of western civilization seem pale. So slavery-in-fact—which was distasteful to some coffee-drinkers and tea-drinkers, who might have read about these things or saw them illustrated in the newspapers the clubs and cafes provided for their patrons, neatly hung on a rack from dowel sticks—slavery-in-fact was abolished, and the freedom which followed on abolition turned into veiled slavery, the model of the rest of the western world. . . . All the forces which worked to keep these people slaves now worked to keep them poor. And poor most of them remained. (*A*, 28)

More important, the novels interrupt the narrative present by staging the heterotemporality of modernity. They recall an even older time, prior to the time of colonial capital, that has left its mark on the postcolonial present as a resource for resistance and the projection of a future, alternative modernity. *Abeng* begins with an invocation of nonhuman geological time, before Jamaica came into being and humans inhabited it, the time of the birth of the island from the sea, where the only measure of time is fossilization. "The island rose and sank. Twice. During periods in which history was recorded by indentations on rock and shell. This is a book about the time which followed on that time. As the island became a place where people lived. Indians. Africans. Europeans" (*A*, 3). In addition to this time *sans* humanity, there were other human times before colonialism: the times of indigenous Indians, who were exterminated, and Africans, before they were transported as chattel slavery. Somehow, something of these times has survived genocide, colonial degradation, and oppression and is present in all descendant Jamaicans as a deep unconscious structure. "They did not know about the Kingdom of the Ashanti or the Kingdom of Dahomey, where most of their ancestors had come from. They did not imagine that Black Africans had commanded thousands of warriors. Built universities. Created systems of law. Devised language. Wrote history. Poetry. Were traders. Artists. Diplomats" (*A*, 20).

Cliff suggests that there is a strong affinity between the temporality of the Jamaican environment and landscape and the temporalities of precolonial Indian and African traditions. They share the common characteristic of wildness, that which cannot be tamed by cultivation and, by extension, colonialism, which has its etymological and conceptual roots in agriculture.[39]

Wildness is the predicate of the natural landscape, which refuses to surrender to the calculative control of human cultivation exemplified by the colonial plantation. The title of *No Telephone to Heaven*'s first chapter gives us the local name for this recalcitrance: *ruinate*, "the distinctive Jamaican term . . . used to describe lands which were once cleared for agricultural purposes and have now lapsed back into . . . 'bush'" (*NTTH*, 1). Wildness is also the predicate of slaves who rebel against slavery. The name of the Maroons "came from *cimarrón*: unruly, runaway. A word first given to cattle which had taken to the hills. Beyond its exact meaning, the word connoted fierce, wild, unbroken" (*A*, 20). Creole subjects who have not been made submissive by the colonial education designed to civilize and make them representatives of the colonizer's culture and revolutionary elements in postcolonial Jamaica are also wild. These wild temporalities form an ecology that undoes the time of (post)colonial capital.

Feminist-Maternal Ontopology: A Postcolonial Dialectics of Place

For Cliff, Jamaica's forests have an anticolonial significance and facilitate the ends of rebellion.

> The civilizer works against the constant danger of the forest, of a landscape ruinate, gone to ruination. . . .
>
> Each word signifies the reclamation of land, the disruption of cultivation, civilization, by the uncontrolled, uncontrollable forest. When a landscape becomes ruinate, carefully designed aisles of cane are envined, strangled, the order of empire is replaced by the chaotic forest. The word *ruination* (especially) signifies this immediately; it contains both the word *ruin*, and *nation*. A landscape in ruination means one in which the imposed nation is overcome by the naturalness of ruin.
>
> As individuals in this landscape, we, the colonized, are also subject to ruination, to the self reverting to the wildness of the forest.[40]

The natural landscape's recalcitrance to colonial cultivation is a symbolic inspiration in the struggle against neocolonialism because it serves as a metaphor for a revolutionary consciousness that will never yield to (neo)colonial power. However, colonial education has obscured and broken the connection between Jamaicans and the power of their landscape. Colonial education plays an important role in colonial cartography by creating representational space in Lefebvre's sense. It scars the minds of colonized subjects by imposing Europe on their imagination. Learning meaningless European geographical and historical knowledge, such as the seasons of the European climate, European mountains, rivers, and flora, actively distorts the consciousness and lived experience of colonized subjects. Colonial education unworlds: it disorientates and alienates subjects by uprooting them from their local environment. "When our landscape is so tampered with, how do we locate ourselves?" Cliff observes. "When the rainy season becomes an unnaturally tempestuous spring; mango season the dog days of summer; hurricane season an untamable autumn?"[41]

The Afro-Caribbean writer's vocation is to produce a different representational space that will reconnect Jamaicans to their landscape and stimulate the cultivation of a revolutionary subject. Where canonical English literature portrays the Jamaican landscape as destructive excess, Cliff's extended pun on *ruination* resignifies wildness as a positive power that frustrates (neo)colonial calculations. In the novels, the landscape has a purposive animistic temporality that harmonizes with the ends of escaping slaves and the resistance movement. Nanny, a mythical female leader of the Maroon slave rebellion against the British from 1655 to 1740 and a sorceress with magical skills from the Ashanti tribe and knowledge about battle tactics from the Dahomey Amazons, sees traces of Africa in the Jamaican landscape. The landscape gives the rebels protective shelter from colonial authorities. "The forests of the island are wild and remind her of Africa. In places the mountains are no more than cliff-faces. The precipices of these mountains often hold caves she can use for headquarters or to conceal the weapons of her army" (*A*, 19).

The description of Clare's maternal grandmother's abandoned farm in the opening chapter of *No Telephone to Heaven* emphasizes the political significance of ruination as the defeat of the monotheistic paternalistic God of Christianity, the highest symbol of colonial cultural control, by Sasabonsam, the forest monster.

> Her carefully planned flowers, a devotion of fifty years, a way, she said, of giving something back to the Almighty . . . —these flowers, chosen for color and texture and how each would set off the next, revealing splendor and glory, her order, her choices, reflecting the order, the choices, of His universe, had been haphazardly supplanted by wilder and brighter ones, exploding disorder into her scheme. A wild design of color was spun through her garden and across her grave, masking the stonecutter's spare

testament to her devotion: SERVANT OF GOD. . . . There was no forgiveness in this disorder. Sasabonsam, fire-eyed forest monster, dangled his legs from the height of a silk-cotton tree. (*NTTH*, 8–9)

Ruination undoes human efforts of cultivation—colonization in the general sense—and transforms the farm into "a wild unhumaned place" (*NTTH*, 9). But it is not opposed to all human purposiveness. When Clare returns to reclaim the land with her fellow guerillas, the ruination protects them from the neocolonial state's gaze, and they find sustenance from surviving precolonial forms of cultivation, wild fruits, fish, and crustaceans in a way that echoes the forests' hospitableness to the Maroon rebels in earlier centuries.

In colonial world literature, Caliban and Bertha Mason exemplify the wild subject who resists colonial cultivation. Drawing on myths and images of the land as powerful mother, Cliff suggests that this revolutionary lineage is maternal.[42] Clare Savage is Cliff's contribution to this series of characters. In the novels, the battle between the teleological temporalities of (neo)colonial capitalist modernity and anticolonial revolution, which is inspirited by the temporalities of the landscape and precolonial Indian and African traditions, is played out in Clare's contradictory heritage. Her paternal family represses its African roots by repeatedly reminding her of her lineage in a Creole plantation-owning family. But through her mother's family, Clare unknowingly carries the African legacy of the Maroon rebels and the knowledge of the Miskito Indians, whom the colonial government had brought in to fight the rebels but who had intermarried with them. In the course of the novels, the reader comes across female characters from the colonial past and from Clare's childhood that are connected to precolonial temporalities and function as inspiration for anticolonial rebellion. However, it is her mother, Kitty, who best personifies an intuitive affinity with the Jamaican soil. Repeating a familiar Romantic topos that opposes the idyllic live-giving country to the stifling influence of the city, Cliff suggests that Kitty's attachment to the bush expresses a patriotic love for Jamaicans who have maintained an authentic relation to their natural landscape.

The country people of Jamaica touched her in a deep place—these were her people, and she never questioned her devotion to them. . . . Kitty had a sense of Jamaica that her husband would never have. She thought that there was no other country on earth as beautiful as hers, and sometimes would take Clare into the bush with her, where they would go barefoot, and hunt for mangoes or avocadoes out of season. . . . For her, God and

Jesus were but representatives of Nature, which it only made sense was female, and the ruler of all. (*A*, 52)

The gendering of the landscape as a female Nature posits a female genealogy in which the wisdom of precolonial traditions is passed on from mother to daughter through the sensuous tactility of corporeal practices instead of the written and spoken logos of patriarchal knowledge. Kitty is a revolutionary *in potential*. Her anticolonial spirit is rooted in her love for black Jamaicans, which she keeps secret because of the chromatist racism of middle-class society.

Clare's struggle is portrayed by a polysemous metaphorics of *passage*, a term with a testamentary connotation. It describes the transmission of Indian and African temporalities to the Jamaican people. But plantation life, the destination of the Middle Passage, which is governed by the temporality of sugar capital, cuts off this legacy. Clare's subsequent movements within Jamaican society and emigration from Jamaica repeat this original cutting of ties to precolonial temporalities and the living soil. The socially normative path for Clare is symbolic death. Cliff figures her paternal Creole legacy and fate of passing as white and being passed on to a white husband as an object of marital exchange as a passage to the otherworld.

> Clare would never gain admission [into the depths of Kitty's soul]—she had been handed over to Boy the day she was born. . . . Perhaps she [Kitty] assumed that a light-skinned child was by common law, or traditional practice, the child of the whitest parent. This parent would pass this light-skinned daughter on to a white husband, so she would have lighter and lighter babies—this, after all, was how genetics was supposed to work, moving toward the preservation of whiteness and the obliteration of darkness. . . . Let her passage into that otherworld be as painless as possible. Maybe Kitty thought that Clare would only want . . . to pass into whiteness. (*A*, 128–29)

As an instrument of colonial education, the bildungsroman prescribes the Creole subject's ascent from wildness into whiteness. It teaches Clare to accept Jamaica's subordinate position in the Eurocentric view of the world and to revere England as the telos of her life-journey.

> England was their mother country. Everyone there was white, her teachers told her. Jamaica was the "prizest" possession of the Crown, she had read in her history book. And she had been told that there was a special bond between this still wild island and that perfect place across the sea.

England was where Charles Dickens had come from. They were studying him in school, reading his novel, *Great Expectations*. She liked Pip and he reminded her of herself in some ways.... Sometimes she felt sure that she would make her own way in the world—would "be" someone, as Pip had wanted for himself. And it bothered her that she would probably have to leave this place—her family's island—in order to achieve anything. England. America. These were the places island people went to get ahead. (*A*, 36)

As a young adult, she feels trapped in Jamaica, which seems to her "one of the saddest places in the world": "She had escaped the island, nothing held her there. Was living, going to university, in London" (*NTTH*, 88–89). But throughout her circulation in America and Europe, her desire to belong to a place remains unfulfilled.

Clare's struggle is resolved by a dialectics of place. The abstract space and homogeneous empty time of the capitalist world market in which she circulates is retemporalized with her repatriation to Jamaica and her reconnection to its landscape's precolonial temporalities. As a student at the University of London, she is fascinated by Aristotle's definition of place (*topos*) (*NTTH*, 117). In book 4 of the *Physics*, Aristotle defines place as a limit, a bounded container that each body requires in order to exist. Place is a "where" in which things exist and that defines their existence such that every body has its own proper place.[43] A body's place defines its existence because the constancy or immovability of place enables the containing limit to stay stable and the same.[44] This stability allows us to define the existence of things that inhabit place. By contrast, space, which is characterized by infinite extension, provides no such stability, and the things within it can only be defined in the meaningless mathematical terms of geometrical location. Aristotle's ideas about place remind Clare of Kitty, who defined her entire existence in terms of her place in Jamaica: "Her point of reference—the place which explained the world to her—would always be her island" (*NTTH*, 68).

Understood in terms of Aristotle's ideas about place, the nation becomes an anchoring frame that provides stability and defines an individual's meaningful conduct. Jamaica's connection to precolonial temporalities provided these stabilizing limits. But these temporalities have been obscured by the temporality of capital, which transforms every place into the abstract space of capital accumulation. Cliff's novels thus undertake a radical postcolonial geography that seeks to destroy the worldless space-time of capital and remake Jamaica as place by reinspiriting it with temporalities that precede and exceed capital. Kitty's final letter exhorts Clare to serve her people: "'I hope someday you make something of yourself, and someday help your people.' A reminder, daughter—never forget who your people are. Your responsibilities lie beyond me, beyond yourself. There is a space between who you are and who you will become. Fill it" (NTTH, 103). Revolutionary action can elevate these forgotten temporalities to a higher form appropriate to the postcolonial present and actualize them as a place of belonging, a world. As Harry/Harriet, another revolutionary model for emulation, tells Clare, Jamaica remains chained to the heteronomous time of colonial capital and must be brought into the present by action. "We *are* of the past here. So much of the past that we punish people by flogging them with cat-o'-nine-tails. We expect people to live on cornmeal and dried fish, which was the diet of the slaves. We name hotels Plantation Inn and Sans Souci. . . . A peculiar past. For we have taken the master's past as our own. That is the danger. . . . Come home. . . . Could help bring us into the present. . . . Jamaica's children have to work to make her change" (NTTH, 127).

Clare's commitment to responsible action begins with her renunciation of England as the revered mother-country of her father's ancestors for the land of her birth mother. Chapter 7, a eulogy that celebrates Jamaica as a magnanimous warrior mother with magical powers to alleviate the suffering of slaves and to battle the colonizer, ends with a question to the implied Jamaican reader that is also an implicit injunction for consciousness-raising as the prelude to political action: "Can you remember how to love her?" (NTTH, 164). This injunction transforms Aristotle's static concept of place into a dynamic account where subjects constitute their place through daily practices and committed political activity instead of being passively defined by a motionless container. On returning to her grandmother's plantation, Clare bathes in the river and undergoes a rebaptism that reconnects her to the temporality of the Arawak Indians (NTTH, 172). Her symbolic purification from colonial ideology signals the closing of the epistemic gap between her younger self and the omniscient narrator. Henceforth, her actions will be driven by her memory of her mother's "passion of place. Her sense of the people. Here is her; leave it at that" (NTTH, 174).

This celebration of the maternal homeland is an ontopology (Derrida), an ontology of present place, where the presence of place is hypostatized through political action as the matricial ground of existence.[45] Nationalist ontopology is not an ideological mystification or recidivist nostalgia for an archaic past. It is continually generated and affirmed by self-conscious universalistic political action in which the revolutionary subject recognizes herself in the history of the nation, especially its struggle against colonial forces. As part of the struggle for Jamaican autonomy, Clare's *Bildung* must be positioned within a larger world-historical struggle against neocolonial capital. In her interview with the guerilla leaders, she observes that in the two years since her return, she has reinscribed herself into place by educating herself about precolonial Jamaican history, Arawak archeology, and local myths and folklore. "I am in it. It involves me . . . the practice of rubbing lime and salt in the backs of whipped slaves . . . the ambush tactics of Cudjoe . . . cruelty . . . resistance . . . grace. I'm not outside this history—it's a matter of recognition . . . memory . . . emotion" (*NTTH*, 194). Her interviewer instructs her to further revolutionize her consciousness by connecting colonialism to the broader system of contemporary neocolonial exploitation: "Do you not realize that this is but one example of contamination from the outside? And you are but one infected nation? . . . Perhaps you will go further. . . . You speak of the knowledge of resistance . . . the loss of this knowledge. I ask you to think of Bishop. Rodney. Fanon. Lumumba. Malcolm. First. Luthuli. Garvey. Mxembe. Marley. Moloise. Think of those who are gone—and ask yourself how, why . . . ?" (*NTTH*, 195–96)

Outside Capital Time

I have argued elsewhere that the early nationalist bildungsroman of Asia and Africa portrayed the development of a revolutionary consciousness to stimulate a corresponding transformation in its implied reader's consciousness.[46] Continuing that tradition, Cliff's Clare Savage novels expose the Eurocentric developmental hierarchy expressed in colonial world literature and accounts of universal world-historical progress and use that critical energy to fuel Jamaica's struggle to become an autonomous agent in world history. This is the political project of anticolonial revolution: the destruction of a world where the colonized cannot develop as autonomous subjects, and the creation of a new common world where they can be at home. However, as a *late* nationalist bildungsroman, Cliff's diptych foregrounds the failure to achieve freedom after postcolonial independence and acknowledges the tenaciousness of capital's abstract space and time. Consciousness-raising through cognitive mapping alone is inadequate to transform the world. Postcolonial literature must reinscribe geography and remake abstract space into place. The novels are therefore world literature in the normative sense. As representational space, they are a part of the production of social space. Moreover, Clare exemplifies emergence in Arendt's sense: the initiation of a newness that disrupts the circuit of (neo)colonial capitalist calculations. By remembering and reappropriating a past free of colonial influence that consists of temporalities outside the time of capital, she opens a new teleological time and projects a free future for the Jamaican people.

Insofar as the temporalities that disrupt capital time are embodied by spiritual and material practices, Cliff subscribes to a spiritualist-materialist conception of literature's worldliness. Literature's power to transfigure the world is primarily that of the imagination to shape the world through images. Secondary criticism has confirmed this by describing the diptych as an example of Caribbean literature that seeks to reveal a new world with "an alternative value system" that, contrary to the plantation economy, regards Caribbean people as persons of value instead of degraded instruments for profit.[47] Another critic describes Cliff's novels as actualizing "a psychic or social space" outside the Manichean world of colonialism, "a geo-political space of memory," "an alternative 'reality' . . . not an imaginary nor an imitation universe but a new kind of reality."[48] But No Telephone to Heaven, I suggest, also puts into question whether the opening of another world in capitalist globalization can be grounded in the imagination's formative power and its processes of Bildung. In so doing, it gestures toward inhuman temporalization as a force of worlding.

Clare's interview with the guerilla leaders is an allegory of the novel's own impossibility as the revolutionary Bildung of humanity. Clare expresses her political commitment in a wish: to give back to the children of Jamaica, a symbol of the future, the imagination's power to create hope through images. But she cannot mention the word "hope." The train of questioning compels her to doubt the imagination's efficacy and withdraw the word: "Look, I want to restore something to these children. . . . And of course you are right: what good is imagination . . . whatever the imagery available to it . . . to a dying child? A child damaged beyond imagining? I . . . it seems I contradict myself" (NTTH, 196).

On the one hand, these novels are literary examples of the power of images to stimulate revolutionary action. Revolution is the process of actualization that raises the imagination's hopeful images to the level of ontological truth. These novels would be part of this material process of actualization where a people reappropriates what has been alienated from it by the (neo)colonial system and creates a new world. On the other hand, the final chapter of No Telephone to Heaven, suggestively titled "Film Noir," underscores the imagination's limits by portraying the global culture industry's prodigious capacity to undermine the efforts of postcolonial world literature by recolonizing the imagination.

Harry/Harriet ominously portends this ending in her observation that "our homeland is turned to stage set too much" (NTTH, 121).

In the last chapter of *No Telephone to Heaven*, a new Jamaican world is stifled at the very moment of its emergence. The memory of Jamaican anticolonial resistance is desecrated by the making of a Hollywood film about Nanny. The historical Maroon leader is replaced by a Hollywood fantasy in leather breeches and a silk shirt played by an African-American actress. The guerillas attack the film set in a symbolic gesture of revolution. This event is framed by a thematization of the extent of Jamaica's degradation by global capital. A fictive excerpt from the *New York Times* sells Jamaica as a beautiful film location, noting the exact features promoted by global tourist capital: the presence of colonial architecture from the British and Spanish eras, the similarity of the landscape to the African plain, and the fact that "it also has a racially mixed population of many hues and ethnic distinctions, which . . . includes a number of people willing to serve as extras" (NTTH, 200). The narrative then cuts to a scene where two film people scouting for locations crudely discuss the prostitution of Jamaica. "You can't beat the prices. And, besides, they need the money . . . real bad. They'll shape up . . . they have to. They're trapped. All tied up by the IMF" (NTTH, 201). As an indication of the state's betrayal of the people to global capital, even the army and its helicopters are available for rent at attractive prices. Indeed, foreigners regard self-prostitution as a national Jamaican trait. "Jamaicans will do anything for a buck . . . Look around you . . . the hotels . . . the private resorts where you have to get an invite . . . the reggae festivals for white kids. . . . The cancer spas for rich people. Everyone from the hookers to the prime minister, babe. These people are used to selling themselves. I don't think they know from revolution" (NTTH, 202).

People can only sell themselves and a state can only sell its people if the world is viewed through the quantitative calculations of capital and life runs according to the temporality of capital accumulation. But the promise of growth is actually an IMF trap. Inflows of foreign tourism capital are touted as the optimal basis for national development, but they result in underdevelopment because they subordinate the Jamaican economy to global capitalism. The film about Nanny takes the time of capital to the extreme. It ironically commodifies Jamaica's culture of anticolonial resistance for foreign consumption to profit neocolonial capital. The irony is all the more bitter because we see all remaining symbols of anticolonial resistance and surviving precolonial temporalities appropriated into the seemingly endless folds of capital time. At the novel's beginning, Christopher, a poor orphan from the slums, had killed his wealthy Creole employers in a gesture of class justice. Now a deranged homeless man, he has been scouted as a film extra to play the part of Sasabonsam, the forest monster who symbolizes resistance to the temporality of colonial sugar capital. Sasabonsam's actions in the film role are to sit in a tree and howl.

The film shoot turns out to be an ambush arranged by the Jamaican state. The intention of the popular nation, embodied by the guerillas, to begin a new teleological time is frustrated by the state's betrayal: "This was not meant to happen; it had not been in the plan" (NTTH, 207). Confused by Christopher's howling and the sudden turning off of the camera lights, they and the forest monster are killed by fire from Jamaican army helicopters. "Some returned the fire—but were no match for the invaders. Some could not—surprise and sadness held them still. There was no time left to them" (NTTH, 208). The resistance fighters are indeed transported beyond the homogeneous empty time of capital. In death, they are literally outside time.

There is, however, a redemptive dimension to Clare's death. She has achieved repatriation by becoming part of her native soil, the substrate from which an alternative future, another world can come. The novel ends with an onomatopoeic sequence that breaks the time of the narrative. The reader "hears" sounds of the whipping and crying of slaves before Clare loses her consciousness and sense of meaningful language. This is followed by various sounds that could be bird and animal cries.

> She remembered language.
> Then   it was gone.
>
> Cutacoo, cutacoo, cutacoo
> coo, cu, cu, coo
> coo, cu, cu, coo
> piju, piju, piju
> cuk, cuk, cuk, cuk
> tuc-tuc-tuc-tuc-tuc
>
> Day broke. (NTTH, 208)

Clare's tragic fate has the resoluteness of heroic action. According to Cliff's authorial interpretation, the final scene is a reunification with precolonial temporalities from which one can project a future that will be free of the colonial past and the neocolonial present: "She ends her life literally burned into the landscape of Jamaica. . . . While essentially tragic, I see it and planned it as an ending that completes the circle, actually triangle, of the character's life. In her death she has achieved complete identification with her homeland. Soon enough she will be indistinguishable from the ground. Her bones will turn to potash as did her ancestors' bones. . . . The forest will grow from her."[49]

Clare's end is certainly more hopeful than the "brutal and messy" death of her counterpart in V. S. Naipaul's *A Way in the World*.[50] Blair, a Trinidadian black revolutionary, is murdered in an African country for offending its political regime. Naipaul does not dramatize the moment of death. The narrator prosaically reports how the corpse was found. There is no unification with his native soil. Blair dies in Africa, his body abandoned on mulch in a plantation built from foreign capital. The narrator imagines the moment of death as a confirmation of the futility of revolutionary ideals. In the final moment of his existence, Blair poses a rhetorical question: "Does this betrayal mock your life?"[51] Although his ghostly voice answers in the negative, it is clearly a denegation (*Verneinung*) in the Freudian sense.

A closer reading indicates, however, that Clare's repatriation is fundamentally aporetic. Onomatopoeia is not exempt from the arbitrariness of the linguistic sign. The sounds following her loss of sentience could well be that of bullet fire from the helicopters. There is a *mise-en-abîme* where the temporality of the Jamaican landscape is enveloped by the rhythms of the Hollywood culture industry. Is the film shoot part of the calculations of the neocolonial state to ambush the guerillas? Or is the real massacre of the revolutionaries a simulation that is part of the culture industry's calculations? It is possible that the deaths have been recorded as part of a filmic retelling of the suppression of resistance in Jamaican colonial history in order to enhance the film's realism, to give it more "atmosphere" with the help of real army helicopters, the firing of real bullets, and the real deaths of revolutionaries. Consequently, at the end of the novel, when the teleological time of revolutionary struggle should have fully unfolded, the narrative becomes split into two. The omniscient narrator generally relates things from Clare's viewpoint. But she also occasionally assumes the perspective of capital and the neocolonial state. It is unclear which emerges victorious from this struggle between narrative viewpoints and temporalities. Far from exposing the falsity of the Hollywood story of Nanny and undermining the fantastic representations of a paradisiacal landscape that tether Jamaica to the temporality of sugar and tourist capital, the deaths of the guerillas are incorporated by them. Hence, the ending can also dramatize the snuffing out of heterotemporality. The tearing of time is here the death of revolutionary consciousness. This is indicated graphically by the gap or spacing in the text in the sentence fragment, "Then   it was gone."

And yet, the same sentence fragment also suggests a certain survival. The temporal adverb, "then," the spacing, and the clause that describes Clare's loss of language and her passing from conscious existence also indicate the persistence of time after the death of any given human individual. This persistence is expressed in a break in the narrative, which transitions from being told from Clare's experience of her gradual loss of consciousness to the omniscient narrator's account of what ensues after her death, namely, the persistence of the world in its diurnal cycle with the sounds of the landscape and the breaking of the day. Cliff puts it this way in her authorial reading: "She is also enveloped in the deep green of the hills and the delicate intricacy of birdsong. Her death occurs at the moment she relinquishes human language, when the cries of birds are no longer translated by her into signifiers of human history . . . but become pure sound, the same music heard by the Arawak and Carib."[52] Indeed, the gap in the sentence fragment recalls the gap between the two stanzas of Wordsworth's "A Slumber Did My Spirit Seal," a poem that also performs the persistence of time in the face of human finitude. Wordsworth is ambivalent about geological time: in death, the only force the female subject has is that of the earth.

> No motion has she now, no force
> She neither hears nor sees
> Roll'd round in earth's diurnal course
> With rocks, and stones, and trees![53]

Cliff, on the other hand, sees geological time as transfigurative. Language is the threshold of a meaningful world, and for each human individual, the world ends with the loss of language at the moment of death. But even if human life as such has come to an end, the world remains and survives because it is held together by other temporalities that constitute place as an envelope that exceeds and shelters us from the denudation of the abstract time of capital. This persistence is epitomized by the earth's orbit around the sun and diurnal effects that express the landscape's ongoing life such as the bird and animal cries. The landscape's vital temporality in turn secures precolonial Indian and African heterotemporalities.

However, Cliff's geo-graphy (literally, the writing of the earth) of the world also suggests the limits of a spiritualist-materialist teleology of the world by pointing to a more radical temporalization of the world. The earth's diurnal course is merely a way that human consciousness reckons with time. Its persistence is dependent on there being time. Hence, what holds the world together is the force that gives time. But this force is inhuman, escapes calculation, and cannot be appropriated by teleological time. In addition to designating the end of human consciousness, the textual blankness in the novel's final passage also indicates time's incalculability. This implies both the irreducible persistence of a world, despite any efforts of calculative reason to destroy it, *and* the impossibility of any teleological guarantee that we can actualize a given normative vision of the world by our actions. The end of Cliff's diptych presents us with the following aporia: When one exits the homogeneous empty time of capital, is this break in time the opening of another temporality or simply the end of the time of a finite human life or human project? What exceeds the temporality of capital is the inhuman force that gives time. This force enables the interruption of capital by heterotemporality. But because of its incalculability, it does not always harmonize with teleological time. In Clare's case, we see the rupturing of the abstract time of capital *and* the frustration of revolutionary teleological time. Heterotemporality is undone by being opened up to contamination and capture by the time of capital. But without this risk of undecidability, there can be no opening of a new world and a new future. There is immanent hope, but without a guaranteed rational practical outcome.

Cliff's novels are concerned with the dehumanizing and world-destroying time of colonial slavery and neocolonial exploitation. However, capital time also operates in actions and processes that purportedly create a more humane world. These humanizing forms of world-making have become widespread today as solutions to the problems of contemporary globalization because of the receding of anticolonial revolution as an effective political alternative. The next two chapters examine two examples of postcolonial world literature that are concerned with the erosion of worlds in the postcolonial South by global flows of funds for environmental preservation and humanitarian aid. How can peoples emerge and what kinds of action can maintain and open a world in such scenarios? What is at stake is a worldly ethics, the ethos of inhabiting and creating a world that is constantly being undermined by global processes, and the fundamental role of storytelling as it conjures with the inhuman force of temporalization that worlds a world.

CHAPTER 9

World Heritage Preservation and
the Expropriation of Subaltern Worlds

After visiting the Dandakaranya refugees in central India and seeing that they were in no position to make an international protest about the Marichjhapi massacre, I sought to put it on record. However, the United Nations Commission on Human Rights in Geneva told me they were flooded with thousands of complaints, indicating nothing would be done. Amnesty International did not respond to my letters, and Human Rights Watch responded with form letters that gave no indication the material had been read.
—ROSS MALLICK

Amitav Ghosh has achieved notable recognition in the world republic of letters. His writings have been translated into numerous languages and honored with numerous prestigious international literary awards.[1] Ghosh's works are also examples of world literature in a normative sense. He sees himself as updating Goethe's ethos of worldly plurality to reflect the multilingual realities of the postcolonial world. As he puts it, with some transcultural hubris,

> I feel writers like me . . . bilingual Arabs and so on . . . in today's world, we are the "universal" people because we have access to wider modes of experience, modes of thought and modes of culture. Westerners are contained within a sense of being which is very particular. . . . People like us . . . have had access to that universality. . . . [People read us because] they recognize that we offer to the reader . . . a much greater dimension of experience; a much greater dimension of history; a much greater vision of the plurality of the world. . . . Indian fiction has found so many readers around the world . . . because our world is richer in the end.[2]

The Hungry Tide is world literature in its most robust normative meaning because it seeks to reworld the world of the subaltern inhabitants of the

Sundarban islands, which is threatened with destruction by the alignment of global flows of funds for world heritage preservation, environmental and ecological movements, global capitalist interests, and economic development. The Sundarbans (literally, "beautiful forest" in Bengali) is a large area of mangrove forest located at the southern end of Bangladesh and in the Indian state of West Bengal. As the site where fresh water from the Himalayas and salt water from Indian Ocean tides meet, it has a complex environmental landscape with many endangered species and rare plants. For the Western world, the Sundarbans is the largest natural habitat of the Bengal tiger. It attained global prominence with the launch of Project Tiger in 1973, a project largely funded by global environmental organizations, such as the World Wildlife Fund, that sought to foster a viable population of Bengal tigers in their natural habitats by preserving the biological ecosystem. It has been a UNESCO World Heritage Site since 1987 and was designated a UNESCO International Biosphere Reserve in 2001.[3]

The Indian Sundarbans has an equally complex cultural landscape that is largely unknown to the outside world and obscure to many Indians outside West Bengal. With a population of around 4 million, it is a place of settlement for different waves of migrants and refugees. These population transfers are determined by the history of the South Asian partition and post-Independence government policies of economic development in West Bengal. The area is as much shaped by linguistic flows (Bengali, Arabic, Hindi, and English) as its unique ecosystem is shaped by the ebb and flow of sea and river. The Sundarbans is the poorest region of West Bengal. The majority of its village inhabitants, especially those in the islands at the margins of the mangrove forests, come from the lowest socioeconomic class, social caste, and tribal groups. Their world is being destroyed by the modernizing projects of the West Bengal state government and the initiatives of international wildlife preservation NGOs. Many have been forcibly relocated in the name of protecting tigers. The livelihood of those who remain is increasingly constrained by forest reserve laws and environmental damage from commercialized prawn seed aquaculture. Their lives are at risk from tiger and crocodile attacks and flood inundation caused by soil erosion from the prawn industry. The Morichjhãpi massacre of 1979 mentioned in this chapter's epigraph is a historical incident in which the ongoing disregard for subaltern lives reached its most violent extreme. Refugees who had fled persecution in East Bengal and settled in the island of Morichjhãpi were forcibly evicted by the West Bengal state for illegally occupying forest reserve land, ending in the displacement of 4,128 families.

Ghosh's novel seeks to give visibility to this subaltern world, to make the larger world aware of the perilousness of daily subaltern life. As Nirmal, a central character who bears witness to the Morichjhãpi massacre, puts it, "perhaps I can make sure at least that what happened here leaves some trace, some hold upon the memory of the world."[4] The novel seeks to disclose this disappearing world in the light of public phenomenality so that it can be retained in collective memory and be part of a shared world.[5] It is hoped that global public recognition will in turn give the subalterns of the Sundarbans light and voice and enable them to renew their world.

The Hungry Tide tries to make a case for the superiority of literature as a modality of worlding over other forms of discursive knowledge. It combines the phenomenological concept of worlding with a neo-Marxist mapping of the Sundarbans's place within the Indian nation and India's position in the global capitalist system. The subaltern's plight is both a universal problem and a problem specific to the Indian subcontinent. Global capitalist accumulation excludes the subaltern from belonging to a common world by denying her visibility. The alignment of colonial legacies and class and caste structures and tribal divisions peculiar to India further obscures the subaltern's phenomenality. Ghosh holds the educated cosmopolitan urban middle class in India responsible. He suggests that the dissemination of stories about divine forces that give meaning to the subaltern's ongoing struggle with the landscape and bind the subaltern world into a whole are fundamental to its reworlding. The novel dramatizes a solution whereby its middle-class protagonists become radically transformed and are moved to responsible action by their contact with subaltern cultural practices and religious rituals. One of the central issues at stake is the efficacy of stories that express subaltern religious and cultural beliefs to continually constitute and maintain a world. As I will argue, against the grain of its authorial intention, the novel suggests that the worlding power of these stories is grounded in a more fundamental force of worlding that cannot be appropriated into a divine figure.

The Memory of the World: Literature as a Power of Reworlding

The task of making the subaltern world visible rests largely on three main characters: Nirmal and Kanai, who are from the Bengali upper caste and middle class, and Piya, a well-meaning but naïve and idealistic American cetologist of South Asian descent. Nirmal is a retired Brahmin schoolteacher who ran the school at Lusibari, one of the most southern inhabited islands of the tide country. The island is the site of the Badabon Development Trust, a welfare organization and cooperative union for women providing medical, paralegal, and agricultural services for its members. It was founded by Nirmal's wife, Nilima, who comes from an affluent Kolkata family devoted to public service. Nirmal was a Marxist intellectual and a promising writer in his youth. The reader is given access to the Sundarbans and, later, the situation at Morichjhāpi through his notebook.[6] The novel suggests that the notebook is one of the very few true witness accounts of the massacre, if not the only remaining one. Written on Morichjhāpi on the massacre's eve, the diary is directly addressed to Kanai, Nilima's nephew, in the style of an extended letter. Kanai is a cosmopolitan bourgeois from New Delhi, a professional translator who runs a thriving translation business that services transnational companies. But the notebook was misplaced and has only recently been found when the novel begins, twenty-three years after the massacre. When Kanai visits the Sundarbans to collect the notebook, he meets Piya, who has come to the Sundarbans to study the patterns of the Irrawaddy dolphins. Fokir, a subaltern fisherman whose mother, Kusum, was killed in the massacre, takes her on his boat to track dolphin routes.

The connection between Ghosh's novel and the concept of worlding comes from Nirmal's obsession with Rilke's *Duino Elegies*.

> *I have nothing with me here except this notebook, one ballpoint pen, one pencil and my copies of Rilke's Duino Elegies, in Bangla and English translation. . . .*
>
> *I am afraid because I know that after the storm passes, the events that have preceded its coming will be forgotten. No one knows better than I how skillful the tide country is in silting over its past.*
>
> *There is nothing I can do to stop what lies ahead. But I was once a writer; perhaps I can make sure at least that what happened here leaves some trace, some hold upon the memory of the world. The thought of this, along with the fear that preceded it, has made it possible for me to do what I have not been able to do for the last thirty years—to put my pen to paper again.*
>
> *I do not know how much time I have; maybe not much more than the course of this day. In this time, I will try to write what I can in the hope that somehow these words will find their way to you. You will be asking, why me? All I need to say for the time being is that this is not my story. It concerns, rather, the only friend you made when you were here in Lusibari: Kusum. If not for my sake, then for hers, read on. (HT, 58–59)[7]*

Rilke's lexis and imagery have completely taken over Nirmal's thoughts. They shape his experiences and interpretation of what he sees and records. Hence, the reader's access to the Sundarbans requires stepping across the framing threshold of Rilke's verse.

Nirmal writes out of fear of the contingency of human existence. He contrasts the leveling force of human violence with that of nature. Government-sanctioned violence erases the achievements of the refugees whose struggles have made Morichjhāpi a meaningful world. This effacement may appear similar to the natural denudation of marks of human habitation by the tide country's silt, which threatens to render memory and history impossible. However, the insular landscape's disappearance when submerged by the flooding tide is part of an endlessly recurring pattern. The islands reappear with the ebbing of the river waters. Hence human settlement is possible, even though it is precarious. The refugees successfully created a world through cultural practices and religious beliefs that helped them to make sense of their constant vulnerability and to establish meaningful relations with the animal species of their hostile environment. In contrast, the massacre is part of a violent design to obliterate their physical presence and wipe out all traces of their existence in the media and historical archives so that no sign will remain that a world once existed on the island.

The novel self-reflexively alludes to its vocation as world literature to preserve a world for posterity in portraying the writing of Nirmal's notebook. Resonating with Arendt's views on the immortalizing power of art, literature's purpose is to ameliorate the evanescence of human life by making a mark in collective memory. Nirmal does not write out of the self-aggrandizing wish to be remembered but in response to the suffering of the subaltern other, Kusum, a displaced young widow born in tide country who has returned among a wave of refugees. Nirmal intends the notebook to be world literature in the narrow sense: an archive of subaltern suffering to be circulated to a global reading public. He entrusts Kanai with the notebook because he "presented a slender connection to the ears of an unheeding world" (HT, 100). Ghosh's novel, however, is world literature in the strongest normative sense. He hopes that The Hungry Tide will aid in reworlding the Sundarbans.

The transposition of Rilke to gloss the perils of the Sundarbans landscape is part of this reworlding. The most important terms in this transposition are "transformation [Verwandlung]" and "translated world [der gedeuteten Welt, literally, 'interpreted world']."[8] "Transformation" refers to the landscape's condition of continual change, its constant process of mutation. Kanai characterizes the landscape's endless transformation as "its epic mutability" (HT, 128). In the episode titled "Transformation," Nirmal visits Garjontola, an uninhabited island, to observe a puja (ritual worship) of a guardian deity, Bon Bibi, the lady of the forest. The forest is the realm of Dokkhin Rai, the demon king. According to subaltern beliefs, Bon Bibi protects humans who venture there. In a metafictional moment, Nirmal compares the landscape to a book that is amenable to multiple interpretations.

> *A landscape is not unlike a book. . . . People open the book according to their taste and training, their memories and desires. . . .*
>
> *To me, a townsman, the tide country's jungle was an emptiness, a place where time stood still. I saw now that this was an illusion, that exactly the opposite was true. What was happening here . . . was that the wheel of time was spinning too fast to be seen. In other places it took decades, even centuries, for a river to change course; it took an epoch for an island to appear. But here in tide country, transformation is the rule of life: rivers stray from week to week, and islands are made and unmade in days. In other places forests take centuries, even millennia, to regenerate; but mangroves can recolonize a denuded island in ten to fifteen years. Could it be that the very rhythms of the earth were quickened here so that they unfolded at an accelerated pace? . . .*
>
> *Nothing escapes the maw of tides; everything is ground to fine silt, becomes something else.*
>
> *It was as if the whole tide country were speaking in the voice of the Poet: "life is lived in transformation."* (HT, 186–87)

Initially, Nirmal distinguishes Rilke's idea of transformation as the radical contingency of human existence from the subaltern religious understanding of the landscape. Echoing Arendt's view of the destructiveness of natural processes, he sees the tide as a force that unmakes what humans have fabricated. The speedy rhythms of natural transformation exemplify the leveling force of finitude. The eternal cycle of natural time devours the world of human achievements, which is governed by historical time. Hence, the Sundarbans landscape is a hostile, menacing process of unworlding that denudes all traces of worldly existence. It is a place of indistinction and incalculability, even malevolence, where human intentions are frustrated by the constant undoing of demarcations between land and water, sea and river. It creates new land, but of swamps and mangroves that cannot support human life. *"At no moment can human beings have any doubt of the terrain's hostility to their presence, of its cunning and resourcefulness, of its determination to destroy or expel them. Every year, dozens of people perish in the embrace of that dense foliage, killed by tigers, snakes and crocodiles. There is no prettiness here to invite the stranger in"* (HT, 7).

Because human existence is inevitably at odds with the natural rhythms of the earth, we can never be at home in the natural world. Nirmal explains this by quoting another passage from Rilke. "*Neither angels nor men will hear us, and as for the animals, they won't hear us either. . . . Because the animals*

already know by instinct
we're not comfortably at home
in our translated world [der gedeuteten Welt]." (*HT*, 172)[9]

Animals have instinctive access to natural processes because as part of the natural world, they exist in an immediate unity with their environment. In contrast, we humans lack secure awareness of nature's patterns and need to interpret nature in our ongoing struggle to make it a habitable world. Hence, we live in a translated or interpreted world, where meaning is artificially imparted by the mediation of human representations. The dangerous Sundarbans environment is a constant reminder of the condition of earthly inhospitality to which we have been abandoned and from which there is no salvation. Transformation is the general predicate of this condition.

The line "life is lived in transformation" comes from the Seventh Elegy, in a stanza where the poetic voice consoles his beloved. The instability of modern constructions, which are transient and imminently replaceable, is an instance of the radical transformation of the external world. However, the beloved is assured that a permanent world can exist, in the invisible inner realm of the imagination that recreates meaningful structures of religious faith.

Love, the World exists nowhere but within.
Our life is lived in transformation. And,
diminishing,
the outer world vanishes. Where a sturdy house
once stood, a fantastic structure rises into view, as much
at ease among the conceivable as if it still stood in the brain.
. . . .
                                               Now we're saving
these extravagances of the heart secretly. Yes, even where
one single thing that was prayed to, served, and knelt to
once, survives, it endures just as it is, in the invisible.
Many don't see it anymore and miss the chance to build it
                                               again,
complete with pillars and statues, greater than ever, *within*.[10]

The elegy refers to the mutability of the artificial built environment and the intrinsic meaninglessness of human existence in the secular God-abandoned modern world. As Arendt notes in her exegesis of the *Duino Elegies*, transience is the movement of passing away that is no longer derived from an immortal being. It is "constant passing and drifting away; it is not an index of the future, but life itself as it is constantly using itself up and living itself out."[11] As a Marxist atheist who subscribes to the view of nature as meaningless raw material that we must collectively master to fulfill human ends, Nirmal regards the unstable world of modernity as continuous with nature's destruction of the meaningful permanence of worldly achievements. Both are cases of the insecure and unstable human condition, whether we explain this in terms of human alienation or the radical mutability of a godless world.

As I will argue, the novel suggests that this despairing view of hostile nature is inadequate. It comes from the limited perspective of a Western-educated middle-class subject who cannot envision the earth as a meaningful realm governed by divine forces. The novel disrupts and displaces this godless world by supplementing it with a subaltern world in which human beings coexist and continually engage with the nonhuman agency of divine and natural forces in their daily survival through religious rituals and folk practices. By the novel's end, nature's agency is no longer viewed as malevolent but is refigured as a moral economy that helps the subaltern survive the unworlding of global capitalist modernization.

How Environmentalism Unworlds: Conflict of Narratives and Images of Nature

It is counterintuitive to characterize the preservation of the natural environment for world heritage as a form of unworlding. However, mainstream environmental movements are embedded in the system of global capitalist accumulation, as evidenced by the development of ecotourism as a source of foreign exchange. Instead of offering a viable solution to late capitalist environmental degradation, they presuppose a world that has already been unworlded by capitalist globalization. Ghosh has spoken passionately about environmental decline caused by prawn fishers and the dangers of ecological disaster in the Sundarbans posed by global warming and projected business plans to transform the area into an ecotourism complex. Most important, he has drawn attention to the inhumane logic of Project Tiger by pointing to a grotesque incident where freshwater wells were created for tigers while impoverished children were dying from a lack of drinking water.[12]

The Hungry Tide is a favored text of ecocriticism because it does not shy away from the critique of environmentalism.[13] Piya personifies the First World environmentalist conscience. Her ethos falls under the biocentric perspective of deep ecology. Three fundamental principles of deep ecology are relevant for present purposes. First, it replaces an anthropocentric view of the environment, where the natural universe is centered on human ends, with a biocentric view of the natural environment as something with intrinsic worth quite apart from its benefits to human posterity.[14] Second, it focuses on preserving pure wilderness and the restoration of degraded areas. Third, deep ecology views Eastern religious traditions as its *avant la lettre* precursors. As Ramachandra Guha notes, "deep ecology, it is suggested, was practiced . . . at a more popular level by 'primal' peoples in non-Western settings. . . . Religious traditions in other cultures are . . . dominantly if not exclusively 'biocentric' in their orientation. This coupling of (ancient) Eastern and (modern) ecological wisdom seemingly helps to consolidate the claim that deep ecology is a philosophy of universal significance."[15] Piya is a deep ecologist par excellence. She thinks that endangered species should be preserved in their natural habitats because "it was what was *intended* . . . by nature, by the earth, by the planet that keeps us all alive" (*HT*, 249). In the tiger-killing episode, she naïvely expects Fokir to stop the other villagers from attacking a trapped tiger because she regards him as "some kind of grass-roots ecologist" (*HT*, 245).

This Northern-centric view of nature as an intentional agent whose intelligent design of a biodiverse wilderness should be respected by environmental preservation movements is premised on an a priori effacement of the peoples who live in designated wilderness areas. Human settlers are viewed through a neo-Orientalist discourse of the noble savage: they are an almost indistinguishable part of the wilderness because of their instinctive attunement to the rhythms of natural processes.[16] Alternatively, one can view the natural wilderness as originally uninhabited and unmarked by human existence. The relationship between humans and nature would then be one of mutual hostility, and our survival and security would involve the despoliation of nature. It follows that preserving animal species in their natural habitats requires displacing human populations so that nature can be shielded from their corrupting touch.

There is a fundamental continuity between the determination of nature as inhospitable to human endeavors in Nirmal's poetic descriptions and Piya's biocentrism. Both presuppose the effacement of the human being. Either nature is seen as originally devoid of any relation to human existence because it precedes human settlement, or local subalterns are seen as an intrinsic part of nature and therefore without an autonomous distinctive identity that would enable a *relation* of coexistence with nature as the basis of rights to resources. Hence, the biocentric idea of nature as "wilderness" is ironically complicit with the international legal fiction of *terra nullius* that European colonial powers used to dispossess native inhabitants so that they could appropriate land and control its natural resources, an instance of what Marx called primitive accumulation. As Ghosh points out, indigenous tribal peoples had rights over forest resources that were taken away by the British colonizers in the 1860s. This expropriation continues in postcolonial India. People who live off the forest are labeled as poachers and victimized by Forest Department officials.[17]

Ecotourism is the alignment of the biocentric idea of natural wilderness with postcolonial economic development projects and global capitalism. It contributes to the destruction of the subaltern world because it leads to the displacement of subalterns who inhabit designated wilderness areas, without financial compensation, and their resettlement in another community. Commenting on Project Tiger, Guha points out that

> because India is a long-settled and densely populated country in which agrarian populations have a finely balanced relationship with nature, the setting aside of wilderness areas has resulted in a direct transfer of resources from the poor to the rich. Thus Project Tiger, a network of parks hailed by the international community as an outstanding success, puts the interests of the tiger ahead of those of poor peasants living in and around the reserve. The designation of tiger reserves was made possible only by the physical displacement of existing villages and their inhabitants; their management requires the continuing exclusion of peasants and livestock. . . . In no case have the needs of the local population been taken into account, and as in many parts of Africa, the designated wildlands are managed primarily for the benefit of rich tourists. . . .
>
> Deep ecology provides, perhaps, unwittingly, a justification for the continuation of such narrow and inequitable conservation practices under a newly acquired radical guise.[18]

Contrary to the view that it lets animals live in their natural habitats, preservation involves the artificial organization of a designated nature reserve for the sake of human beings. The idea of an unspoiled wilderness underwriting Northern environmental organizations such as the Sierra Club and Friends of the Earth is an ideological reflection of Northern postindustrial consumer societies, where the experience of leisure is an important avenue of escape from the urban work-world.[19] Hence, wilderness preservation is a function of the commodification of nature as an object for human enjoyment and consumption. Northern-style environmentalism is a cosmetic bandage for a world that has already been unworlded by industrial capitalism.

The expropriation of the subaltern world is symbolic in the primary instance. It involves narratives and images that represent the area as an uninhabited wilderness rich in interesting flora and fauna. This investment of nature creates a representational space (in Lefebvre's sense) in which nature is symbolically expropriated from human habitation. This representational space is then used to justify the legal exclusion of marginalized peoples. The Indian government can expropriate that space at the behest of environmental groups who represent a cosmopolitan humanity seeking to preserve the world's natural heritage.[20]

As a result of an alignment of Northern environmentalism, Indian political history and local relations of inequality and socioeconomic exploitation, global funds from environmental preservation movements became a contributing cause to the tragic massacre of refugees at Morichjhāpi. The influx of Hindu refugees from East to West Bengal dates back to the partition of British India.[21] The majority of these refugees are peasants, laborers, and fishers from low-status social groups, the "depressed" or "Scheduled" castes. The West Bengal government saw the refugees as a threat to the fragile stability of postpartition society and directed them to areas outside West Bengal, resettling them in refugee colonies on empty tracts of poor-quality land shunned by locals. Among these resettlement schemes, the Dandakaranya Project of 1958 was the most spectacular failure. Augmented by more recent migrants from Bangladesh, the East Bengal refugees who were sent there deserted in droves in the 1970s to return to West Bengal.[22] Starting in May 1978, around thirty thousand escapees arrived at Morichjhāpi and established a settlement there. In *The Hungry Tide*, Kusum joins this wave of migration.[23]

Morichjhāpi is part of the designated Reserve Forest, and the refugees defied government directions concerning resettlement. In the first half of 1979, the Communist government of West Bengal began to remove them for violating the Forest Act. Numerous acts of violence were committed against the refugees, including teargassing the community, razing their huts and destroying their fisheries and wells, and depriving them of food and water. Boats attempting to cross the river to obtain sustenance were scuttled, leading to deaths by drowning. "With their food and water supplies cut off or destroyed, the refugees were forced to eat wild grass and drink from improvised wells. . . . In all thirty-six refugees were killed by police firing, forty-three died of starvation as a result of the blockade, twenty-nine by disease and 128 from drowning when their boats were scuttled by the police. . . . [After the operation for forcible evacuation of May 14–16] several hundred men, women, and children were believed to have been killed by the police in the operation and their bodies dumped in the river to be washed out by the tide."[24]

Because their interests intersect with those of business enterprises and local elites, there is an irresolvable contradiction between transnational environmental movements and the rights of subalterns whose survival is directly impacted by ecological projects. The denial of the possibility that Morichjhãpi could have been inhabited by the environmentalist image of nature is an a priori dispossession of subalterns. Its obliteration of the meaningful relations to the natural environment found in subaltern religious and folk beliefs paves the way for the violation of subaltern rights. As Mallick notes,

> there are costs from environmental preservation to people who are displaced as a result or who lose opportunities for life improvements through denial of land access. In the case of Marichjhapi it was the poorest people who paid with their lives, while the benefits went to the animals, tourists, and tourist operators. Tourism, in requiring pristine environments, creates an incentive for big business and the state to set aside areas that might otherwise be used by poor people for subsistence. While this may generate economic benefits, they rarely are realized by the people being displaced and certainly not by the Marichjhapi inhabitants.[25]

As the privileged synecdoche for the Sundarbans natural reserve, the tiger is an objective correlative for the Northern environmentalist image of nature. In her illuminating study of relations between tigers and human beings in the Sundarbans, Annu Jalais, an anthropologist who accompanied Ghosh on his travels, suggests that the tension between subaltern relations to nature and global conservation is a conflict between two different images of tigers.[26] "Transnational animal-centric charities and development agencies like the World Wildlife Fund (WWF) or the Asian Development Bank (ADB)" deploy the image of a cosmopolitan tiger as an endangered species threatened with extinction by "poaching, retaliatory killings and habitat loss" as an icon for "moral and ethical debates around wildlife" in their bids for funding.[27] As opposed to the local Sundarbans tiger, which coexists with subaltern islanders, the cosmopolitan tiger presupposes the effacement of subaltern inhabitants from the landscape because they are seen as originally absent from and encroaching on the tiger's natural habitat. Because this image is used to mobilize action for preservation, it leads to the displacement and disappearance of the islanders in a manner that is continuous with the discriminatory treatment of subalterns by national elites and the forces of global political economy.

The Hungry Tide counters Northern environmentalism's unworlding of the subaltern world by cognitively mapping the position of the Sundarbans in the fabric of global relations. The novel reveals to the wider world that the forest islands are not uninhabited wilderness but always already a world with a subaltern population, a place constituted and continually held together by a web of meaningful relationships that can be rightfully claimed by subalterns as *their* world. The legend of Bon Bibi is a worlding through storytelling and folk performance. It generates a world in which the local tiger coexists with humans as part of a moral economy.

The novel draws on Jalais's analysis of the Bon Bibi myth. Three fundamental principles of the myth's moral economy are important for present purposes. First, as exemplified by the tale of Dukhey, a young boy who is sold by his greedy village uncle to the demon king and subsequently saved by Bon Bibi, Bon Bibi protects the weak, oppressed, and underprivileged. Second, under Bon Bibi's influence, the forest is governed by an egalitarian ethos. Unlike the land, which is based on the selfish principle of ownership and sanctions division according to economic status and social hierarchy, the forest equalizes and unites because it belongs to and supports everyone.[28] As Jalais notes, "anyone can lay claim to Bonbibi. . . . For those who live in the 'down' islands and work in the forest she remains an 'egalitarian' entity accessible to all. Not only must her shelters be placed on public roadsides but they should be open, either without a door or, if there are doors, they should always be unlocked."[29] Because she is open to all in the generosity of her protection, Bon Bibi personifies openness itself. She is worldliness as such, a divine figure for worlding, because she brings all the inhabitants of the forests into relation and unites all humans into a meaningful whole. Third, the world created by her openness is not exclusively human. It entails relations of equality, kinship, and community between human beings and animals, especially tigers, in the sharing of food and resources. Bon Bibi is an "'interstitial' being—mediator between Allah and humans, between village and forest, and between the world of humans and that of the tigers."[30]

In stark contrast to Nirmal's atheistic vision of an inhospitable nature, humans do not relate to tigers in a mutually destructive manner in Bon Bibi's world. And unlike the natural world of deep ecology, humans are not deprived of autonomous agency by an identity-destroying symbiosis with nature. Human-tiger "relatedness" involves the ongoing negotiation of a necessary coexistence in a common world of shared resources, where nature is dangerous and relatively barren but also a source of livelihood. Because tigers are viewed as equal agents, these negotiations are guided by what Jalais calls an "economic morality of the forest."[31] This morality is characterized by production for use. It prescribes restraint on the part of humans so that they share forest resources with tigers instead of depleting them out of greed. This relatedness differs from Heideggerian being-with others in two significant respects. First, the being-with is with nonhuman beings. Second, the world is held together not by the force of temporalization but by divine forces of Islamic and Hindu religious cosmology and folk belief, namely, Bon Bibi as the common symbolic mother of human and nonhuman beings alike. The subaltern moral economy is not a superstitious traditional response to the shaping of the environment by global forces. It is a nuanced ethical interpretation of the impact of global political-economic and local social forces on the environment that expresses subaltern needs and interests. Jalais notes that the subalterns believe that the environment shapes the characters of humans and tigers even as humans have the capacity to affect the environment and the character of the tigers through their ethical conduct. The government betrayal of the subalterns in the massacre has destroyed the relations between humans and the nonhuman inhabitants of the forests and rivers: it changed the tiger's character and turned it against the people.[32]

The Poetic Magic of Morichjhāpi: The Transfiguration of Cosmopolitan Middle-Class Consciousness by Subaltern Stories

Such ethical interpretations can be the basis of local popular movements in defense of community rights to natural resources. Ramachandra Guha has described this political alternative to Northern environmentalism as "the environmentalism of the poor," a new form of class conflict that corresponds to the global capitalist appropriation and exploitation of natural resources.[33] In a similar vein, Nirmal's diary poignantly evokes the violent denial of the subaltern's attempt to emerge as a subject in the world. When the refugees are prevented from returning to the island, they address the world in a cry of despair: "*Amra kara? Bastuhara.*' *Who are we? We are the dispossessed. How strange it was to hear this plaintive cry wafting across the water. It seemed at that moment not to be a shout of defiance but rather a question being addressed to the heavens, not just for themselves but on behalf of a bewildered human-kind. Who, indeed, are we? Where do we belong?*" (*HT*, 211). Similarly, Kusum protests against the dehumanizing logic of Northern environmentalism. The settlers have been reduced to eating grass and drinking from puddles of water because their food supply has been exhausted and the police have destroyed their wells. Their dehumanization to a status lower than tigers is a conse-quence of being deprived of world. They are not recognized as members of a common humanity because environmental preservation has ironically eradi-cated humanity from the island and reserved it exclusively for tigers.

> *The worst part was not the hunger or the thirst. It was to sit here, helpless, and listen to the policemen making their announcements, hearing them say that our lives, our existence, were worth less than dirt or dust. "This island has to be saved for its trees, it has to be saved for its animals, it is part of a reserve forest, it belongs to a project to save tigers, which is paid for by people from all around the world.".... Who are these people, I wondered, who love animals so much that they are willing to kill us for them? ... It seemed to me that this whole world had become a place for animals, and our fault, our crime was that we were just human beings, trying to live as human beings always have, from the water and the soil. No one could think this a crime unless they have forgotten that this is how humans have always lived—by fishing, by clearing land and by planting the soil.* (*HT*, 217)

But poor environmentalist movements require organizational help. This means that the collective consciousness of the urban middle class within and outside India must be changed to create new sociopolitical subjects who are cognizant of subaltern interests. Subaltern dispossession occurs because sub-alterns do not count in the eyes of a self-serving national middle class who see the world filtered through their particularistic agenda of economic accu-mulation and progress. Kanai personifies this class. His perspective, Piya points out, is "a looking glass in which a man like Fokir could never be anything other than a figure glimpsed through a rear-view mirror, a rapidly diminish-ing presence, a ghost from a perpetual past that was Lusibari" (*HT*, 183).

Kanai, Nirmal, and Piya, the key urban middle-class characters, are modern cosmopolitan and secular subjects. Their world is lubricated by two types of money. Piya's research is financed by Northern environmentalist funding for forest and wildlife preservation, and Kanai's translator and interpreter agency, which "specialized in serving the expatriate communities of New Delhi: foreign diplomats, aid workers, charitable organizations, multinationals and the like," thrives because flows of global capitalist investment have turned India into a major location for call centers and a leading conference city and media center (*HT*, 17). These two types of money roughly correspond to two kinds of cosmopolitanism: a cosmopolitanism based on bourgeois consumption and a universalistic humanist cosmopolitanism. Kanai exemplifies bourgeois cosmopolitanism. He is self-centered and predatory, especially in relation to women. His business, which traffics in the traffic among languages, is a travesty of Goethe's project of world literature. Nirmal's Marxism, Nilima's ethos of social service, and Piya's extension of humanitarian sentiment to the animal world are examples of the universalistic humanist type of cosmopolitanism.

According to the norms, values, and conceptual categories of cosmopolitan bourgeois secular modernity, the religious practices and folk beliefs that hold the subaltern world together by affirming nonhuman agency are vestiges of traditional superstition that need to be eradicated because they obstruct universal progress. Hence, bourgeois subjects need to be transformed so that they will accept and respect subaltern beliefs and practices as viable ethical principles for living.[34] *The Hungry Tide* offers a fictional expiation for the urban Bengali middle class's disregard for the subaltern population by having Piya, the cosmopolitan environmentalist, and Nirmal and Kanai, representatives of the Bengali middle class, cross the divides of class, caste, and cultural worlds. They are touched by the subaltern world, and this triggers a radical change in consciousness that causes them to recognize the structural limitations of their lives and their culpability in subaltern suffering.

At the level of plot, the subaltern touching of bourgeois consciousness occurs through affective libidinal intimacy. There are three romantically charged or potentially romantic pairings of characters from the two worlds that involve socially inappropriate sexual desire: Fokir and Piya, Nirmal and Kusum, and Moyna, Fokir's wife, and Kanai. Each of these pairings is chiasmically related to corresponding pairings of one character in the first pairing with a counterpart from the same world to form two constellations of four characters. For example, the relationship between Fokir and Piya stands in a chiasmic relation to the relationships between Piya and Kanai and Fokir and Moyna (see fig. 9.1). These couplings provide the dramatic tension that drives the novel's plot and subplots.

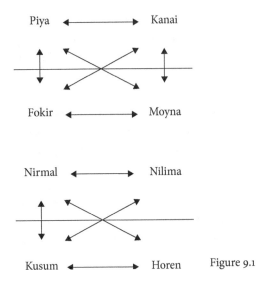

Figure 9.1

The disruption of bourgeois consciousness also occurs in the novel's narrative structure. In the first part of the novel, the narrator alternates in consecutive episodes between presenting events that happen in the novel's "present" from Kanai's and Piya's perspectives. This alternation occurs from the moment they meet at the Kolkata train station and continues through the duration of their separation. The episodes where Kanai's perspective predominates have an additional temporal dimension. He recalls through flashbacks his initial visit in 1970 to Lusibari as a ten-year-old, where he first befriended Kusum, heard of the Bon Bibi legend, and learned from Nirmal of Sir Daniel Hamilton's establishment of a classless and casteless society run by cooperatives. Echoes of his earlier visit shadow his present visit. More important, portions of Nirmal's diary are embedded in these episodes as Kanai reads it and learns about the events leading up to the massacre. Written in 1979, the diary is a ghostly voice from beyond the grave that refers to another ghost, Kusum, who died in the massacre. Her shadow disturbs Kanai's memories of her as a young girl. These repeated hauntings make him uneasy. Even when the alternation between the protagonists' perspectives is suspended with Piya's arrival at Lusibari at the beginning of the novel's second part (titled "The Flood"), the narrative about Kanai and Piya is persistently interrupted by the voice of Nirmal's diary. Parallels between events taking place in the narrative present of the novel's second part and the violent events recorded in the notebook, especially the echoing of Kusum's death by Fokir's death in the cyclone storm, signal that very little has changed between 1979 and the present.

Nirmal's transformation is the most important, because we see his initial elegiac experience of loss in a godless world give way to a radical idea of transformation that fuses redemption through subaltern religious beliefs with revolutionary fervor. Transformation no longer refers to the persistent mutability of a nature that is hostile to human existence but to the resilient ability of subalterns to survive by transforming themselves and the harsh landscape in their negotiations with it. We see this understanding of transformation as worlding activity in two moments: when Kusum and Fokir move back to the Sundarbans with the wave of deserting Dandakaranya refugees and the refugees' successful endeavors on Morichjhāpi. The migration to Morichjhāpi echoes the original migration initiated by Sir Daniel Hamilton. Nirmal describes the worldlessness of the dispossessed refugees using lines from the Seventh Duino Elegy. *"I saw them coming, young and old, quick and halt, with their lives bundled on their heads, and I knew it was of them the Poet had spoken when he said:*

> *Each slow turn of the world carries such disinherited*
> *ones to whom neither the past [das Frühere] nor the future [das Nächste]*
> *belongs."* (HT, 137)

The stanza continues:

> For even the immediate future is far from mankind. This
> shouldn't confuse us; no, it should commit us to preserve
> the form we still can recognize. This stood among men,
> once, stood in the middle of fate, the annihilator, stood
> in the middle of Not-Knowing-Where-To, as if it existed,
> and it pulled down stars from the safe heaven toward it.[35]

For Rilke, the world's endless mutability leaves us stranded and bewildered, without direction, as though we have been expelled from the continuity of time itself and do not possess a "before" (*das Frühere*) and an "after" (*das Nächste*). In this radical uncertainty, we can only find refuge in the eternal forms of the mind.

However, Kusum does not experience her migration as a purposeless wandering. Although she initially describes the refugees as ghosts, she discovers that their situation is not one of worldless despair. It is instead an occasion for world-making through human interlocution and action. Through her recognition that the refugees speak the same language, Kusum forms a world with them in their shared worldlessness. "Did you notice the words? See: I'd spoken in Hindi, but it was in Bangla they spoke back to me. I was amazed: the very same words, the same tongue! 'Who are you?' I said. 'Tell me, where are you headed?' 'Listen, sister, we'll tell you. This is the story'" (HT, 136). The world they intend to make on Morichjhāpi is an active commemoration of the previous worlding of Hamilton's cooperative society. When Kusum hears their story, she becomes transfigured and decides to participate in their project.

> "Our fathers had once answered Hamilton's call: they had wrested the estate from the sway of the tides. What they'd done for another, couldn't we do for ourselves? . . .
>
> I listened to them talk, and hope blossomed in my heart; these were my people, how could I stand apart? We shared the same tongue, we were joined in our bones; the dreams they had dreamt were not different from my own. They too had hankered for our tide country mud; they too had longed to watch the tide rise to full flood." (HT, 137)

Nirmal's perspective on the refugees undergoes a rapid change. When he witnesses the orderliness of the refugee settlement, he concedes that they have made a world on the island. Instead of a random apposition, people and things are held together as a meaningful whole.

> These were huts, shacks and shanties built with the usual materials of the tide country—mud, thatch and bamboo—yet a pattern was evident here: these dwellings had not been laid out at random.
>
> What had I expected? A mere jumble perhaps, untidy heaps of people piled high upon each other? That is, after all, what the word rifugi has come to mean. But what I saw was quite different from the picture in my mind's eye. Paths had been laid; the bādh—that guarantor of island life—had been augmented; little plots of land had been enclosed with fences; fishing nets had been hung up to dry. . . . Such industry! Such diligence! (HT, 141)

Unlike the invisible spiritual world that Rilke regards as our shelter from time's corrosiveness, the order created on the island is something actually created by material activity. As Nirmal notes, "it was an astonishing spectacle—as though an entire civilization had sprouted suddenly in the mud" (HT, 159).[36] The refugees regulate finitude by appropriating time through their industry and giving a meaningful pattern to what would otherwise be wasteland. More significant, unlike Sir Daniel Hamilton's project, the subaltern worlding of Morichjhāpi is not a vision imposed from above but a communal effort from below that overcomes the division of spiritual and material labor.

> *I felt the onrush of a strange, heady excitement: suddenly it dawned on me that I was watching the birth of something new, something hitherto unseen. . . . This dream had been dreamt by the very people who were trying to make it real. . . . How astonishing it was that I, an aging, bookish schoolmaster, should live to see this, an experiment, imagined not by those with learning and power, but by those without!* (HT, 141)

Nirmal is transfigured. He feels "all of existence swelling in [his] veins" (HT, 141) and overcomes the socioeconomic divisions that separate him from the refugees. His empty existence is now filled with purpose: the commitment to help the community. He stays on as a teacher, documents its life, and later records the events of the government siege. Kanai will later tell Nilima that for Nirmal, "Kusum . . . was the embodiment of the idea of transformation" (HT, 233).

Kanai's and Piya's transformations are fundamental to the transmission of Nirmal's diary and its injunction to improve the situation of the subalterns. The changes in them illustrate the worlding force of subaltern cultural practices and stories, their power to move bourgeois subjects to assist in maintaining and re-newing the subaltern world. When Kanai and Fokir help Piya to track dolphin movements, he accuses Fokir of duplicitously exaggerating the dangers of tiger attacks on Garjontola and verbally abuses him. This incident develops into a moment of self-revelation where Kanai is thrown back onto himself, sees in full transparency how he appears in Fokir's eyes, and judges himself from a subaltern perspective. He is stripped of concrete individuality and be-comes a caricature of the privileged educated Bengali middle class.

> In Kanai's professional life there had been a few instances in which the act of interpretation had given him the momentary sensation of being trans-ported out of his body and into another. In each instance it was as if the instrument of language had metamorphosed—instead of being a barrier, a curtain that divided, it had become a transparent film, a prism that allowed him to look through another set of eyes, to filter the world through a mind other than his own. . . . It was exactly this feeling that came upon him as he looked at Fokir: it was as though his vision were being refracted through those opaque, unreadable eyes and he were seeing not himself, Kanai Dutt,

but a great host of people—a double for the outside world, someone standing in for the men who had destroyed Fokir's village, burnt his home and killed his mother; he had become a token for a vision of human beings in which a man such as Fokir counted for nothing, a man whose value was less than that of an animal. (HT, 270)

Kanai compares this moment of complete access to Fokir's mind to a perfect act of translation where language has become invisible. It is literally a process of perfect cultural "translation" in which the subaltern world penetrates and prevails against the modern secular world of the cosmopolitan middle class. In local traditions, Garjontola is a sacred site of self-knowledge where Bon Bibi reveals to believers what they wish to know. Kanai's experience of being judged in the forest confirms the magic of Garjontola and the ethical viability of subaltern tales and practices.

His parting gift to Piya, a translation of the chant of Dukhey's tale sung by Fokir, confirms the power of subaltern traditions to overcome caste and class divisions. In the tiger-killing episode, Piya becomes aware that Fokir does not share her deep ecological sympathies and that his relation to the landscape and its fauna is governed by animistic beliefs. He justifies the burning of the tiger by saying that it came into a human settlement because it wanted to die. However, because Piya has almost no knowledge of Bengali, her transformation, that is, her recognition of the subaltern moral economy as a viable ethos requires the agency of linguistic translation into English and cultural translation across different worlds. With Kanai's help, she learns that Kusum's tales and songs have transformed Garjontola into an enchanted place with its own code of conduct for Fokir (HT, 254). Fokir lives his life according to these texts of local practical knowledge. As Nirmal notes in his diary, "*the words* [telling of the Bon Bibi myth] *have become a part of him*" (HT, 206). They have created a world between Fokir and the dolphins, which he regards as friendly messengers of Bon Bibi. Indeed, all of his actions in relation to Piya are determined by his beliefs. Kanai's prefatory letter and postscript to the translation emphasize the song's axiomatic status in Fokir's everyday practices. Indeed, it is part of the worlding of the Sundarbans: "In those words there was a history that is not just his [Fokir's] own but also of this place, the tide country" (HT, 291).

The transformative power of subaltern stories indicates that the Sundarbans have not been completely saturated by the imperatives of global capitalist accumulation. The region is constituted by relations of poetic meaning at a more fundamental level. In other words, the subaltern world of the Sundarbans is held together by forces more powerful than instrumentality. As poetry, these stories are not merely a force that discloses the worlding of a world but modalities of worlding itself. Nirmal, who has lived his life through poetry and recognizes Fokir as a kindred spirit, comments that *"for this boy those words were much more than a part of a legend: it was the story that gave this land its life"* (HT, 292). We should here understand poetry in the Arendtian sense of the creation of something permanent that transcends the ravages of temporal finitude.

Deep Time and World Literature as Deep Communication

The moral economy of the landscape formed by these stories is an unconscious historical substrate that motivates the desires and determines the actions of individual subaltern subjects. Quoting from the Third Duino Elegy, Kanai describes this substrate as

> a multitudinous brew; not just one
> child, but fathers, cradled inside us like ruins
> of mountains, the dry riverbed
> of former mothers, yes, and the whole
> soundless landscape under its clouded
> or clear destiny . . .[37]

In the next stanza, Rilke calls this "prehistoric time [Vorzeit]."[38] Elsewhere, Ghosh uses a geological metaphor to describe the fundamental religious ideas and traditional beliefs that shape individual lives. He notes that he does not merely write about the individual in his or her immediate situation but "about what is there, the geology, the deep time that exists outside the individual, and the immediacy of time, and the times that make up every aspect of the circumstance."[39] Like *Vorzeit*, the "deep time" that animates subaltern agency refers to a temporal order different from the time of the clock and the calendar by which modern Westernized subjects measure our immediately appearing individual lives. The coexistence of deep time, conventionally stigmatized as premodern, with clocked time is akin to the notion of heterotemporality I critiqued in chapter 7.

In Ghosh's view, literature can world a world and impart permanence to everyday existence because it reveals the deeper connections between finite life and fundamental historical forces. Although informed media coverage and social scientific research are important avenues for making us aware of the destructive impact of Northern environmentalism on the subaltern world, Ghosh suggests that literature is a superior form of discourse because of its special connection to "deep communication," a type of understanding that is more effective in rendering deep time. Here the import of Ghosh's reenvisioning of the pluralistic ethos of world literature in terms of the multilingual complexity of postcolonial life-experiences becomes clearer. The plurality of languages resists the cultural homogenization of globalization because it implies the need for "deep communication," as opposed to the "shallow communication" of e-mail, the paradigmatic case of human exchange in our contemporary speeded-up global era.[40] E-mail can be translated instantaneously because it conveys mere information and not a "deeper, resonant" meaning. In contradistinction, genuine worldly understanding requires "deep communication between languages and experiences," a sense that words from other languages can resonate with deeply sedimented meanings even if the reader does not understand their precise lexical content or denotation.[41] Deep communication is not about determining semantic content. It does not give rise to positive factual information or even determinative conceptual knowledge. Instead, it elicits a richer evocative "knowledge," the constitutive imbrication of words in the larger web of relations that make them meaningful, the associations or "resonances and meanings that words have."[42] Only deep communication can effectively convey the deep history that animates subaltern agency, such as the Bon Bibi myth, and facilitate the transformative contact between the novel's elite middle-class and subaltern subjects.

For Ghosh, literary writing exemplifies deep communication. Rightly or wrongly, he links the birth of the novel to "the development of monolingual cultures in Europe" that followed from the rise of vernacular print at the beginning of the seventeenth century.[43] Only multilingual and "interlingual" works of literature are worldly in the normative sense because they are constituted by deep communication across different languages. Although *The Hungry Tide* is written in English, it exemplifies world literature because it foregrounds the complexity of translation by giving it a central role in its plot. Moreover, the novel attempts to make the reading experience one of deep communication to give the reader a sense of the depth of the religious and cultural meanings that constitute the subaltern world's deep time. Literature is better able to portray and enact deep communication than conceptual knowledge and information because it is an intertextually constituted linguistic artefact.

First, the novel's interruptive narrative structure is a literary mode of deep communication that gives the reader a heightened sense of deep time. In addition to the oscillation between narrative viewpoints, the flow of the narrative present is also repeatedly interrupted by flashbacks, such as Kanai's memory of Kusum, and various acts of reading, such as Kanai's reading of Nirmal's diary, which is written in Bengali, and Piya's reading of Kanai's translation of Fokir's song. The interruptive reading experience suggests that there is something deeper than the values of secular modernity according to which the cosmopolitan middle-class characters process their immediate perceptual experience.

Second, Ghosh's disruption of the reader's conventional expectations of the novel form by a complex intertextual mixing of forms and genres achieves a related defamiliarization of the reading experience. In addition to the use of different diegetic modes, such as the letter and diary, Ghosh introduces Indian vernacular cultural forms, such as songs, chants, and ritual performances, into the form of the novel. One commentator has suggested that in addition to presenting local cultural resources that challenge the "normative understandings of knowledge, civility and progress" of its elite characters, the novel's use of these local vernacular forms is an effective way of solving the dilemma faced by the postcolonial writer who seeks to portray in an elitist literary form the complicity of the Western-educated postcolonial elite in the destruction of the subalterns and their environment.[44] Incorporating local cultural elements, especially the Bengali folk-theater form of Jatra, explodes the form of the Western novel and renders it improper, and adequately represents the novel's "own distinctive historical environment."[45] This interpretation is similar to the argument of the Kenyan novelist Ngũgĩ wa Thiong'o, in his famous manifesto, *Decolonising the Mind*, that the African novel must incorporate elements of orature, popular music, and culture so that it will become organic to African peoples through oral performance and help to organize them into a collective subject of resistance.[46]

The attribution of a "localizing" intention to the novel, however, ignores the fact that Rilke's poetry is the novel's most pervasive literary resource. The portrayal of the deep history of subaltern characters is part of a larger vision of a world made up of plural histories. Ghosh's obsessive use of a European poet suggests that this vision can only be adequately portrayed by a novel with an equally deep *textual* history: a literary intertextuality that is worldly because it weaves together European and non-European texts—Rilke, Bengali oral folk poetry, chants of Islamic-Arabic origin, and so on—in a manner that reflects the Sundarbans's complex cultural landscape. In a remarkable metafictional passage where Nirmal is shown a printed booklet that tells the Bon Bibi legend, Ghosh unsettles the idea that subaltern beliefs are indigenous. The legend itself is an example of world literature in the narrow sense, a text that circulates across linguistic and territorial boundaries. Nirmal guesses that the story is a refugee import. The printed text is written in the prosody of Bangla folklore, in a verse form with rhymed couplets, but its pages, like Arabic texts, open to the right.

> It struck me that this legend had perhaps taken shape in the late nineteenth or early twentieth century, just as new waves of settlers were moving into the tide country. And was it possible that this accounted for the way it was formed, from elements of legend and scripture, from the near and the far, Bangla and Arabic? How could it be otherwise? For this I have seen confirmed many times that the mudbanks of the tide country are shaped not by rivers of silt but also by rivers of language: Bengali, English, Arabic, Hindi, Arakanese and who knows what else? Flowing into one another they create a proliferation of small worlds that hang suspended in the flow. And so it dawned on me: the tide country's faith is something like one of its great mohonas, a meeting not just of many rivers, but a roundabout people can use to pass in many directions—from country to country and even between faiths and religions. (HT, 205–6)[47]

More important, Nirmal uses the metaphor of ecological biodiversity to connect the diverse sources that go into the story's making, the syncretism of religious belief in the area, and the linguistic diversity of different groups of settlers. In an earlier passage, Piya used the same image of the biodome to characterize the area's biodiversity: "Each balloon was a floating biodome filled with endemic fauna and flora, and as they made their way through the waters, strings of predators followed, trailing in their wake. This proliferation of environments was responsible for creating and sustaining a dazzling variety of aquatic life forms—from gargantuan crocodiles to microscopic fish" (HT, 105). These figural associations between linguistic diversity, the plurality of cultural forms and practices, and the infinite variety of biological forms bring out in the sharpest relief the novel's conceit: a vision of the world as the harmonious gathering together of different languages and cultures that also holds together the human world with the natural world of nonhuman beings. This unity is the solution to environmental degradation and the destruction of subaltern communities by capitalist globalization.

*Inhuman Textuality: Translating the Blankness at the Heart
of the Novel's Moral Economy*

The Hungry Tide resonates with Arendt's idea of a plural human community constituted through speech and action and Goethe's idea of spiritual intercourse across cultural diversity. In an interesting twist, it extends the reach of worldliness beyond human community to include nonhuman life forms. These different spheres are held together as a world by subaltern beliefs in meaningful relationships between human and nonhuman life forms. For Ghosh, all literature is poetry in the broad sense of discourse with a creative power. The stories that are part of subaltern cultural practices are poetic. They provide an ethical counterpoint to modern scientific explanations of the Sundarbans landscape, such as geology, geography, biology, and ecology. The novel clearly favors poetry over the prose of science and pragmatic social service in the reworlding of the subaltern world. Near the novel's end, Nilima melancholically notes that because Nirmal wanted to deal "with the whole world's problems," "he ended up with—nothing," instead of "making a few little things a little better in one small place" (*HT*, 319). "Nothing" refers disparagingly to the poetic approach's lack of practical efficacy, literature's negligible causality in the world. When Kanai reminds Nilima that Nirmal produced the notebook and she points out that it has been lost in the storm, he responds by saying that it has not gone "in its entirety. A lot of it is in my head, you know. I'm going to try to put it back together" (*HT*, 319). This consolation echoes the inspiration of Fokir's life by the Bon Bibi myth. Kanai, the translator of prose, has also been taken over by poetry. Because the missing notebook has left a trace in his memory, he can save the subaltern world by reassembling it and telling how it was torn apart.

At the end of the novel, Fokir dies a meaningful death in the cyclone storm. His death is partly caused by his dream about Kusum, and he heroically sacrifices himself for Piya. The repeated association of Fokir with Dukhey suggests that his death is part of the meaningful world created by the Bon Bibi myth. The aftermath of his death has a strained sense of poetic justice and gives aesthetic completion to the novel. His death enables Piya and Kanai's relationship to progress in a future beyond the novel's frame. At the same time, his death maintains the structure of memory and recollection so fundamental to the narrative. First, traces of Fokir are perpetually encrypted in Piya's and Kanai's lives in the same way that the novel's narrative was persistently interrupted by Nirmal's portrayal of the subaltern world and the massacre. Second, Fokir's local practical knowledge is neatly converted into scientific knowledge.

Although Piya has lost her notebook, the routes that trace dolphin migration patterns have been preserved as data on her GPS device. She intends to establish a subaltern-friendly conservation project named after Fokir with the sponsorship of the Badabon Trust and the participation of local fishermen (*HT*, 328). Ironically, his death also brings economic security to his wife and son. Piya has raised money to buy them a house and give Tutul a college education by circulating an email chain letter about his heroic death.

But despite its literary complexity, *The Hungry Tide* subscribes to a simplistic ethical view of translation as the perfect conveyance of meaning that brings about a transparency between minds and cultures. As an example of deep communication, the novel aims to expand the circle of the subaltern moral economy and give subaltern stories wider circulation so that the subaltern world can be presented more cogently to modern reading subjects. The novel presents itself as a mere auxiliary aid for relaying these stories. The stories are the true force of worlding that can save the subaltern world by moving bourgeois subjects to responsibility. The novel merely communicates them through the mediation of fiction. But at the same time, against its authorial grain, the novel also problematizes its function as deep communication and puts into question the power of stories to mend and hold the world together by pointing to the impossibility of arriving at a condition of perfect meaningfulness. For at its heart, there is a blankness that is at once utterly meaningless and also the condition of possibility of the novel's complex layers of meaning.

Although Nirmal remains on the island as a witness during the siege, his notebook does not in fact tell of the atrocious violence, since it was delivered to Kanai before the massacre. "*Maybe you will know what to do with it,*" Nirmal writes, "*I have always trusted the young. Your generation will . . . be richer in ideals, less cynical, less selfish than mine*" (*HT*, 230). This hopeful gesture of sending something to posterity to build for a better future opens up the relay of stories and narratives that gives the subaltern world public phenomenality. But because Kanai loses the diary, what we have at the heart of the novel is quite literally a blank that is a direct consequence of another blankness that shapes the Sundarbans landscape, the eye of the cyclone storm.

Why is the novel so studiedly hesitant to represent the massacre when it is patently an attempt to represent the suffering of the subaltern? Why this coy withholding of the representation of the events epitomizing subaltern oppression in a lengthy novelistic representation? In line with Ghosh's faith in the worlding power of stories, we can understand this withholding of representation in terms of an ethical exigency to maximize the public phenomenality of the refugees. It is impossible to represent suffering without objectifying the unfortunate into passive victims and speaking in their place. But the mere intimation of suffering without representation can set off a proliferation of stories and narratives about the events. In the novel, the tragedy is hinted at by the representation of surrounding circumstances—Kanai learns about what happened in Morichjhāpi from the rumors that Horen hears.

In turn, the reading experience can create a desire in the reader to find out more about what happened by reading beyond the novel. This is, in fact, what any careful study of the novel will have to do. Beyond this, the withholding of the representation of the refugees also creates a desire for interlocution, to address the imagined sufferer as a subject who can speak back and tell the story of who she is. This engenders an imaginary structure in which a slot is opened up for the emergence of a series of similar subaltern actors who can reply. It transforms the reader from a voyeuristic observer of portrayed suffering to a patient listener who awaits a response. What is at issue here is not the portrayal of the material conditions of global inequality that lead to suffering. By itself, such a portrayal does not set up a structure for us, cosmopolitan middle-class readers, to understand and deliberate about these conditions, their effects on those who suffer, and how they can be eliminated. As the necessary prelude of action, we first need to address and enter into interlocution with these others, thereby allowing them to emerge and belong as part of a common world so that we can act in concert.

However, the nonrepresentation of the massacre has a more disturbing significance. Given that Kanai has been portrayed throughout the novel as a selfish, egotistical Western-educated upper-middle-class cosmopolitan consumer, it is unclear that he would have "done the right thing" with the notebook. His shameful recognition of his class-based abuse of Fokir does not guarantee that he will act responsibly. It is instead the guilt he feels for losing the notebook that drives him to fulfill Nirmal's injunction to transmit the notebook's contents and give its moral message a future. Kanai decides to restructure his translation business so that he can spend more time in Kolkata and "write the story of Nirmal's notebook—how it came into his hands, what was in it, and how it was lost" (*HT*, 329). His decision to write this story is the novel's condition of possibility. Hence, it is a blankness, a narrative that became lost because of a natural catastrophe beyond human explanation, that provides a resolution to the plot and narrative closure.

The novel figures these blanknesses—the lost diary and the storm that leads to its loss—as something meaningfully destined by divine forces. But they are utterly devoid of meaning, because there is no reason why the storm takes place. At the same time, the storm is the origin of meanings and interpretations and, indeed, the condition of possibility of the novel's meaning. The blankness gives rise to the layers of narratives we experience as readers and opens up a meaningful world on Lusibari after the storm that helps to maintain the subaltern world. These blanknesses are instances of the inhuman alterity of time elaborated in the deconstructive account of the world: the inappropriable other from which time comes is both a force that opens a world by unifying it and letting it be present and that which leads to the world's disappearance. The subaltern settlers' imminent danger of losing their world is an example of the radical alterity of time. They cope with the contingency of finite existence by instituting a moral economy that appropriates and figures time's otherness as the power of gods and deities, thereby giving meaning to existence. The stories that performatively express this moral economy need to be given public phenomenality through the assistance of a cosmopolitan middle class whose conscience has been moved if they are to survive as a force of worlding. But this structure of maintaining and reopening the subaltern world always runs the risk of corruption and contamination. The blanknesses in the novel indicate that the divine presence that subaltern stories celebrate is constituted by something radically other that escapes the appropriation of human reason or belief. Hence, the meaningful stories that the divine presence gives rise to, like any meaningful presence, are open to interpretation and even refutation. They are subject to a law of contamination. For example, there is no guarantee here that particularistic bourgeois interests are not at work in the giving of public light. If we accept the novel's suggestion that Nirmal's notebook and the oral narratives and memories of the event are the only available records of the Morichjhāpi incident, then Kanai's planned narrative, which may or may not be the novel, is the only way of giving voice to the refugees who were killed. Hence, the structure of emergence can also be a gesture of appropriation and ventriloquism that usurps the subaltern's announcement of who he is.

The fundamental ambivalence of translation is a relay of the aporia of giving phenomenality to the subaltern world. The novel explicitly emphasizes that translation is premised on finitude, in this case, that of languages and cultures. There are barriers between languages and cultures, but because these barriers are porous, translation and communication across cultures is possible and can even lead to an augmentation of meaning, as celebrated by recent theories of world literature. The common and metaphysical explanation of translatability is that different languages are the particular sensuous expressions of universal and infinite ideas and concepts. But if language is understood as a system of signification and not as the mere expression of preformed atemporal concepts, then there is no *reason* why translation is possible. Translation occurs, but it will always be marked by the irreducible possibility of uncertainty and loss of meaning.

More important, the structural contamination of meaning in translation is grounded in the lack of a rational basis for meaningfulness in radically finite existence. The strangeness of a foreign tongue or culture is a synedoche of the strangeness of the world for finite humanity. The novel makes this point through Kanai, a professional translator. For him, the translator is a prophylactic defense against finitude: "[the translator-guide] was the life preserver that held . . . [travelers] afloat in a tide of incomprehension. . . . His job sometimes made him a proxy for the inscrutability of life itself" (*HT*, 269). Some mystification of the foreign is structural to the translator-guide's role as a mediator between a traveler and a foreign land because a translator's value is premised on the mysteriousness of the foreign. Ethics, however, requires that a translator accurately convey the degree of unknowability. Exaggerating the inscrutability and dangers of the foreign would give the lie to the necessity of the translator's mediating function.[48]

The translator is thus an ambivalent figure. He is potentially an aid to mutual comprehension and coexistence with other cultures. But deficient translation or translation with malicious intent can be destructive. Accordingly, the novel repeatedly cautions us about the contaminating character of translation, that it does not always lead to the transparency of deep communication. When Moyna asks Kanai to actively place himself between Piya and Fokir as the translator of their intercourse, she pointedly observes that the translator has the power of creative mediation through distortion: "It's you who stands between them. . . . Their words will be in your hands and you can make them mean what you will" (*HT*, 213–14). The important point, however, is not that translation or, more generally, mediation can distort but that the possibility of distortion is structural to meaning itself because in a radically finite world, we cannot explain how the unity that constitutes meaningfulness arises. Simply put, because this unity comes from what is entirely other to reason, it is always unstable and cannot be guaranteed.

In the case of the giving of phenomenality to the subaltern world, the irreducible possibility of filtration and distortion through translation is heightened by the fact that the stories that constitute this world can only be disseminated and circulated in the wider world through forms of technological recording and mediatization that are inseparable from the processes of global capitalism. The preservation of subaltern knowledge of dolphin migration patterns on Piya's GPS device is an objective correlative for this heteronomy. It implies that the solution to the unworlding of the subaltern world the novel imagines can always be captured and co-opted by global capitalism. Establishing a conservation project in Fokir's name that is sensitive to local community needs and interests may well be a naïve deployment of eco-friendly ideas, such as strong local community participation and sustainable socioeconomic development for the local people, that can be easily appropriated by global corporations as part of their rhetoric to promote ecotourism.

Indeed, what is Ghosh's novel but a complex labyrinth of interwoven translations? It is written in English. Nirmal's notebook is full of English translations of Rilke's poetry. Kanai loses the notebook and writes the story of the notebook in which he translates for Piya, among other things, Fokir's rendition of the song about Dukhey's Redemption, which comes "from the epic of the tide country, as told by Abdur-Rahim—The Miracles of Bon Bibi or the Narrative of Her Glory" (*HT*, 292). We are constantly reminded that the material production of world literature in the strong sense—including Ghosh's novel—necessarily involves translation and that this is a commercial business that weaves it into the structures of global capitalism.

In all rigor, one must also ask whether Ghosh's novel is a benevolent distortion that gives an idealized homogeneous picture of the subaltern world. By portraying the subaltern moral economy as being governed by laws different from those of secular modernity, the novel follows the Subaltern Studies view of subalternity as a space of difference formed from elements of society that are excluded from the logic of global capitalist accumulation. This effectively homogenizes subalternity in a way that obscures the subaltern desire to exit the subaltern world and be integrated into the space-time of capitalist modernity as a willing participant. Moyna personifies this desire for modernity. Despite being thwarted in her plans to obtain a college education by her parents, who married her off to the illiterate Fokir, she moves to Lusibari to train to become a nurse. She also wants her child, Tutul, to have an education because she realizes that there is no future in fishing. Moyna is not portrayed in a sympathetic light. She is characterized as worldly. But her worldliness is not that of the subaltern world with its sense of deep time but that of upward class mobility. Her worldliness is driven by a foresight in making plans for the future, that is, the linear temporality of progress and the calculative management of time needed to get ahead. In an exchange between her and Kanai, we clearly see that the ideological opposition between backward tradition and progressive modernity is *internal* to subaltern space. Moyna wishes to quit this space with her son and leave her husband behind.

> "It's people like us who're going to suffer and it's up to us to think ahead. That's why I have to make sure Tutul gets an education. Otherwise, what's his future going to be?" . . .
>
> It occurred to Kanai, as she was speaking, that for someone in her circumstances, Moyna possessed a sure grasp of the world and how to get by in it. It was astonishing to think of how much had changed in the tide country since his last visit, not just in material matters but in people's hopes and desires. . . . This made it seem all the more unfortunate that someone with Moyna's talents should be held back by a husband who could not keep up. . . .
>
> Kanai could tell from the sound of Moyna's voice that her dream of becoming a nurse was no ordinary yearning: it was the product of a desire as richly and completely imagined as a novel or a poem. It recalled for him what it meant to be driven to better yourself, to lay claim to a wider world. It was as though, in listening to Moyna, he were looking back on an earlier incarnation of himself. (HT, 112–13)

Left on their own, the stories of the subaltern world are not enough to hold it together in capitalist globalization. The subaltern world risks being distorted by the various forms of mediation that afford it public phenomenality. It is also undermined from within by the subaltern desire for modernity. However, the blankness at the heart of *The Hungry Tide* as *textuality* also points to an inappropriable otherness that resists the calculations and desires of capitalist modernity because it cannot be appropriated by human rationality. This otherness opens a world and is the promise of a future because it is the condition of possibility of telling stories about the subaltern world, including Ghosh's novel. But this alterity is also the nonerasable possibility of the contamination of the world it opens up, because it escapes progressive rational control, including the novelist's authorial desire for the pure difference of subalternity. The narrative form, I suggest, has a special affinity with this inhuman force that opens a world without the secure guarantee of an ideal telos, because the giving and coming of time is fundamental to its structure.

CHAPTER 10

Resisting Humanitarianization

Somalia's lasting image on the world stage is a famine-ridden, impoverished country of starving children. The plight of the Somali people has been exacerbated to the point of tragedy by the repeated failure to establish a functional state after the fall of Siad Barre's dictatorship in May 1991 and a series of civil wars based on clan divisions and sectarian Islamic differences that continue to the present.[1] The United Nations and the United States responded to the Somalian crisis with humanitarian initiatives to provide relief aid at the end of the Cold War: the United Nations Operation in Somalia (UNOSOM) and the US-led Operation Restore Hope, which was charged to create a protected environment to facilitate the work of relief agencies in delivering humanitarian aid. The Somalian situation left enough of a mark on global popular consciousness that the Battle of Mogadishu, the war waged by US troops against the Somali warlord General Aidid on October 3–4, 1993, was the subject of *Black Hawk Down*, a Hollywood movie with a star-studded cast.

Prima facie, humanitarian relief aid seeks to humanize the globe, to make it into a humane world, a place more hospitable to humanity, by giving succor to the needy regardless of national affiliation. Transnational humanitarian NGOs purport to world the world in the image of humanity. As Jonathan Benthall has noted, their logos are mappings of the globe in terms of the suffering parts of a world in need of salvation, spaces of injustice that require the intervention of humanitarian justice.

> The United Nations uses a map of the globe . . . surmounting Olympic laurel leaves—to which the World Health Organization adds a medical caduceus. UNHCR adds to the laurels a pair of hands offering shelter to a "lego" man; UNICEF a mother holding up her baby. . . . World Vision uses a Christian cross apparently impaling the globe like a sword from North to South Pole. . . . In 1992, to mark its fiftieth anniversary, Oxfam [adopted] . . . a new logo,

"OXFAM: Working for a Fairer World," in which the capital O has become a globe with cross-hatchings presumably representing divisions and injustice, the X possibly expresses anger, the F slopes backwards, the A and the M stand four-square on their feet. Christian Aid again uses a stylized image of the globe, but viewed, unlike the UN's, from somewhere above the Equator. Spreadeagled from the North to the South Poles is a thin human figure with tapering arms and legs. This symbol was designed for a poster by Maurice Rickards. . . . [His] name for his concept was "The Victim." "This figure . . . is a monument to millions. It represents the concentration-camp victim, the refugee, the oppressed, the outcast and the disaster-stricken."[2]

In fact, humanitarianization unworlds the world of an aid-receiving people. In the case of Somalia, the US Department of State attached a paramount importance to the provision of humanitarian relief for reasons of realpolitik. This led to the sanctioning of military action by UN forces according to the concept of humanitarian intervention—here, foreign intervention in a sovereign nation-state to facilitate the right of humanitarian access to famine victims—such that the actions of UN forces clearly violated the international legal standards for humanitarian treatment in wartime established by the Geneva Conventions.[3] From June 5 to October 3, 1992, clashes with UN forces and fights between rival Somali armed groups claimed the lives of six to ten thousand Somalis.[4]

Nuruddin Farah's *Gifts* is concerned with the devastating consequences of humanitarian relief aid in Somalia. Although it is set in a period before the fall of the Barre regime and the concentration of global public attention on Somalia as the target of humanitarian care, it presciently explores the underlying logic of transnational aid that led to the tragedy of humanitarian intervention.[5] International philanthropy creates an asymmetrical relationship of inequality, dependency, and even domination between donor and recipient nations that undermines the dignity and self-determination of peoples receiving aid by making them into passive suffering victims and objects of pity. The ethics of international philanthropy, the novel suggests, is continuous with the capitalist world-system's exploitative logic of commodity exchange.

But there is no indulgent breast-beating about how abject populations in the peripheries, the contemporary equivalent of peoples left behind by the march of Hegelian world history, have suffered from famine, poverty, and human-made disasters. The novel's central question is affirmative: How can a people in situations of need achieve self-determination and become the active subject of their own history and self-directed future? How can a people announce themselves as a subject so that they can be a participating member of a plural humanity when the global system deprives them of having a world by creating structural relations of dependency that infantilize them into a prolonged "minority" (*Unmündigkeit*), as Kant would have said? Responding to the charge that US intervention is justified because Somalia has become a post–September 11 terrorist haven, Farah notes that "to own Somalia's problems and eventually its solutions, we must take possession of our country, and everyone must return our property to us, and all interferences in our affairs must stop."[6] The permanent receiving of foreign aid undermines a people's self-possession. Hence, the question of emergence is tied to the issue of how to receive with dignity. Conversely, for donor nations, the global philanthropic public, and humanitarian agencies, the question is how to give in a manner that does not disable the recipient through perpetual indebtedness and dependency.

Like Ghosh, Farah sees himself as a practitioner of world literary exchange à la Goethe. Reflecting on his choice to write in English, he emphasizes the importance of a worldly ethos of respect for different literary traditions and the values of multilingualism and multiculturalism for expanding his mind.

> With our minds open, our hearts likewise, we received the world, and along with it the knowledge that made the world larger and more varied too. There is something forward-looking about knowing other languages, something outward-looking about studying the cultures of other peoples: not only do you enrich your understanding of your own culture, but it makes you appreciate yours all the more. . . . Writing in foreign tongues was as much fun as reading had been entertaining and edifying too. I felt encouraged by what I read, stories whose cunning and sophistication enabled me to get in touch with the narrative genius that is the African folktale. Literature of the written and oral variety became a mansion in which I moved with self-edifying ease, reading books in foreign tongues and listening to the oral wisdom transmitted in Somali. . . . I was elated by this multicultural encounter, the world now unitary, and now boasting of a wealth of differences, each expressive of a human need: the need to gain more knowledge about myself and about the lives of others, in order to be fulfilled.[7]

In the spirit of Goethean *Spiegelung*, Farah notes that encountering other languages and literatures and writing in a language that is not his mother tongue is a process of wondrous estrangement. It leads to a self-reflexivity that enables one to better understand one's own literary traditions and overcome the limitations of ethno-nationalist insularity and particularism.[8] Hence, despite the fact that his works are primarily concerned with Somalian politics, critics have described Farah as "a writer in the tradition of cosmopolitan modernism" and as "Africa's most cosmopolitan writer."[9] Simon Gikandi notes that through a complex intertextuality that connects African literature, Asian poetry, and religion to high European literary culture, Farah "extends his literary and philosophical referents to make postcolonial Somali culture part of a cosmopolitan discourse that is a crucial ingredient of what it means to be African in the modern world."[10]

Gifts seeks to hold together a Somali world stifled by humanitarian aid. Farah suggests that storytelling is itself a generous form of giving that worlds a world. It disrupts the calculative logic of humanitarianization and creates a worldly domain of ethics. This world, a dynamic place where social solidarity repeatedly emerges from the quotidian activity of Somalians coping with famine and civil war, gives the lie to the representation of Somalia as a political wasteland in desperate need of humanitarian intervention.

I first outline the main features of "humanitarian dehumanization"—the dehumanization of recipients of aid in the humanitarian imaginary—and its calculative logic of the quantification of life and the role of literature in challenging the media narratives at the heart of the humanitarian imaginary that portray the Somali people as victims of famine, social dysfunction, and civil war. I then consider Farah's transformative use of Mauss's theory of the gift as a solution to geopolitical problems and his celebration of African folk traditions of giving and Somali cultural practices of communal self-help as an alternative to Abrahamic-based humanitarian ideas of philanthropy. The novel provides a literary solution to the obstruction of the emergence of the Somali people by existing geopolitical gift relations by exploring the phenomenological and diegetical dimensions of giving. At the thematic level, it suggests that the Somali people can achieve self-determination through their tradition of reciprocal giving because it is their gift to world culture and should gain the world's respect. The novel's intertextual borrowings from multiple discourses and literary traditions enact reciprocal giving at the formal level. *Gifts*, however, exemplifies the structurally aporetic character of *postcolonial* world literature. As a modality of reciprocal giving, storytelling facilitates the emergence and self-determination of peoples in the postcolonial South. But the force of worlding it draws on—the inhuman gift of time as the condition of possibility of narrative—also renders self-determination problematic.

Writing against Humanitarian Dehumanization: Somalia
in the Humanitarian Imaginary and the Role of Media Narratives

In Farah's view, there are two reasons why a solution to the Somali situation needs to have recourse to literature. First, the existence of a sovereign nation that can participate fully as a member of the fraternity of nations requires a collective political personality, the state. The state's legitimacy comes from the corporate truth of the popular imagination. Where this truth is absent, as in the case of the Barre dictatorship, the state is sustained by a shabbily crafted fiction. Somalia is a poor piece of literature. "The body politic whose sinewed muscles, strong as pillars, embodied the collective strength to which every member of the community contributed: in Africa this was sadly absent. And so was the 'groomed' truth, the nursed truth so to speak, a truth mended as though it were a broken pot, a truth plastered with a 'cured' cloth. Somalia was a badly written play . . . and Siyad Barre was its author. To our chagrin, he was also the play's main actor, its center and theme; as an actor-producer, he played all the available roles."[11] For Farah, as for other Asian and African writers, such as Ngũgĩ wa Thiong'o, Pramoedya Ananta Toer, and Salman Rushdie, literature's political vocation is to expose the cracks in the dictator's art by narrating "the true history of the nation."[12] Literature resists authoritarianism through world-public phenomenality. But after the fall of the Barre regime and the concentrated inflow of humanitarian aid, literature's vocation is to understand the nation's crisis in a scenario where the larger world has become part of the problem. Literature challenges fiction of another kind: representations of Somalia in global media narratives that shape the humanitarian imaginary. Such narratives deprive the Somali people of their capacity for world-making by reducing them to irrational perpetrators of clan-motivated civil war, hapless victims of famine and internal strife, and passive recipients of foreign aid.

The problematic of *Gifts* resonates with recent critiques of humanitarianism.[13] Their overarching theme is the threat of heteronomy. Heteronomy takes two forms: first, the material subjection of recipient nations to the economic and political imperatives of donor nations and the self-interested motives of humanitarian agencies, and second, the incapacitation of peoples receiving aid at the level of subjectivity, because they live in a global environment structured by relations of dependency that deprive individuals of the will for self-determination.

In the later part of the 1980s, Africa became the world's largest regional recipient of food aid and humanitarian assistance. I use the phrase "the humanitarianization of the world," to refer to the growing trend whereby Western donor governments divert official aid away from states in the South and channel funds through transnational humanitarian NGOs, who become the primary subcontractor for the large-scale delivery of basic services such as health, agricultural extension, and food rationing to needy people in the South.[14] By the end of the Cold War, NGOs had achieved a greater net transfer of resources to the South than the World Bank.[15] In principle, philanthropic humanitarianism should transcend the self-interested imperatives of market exchange because it only enters a space to satisfy needs that are left unfulfilled by a total absence of market institutions or in an environment that is not amenable to healthy market activity such as famine or civil war. In fact, flows of humanitarian aid actively integrate recipient countries into a neoliberal regime of global market exchange.

First, contemporary humanitarianism is a symptomatic expression of the power of transnational market mechanisms to undermine the self-determination of peoples in the South. As Alex de Waal has provocatively claimed, the rise of humanitarian internationalism in the 1980s–1990s is isomorphic with neoliberalism, because its underlying logic is a retreat from political accountability to the people in need of aid. Although NGOs may be critical of the harsh consequences of structural adjustment, they do not provide a coherent alternative political and economic program. Their philanthropic efforts as service deliverers merely create a charitable human face to supplement neoliberalism: "The internationalization of social welfare is closely linked to the decline of state authority, which is central to the neo-liberal project. . . . Both neo-liberalism and international humanitarianism are justifications for foreign institutions to intrude into the domestic politics of African countries. . . . Even when the intrusions have succeeded on their own terms, they have rarely supported progressive political contracts."[16]

Second, humanitarianism is an ideological mask for the self-interested political motives of donor countries. It reinforces relations of inequality between giver and recipient countries within the framework of global capitalist market exchange. Even when there are no explicit strings attached, aid can be used to indebt grateful recipients and bend them to the wills of donor nations or as a form of reward that perpetuates the cycle of obligation. Henry Kissinger publicly spoke of disaster relief as an important US foreign policy instrument. The 1950s US "food for peace" program illustrates the manipulative use of international aid to dispose of surplus grain production from the US Midwest and to reward Cold War allies.[17]

Third, the corrosive force of world marketization is also at work in NGO practices. Although they claim to be the institutional objectification of disinterested humanitarianism, NGOs need to compete for funding. Humanitarian workers are also driven by the desire for career security, prestige, and job satisfaction. In their struggle to survive and justify themselves in the global market of philanthropy, NGOs often act in a manner that undermines their humanitarian ideals.[18] To achieve success in this marketplace, they have to produce the best charitable product to sell to donors. Humanitarian workers then frequently assume that their interests are identical to those of the subjects they wish to help, thereby blocking out the latter's needs and interests through ventriloquism.

The humanitarianization of the world leads to a vicious form of dehumanization where providers of aid fail to affirm the humanity of the people they purportedly serve and, indeed, actively dehumanize them. Humanitarian dehumanization's underlying logic is the quantification of human life. Because the charitable solution to famine focuses on material assistance, it views human life as something that can be measured and improved by human calculation. In Somalia, this led to the privileging of the logistics of resource delivery, the protection of relief agencies, and the demotion of the needs and suffering of subjects requiring aid. Instead of regarding Somalis as full human personalities and responding to local demands, philanthropic agencies reduced Somalis to passive recipients of aid and victims of self-inflicted civil war.

The emphasis on immediate material existence is politically naïve and ends up prolonging human suffering, because it treats the symptom (hunger) instead of the disease (the political-economic system and global power relations that lead to the violation of human rights).[19] Moreover, this approach to famine has the ironic effect of bolstering corrupt regimes. Humanitarian relief can shield authoritarian governments from the possibility of popular unrest and enrich local elites.[20] Wars give rise to their own distinctive informal economy in which oppressive dominant extrastate groups, such as warlords and gangsters, thrive in the environment of a collapsed or dysfunctional formal economy.[21] Such predatory groups control irregular economic activities, expropriate the assets of the population, and manipulate relief aid. They thrive on "the displacement and impoverishment" of the masses and are "intrinsically disaster-producing."[22] Relief operations have often fueled conflict among predatory groups seeking to profit from aid distribution. Moreover, by operating through informal channels, NGOs fuel the further erosion of remaining civil society institutions, because informal activity retards the development of the national capacity for coordinated relief and economic development.[23]

Philanthropic imperialism and militarized humanitarianism are the culmination of humanitarian dehumanization. Critics have rightly noted that exercises of the so-called right of humanitarian intervention have involved a demand for access to victims for the efficient delivery of aid resources that has ironically disregarded the rights of victims, who are viewed as objects of assistance.[24] This leads to the ultimate irony where the primary aim of military intervention is to protect humanitarian workers so that they can better deliver aid. As Alex de Waal astutely points out, UN resolutions concerning Iraq, Bosnia, and Somalia transformed the way the right of humanitarian access was interpreted, "so that material relief was given legal pre-eminence over human rights; assistance was given priority over protection. . . . In the 1990s, the right of 'humanitarian access' has come to refer primarily to the desire of humanitarian agencies to be operational in conflict zones. The needs of the relief agency are conflated with those of the suffering civilians. . . . As a consequence, international military intervention in Somalia and Bosnia was primarily aimed at protecting aid givers, rather than the populace in the area."[25]

Whereas the emphasis on the logistics of resource delivery dehumanizes subjects needing relief, the critique of humanitarianism enjoins responsibility to the humanity of the suffering considered in the full complexity of concrete situations. Literature can play an important role in increasing awareness of local contexts. Humanitarian organizations use global media narratives about famine to stimulate interest in an area of suffering for the purpose of eliciting large-scale transnational relief. These dramatic narratives package suffering into an urgent philanthropic cause, a commodified charitable product that can attract intense demand from donors, ranging from states to transnational institutions and the wider public in other countries. They are the primary means of transmitting knowledge about disaster in the postcolonial South to the larger world. Global media and humanitarian NGOs are symbiotically related by mutual self-interest. The media is dependent on NGOs for access to the country and for conveniently condensed information for stories and soundbites; NGOs serve as guides and cultural translators to help the media navigate a hostile environment. Conversely, NGOs rely on journalists for publicity to attract philanthropic funding for their professional activity. Unfortunately, these news stories are not based on careful investigation and extensive observation but on "disaster tourism."[26] As de Waal notes, "relief agency guides take visitors to the worst places (relief shelters) and are keen to stress the hunger and dependence of the people and the importance of relief. This leads to exaggerated, dire predictions and stereotypes of pathetic dependency."[27]

The photojournalistic images portraying disaster in Africa that humanitarian agencies depend on when appealing for public funding range from compassionate realism to predatory sensationalism and to aestheticism.[28] Jonathan Benthall points out that these images efface the viewpoint of Africans and reinforce "stereotypes of a doomed and helpless continent" that originate from the colonial era.[29] The publicity of disaster relief follows the narrative convention of a folktale.

> The central character of the narrative is the travelling *hero*, who may be an expatriate fieldworker, such as an officer of Oxfam or MSF, or a foreign correspondent. There is also in some cases a *villain*—a Pol Pot in the Cambodian crisis of the late 1970s. . . . But . . . in those tales where no villainy is present, "lack" or misfortune can serve instead, and it is noticed by a *dispatcher*. . . . [The *donor*] is another essential character. The donor provides the hero with a *magical agent* sometimes in the form of a *magical helper*— clearly, in our case, the embodiments of Western abundance and technology in its various forms. After the hero has undergone various ordeals and solved difficult tasks, the misfortune or lack is liquidated. . . . Fairy tales . . . have to have a happy ending. The agencies try to provide this, especially in their annual reports to donors and staff, with a favored alternative to the image of distress: the image of gratitude.[30]

These fairy tale elements were present in the media coverage of Somalia prior to US intervention. As the tale progressed into 1993, the villain, initially the misfortune of famine coupled with the authoritarian Barre regime, now included the warring factions that succeeded his downfall. The NGOs entrusted with delivering relief were the hero. They were assisted by the UN and the US-led taskforce of the aptly named Operation Restore Hope. The media coverage of Somalia has been described as a form of "disaster pornography."[31] Through the narrative manipulation of emotionally charged visual images— the juxtaposition of gunmen on jeeps amid ruins with pathetic malnourished children—Somalia was portrayed as teetering on the edge of an apocalypse and the Somali people as an assortment of victims in distress, corrupt profiteers, and violent elements who prevented relief aid delivery. This picture of a place crying out for US-led humanitarian imperialist intervention did not correspond to the real Somalia. As Rakiya Omaar notes, even in the areas of the country stricken by famine, outright starvation is the exception. Most deaths are the result of disease. The great majority of people will survive—largely due to their own efforts. International food aid is much less important than food grown by local farmers, the maintenance of animal herds, having roots and berries to eat and the charity of relatives and friends. . . . The total impact of our charitable giving is less than what can be achieved if the stricken people are enabled to assist themselves. If "Operation Restore Hope" is to live up to its name, first it must restore humanity, self-respect and dignity to the Somali people. This cannot be done while the press corps makes disaster pornography pass for a true portrait of the Somali nation.[32]

The one-sided global media folk narrative about Somalia creates despair and obscures internal political efforts of reconstruction.[33] Humanitarianism undermines the self-determination of Somalis and the establishment of local political accountability by replacing local political contracts for coping with disaster with a relationship between nonaccountable relief agencies, media, and the donating public.[34]

Humanitarian aid constantly encroaches on the lives of the characters of *Gifts*. It is the background for their daily acts of giving and receiving. Set in a Mogadiscio "of galloping inflation, famines, foreign currency restrictions and corrupt market transactions" (*G*, 160), the novel provides a cognitive mapping of 1980s famine-stricken Somalia within the totality of global capitalism. It critically portrays humanitarian dehumanization by inserting in its narrative fictive international news reports about drought, famine, civil war, campaigns of Third World governments for foreign aid, and various "gifts" from Northern states and international NGOs. The juxtaposition of the reports with the narrative suggests that the reality they describe is constituted in narrative time. The citation of media reports, which are discontinuous with the narrative and abruptly punctuate the ends of chapters, reframes their content in terms of the characters' daily lives, problematizes their facticity, and denatures the world they create.

The clippings function like a media version of a Robert Browning dramatic monologue: Northern powers and humanitarian organizations are condemned through the dramatic irony of global media reports meant to serve as mouthpieces extolling their generosity. They contain knowledge that justifies the reluctance of Third World countries to receive gifts of foreign aid. In a Reuters report, a UNDP spokesperson notes that "millions of people in the developing world have starved to death because of the policies of Western creditor nations" and that "it was unfair ... that poor countries have been made to depend totally on what happens not in their own economies but in those of richer, more economically developed countries" (G, 33). Another report suggests that foreign aid is a form of foreign intervention that undermines the recipient's sovereignty: "After economic and political pressures (and no doubt delicate negotiations), the European Community has finally imposed its mighty will on the Ethiopian President Mengistu Haile Mariam by making him accept that a team of EC officials oversee the distribution of food aid in the country's northern provinces" (G, 148). Yet another report points to the contradictions of African aid: aid is given to Mozambique because it is in an economic crisis caused by a rebel uprising assisted by the United States and South Africa (G, 181–82). Other negative effects include the strings-attached character of aid—the extraction of concessions from recipient countries under the rubric of "structural adjustment," aid as a way for economically developed countries to dump surplus or harmful agricultural products (such as Chernobyl-contaminated milk). The encouragement of cash crop farming for an international market is a way of manufacturing famine.

The novel's often heavy-handed critique takes the form of didactic commentary. A fictional newspaper article entitled "Giving and Receiving: The Notion of Donations" suggests that current practices of foreign aid make the economy of a receiving country totally beholden to economically developed countries. Foreign food donations can even create a buffer zone between corrupt leaderships and the starving masses, thereby preventing the overthrow of authoritarian regimes. But worse still, foreign aid is a structural form of expropriation. Somalia becomes chronically dependent because it cannot refuse to accept or return an unwanted donation.

The clash between the novel's main narrative and the news reports is a conflict between two forms of representational realism: reportorial and critical. Reportorial realism conveys bare facts and information, often in a quantitative manner, and facilitates the reductive determination of human life in terms of economic value in the worldless world of capitalist globalization. Critical realism exposes the lie of reportorial realism through fuller mimetic representation. The vivid ethnographic detail of the novel's portrayal of Somali characters engaging in gift relations in their everyday lives presupposes local knowledge of the physical environment, sociopolitical context, and cultural traditions. This cognitive mapping of concrete Somalian existence seeks to reshape global public perceptions of Somalia. It fractures the existing world's factical solidity. It shows that the world does not have a predetermined linear path of development, namely, economic and political progress along the lines of Western modernity, which dictates structural adjustment for the postcolonial South, but is only *a* world that can be contested and remade. In addition, the novel is composed of many narrative voices and styles and diverse forms of literary representation, some of which draw on non-Western cultural traditions. This discursive heteroglossia, which has been described as a verbal potlatch that explodes the boundaries of the conventional novel through formal excess and intertextual collage, expresses at the formal level an alternative kind of giving based on reciprocity derived from the thought of Marcel Mauss.[35] I will now consider how the novel develops Mauss's ideas into a practical basis for Somali popular self-determination.

In a Maussian Spirit: Local Traditions of Giving with Reciprocity, Popular Self-Determination, and Emergence

Gifts distinguishes between four modalities of giving: geopolitical, anthropological, phenomenological, and narrative. By drawing an extended analogy between geopolitical gift relations and anthropological practices of giving, the novel elucidates humanitarian aid's underlying logic and offers an alternative model of giving in its characters' actions and the resolution of its plot. Duniya, the novel's protagonist, personifies the Somali people. Her entire life has been governed by masculinist-patriarchal relations of dependency that have placed her in the position of a gift, an object of exchange between men.[36] As the narrator tells us,

> it was when she thought of herself as a woman and thought about the female gender in the general context of "home" that Duniya felt depressed. The landmarks of her journey through life from infancy to adulthood were marked by various "stations," all of them owned by men, run and dominated by men. Did she not flee Zubair's right into Shiriye's? There was a parenthesis of time, a brief period when she was her own mistress and the runner of her station, so to speak, as a free tenant of Taariq's, only for this to cease when they became husband and wife. Meanwhile, her elder brother Abshir's omnipresent, benevolent and well-meaning shadow fell on every ramshackle structure she built, pursuing every move she made, informing every step she took: Abshir being another station, another man. Now there was Bosaaso. *Morale della storia?* Duniya was homeless, like a great many women the world over. And as a woman she was property-less. (*G*, 172–73)

In the resolution of the novel's plot, Duniya successfully breaks away from these dependency relations and emerges as an autonomous agent who participates in reciprocal giving in her romantic relations with Bosaaso, a well-to-do widower. She sums up the meaning of her life story by stressing her resolve to be independent: "'To know who I am and how I have fared, you must understand why I resist all kinds of domination, including that of being given something. As my epitaph I would like to have the following written: 'Here lies Duniya who distrusted givers'" (G, 241–42).

The violence of foreign aid stems from its unilateral and hierarchical character, the fact that it has not been willingly requested, cannot be returned and is received under the compulsion of crisis. Such giving is a form of aggression and domination that undermines the establishment of genuine sociality. Because there cannot be a reciprocal relation between donor and donee, the donee is placed in a cycle of perpetual indebtedness that causes indignity and humiliation. As Duniya puts it, "unasked-for generosity has a way of making one feel obliged, trapped in a labyrinth of dependence. . . . Haven't we in the Third World lost our self-reliance and pride because of the so-called aid we unquestioningly receive from the so-called First World?" (G, 22)

The novel draws directly on Mauss's famous essay on the gift, which emphasizes an unreciprocated gift's injurious and humiliating effects: it "makes the person who has accepted it inferior, particularly when it has been accepted with no thought of returning it. . . . Charity is still wounding for him who has accepted it, and the whole tendency of our morality is to strive to do away with the unconscious and injurious patronage of the rich almsgiver."[37] Institutions of giving in Polynesian, Melanesian, and American northwestern tribes, however, are unlike modern capitalist relations because they are characterized by reciprocity between independent parties who compete and vie with each other. Unlike the self-interested exchange of commodities, which presupposes the atomistic individual without social ties and obligations, agonistic practices of giving are disinterested and create social obligations. Hence, Mauss argued, a gift economy is an originary sociality. A return to "archaic society's" gift relations can solve the problems of capitalist modernity by helping us arrive at an optimum balance between individual interests and self-reliance and public generosity and care for others and by furnishing the moral basis for world peace and solidarity.[38]

In a gesture typical of postcolonial world literature, Farah transposes Mauss's ideas to postcolonial Somalia and transforms them in three respects. First, where Mauss suggests that charitable impulses are originally rooted in a gift economy, *Gifts* depicts humanitarian relief aid as an insidious type of giving that has greater affinity to commodity exchange than the gift because it incorporates recipient countries into the global market. Humanitarian giving is self-interested. It does not occur out of affection and generosity or with direct knowledge of the needs of a particular recipient community but creates a condition of indebtedness marked by structural inequality in power and status between donor and recipient.

Farah portrays the values of Western humanitarianism with dramatic irony in a didactic conversation between Bosaaso, his first wife, Yussur, and Ingrid, a Danish woman who worked with a Scandinavian voluntary organization in Somalia. Yussur notes that Western aid consists of things the donor no longer needs and values (*G*, 48). A large part of US financial aid to Somalia consists of surplus agricultural produce that needs to be dumped. Much of US aid never benefits Somalians but supports the salaries of American relief workers who live luxuriously in Somalia. Moreover, a calculated return is built into such gifts. Wheat donated by the European Community is a "free sample" aimed at creating a future generation of African consumers, and wheat given by a charity from the US Bible Belt leads to earthly vainglory (*G*, 197). As epitomized by the stereotypes of starving African children in disaster pornography, giving is here an act of self-aggrandization on the part of the donor and even a form of aggression that involves the belittlement of the recipient through benevolence. The gifts are not objects of genuine need, and one gives so that one can occupy a superior position and place the other in the inferior receiving position. Because the recipient's gratitude is compelled, no reciprocity is possible.

At its most damaging, foreign aid subjects a people in dire need to a process of expropriation. It leads to a corrosive loss of dignity and identity at the subjective level. Foreign gifts of food inflict psychical injury to the citizens of receiving countries. As Taariq, Duniya's former husband, puts it, they "sabotage the African's ability to survive with dignity" (*G*, 196). Foreign aid can also undermine the legitimacy of government efforts to deal with famine when the population regards foreign relief programs as superior to government programs. At the objective level, it leads to a material condition of impotence. It creates an illegal informal economy that cannot be sustained and that leads to violence and corruption on the part of elites when foreign aid is cut off. The abundance of food from relief agencies threatens to destroy the local agricultural economy and undermine local employment because it undercuts demand and prices for local produce.[39] Hence, relief aid opens recipient peoples up to the foreign without the possibility of a return to self. It makes them utterly helpless and dependent instead of fostering social solidarity and self-determination.

Second, whereas Mauss argues that the fundamental principles of a gift economy have survived in ancient Indo-European legal systems, *Gifts* posits a sharp distinction between giving in African cultural traditions and in the Abrahamic religions. The latter is at heart a form of exchange without reciprocity and constitutes the religious-ethical basis for Western humanitarianism and the exploitative global capitalist world-system. In contrast, the former leads to reciprocal social relations and should be taken as a model for international relations. By insisting on the unique world-historical contribution of gift practices from the Somalian cultural tradition, Farah's novel resonates with recent social scientific studies that have responded to the critique of Western humanitarianism by exploring alternative traditions of contemporary charitable organization that are rooted in non-Western religions.[40] This also makes *Gifts* an example of the discourse of non-Western modernity discussed in chapter 7. Unlike Mauss, Farah does not advocate a nostalgic return to archaic society. Just as Cliff harkens back to precolonial African traditions transplanted to Jamaica and Ghosh celebrates the Bon Bibi myth, Farah portrays Somalian practices of giving as living traditions that inform daily existence in contemporary Somalia.

The distinction between Somali and Western traditions of giving is primarily the difference between the religious ethics of a polytheistic animistic worldview and that of Abrahamic monotheism. According to Dr. Mire, Bosaaso's close friend and Duniya's boss at the hospital, the difference between the religious ethics of the peoples of the Book and African beliefs lies in how one understands the finitude of worldly existence and whether one believes that the world is created by a transcendent absolute power. "The starting-point is this: *who* or *what* do we worship? In the case of the Somali who deifies crows, the answer is clear: Somalis defer to death, crows being associated with the ending of life, a termination of this existence. What the Judaeo-Christian and Islamic systems offer is a forward-looking, reward-offering life-after-death rationalization, a credo in which you are guaranteed paradisiacal delights after death" (*G*, 96). The Abrahamic religions respond to finitude by means of a restricted ethical economy of self-return that is specular and speculative. The specular processes of religion project the human being onto a higher plane by creating an ultramundane God in man's image. This projection is also a movement of speculative self-return, an investment from which one reaps profits. Belief in an absolute infinite being enables individuals to transcend their finite existence in a higher form of life (divine life) that lies beyond the mortal world. One works hard in this world and trusts that the ultra-mundane God who gives us being will reward us in an eternal world. Salvation is thus essentially a process of reflective self-worship. It is highly individualistic and personal in character and confirms the absolute power of the human self. As Mire puts it, "you invest your efforts in your daily activities of self-worship . . . and are promised heavenly dividends worthy of your trust in a god who gives and takes away life" (G, 97). This view is supported by social scientific scholarship that argues that Western humanitarian and development NGOs are informed by a Christian tradition of giving such that charity is accompanied by the implicit expectation of repayment in another life or the affirmation of good conscience.[41]

In contradistinction, the Somali belief system is not based on the transcendence of finitude through self-worship but instead accepts the limited term of life. Crows mark the term of a mortal life. Being "unlike man's idea of himself," the crow is not an anthropomorphic projection of man's image but a figure for the inhuman, inappropriable other (G, 97). Hence, the Somali ethical economy is characterized by an openness to what is radically other to and beyond the control of human beings. A worldview grounded in the acceptance of human finitude gives rise to a superior ethics where we cope with finitude through worldly cooperative activity or the shared negotiation with crises and emergencies. For example, in Somali custom, food should be shared because it is perishable (G, 198). Such an ethics gives rise to communal forms of giving that can be the basis for solidarity: extended families form a system of needs that are fulfilled by the exchange of potlatches. This type of giving is characterized by collective self-determination in the face of need and reciprocity. Taariq's article notes that

> there is a tradition, in Somalia, of passing around the hat for collections. It is called *Qaaraan*. When you are in dire need of help, you invite your friends, relatives and in-laws to come to your place or someone else's, where, as the phrase goes, a mat has been spread. But there are conditions laid down. The need has to be genuine, the person wishing to be helped has to be a respectable member of society, not a loafer, a lazy ne'er-do-well, a debtor or a thief. Here discretion is of the utmost significance. Donors

don't mention the sums they offer, and the recipient doesn't know who has given what. *It is the whole community from which the person receives a presentation and to which he is grateful.* It is not permitted that such a person thereafter applies for more, not soon at any rate. If there is a lesson to be learned from this, it is that emergencies are one-off affairs, not a yearly excuse for asking for more. (*G*, 196, emphasis added)

[In] a familiar or tribal society . . . obligatory or voluntary exchanges of gifts are part of the code of behaviour. In such a context, the exchange is direct. You give somebody something; a year later, when you are in need, today's recipient becomes tomorrow's giver. (*G*, 197)

This kind of gift economy involves ad hoc negotiations with finitude as it erupts without anticipation into the regular rhythms of social life. The characteristics of reciprocity and collective self-determination follow from the gift's anonymity and incalculability. First, because we do not know the specific donor and the sum that is given, the recipient is not directly indebted to a given individual but to the entire community. Second, the donation is not a continually recurring and fixed process but a singular event that arises in response to an unexpected emergency. Hence, the possibility of reciprocity is inscribed in the act of giving. This form of giving makes long-term structural dependency impossible. There is collective self-determination because the donor is the whole community and it is the community that helps itself. There is an ongoing reciprocity because the positions of donor and recipient are not fixed in perpetuity but are reversible and can change according to contextual contingency. It gives rise to a cooperative communal interdependence that is immanent to the world.

Conversely, the hierarchical structure of global capitalism derives from the ethics of the Abrahamic religions. The individualistic belief in salvation beyond this world is premised on an omnipotent creditor to whom we are indebted for our existence. We are in permanent debt to God and can only discharge this debt in the eternal world. The gift of life is thus a hierarchical unilateral relation without reciprocity because reciprocity between an absolute being and its creature is impossible. The unilateral character of humanitarian relief is a relay of this hierarchy, which is the foundation of a larger web of relations of chronic economic dependency and underdevelopment that determine postcolonial Africa's place in the world-system. Indeed, Taariq suggests that the destruction of the plurality of African gods by the Middle Eastern philosophical conception of a monotheistic God as transcendence epitomizes the drive toward unilateral control (G, 198).

Third, contra Mauss, Farah suggests that gift relations are not part of an agonistic competition but a matter of mutual help among a given people and between different nations. The point here is not that one should always reject the generous help of others when one is in need but that one should exercise critical judgment over which gifts to ask for. A recipient who accepts a gift with the element of critical knowledge exercises self-determination and is not subjected to others. The passive acceptance of humanitarian aid is not the only available response to crisis. Famine can be a stimulus for revolutionary action. Reenvisioning humanitarian aid along the model of communal self-help will create a global community of interdependence where reciprocity is deferred into the future, in a possible situation where Africa may be able to help Northern countries.

These alternative models of giving are not utopian. They exist in Somalia alongside the more publically visible attention-seeking operations of global humanitarian organizations. As Cindy Horst notes, although "the international aid regime claims a monopoly on assistance based on the perception that the UN and NGOs are the sole providers of aid and that refugees are solely receivers," there are, in fact, agencies that operate with different principles from that of charity, such as principles of human rights and the gift-giving norms of local communities.[42] "Somalis see assistance to those in need as an absolute responsibility of the individual as a member of a larger whole, whether this is the family, clan, community, or umma. It is a religious and cultural obligation to assist those who are struck by a crisis situation and to contribute to the livelihoods of one's close relatives in need."[43] These norms explain why Duniya willingly receives Abshir's financial gifts without feeling trapped in dependency. Such acts of reciprocal giving and mutual self-help in the novel tie its characters together and form a world. Beyond the novel's frame, Somali traditions of giving also lead to self-determined popular political action. Local relief work and other existing social resources, such as the clan system, indicate the presence of opportunities for nascent political contracts that can effectively deal with the crisis and reconstruct social services and a new economic system.[44] Somalia is not a political desert, as Arendt would have said, that needs to be filled by humanitarian agencies, especially when actually existing humanitarianism destroys local openings for world-building.

Farah's critique of humanitarian dehumanization is at heart a discourse of sovereign self-determination. Humanitarianism asserts humanity's sovereignty against the self-determination of the failed Somali state. But this assertion of sovereign humanity actually destroys the self-determination of the Somali people and their world by creating dependency. Farah wishes to restore self-determination to Somalians by arguing that their traditional practices of reciprocal giving are an alternative to chronic dependency. This gift economy is Somalia's contribution to world culture and can serve as a model for international relations. By thematizing this contribution, *Gifts* is postcolonial Somalia's contribution to world literature in the narrow sense. It is an example of world literature in the normative sense because it self-reflexively foregrounds the worlding power of stories by suggesting that we emerge as self-determining agents and engage in reciprocal relations with others by telling stories.

The novel repeatedly suggests that the coming into presence of a world is a gift in the phenomenological sense. The perceived world is literally a present, something that is given. The first chapter is titled "In which Duniya sees the outlines of a story emerging from the mists surrounding her, as the outside world impinges on her space and thoughts" (*G*, 3). Giving is the impingement of the outside world, of things and other people on our consciousness through our senses. But, more important, we are given the light of phenomenality without which experience would be impossible. Even merely waking up and seeing the world is already to receive a gift that opens a world. The fact that Duniya first sees a story and not objects or things suggests that our initial response to the gift of the world is to tell a story about it. In ways that recall Keats's poetry, it is unclear whether she is awake or asleep. A cat has appeared in her dreams and she fully awakens only when it falls asleep. The novel contains many sequences of such liminal states, where neither reader nor character is certain whether events are part of a dream. In these sequences, Duniya and Bosaaso tell stories of a fabulous nature involving animals with magical powers, such as dragonflies, butterflies, and cats. If we add to this the reflexivity that derives from the fact that Duniya means "world," then the chapter title suggests that a story comes into being when an inner world of imaginary space and thoughts interacts with the external world. It suggests, moreover, that the world is constituted by, or better yet, is nothing but an auto-poetic process of narration about itself.

The juxtaposition of these scenes of phenomenological giving with human-itarian giving has a different function from the contrast between the reporto-rial realism of media discourse about humanitarianism and the critical realist representation of anthropological giving discussed earlier. Phenomenological giving constitutes experience. As the process that gives us the reality we take as given, it has a dreamlike, fabulous character. The giving and receiving of a world is marked by indeterminacy and incalculability, because it is a process whereby reality is being (re)constituted and has yet to achieve (re)stabilization. Hence, scenes of phenomenological giving exceed and undermine the calcula-tive and instrumental relations based on self-interested commodity exchange. The juxtaposition of these scenes with the reportorial realism of the media evokes the puncturing of reality by the process that constitutes it. This open-ing enables critical realist narrative to contest and remake the existing world.

Gifts uncannily echoes Arendt's account of the world as a web of authorless stories in its suggestion that the world opened by phenomenological giving is sustained by the telling of stories. Because our habitual relations to things and intercourse with others hold a world together, the existing world is dis-rupted and a new world is opened up whenever someone new enters our lives. Duniya's encounter with Bosaaso is such an irruptive event.[45] It generates a story, and the subsequent relating and receiving of other stories create and sustain the new world that is formed.

The first part of the novel is titled "A Story Is Born." Duniya is conscious of herself as a storyteller: "Stories pursue audiences to their hiding-places, she told herself. Bosaaso had become her narrative" (*G*, 23). But stories are in themselves also gift relations. A story begins when the other is given to me, enters my world, and draws me into his or her world. The telling of a story in response to this gift is also an act of giving that requires a receiver. The positions of teller and audience, giver and receiver, are endlessly revers-ible. Initially, Duniya is the receiver who is pursued by the story announcing Bosaaso's appearance as a subject in her world. But when she assumes the role of narrator by claiming him as her narrative, she becomes an agent who tells her own story. He becomes a part of her story, and they share a common world formed by her telling of the story about them. Duniya's opening of a world through storytelling is reciprocated when Bosaaso dreams of Duniya and tells her a story about his life history: "He diverted his mind by telling himself (and Duniya in her dream, of which he is a part) the story of an only son of an only parent" (*G*, 42). Their ability to tell stories to each other telepathically and in dreams maintains their shared world.

Gifts teems with a multitude of narrators and storytellers. The omniscient narrator who informs the reader of the actions of characters and the plot's social context is the most obvious of these. The novel's main characters are also storytellers. Some, like Bosaaso and Nasiiba, Duniya's older daughter, tell stories about what happens in their daily lives or their history. Others recount Somali and African folktales with edifying morals.[46] These two types of narration, which interrupt and complicate the omniscient narrator's main narration, enact Somalian self-determination.

By telling her own story and life history, a character attempts to take control of her life and give it a meaning and direction that is different from the constraining and even oppressive role given to her in the narratives of others.[47] This is clearly so for Duniya, who attempts to break away from the hierarchical patriarchal-masculinist relations of traditional Somalian society. As she puts it in an episode where she achieves control over her body by learning how to swim, "*I am the story, I am success*" (*G*, 188). These are stories of self-determination in the fullest sense, where the act of narration is in itself an expression of freedom whereby one claims ownership of one's life and the power to determine its meaning. However, the selves that are created are not the atomistic individuals of Western liberalism. The insertion of local moral folktales foregrounds the continuing existence of local religious ethics and their moral economies as resources for self-determined action. More important, the various acts of storytelling create a larger community characterized by reciprocal care in the spirit of communal self-help that the novel identified with Somalian traditions of giving.

There is a twofold connection between telling stories and generous giving. First, stories do not originate from the teller. They come into being in response to the gift of the world and the coming of the other. Second, stories can only be told if there are listeners. Arendt emphasized the agonistic structure of an intersubjective world constituted by competing stories. Farah suggests that storytelling is a relation of reciprocal generosity. The act of telling presupposes a corresponding commitment on the part of another subject to listen. Receiving a story can be as generous an act of giving because it requires patience and attention. One of the signs of Bosaaso's generous accommodating spirit is his ability to listen to Duniya's stories (*G*, 181). The telling of stories therefore implies a relation to others that is characterized by equality and reciprocity, where autonomy coexists with our heteronomous relations because we exist as unique selves within a communal whole consisting of interdependent members.

In the course of the novel, two new worlds are opened up that epitomize this coexistence of self-determination and heteronomy: the community of care created around an abandoned infant whom Duniya finds and the new family formed from her romantic love with Bosaaso. The foundling's coming is the irruption of a pure event that changes her life and catalyzes her decision to break out of a condition of dependency. A baby recalls the mystery of the giving of the world and its continuing existence because its very presence is the occasion of questions about its origins and its future: how it came into being, to whom it belongs, will it live to adulthood? Stories are told to enable others to understand the conditions of an infant's existence, such as its family background. We may attribute a meaning to its life through the determination and calculation of expectations and probabilities based on these conditions, just as we try to determine the world through our cognitive powers. But just as the giving of the world evades and exceeds our rational powers, the foundling in the novel also resists the efforts of the novel's characters to determine it. He is simply "the Nameless One."

The atmosphere of undecidability surrounding the foundling leads to a proliferation of stories narrated by Duniya and those around her as potential givers of care. He shakes up Duniya's world by frustrating the teleological time of her intentional plans of freedom, and she tries to attribute an intended design to his entry into her life. She had "always looked forward to the day when her children had grown up so that she could do what she desired with her own time and freedom. . . . The foundling was now a reality. It remained to be seen if Duniya would now have more time to herself, more physical space and liberty" (G, 66). But at the same time that the foundling takes time away from her and disrupts the turning of her world, he also creates a new world. Caring for him requires cooperation with others. His presence enables Duniya to exercise her giving spirit, which generates stories in her praise and earns her the friendship of neighbors. But, more important, the common care for the child consolidates the world opened by Duniya's and Bosaaso's romantic attachments. He is a pretext for Bosaaso's visits, and Bosaaso begins to habitually refer to himself and Duniya as a plural self, a "we." The baby's coming, a gift in the phenomenological sense, thus leads to a series of acts, such as the telling of stories and gestures of care, that establishes reciprocal bonds. The community that is formed brings to fruition Duniya's and Bosaaso's sexual attraction and gives Duniya's life story a new telos. The promise of negative freedom from parental responsibility is replaced by the reciprocal heteronomy of love in her future with Bosaaso. This future is figured as a gift of time: "There was no rush, she said to herself. They had all the time in the world to explore the depths of their feelings for one another" (*G*, 78).

However, true to the foundling's significance as an event that cannot be rationally explained, he confounds all expectations by suddenly dying. His departure creates uncertainty in the world Duniya and Bosaaso have built around his care and even threatens to destroy it. "The foundling's death shook Duniya profoundly. . . . She asked herself what would become of Bosaaso and her myth-construct? . . . Duniya wondered what would become of Bosaaso and her? Would something irrational like the foundling's death demolish the symmetries they had constructed together?" (*G*, 128–29).

But just as his birth creates a world of care, his death also serendipitously sustains that world by becoming a further source of stories. Duniya's family and friends gather at the foundling's wake and relate "anecdotes about death and creation myths" (*G*, 129). The plural self or "we" she has formed with Bosaaso is transformed by reciprocal grief and consolation into something newer and stronger. "And people came, visitors arrived in hordes, to play cards, to consume tea, to tell each other stories and to become friends. Duniya couldn't help taking account of the fact that the foundling's death imposed a compulsory set of grammatical alterations on their way of speaking, producing a *we* that had not been there before, a *we* of hybrid necessities, half real, half invented" (*G*, 135). The foundling continues to give life even in his death. Memory and storytelling nourish the world opened up by his coming. "Duniya thought that at the center of every myth is another: that of the people who created it. Everybody had turned the foundling into what they thought they wanted, or lacked. In that case, she said to herself, the Nameless One has not died. He is still living on, in Bosaaso and me" (*G*, 130).

The Time of Stories and the Aporia of Postcoloniality

For Farah, the world is the force of existence. It is repeatedly manifested in and renewed by the power to tell stories, which is an integral component of the mutual self-help required to form an autonomous Somali community. Fanon also gave storytelling an important role in creating a new world. Stories had a revolutionary force in Algeria. After storytellers "radically changed their methods of narration and the content of their stories," they stimulated people to anticolonial action by showing the emergence of a new subject.[48] "Every time the storyteller narrates a new episode, the public is treated to a real invocation. The existence of a new type of man is revealed to the public.

The present is no longer turned inward but channeled in every direction. The storyteller once again gives free rein to his imagination, innovates, and turns creator." Farah's account of storytelling is different in two respects. First, instead of being associated with political action that seeks to destroy the colonial world, storytelling is a process of ethical resistance to humanitarianization. Second, storytelling is not part of the teleological emergence of a revolutionary political subject. It gives rise to a community of reciprocal self-help that seeks to inhabit the world-system with the least heteronomy or the most tolerable degree of heteronomy, in the hope that the world will gradually be ethically transformed. Because this genesis involves the Somali people's return to itself, it can be considered teleological but only in the lower case.

However, because stories arise in response to the incalculable gift of a world, their worlding power also radically undermines sovereign self-determination. To take the foundling's passing as an example, his departure is only irrational because we rationally expect that beings who come into the world will continue to live just as we expect the world to continue to exist. But from the perspective of radical finitude, birth is an inexplicable gift. Like existence itself, death is a mysterious secret that prompts us to ask questions. We inevitably respond to the gift of existence by telling stories that try to decipher the secret and give the mysterious event a meaning or by producing knowledge that destroys its eventness by explanation. Accordingly, the teleological meanings found in this novel appropriate and convert the eventness of world-opening to teleological time. For example, in the final section, titled "Duniya Gives," Duniya posits a telos for her life. She decides to receive Bosaaso's gifts because they show genuine affection. They do not create dependency because he has not imposed himself or demanded anything in return. More important, she receives his gifts because she can reciprocate by giving herself to him in erotic love. As what is propitiously right, love is teleological. Its time is one that has come: "Tonight, Duniya had a deep-seated wish to give herself to him, a wish that had taken days to mature. She was glad he hadn't rushed her. Now the timing was right, and its suddenness lent her decision more power, like unexpected thunder in a season of awaited rains" (G, 205).

Similarly, each narrator-character attributes a deep significance to the foundling and regards his presence as a synecdoche that will explain the mysterious gift of life and give existential direction to members of the community. For Taariq, the foundling is a miracle baby or divine gift in the genre of Moses or Jesus. His "beginning shared the timelessness of fables, expiring in the inexactness of legends" (G, 116). In order to preserve his magical powers to redeem the world, he must be shielded from the gaze of empirical knowledge, which reduces everything to the brute ordinary facts of quotidian reality (G, 124). Taariq exhorts Duniya not to give the baby to Muraayo, her sister-in-law, because she "live[s] on the surface of things, in the glitter of false beauties, easily contented with the superficiality of things," and "has little in-depth understanding of symbols" (G, 124).

What literature shares with myth is the suspension of disbelief, or more precisely, of quotidian empirical reality, that enables faith in the magical and fabulous. This can lead us in two different directions. On the one hand, we can view objective reality as a surface, a mere shell that harbors a deeper symbolic meaning. The meaning points to a telos, the full presence of an absolute divine being that transcends the mundane world and will be revealed to us through religious faith. Faith gives a religious determination to the mystery of the world's origin as the ultra-mundane working of an unknowable divine providence. As Taariq puts it, "I'm increasingly beginning to think that humankind must have faith in abstractions, and on this foundation we must reconstruct the world as we know it from the myth we have faith in, but not know, not really know. There's sustenance in myth, of an enriching kind" (G, 125). The normative conception of world literature in secular humanist criticism as the construction of a higher spiritual world through the expression of the highest ideals of humanity is continuous with the believer's faith in divinity. Literature is an expression of the human tendency to construct the world according to teleological time by interpretation and the conferral of meaning.

On the other hand the literary suspension of factual reality can also disrupt any reference to a transcendent absolute being by pointing to the worlding of the world by the sheer coming of the event. Here, world-opening is not closed off by any determination but is simply affirmed as the sheer persistence of finite existence. Although the foundling dies from an empirically determinable biological cause (illness), his "magical work" inexplicably survives and continues beyond his factual death: "He'll have assumed a different kind of motif in our story; everybody will get something different out of him. . . . At worst, he'll have served to make some of us think seriously" (G, 125). Literature is that thinking that affirms the inhuman incalculability of temporalization as a force of worlding.

Here, the novel gives us a key for how to read it as an example of postcolonial world literature. The aporia between the two views of literature's relation to the world is a version of the political aporia between the teleological time of self-determination and the opening of a world by the coming of time.

Postcoloniality exemplifies and brings out in the sharpest relief this political aporia. As Samir Amin puts it, the structural inequality of contemporary globalization is such that "the victims of the project of the new right exist in incomparably greater numbers in the peripheries. There, hundreds of millions already live in poverty in shantyized urban areas, and hundreds of millions of peasants will soon join them as a result of the liberalization of agriculture."[49] It is imperative for postcolonial peoples to assert their sovereign self-determination in the cultural, political, and economic spheres. But despite the proliferation of protest movements against capitalist globalization that take as their rallying cry "Another World Is Possible," the project of delinking from the calculative logic of the capitalist world-system and building a multipolar world is fragile. Because we largely inhabit the homogeneous space-time produced by the calculations and technologies of capitalist accumulation, how can disruptive openings of the system be maintained long enough to cultivate new subjects of transformation?

As an example of politically committed world literature, *Gifts* does not envision the revolutionary transcendence of the world-system. It contributes to Somalia's search for self-determination by means of a cognitive mapping that grounds capitalist accumulation in the religious ethics of Abrahamic monotheism and suggests that the Somali gift economy is a viable ethical alternative to global market exchange and the Somali people's normative contribution to global politics. By enabling us to resist humanitarianization, these gift practices are the first step toward global change. The assertion of Somalian self-determination relies on the view of literature as the repository of a deep meaning that reveals the world's teleological organization. Somali practices of giving open a world because they are based on an acceptance of human finitude. However, by characterizing these practices as proper to the Somali people, Farah posits an ethical identity that returns to itself. He converts the opening to teleological time and regulates worlding toward the end of remaking the world *for* Somalia in defense against capitalist globalization. The novel's intertextuality formally enacts the gift economy. Its use of Western literary forms, its reinscription of Mauss, its references to biblical sources, and so on are literary relations of reciprocal giving that do not lead to cultural dependency and the blind imitation of foreign cultural forms. Just as its characters express their self-determination through their stories and act as free agents in the common world formed by storytelling, the novel preserves its unified identity as a distinctively Somalian contribution to world literature, a text of the Somali people's emergence, throughout its gift of narration. The novel's fictional world moves us as readers when we arrive at its meaning by understanding its themes, appreciating its formal complexity, and grasping the unity of content and form. We facilitate Somalia's emergence by carrying this world beyond the reading experience.

But in the face of the pervasive power of capitalist calculations to level off openings, the novel also points to the gift of time as an indestructible force of world-opening to prolong the teleological time of Somalian self-determination. Because capitalist processes require time, the gift of time that inheres in the processes that constitute and maintain the world-system is the original ground for its disruption. As the pure event that opens a world and lets new subjects emerge, this incalculable force is the most important resource for resisting capitalist unworlding. However, the same incalculability also problematizes the novel's attempt to limit the world's openness by conserving a Somali subject of cultural and religious difference as a solution to humanitarian dehumanization. The incalculable gift of time resists the teleological movement of self-return and makes the reader think the world's openness by suspending any sense of narrative ending.

Narrative is a direct intimation of the gift of time. First, the accomplishment of the act of narration takes time. Second, narrative as the recounting of something to someone is a form of repetition that requires a lapse of time between what is narrated (phenomena or occurrences), the act of narration, and the account generated by narration (discourse). This temporal lapse is the condition of possibility of narrative. Narrative would be impossible if the narrator and listener were simultaneously present when the recounted phenomena took place and there was no lapse of time. Narrative would be redundant because there would be no need for remembrance. However, unlike a fact or datum, which can be made the subject or theme of narrative, the gift of time itself cannot be narrated, since it is the very origin and condition of narration even as it demands narrative. As I noted in chapter 6, because the incalculable gift of time cannot be rendered present except by its effacement, it only takes place in narrative, as a repetition or simulacrum that refers to an otherness that exceeds presence. Literary narrative always comes up against its own impossibility when it touches on the gift of time. But since the gift of time is narrative's condition of possibility, literary narrative that is self-reflexive about its narrativity necessarily confounds the telos of any narrative ending. *Gifts* undertakes this self-reflection on narrativity or the impossibility of narrative self-reflection. Its final chapter repeatedly undercuts its attempt to reveal a deeper meaning and organize the world according to teleological time. It emphasizes instead the world's open-endedness as a story to be told and retold / that tells and retells itself through us.

The novel's self-reflexivity as narrative revolves around the fact that Duniya, its main protagonist and storyteller's proper name, is Arabic for world. In the last chapter, the omniscient narrator's recounting of how Duniya achieves spiritual rebirth turns out to be about an impossible narrative. The narrative is rendered from Duniya's perspective as a storyteller who recounts her meeting of Abshir at the airport and their celebratory dinner. The endpoint of her *Bildung* is the emergence of a new subject in the world *and* the coming of a new world. Initially, she is likened to an infant receiving the coming of a world at the moment of birth. This changes into the image of a convivial encounter with a traveler that transforms the existing world and opens a new one. But Duniya's narratorial gaze cannot capture this opening in its totality. Although she imagines herself in Abshir's place in order to give a full account of the event from multiple aspects, the omniscient narrator notes that her memory "was fragmentary and full of hiatuses, like a photographer who, while the group of which she was a member posed in front of a camera, adjusted the timing wrongly, giving herself insufficient time before taking her own place in the group portrait" (*G*, 233).

Duniya cannot achieve omniscience because she does not have enough time. The photography analogy implies that one can give oneself enough time by treating it as quantifiable and making the right calculations. However, the hiatus in the continuous flow of her memory is a suspension of her mental capacities by a disruptive force that puts time out of joint. Moreover, this temporal suspension can only be explained after the resumption of time and a lapse of time. "There is nothing like heightened consciousness to make one's center shift. Duniya would explain to Bosaaso later that evening that she had suffered from some form of psychic disturbance, of the kind likely to demonstrate itself when one's brain cells receive a greater amount of impressions than they can cope with. She didn't know how else to describe what she felt" (*G*, 233). We explain this force as an overload of sense stimuli, but it is the giving of time that is prior to and exceeds sense-perception, a force that is simultaneously the condition of possibility and impossibility of experience. Only "after" time has been given and received and a world has been opened can our cognitive faculties work on the world as factical reality, give it thickness through the associations of memory, determine its specificity, calculate and master it, and make events the material of a narrative. "Once Duniya came to, the universe of her imagination was at her beck and call. She could now see Abshir properly, hear his deep voice, remember all kind gestures, his unlimited generosity" (*G*, 234).

The omniscient narrator implies that while Duniya cannot comprehensively capture the gift of time because her power of narration is limited, he can. He wishes to be a relay of an absolute being, to give the time of the whole narrative and bring it to its proper meaningful end where telos and eschaton coincide such that all the novel's teloi are tied together and the world as a whole is given a telos. But the novel refuses this punctual sense of ending and instead evokes the world's unfinished character.

The final dinner scene presents us with a Duniya who is no longer a storyteller but a passive receiver of a revelatory story about herself from a mysterious higher power that can create through a performative utterance. "Duniya thought to herself that little is revealed to oneself directly. Revelations are received from out of a mist of doubts, in caves, in the dark, out of a child's mouth, or via the wise utterances of an elderly or mad person. She decided that her own epiphanic instant had occurred at a moment, on a morning, when a story chose to tell itself to her, through her, a story whose clarity was contained in the creative utterance, *Let there be a man*, and there was a story" (*G*, 245). Duniya likens this power to the God of Genesis. It gives the time that makes stories possible. However, as the novel winds to its close, she becomes the teller of stories in response to another coming of the event. Although she assumes agency for the story about herself and the power of opening a world by viewing herself as a character in her story, she does not have the power of absolute creation. She is not the narrator. The narrative is merely focalized through her, and she does not know how to end the story about herself.

> Duniya's centers shifted. The skin on her face felt too tight, like that of a woman half-way through washing her make-up and who receives a visitor. She was thinking that beginning the story had been easy, like extracting a milk-tooth. But how was she to end it?
>
> Here, she paused. . . . Looking at the pepper-steak, she told herself that it was not she who had ordered it, but another Duniya. But where was this other Duniya? . . .
>
> She was asking herself if she was content that her guests could get on with the telling of their respective stories without her. And *the other* Duniya with *her* tale? . . .
>
> Whom was Bosaaso married to?
>
> Which Duniya?

This or the other?
She wished she knew.

> Duniya, the chronicler, is no longer certain how to go on, and nothing
> short of a much longer pause will enable her to look back on the events as
> they took place in order for her to describe them accurately. (G, 245–46)

What is needed for her narrative to go on is precisely time. But here, time
becomes irreparably split. Duniya's act of narrating is contemporaneous with
the actions and events of the story. But the time of her narration, which is simultaneously the time of the omniscient narrator's story, must be dissociated
from the time of the events Duniya recounts. If her narration is to continue,
her narrative time cannot cleave closely to the time of what she recounts—the
time of her actions and what happens to her. As a narrator, she has to first
pause and put narrative time on hold before she can resume the narrative
because she needs to repeat and mentally reenvision the events that happened
to her as a character to attain greater descriptive control. In other words, even
as Duniya, the storyteller, needs to freeze the time of her narration, she also
needs time to continue so that she can repeat in memory the past flow of the
time of events before the time of her narration can rejoin the time of events
and the storyteller can be united with the character. But she is paralyzed because the split between storyteller and character is irreparable. The former
Duniya cannot find and place the latter, much less determine her or identify
(with) her.

We can give a psychological-linguistic explanation to this splitting following Benveniste's account of the enunciative split by pointing out that a narrator
who is also a character can never quite coincide with herself qua character
because however close they may be, the narrator must always follow the character's lead, just as the act of narration must always take place after the events
that are recounted. The problem is, however, the more fundamental ontological problem of radical finitude. In the act of narrating, the narrator is the
present self, and as character, she is the past self. However, a narrator-character
cannot give a convincing or "natural" ending to her story while she is alive,
because her life's meaning will not be clear until after her death, when she can
no longer recount what happened to her. She can try to anticipate this meaning
by the projection of a hypothetical end. But this will lead to another splitting
between the present self and a possible future self whom we can view as a past
self through the resources of literature. However, even here, the present self can
only identify and be reunited with this possible-future-but-seen-as-past-self

if she continues to receive the gift of time. In other words, the identity and unity of the two Duniyas can only be guaranteed by the persistence of time, the promise that Duniya, the storyteller, will remain the same as the Duniya whose story she tells. But this promise is inhuman and exceeds human calculation. It leads to an abyssal questioning that paralyzes Duniya.

The omniscient narrator intrusively halts this endless questioning with a thematic proposition that simply states Duniya's uncertainty. Because radical uncertainty is intolerable, two other characters attempt to impose a teleological meaning. Nasiiba, Duniya's daughter, asks a rhetorical question: "Don't all stories end in marriage or the dissolution of such a union?" (*G*, 246). Abshir is described as saying that "all stories are one story, whose principal theme is love. And if the stories feel different, it is only because the journeys the characters are to undertake take different routes to get to their final destination" (*G*, 246). But the novel immediately undercuts this eschato-teleological tendency by suspending all ends: "'All stories,' concluded Abshir, 'celebrate, in elegiac terms, the untapped source of energy, of the humanness of women and men.' . . . The world was an audience, ready to be given Duniya's story from the beginning" (*G*, 246). This untapped source of energy is not the calculative power of human reason or any of its capabilities for action, the edifying attributes of enlightened humanity. For, pace Arendt, what is human about men and women is their radical finitude, which points to the inhuman other in us. Hence, the celebration of humanness is always elegiac. Yet it is in response to this inhuman gift that cannot be reduced to an absolute ultra-mundane being that storytelling occurs and the world survives through narrative.

The novel's last sentence safeguards the inhuman coming of time by derailing the omniscient narrator's power to place Duniya/the world in a fixed place and time and give her story a final determination. The sentence can indicate that Duniya's story, as told by the narrator, is completed and can be disseminated to the larger world in its finished form. But who is the narrator here? We can neither fully identify the teller of her story nor Duniya herself. The sentence places everything in suspension. The world is not an indivisible whole, a closed totality. It is divided into at least three, simultaneously: audience, subject of a story, and teller. What narrates or gives the world's story to itself is the gift of time. The gift, however, does not come from a presence beyond but inheres in the world. It constitutes the world by repeatedly dividing and opening it up. The world is a movement of opening, an endless process of narration that tells its own story. It is transformed and transforms itself in that telling precisely because it is fractured by the gift of time and cannot enclose itself as a sovereign whole. The world is in a state of receptibility, ready to be given and to receive its own story again and again. Such receptiveness is not ethical action in an already constituted world but attentiveness to the opening of a world and the readiness to act in response to and with the propulsive force of this opening.

Where world literature's vocation is to think the force of worlding, postcolonial world literature's normative task is to enact the unending opening of a world as a condition for the emergence of new subjects in spite of capitalist globalization. Its non-utopian promise is that we can belong otherwise, in different ways, because quivering beneath the surface of the existing world are other worlds to come.

Without Conclusion

Stories without End(s)

Against recent theories of world literature, I have proposed a normative conception that does not simply revive the older vision of world literature as the expression of universal humanity. That vision, which received its canonical articulation by Goethe and which I have described as spiritualist, is not confined to the West. Here is Rabindranath Tagore's description of how world literature gives us access to humanity's eternal ideals.

> Among different ages and people, only those things survive in which all human beings can discover themselves. The things that pass this test are the permanent and universal human treasures.
>
> Through this process of making and breaking, a timeless ideal of human nature and expression gathers of itself in literature. . . .
>
> A work is admitted to the ranks of literature only when the author has realised the ideas of the human race in his own thoughts and expressed humanity's pain in his writing. We have to regard literature as a temple being built by the master mason, universal man; writers from various countries and periods are working under him as labourers. . . .
>
> The mass of matter at the sun's core is forming itself in many ways, both solid and liquid. We cannot see the process, but the surrounding ring of light ceaselessly expresses the sun to the world. It is thus that the sun gifts itself to the world and links itself to all else. If we could make humanity the object of such an integral view, we would see it like the sun. We would see that the mass of matter was gradually forming itself into layers, and around it, perpetually, a luminous ring of expression spreading itself joyously in every direction. Look at literature as this ring of light, made of language, encircling humanity.[1]

Our timeless ideals are the unifying basis of the higher spiritual world that we make. Indeed, by placing humanity at the center of the solar system, Tagore's heliocentric simile suggests that we are the giver of time and phenomenality. I have argued that what originally opens and holds a world together is the coming of time from the inhuman other. World literature intimates and participates in processes of worlding.

In an obvious sense, literature opens a world because it magically gives a world or makes one "appear" in the imagination in a manner similar to evocation or conjuration. We conventionally regard the world depicted by literature as a copy of the existing world in representation, memory, or the imagination. In the spiritualist conception, we can remake the existing world according to the modular image of an ideal world that literature creates. I am suggesting, however, that "literature" is ontologically infrastructural to the existing world because the existing world's solidity is constituted by the giving of time. Literature in the narrow sense, especially stories and narratives, help us understand the process of worlding because, as forms of recounting, they depend on and express the world's temporal structure. The world's "literary" structure is not reducible to the discursive construction of experience, namely, the overlaying of factuality by meanings and values that occurs because discourse frames and shapes our sense of reality. The world's "literary" structure is instead what enables the world to persist and achieve stability. The reason why discourses play a part in the making of worlds is because worlding destabilizes any existing world and opens up reality to interpretation. This force is the condition of possibility of the interpenetration of factual reality, value, and discursive meaning.

Of all literary forms, narrative has the closest affinity to the opening of a world by the gift of time because, as the recounting of events, time is structural to its form. Caution must be exercised whenever we speak of the time of narrative. The time of narrative as discourse (*Erzählzeit*), the time of the *sjuzet*, cannot be equated with the time of the events recounted (*erzählte Zeit*), the time of the story (*fabula*). As Gerard Genette notes, there cannot be an isochrony between narrative and story because of the former's secondary or derived character. Narrative cannot approximate and simulate the time of the occurrence of real or fictional events. Written narratives complicate matters further. Whereas oral narratives are themselves acts that unfold in time and have a measurable duration, the time of written narratives can only be determined metonymically by measuring the time of its consumption through reading. "Written narrative," Genette observes, "exists in space and as space, and the time needed for 'consuming' it is the time needed for *crossing* or *traversing* it, like a road or a field. The narrative text, like every other text, has no other temporality than what it borrows, metonymically, from its own reading.... We must take that [metonymic] displacement for granted, since it forms part of the narrative game, and therefore accept literally the quasi-fiction of *Erzählzeit*, this false time standing in for a true time and to be treated ... as a *pseudo-time*."[2] Even with dialogue, written narrative cannot "restore the speed with which those words were pronounced or the possible dead spaces in the conversation. In no way, therefore, can it play the role of temporal indicator; it would play that role only if its indications could serve to measure the 'narrative duration' of the differently paced sections surrounding it. Thus a scene with dialogue ... cannot serve us as reference point for a rigorous comparison of real durations."[3] There cannot be equality between the durations of narrative and story because it is unverifiable.

Narrative theory conceives of duration in quantitative terms. It spatializes time by understanding it as the measure of movement. Genette speaks of the time of the written narrative as the time needed for the reader's consciousness to pass through a text, which he likens to the geographical phenomena of field and road. The duration of narrative is its speed, "the relationship between a temporal dimension and a spatial dimension (so many meters per second, so many seconds per meter): the speed of a narrative will be defined by the relationship between a duration (that of the story, measured in seconds, minutes, hours, days, months and years) and a length (that of the text measured, in lines and in pages)."[4]

A literary narrative, I suggest, does indeed touch on the "real" time of events when it is concerned with its own status as narrative. But this is not time as quantified duration, the measure of how long occurrences take, but instead the giving of time as the force of worlding. The stability of the world requires the persistence of time, which is also the condition of possibility of narrative. Better yet, in its very being, narrative is a simulacrum of temporalization. But because time's persistence can only be understood in terms of the incalculability of the gift or the coming of the pure event, it is also that which cannot be narrated. It is a force, both creative and disruptive, that cannot be ordered and placed in sequence by rational calculation. The novels I discussed in part III draw on this force to frustrate the calculations of colonial and neocolonial global capital and the linear time of Western-centric modern progress and to open new worlds. These envisioned worlds are governed by heterotemporalities, that is, alternative teleological times to that of capitalist modernity.

But the gift of time also destabilizes the temporal reckoning of teleological time and disrupts its self-returning closure. This is manifested at the level of narrative form in the open-ended character of the novels, their inability to achieve a conclusive end with a clearly determinable meaning that indicates the transcendence or regulation of the world made by capitalist globalization: the undecidability of Clare Savage's death, the unconvincing assurance that the story about Nirmal's diary will be faithful to its vocation of recording subaltern suffering, and the paralysis of Duniya as the sovereign teller of her narrative of self-determination.

Telling Tales of the World

In his study of the bildungsroman, Franco Moretti noted something similar in the plots of classical European novels governed by what he calls the transformation principle. The protagonists in novels by Stendhal, Balzac, Pushkin, and Flaubert do not conform to social norms but endlessly seek to change society and remain alienated from it, sometimes to the point of their destruction. Moretti suggests that "what makes a story meaningful is its narrativity, its being an open-ended process. Meaning is the result not of a fulfilled teleology, but rather . . . of the total rejection of such a solution. The ending, the privileged narrative moment of taxonomic mentality, becomes the most *meaningless* one here. . . . [The narrative logic is such that] a story's meaning resides precisely in the impossibility of 'fixing' it."[5] What is distinctive about the postcolonial novels I have discussed is that they associate this open-endedness with the premodern narrative form of the story, either by embedding stories from oral folk traditions within their novelistic frames or by pretending to be tales. Salman Rushdie's *Midnight's Children* is exemplary of the latter tendency. Not only does the novel playfully allude to *One Thousand and One Nights* in the number of magical children born during the first hour of Indian independence. Saleem Sinai, the protagonist and first person narrator of the novel who personifies the nation, also self-consciously identifies his fate as that of a storyteller in comparison with the younger generation: "From now on, mine would be as peripheral a role as that of any redundant oldster: the traditional function, perhaps, of reminiscer, of teller-of-tales."[6]

It would be too easy to explain this obsession with tales and stories by suggesting that postcolonial novels committed to an anti-Eurocentric reworlding of the world are nostalgically drawn to precolonial narrative forms. Nor is it just a matter of an epistemological crisis, where according to Jean-François

Lyotard, the loss of credibility of grand narratives that legitimate knowledge by reference to humanity as the universal subject of freedom or speculative truth has led to the reaffirmation of flexible small stories (*petit récit, petite histoire*) tied to specific places, times, and locally situated subjects, the precursors of which are premodern oral narratives.[7] Instead, I submit that of all narrative forms, the story has the most intimate connection with the force of time as an inexhaustible resource for opening other worlds because being grounded in the experience of finitude, it is a narrative without a rationally determinable end. I end with a brief look at two novels about the postcolonial Philippines that illustrate this point, Ninotchka Rosca's *State of War* and Timothy Mo's *Renegade or Halo²*.

The Philippines has been subject to the (un)worlding of Old and New World colonialism and neocolonialism. It was integrated into the European world economy when Magellan claimed possession of the islands for Spain in 1521. It remained a Spanish colony until 1898, when it was sold to the United States for $20 million by the Treaty of Paris, which concluded the Spanish-American War. After a period of Japanese occupation during World War II, the Philippines achieved full independence on July 4, 1946, following the schedule set by the Tydings–McDuffie Act of 1934, which had established the Commonwealth of the Philippines and a transitional period to independence.

For present purposes, three features of this worlding are noteworthy. First, as Benedict Anderson has noted, clerical domination under Spanish colonialism created a Christianized mestizo stratum, from the descendants of the illegitimate children sired with local women by friars, other Spaniards, and Chinese migrants, that formed an economically powerful landowning group.[8] Second, under US colonialism, this group benefited from the American expropriation and sale of rich agricultural land owned by the friars and the free trade laws that gave preferential access for Philippine agricultural products in US markets. "After 1909," Anderson notes, "by the terms of the Payne-Aldrich Act, the Philippines were enclosed within the American tariff wall, so that their agricultural exports had easy, untaxed access to the world's largest national market—where, in addition, prices, especially for sugar, were often well above world norms."[9] Sugar exports increased seven times in the twenty-five years following this tariff act.[10] American colonialism was so nurturing to the emerging national oligarchs that although they "could not decently say so in public, independence was the last thing they desired, precisely because it threatened the source of their huge wealth: access to the American market."[11]

Third, the Philippines remained heteronomously tethered to America as a neocolony after formal independence in 1946. The 1947 Military Bases Agreement permitted the United States to maintain and operate twenty-three land, sea and air bases, including the Clark Air Base and the Subic Bay Naval Complex, until 1991. The Bell Trade Act (1946), a bilateral free trade agreement, gave U.S corporations a significant presence in the Philippines through preferential tariffs that weakened the control of the Philippine government over imports and exports. A "parity" clause in the Bell Act gave US corporations and citizens equal access to "exploit" minerals, forests, and other natural resources as Philippine citizens. This required the amendment of a provision in the 1935 Philippine Constitution that had mandated Filipino ownership of 60 percent of each corporate business. In return, the Philippines was allowed to continue free trade with the United States until 1954, after which it would have declining preferential access to the protected American market until 1973, when full duty would be paid on its exports to the United States. In addition, the Philippine Rehabilitation Act (Tydings War Damage Act) (1946) provided full payment of more than $620 million of rehabilitation assistance for damages to parties able to demonstrate a loss of a minimum of $500 because of World War II.[12] As one commentator notes, "although the Philippines received considerable aid, the Bell Act also forced the Philippines to make major concessions to the United States on trade and investment in order to receive that aid. . . . US companies quickly dominated the Philippine market in such diverse sectors as automobiles, power generation, textiles, and consumer goods."[13]

These features of political-economic history determine the Philippines' subsequent development, from 1954 to the years of the Marcos dictatorship, into a country with a dependent neocolonial economy run by a patrimonial oligarchic state according to the theft and corruption logic of crony capitalism, where economic growth is primarily fueled by foreign debt. As Benedict Anderson notes, the oligarchy compensated for the declining access to the US market by plundering the state's financial instrumentalities. "Under the guise of promoting economic independence and import-substitution industrialization, exchange rates were manipulated, monopolistic licenses parcelled out, huge, cheap, often unrepaid bank loans passed around, and the national budget frittered away in pork-barrel legislation."[14] The patrimonial state in the Philippines shares with the strong developmental state at the helm of the

East Asian economic miracle a relative lack of distinction between the state apparatus, personal power, and the interests of dominant economic groups. Its inability to stimulate economic development and fulfill basic administrative functions such as providing electricity and other infrastructure services means that it is only one step away from a failed state.[15]

The Philippines is a combination of something close to the failed state of Somalia and the dependent sugar economy of Jamaica at the end of its halcyon days. The gradual closing of access to the US market was accompanied by more plunder of national wealth and increased weakening of state bureaucracy. Following Max Weber, Paul Hutchcroft has pointed out that rational capitalism cannot develop in a political environment with a low degree of calculability in the legal and administrative sphere, a feature of state apparatuses that are unable to control arbitrariness in decision-making. "The weak degree of calculability in the political and legal sphere inhibits the fuller development of calculability in the sphere of production—particularly by impeding the clear separation of the household and enterprise."[16] Businesses must pay unofficial "taxes" to get results from state functionaries, and "this variability quite dramatically inhibits the development of rational capital accounting at the level of enterprise."[17] This weak calculability, which explains the failure of developing rational capitalism at the *national* level in the Philippines, is part of a larger set of calculations that further *global* capitalism's systematic exploitation of the peripheries and perpetuate inequality among peoples in the world-system. Rosca and Mo write against the world created by global capitalism and the patrimonial state.

Revolutionary Stories

State of War is set in the Philippines of the 1970s–1980s. Anna Villaverde, its central character, is the counterpart of Clare Savage and personifies the popular Philippines nation. She is a mestiza Chinese who has joined a guerilla struggle against a Marcos-like dictatorship. Like Cliff's novels, *State of War* distinguishes among three different times: the homogeneous time of contemporary global capital, the time of colonial history inaugurated by Magellan's landing in Cebu, and a precolonial time. Although colonialism is a function of capitalist calculations, colonial time constitutes a web of karmic fate that engulfs and determines the lives of the novel's characters. Precolonial time is the time of a world that is innocent of the contaminations of European colonial cartography. A refrain in the novel observes that it is "a time when the world

was young, the sea was simply the sea, and names were but newly invented";
"when the archipelago's song was just beginning, in a still-young world of
uncharted seas."[18] This time is conveyed through visions that are stimulated by
tactile bodily contact and oral narratives. It provides resources for revolutionary reworlding.

State of War is divided into three parts. The first and third parts are set in
the present. The second part, "The Book of Numbers," takes us back to a complex web of interpersonal relations among the ancestors of the main characters
that spans the entire history of the various colonial regimes in the Philippines,
from the arrival of Magellan and Spanish colonialism to American colonialism
and the Japanese occupation during World War II. Unbeknownst to the main
characters, this web of historical relations influences their actions and choices
in the narrative present. Hence, the middle section stages the interruption of
the homogeneous time of the neocolonial present by a temporality that is governed by fate, retribution, and poetic justice and pregnant with meaning. The
second part begins with the rape of a Malayan girl by a Capuchin monk at
the dawn of Spanish colonialism, the forefather of the Villaverde clan. This
original violence, which inaugurates the history of the Villaverdes, is a synecdoche for the beginning of colonial history. But before his violent act, the
priest experiences another tearing of time: the rending of colonial history by
meteorological time, the chaos and destruction of which make a mockery of
colonial appropriation.

> The land he passed through—from horizon to horizon—though still un-
> named, was already owned by the Church.... A monologue of despair
> went on in his mind. He saw himself dying in this forgotten corner of the
> world, this archipelago floating in an ocean which, to mock its name of
> peace, periodically unleashed the terror of typhoons throughout South-
> east Asia.... His bones would rot far from civilization and nothing would
> remain of his memory, despite all his efforts, for *time was impossible in this*
> *country*, existing in all the true meaning of eternity. Things fell apart with
> the heat and the rain, and the incessant mastication of insects, and he had
> no doubt that the great stone bridge he was building across the seasonally
> rampaging river would, at one time or another, encounter a torrent too
> strong to withstand and thus be swept away. (*sw*, 154, emphasis added)

Colonialism represents itself as having brought historical time to the Philippines through the introduction of written records. The arrival of Spanish
ships is a movement "along the rim of time" (*sw*, 31). However, from the

priest's viewpoint, the elemental forces of the environment and landscape make colonial time impossible. These forces thus open up the time of a precolonial world. This heterotemporality is an eternal resource for resisting both the neocolonial present and the retributive fate imposed on the present by the history of colonial violence. Various characters yearn for a forgotten innocent past, a lost presence uncontaminated by colonial culture. This past has somehow left traces in popular culture, despite the shortcomings of popular memory. It persists as the animating force of all wars of anticolonial resistance in Philippine history, beginning with the native chieftain Lapu-Lapu's killing of Magellan. Old Andy, the grandfather of Adrian Banyaga, Anna's love interest, is the patriarch of an oligarchic family that seeks to undermine the Marcos-like Commander. He sends his agents to accumulate relics of the 1896 Revolution, the 1902–1908 Philippine-American War, the 1930s uprising, the 1940s anti-Japanese resistance, the 1950s Huk rebellion, and the current insurgency. The piecing together of these relics as an interconnected whole, he hopes, will give positive proof of the historical reality of anticolonial revolution and stimulate a successful revolution today: "No one remembered the totality of it, its entirety, only bits and pieces, that battle, this confrontation, that siege—but not, no never, the monstrous carnage of four hundred years, from the very first dawn when Lapu-lapu skewered that vagabond poacher Magellan" (sw, 89).

Because Anna's ancestry takes her back to the history and birth of the Filipino nation, her personal memory of her genealogy symbolically reenacts the archipelago's collective memory of struggles against Spanish, American, and Japanese colonialism. The different colonial regimes have obscured and marred this collective memory. By imposing alien languages and renaming the landscape, they have made the people so confused about where they are that they no longer know who they are and where they are heading. As Anna puts it, "they monkeyed around with language . . . while we were growing up. Monkeyed around with names. Of people, of places. With dates. And now, I can't remember. No one remembers. And even this . . . even this will be forgotten. They will hide it under another name. No one will remember" (sw, 149).

This "mangled history" can be set right by the wisdom from precolonial times, which Anna receives through visions (sw, 336). However, this wisdom cannot be communicated through the discursive language of patriarchal genealogy, which originates in colonial rape. It can only be passed on through the immediate, tactile corporeal intimacy between mother and daughter in the manner of the sensuous intuitive chants of priestesses from the precolonial world.

> [Maya, Anna's great grandmother] had lain with her own mother in exactly the same manner, absorbing the older woman's knowledge through this means, opening a channel to the past. . . . Through her mother's flesh, she had met her own grandmother who was still raving against what the Spaniards had done, her voice joined by the voices of other women who spoke of a time when the world was young, the sea was simply the sea, and names were but newly invented, and when women walked these seven thousand one hundred islands with a power in them, walking in single file ten paces ahead of the men, their gold bracelets and anklets tinkling, warning that the women were in passage so that strangers would stay clear, for women then were in communion with the gods, praying to the river, the forest spirits, the ancient stones. . . . They walked with wisdom, dressed simply in an ankle-length piece of cloth wrapped and knotted about the hips, breasts left bare—until the Spaniards infected them with shame and made them hide their strength beneath layers of petticoats, half-chemises, drawers, skirts, blouses, shawls, and veils. (SW, 191–92)

Cliff's novels stage a similar feminized heterotemporality. Anna is urged by this force to perform heroic deeds in the novel's final part, which has the apocalyptic, eschatological title "The Book of Revelations." Here, the weak calculability of the internally divided patrimonial oligarchic state becomes ironically aligned with the interests of revolutionary forces and causes disruptions to the neocolonial state's calculations. Revolutions "do not happen without wherefores and whys" (SW, 129). They require arms. To prevent the Commander from destroying the Banyaga family, Old Andy funds trafficking in explosives and arms to create disturbances that will deflect the Commander's attention from the Banyagas. He also searches out enemies of the state and puts these revolutionary elements in touch with the arms supplier. Unlike the guerillas in *No Telephone to Heaven*, these guerillas win the immediate battle in the long war against neocolonialism in Rosca's novel. The explosion set off by the resistance inflicts damage on the dictator's forces. The dictator retaliates, but the resistance endures and waits to strike again. It withdraws itself from phenomenality and time before it erupts and tears neocolonial time again. "It absorbed its losses, withdrew its people from exposed positions, clothed itself in anonymity. In *due time*, it saw the flagging of the enemy's zeal, saw its attention waver and, at last, turn to other matters. Then the resistance stirred and reached out" (sw, 379, emphasis added).

What is significant is the temporality of the revolutionary movement's survival. Precolonial time is always characterized as a past presence. Accordingly, its resurrection and reincarnation in the resistance are understood as a modality of teleological time—the inevitable negation of neocolonial forces, which negate the life of the Filipino people. Yet the novel does not portray the endurance of revolutionary struggle as a form of presence. It is instead a promise with the temporal mode of the to-come. The novel's concluding chapter is formally distinguished from the rest of the narrative because it is a list of punctual intelligence reports preceded by the heading "Item." Anna has retired to a small village by the ocean, where she is now a teacher in a children's school. She has inherited tape recordings of the guerrilla leader, Guevarra, in which he speaks of his life and the reasons for his actions. She is carrying Adrian Banyaga's child, who will be free of the colonial past because he will be nourished by stories of Philippine legends, including that of Guevarra.

> He would be nurtured as much by her milk as by the archipelago's legends—already, she was tucking Guevarra's voice among other voices in her mind—and he would be the first of the Capuchin monk's descendants to be born innocent, without fate. . . . She knew all that instantly, with great certainty, just as she knew that her son would be a great storyteller, in the tradition of the children of priestesses. He would remember, his name being a history unto itself, for he would be known as Ismael Villaverde Banyaga.
>
> Time passes. (sw, 382)

We see here the intentional structure of an oracular prediction of a future beginning that claims the status of knowledgeable certainty. But this structure is complicated in two ways. First, given that *State of War* is a novel, why does it privilege the premodern, primarily oral form of narrative, the story, which characterizes a face-to-face community that was superseded by the imagined community of the modern nation as the means and medium for the survival of resistance? The easy answer, one that Rosca's novel suggests and also accords with conventional literary history, is that the novel is a European colonial import. Novelistic memory and narrative, as exemplified by the Villaverde family history, will always be determined by colonial history and tainted by the shame of colonial violence. The more interesting suggestion, however, is that novels, unlike stories, come to an end because they are print commodities. By this, I do not only mean that their plots, like all plots, have endings. Rather, they end in a definite way, have this or that purpose or telos that we try to fix as a meaning. They can be arrested in this way, and this is their end because the narrative is fixed by print.

Walter Benjamin's essay "The Storyteller: Reflections on the Works of Nikolai Leskov," which was first published in English translation in a volume edited by Hannah Arendt and resonates with her views on stories, elucidates how stories open a world by suggesting that finitude is structural to their form. Benjamin makes two important points. First, the story is a literary form that "contains . . . something useful," whether this is moral, practical advice or a proverb.[19] A storyteller instructs and gives counsel (*Rat*) to his readers. Counsel has a temporal dimension because it necessarily involves narrative. It is not an answer to a question but "a proposal concerning the continuation [Fortsetzung] of a story [Geschichte] which is just unfolding. To seek this counsel one would first have to be able to tell the story" ("S," 86; 106). Counsel is not just this or that singular act of narration but the continuing power of narration, narration to the nth degree. To receive advice, the receiver of the first narration has to commit to continue the story because it is only in the act of narrating it a second time that he or she learns something. What is communicated, or better yet, transferred through storytelling is not merely a message but experience (*Erfahrung*) itself. Experience refers to what has been directly witnessed and what has been received through a story, because both the proficient telling or crafting of a good story and listening to one are experiences in themselves. They communicate an initial experience in such a way that it can be reexperienced. This is why, Benjamin emphasizes, the source of stories is oral narrative, where telling and listening are sensuous acts. The two archetypes of storytellers are the resident tiller of the soil, someone who has remained at home and "knows the local tales and traditions," and the trading seaman, someone who has come from afar and has a lot to tell ("S," 84; 104). The temporal dimension of counsel is further enhanced when we heed and use it to guide our lives and make it into living activity. Wisdom is the name that Benjamin gives to "counsel woven into the fabric of a life that has been lived [in den Stoff gelebten Lebens]," that is, practical knowledge or ethics ("S," 86–87; 106, translation modified). Telling and listening to stories should not be confused with temporalization because they take place in time. But they are analogues of the force of temporalization because a quasi-epigenetic power of auto-continuation and auto-prolongation is part of their structure.

The contrast Benjamin draws between the story's wisdom and the novel's and mass information's lack of it emphasizes the connection between the story's meaning and the power of temporalization. The novel is poor in wisdom because it is produced by the isolated individual of modernity, read in solitude, and disseminated in a form that fixes and limits its meaning. Because its narration and reception do not involve the sensory experience of other living beings, it cannot be a continuing experience. It does not contain a force akin to temporalization and hence cannot enter into living activity. "The birthplace of the novel is the individual in his solitariness, who is no longer able to express himself by giving examples of his most important concerns, is himself uncounseled, and cannot counsel others" ("S," 87; 107, translation modified). But although the novel cannot enter into life, it is at least still able to represent life. Mass information is almost lifeless. It is immediately stillborn. "It is half the art of storytelling," Benjamin writes, "to keep a story free from explanation [Erklärungen] as one renders it again [wiedergibt]" ("S," 89; 109, translation modified). The vitality of life is here understood in terms of the richness of meaning that arises from the listener's freedom to interpret. In contradistinction, news information is poor in meaning because it is stifled by explanation and leaves the reader with no interpretative freedom. Consequently, it is tethered to and cannot exceed the punctuality of the immediate moment of its production and reception. "The value of information does not survive the moment in which it was new. It lives only at that moment; it has to surrender to it completely and explain itself to it without losing any time" ("S," 90; 110). In comparison, the story's experiential and communal character leads to an inexhaustibility in meaning. It survives beyond its initial moment of telling and can be retold again in a different setting, thereby always gaining in meaning. This is the story's vitality. Its germinal power resembles the force of temporalization: "It does not expend itself. It preserves and concentrates its force [Kraft] and is capable of releasing it even after a long time" ("S," 90; 110, translation modified).

The experiential origin of stories may imply that their mode of temporality is one of presence. In fact, their temporality is that of an unending promise, because the paradigmatic experience at the origin of stories is the aporetic experience of the finitude of human existence. The stuff that all stories come from is life that has been lived (*gelebtes Leben*) ("S," 94; 113). A "life that has been lived" is an eventful life, one to which things have happened, a life that has involved experiences. Unless one has lived or gone through something significant, one's life would be unworthy of being recounted in and as a story. Hence, a life that provides material for a story has more or less passed by. Benjamin notes that "a man's knowledge or wisdom, but above all, his life that has been lived . . . first assumes transmissible form at the moment of his death" ("S," 94; 113). There are two moments in the constitution of this transmissible form. First, when someone's life comes to an end, "a sequence of images is set in motion" in his interior consciousness, "unfolding the views of his own person under which he has encountered himself without being aware of it" ("S," 94; 114, translation modified). One goes through life without true self-knowledge. This only comes when one sees and grasps one's proper self as the sum of all the fleeting selves that one is and has been. Self-knowledge gives meaning to one's life and makes it worthy of transmission. But one can only gather together these selves, see this state of wholeness that is the precondition of self-conscious knowledge of one's self, at the moment of one's death, because only then will one's life be completed.

Second, because I only attain self-knowledge at the moment of my death, I cannot tell others the thematic content of my life's meaning. However, the fact that I have attained self-knowledge and grasped this meaning can be seen in my expressions. They communicate my life's meaningfulness to those around my deathbed but not its precise meaning. In Benjamin's words, "suddenly in his expressions and looks the unforgettable emerges and imparts to everything that concerned him that authority which even the poorest wretch in dying possesses for the living around him. This authority is at the very source of the story. Death is the sanction of everything that the storyteller can tell. He has borrowed his authority from death" ("S," 94; 114). The experience of finitude at the origin of stories is radically aporetic. Those who witness another's death experience sheer meaningfulness without determinate meaning, or better yet, without absolutely determinable meaning. (Kant similarly described aesthetic judgment as expressing a purposiveness without determinate purpose, and Derrida spoke of the messianic without messianism.) But it is precisely this lack of determination in meaning that engenders a story. First, the unforgettable meaningfulness of a life makes it worthy of relating. Second, the nondeterminability of meaning is a lure that makes us endlessly interpret and decipher the meaning of the dying person's signifying face, despite the fact that this meaning can never be confirmed or revealed, because the only person who possesses this knowledge has departed. This aporia is the source of the story's open-ended character, its structure as a promise that keeps on promising. Its unending germinal character makes it an analogue of the opening and worlding of a world by the force of time.

Without naming it, Benjamin elucidates this aporia as the undoing of sovereignty. The sovereign has authority and the power of sanction. Someone who attains self-presence in the knowledge of his or her proper self is a figure of sovereignty. But since this is attainable only in death, sovereignty is ushered in by its impossibility, the absolute loss of self-presence. This is the same as saying that death is the true sovereign. Death undoes the sovereignty of every human life and that of the storyteller, who merely borrows his power of narration from death. Arendt had pointed to a related nonsovereignty of stories: we can never be the sovereign authors of the stories we tell about ourselves but only their agent and sufferer because we cannot control the outcomes of our actions. But precisely because of this lack of sovereignty, stories are unending. What is without end is not the infinite but the finitude of temporalization itself. This is the origin of ethics, that is, storytelling and action in response to finitude.

To return to Rosca's novel, one explanation for why *State of War* ends with the figure of the storyteller is because stories not only create worlds that endure beyond the lives of their tellers but also point to the opening of worlds by the force of time. Second, the novel further elaborates on the undoing of sovereign intention by questioning the privileging of precolonial oral narrative. The stories Anna tells her child are repetitions, not of an oral presence, but of a technical archive, a tape recording, that comes to her from beyond the grave. This voice is also a promise of a revolutionary force that survives. But although it partakes of a precolonial spirit, this force is not merely precolonial, because its survival involves intermediality, the transmission-contamination of oral narrative by non-oral forms of mediation. It survives by means of a technological device of capitalist modernization: the consumer electronics assembled in free trade zones in the developing world. Instead of being fully reincarnated in and as a present world, the precolonial spirit's purity is necessarily contaminated by that which it resists even as it finds a way to survive in and through the instruments that contaminate it. But precisely because of this contamination, it has the structure of a promise, that which is always yet to come.

Outsider Worldliness: Cosmopolitan Consciousness from Below

The opening of a world, however, does not always lead to revolutionary action that affirms a people, especially in contemporary globalization, where a successful revolutionary worlding often appears unlikely. Timothy Mo's *Renegade* proposes as an alternative worldly ethics a detached critical involvement that seeks to change the world through a refusal of what it calls "tribalism," belonging to existing communities that are constituted through separation and exclusion and organized by internal hierarchies. This is the perspective of the outsider, the marginal. As Rey Castro, the novel's protagonist and first person narrator, puts it, this is "the ability to be dispassionate about myself, to see things cold-eyed from the outside."[20] One becomes an outsider by a process of self-detachment, which enables one to view oneself and one's immediate situation from the outside. But the outsider is not a mere observer. He also relates what he sees to others. In the act of testimony, he transcends the limits of the immediate conditions of his existence and attaches himself to the wider world. He becomes immersed in the world as a participant who endures and suffers what happens in it. Hence, telling stories and giving testimony are heroic interventions. In Rey's words, the outsider has "a cool heart and a permanent emancipation from tribalism. Funnily enough, the former was the most enigmatic, the most Eastern of all virtues—I should say Buddhist rather than Christian. It was something to prize more than a mere code of silence, which is just an abstention and represents neither a doing nor the enduring fortitude of the true hero" (Re, 40).

The outsider's worldly ethics belies the revolutionary connotations of the novel's title and its epigraph's revolutionary spirit. The epigraph, "El demonio de las comparaciones," is a phrase from José Rizal's Noli Me Tángere (1887), the famous novel written in Spanish by a Filipino ilustrado that is widely regarded as having inspired the nationalist revolution against Spain. The phrase is used to describe how the consciousness of the main protagonist, Ibarra, a young man from a wealthy mestizo family who has returned to Manila after several years of foreign study in Europe, is haunted by the endless comparison of his experiences of modernity abroad with the degraded situation in the colonial Philippines, where the civil and political liberties celebrated in secular enlightened Europe are not available because the Philippines is governed by an anachronistic and oppressive quasi-feudal administration that does not subscribe to the separation of church and state.[21] In Rizal's novel, this process of comparison stimulated revolutionary consciousness because it made palpable to the educated native that he must overthrow the yoke of colonialism if native society was to survive and thrive.

In Renegade, the phrase refers to the burden of a cosmopolitan consciousness, "the restlessness and uncertainty brought on by too wide a knowledge of the world" (Re, 36). Its use in relation to Rey suggests that comparison as a force of worlding is transformed in postcoloniality because the ideals of revolution have been betrayed. This is a worldliness from below, of a new type of mestizo. Unlike Rizal's protagonist, Rey is from the lowest social stratum of postcolonial Philippines. The illegitimate child of a Filipina prostitute and an African-American GI from the Vietnam War period, his very being bespeaks the worlding of the Philippines by the informal empire of US military and economic neocolonialism and global capitalism: the US military bases that led to flows of military personnel, the condition of possibility of the sexual exploitation of local women who initially served GIS on rest and recuperation and, later, foreign sex tourists. Rey enters the world in Mactan, where the local chieftain, Lapu-Lapu, who is retroactively considered to be the first national hero, killed Magellan in 1521. *State of War* mentions this act in a persistent refrain. But whereas Rosca's novel attempts to resurrect the precolonial past and the history of anticolonial resistance as resources for revolution, *Renegade* does not endorse nationalism of any kind. At the end of *Renegade*, Rey identifies with Magellan and describes his departure from the world as respite for a worldly soul weary from travel and exploration. "The sun starts to set over Olango island to the west of my native Mactan, as it must have set the day Magellan got chopped to pieces by Lapu-Lapu's homeboys in the gory froth of the reef shallows. Magellan and my bad-self, finding a quietus after our globe-trottings" (*Re*, 538). In Benjamin's taxonomy, Anna Villaverde is a storyteller who is rooted to the soil and tells local tales of revolutionary struggle. Rey is the second archetypal storyteller: the seafarer who shares the wisdom of strange experiences from foreign lands. Educated by Jesuit priests and framed for the murder of a young girl after his well-to-do college mates gang-raped her, he flees the Philippines and travels the world in steerage, working in menial jobs that take him from Hong Kong to Singapore and then to the Middle East, India, Thailand, Britain, and Cuba, before returning to the Philippines after he is cleared of criminal charges.[22]

Renegade is a picaresque novel that alludes to the European tradition of travel literature and satire, particularly Swift's *Gulliver's Travels*.[23] While in Havana, Rey finds an antique leather-bound copy of Hakluyt's *Voyages* in the rubble of a fallen building (*Re*, 492). The tales he tells of his adventures as an underclass migrant in strange lands contain cultural-psychological portraits of the different peoples he has encountered in the manner of eighteenth- and nineteenth-century discourses on the characteristics of different national types. His moral lessons condemn evil and selfish behavior, for example the cruelty of Middle Eastern peoples toward overseas contract workers, the pitiless character of Indians, and so on. His experiences as a biracial person and his marginal social position, however, problematize any clear identification with the Filipino people. Because he assumes an outsider position with regard to all tribes or group identities, he develops a moral code of conduct that is not compromised by a self-aggrandizing sense of his own people's cultural superiority. A renegade, Rey tells us, is someone who does not like his own tribe and can take a distance from its values.[24] He permanently refuses to belong or only belongs problematically to a group. The renegade thus occupies a position from which one can undertake a critical destabilization of tribal identity. *Renegade* is a synonym for *picaro*. Rey's storytelling is a movement of swerving away (*clinamen*) from tribalist principles, such as ethno-nationalism and the official nationalist idea of Asian values. At the same time, he does not present himself as more noble-minded than those he judges. Undertaking sly acts to survive and to protect those he believes are worthy, he describes himself as "a benevolent Iago who watched and listened and never snitched" (*Re*, 363).

Rey's storytelling is part of a worldly ethics, in the sense of activity that holds a world together across the extensiveness of global space. His travels turn him into a node that connects characters in different places across the globe, even though they may not know each other. Two chapters take the form of missives to him from locations as diverse as Karachi, Perth, Honolulu, Hong Kong, Ho Chi Minh, Quezon City, Surrey, Mactan, Naples, Bohaiden (a fictional Middle Eastern country), Southampton, and London. Moreover, his actions and the moral counsel of his stories constitute an honorable code of conduct that gives his world a meaningful ethical form. This attempt at worlding is clearly not as radical as the revolutionary worlding Rosca envisions. It does not aim at overthrowing the capitalist world-system but forages for resources in the unexpected linkages and alignments made possible by circulation within the circuits of global capitalism. The objective correlative for this complex interconnectedness and mixing of members of the human species that transcends tribal belonging and hierarchical divisions between and within groups is the halo-halo, a Filipino dessert made of a mound of shaved ice mixed with evaporated milk to which various sweet ingredients and toppings are added to create a "many-hued and multi-textured confection of ice-cream, cereals, neon syrups, crystallised fruits, frosty shavings, leguminous preserves and bloated pulses" (*Re*, 11).[25] The types of ingredients and toppings are potentially inexhaustible. The dessert is eaten by mixing everything together. Much of the pleasure is in the unusual flavors, tastes, and smells that come from the unexpected combination of ingredients. Rey characterizes the historical connections between different islands of archipelagic Southeast Asia as "the intraspecies global *halo-halo*" (*Re*, 67). As a supplement to *Renegade* in the novel's title, *Halo²* suggests that demotic everyday social intercourse among members of the human species gives rise to an infinite creativity that undermines the oppressive exclusions of tribalism. This creativity is an incalculable force immanent to global capitalism.

Renegade embodies this creativity. The inventive linguistic hybridity of its vocabulary, which incorporates words from many languages, especially Cebuano and Tagalog, and creates puns from them; its style, which mixes the syntactic structures of verbal English with those of other languages; and its heteroglossic range of cultural references enact the undoing of tribalism. Here is a random self-reflexive example:

> One day Dant used the word [incorrigible] as an adjective before a verbal noun, "Da kid is an incorrigibles puck-up, mans." A stylistic trick of higher-class English speech that came absolutely naturally to native Visayan-speakers like ourselves was the pattern of repeating the definite article before two qualifiers, separated by a comma. . . . We were used to repetitions, but repetitions that weakened, not strengthened: *init* was hot but *init-init* was luke-warm, *amahan* was father, but *ama-ama* was step-father. When I played aimless pursuit with Bambi as a kid it was running-running, definitely not just running when I could have been after her for sweets or her cherry. And, of course, *halo-halo* was a fun, a dolly-mixture. (*Re*, 35)

On a quick first reading, the passage makes sense. It is only when we pause to think about it that we marvel that it does make sense notwithstanding its hybridity. The porosity of languages—their inherent tendency to hybrid creativity—exemplifies a cosmopolitanizing force from below. Elsewhere, Mo compares the multiplicity of English language-use to the process of vernacularization that opened up multiple worlds in Europe: "If we can say the US is the Roman Empire of our day, English is the Latin. And . . . when the political sway of Rome ended, the territories fragmented and so did the languages: Latin became the modern Romance languages of French, Italian, and Spanish. Perhaps Taglish or Singaporean English will become languages in their own right."[26] The breaking-down of the empire of a given dominant language is inevitable. And if walls are built around a given vernacular, they too will be undermined by the linguistic porosity and incalculable creativity set off by intercultural intercourse.

It would be too easy to say that *Renegade* and the stories that it consists of are examples of world literature in the narrow sense of a linguistic object that circulates globally. This would beg the following questions: What enables a linguistic artifact to circulate? Why are languages porous in the first place? We tacitly use the anthropologistic thesis of human intercourse to understand circulation and porosity—human subjects put things into circulation in their social relations. Even so, we still need to explain how human beings have access to things, how they are open to each other in the first place, and where the time required for circulation comes from. To take the story as an example of a linguistic artifact, how are we able to tell stories to others in the first instance? Where does the time of storytelling come from? I have argued that this opening and access, worldhood in the original sense, comes from the incalculable giving of time.

The closing chapter of Mo's novel squarely confronts radical finitude by broaching the historical decline and end of the story form and its narrator's departure from the world. Echoing Marshall McLuhan's distinction between the mechanical and electric phases in the history of technological development, Rey ponders whether the time of stories (and his time as a storyteller) is over because in the era of microelectronic global information and teletechnomediation, we no longer have the time to tell and listen to stories.

> Cable had come to Cebu. Nobody was interested in traveller's tales. You didn't have to move two feet from your set or your more affluent neighbour's to see either a pageant of the world's great cities or its seamier spots. (*Re*, 534)
>
> There was no need to leave the discomfort of your own hooch to see the world; the world would come to you at the touch of a button. (*Re*, 536)

This is the world as picture in the Heideggerian sense, the world as quantified, measured, and pictured by human calculative reason. The triumph of teletechnomediation and the end of storytelling are, however, arrested by Rey's final words, which emphasize that clocked time is itself inadequate and limited.

> I check my watch, my Bambi-purloined, my Bambi-bestowed Timex. It's already 23:00. It's my eleventh hour, Brod, but I don't think the US Cavalry will be coming, more like the Horsemen of the Apocalypse.
>
> I stand, I lurch. (*Re*, 539)

The world governed by clock and calendar must eventually give way to the coming of another world beyond it. What is intimated is a stronger and more powerful because eternal presence. But although we will all eventually escape the dictates of clocked time, we can never know in advance when this will be. In this case, we are unsure whether Rey's end has come, what the meaning of his life is, and, therefore, how the novel ends. Put another way, the novel's ending leaves the reader unsure about whether anything or anyone does indeed come. We are left with the suspension of a sheer opening that is incalculable, precisely the open-ended, germinal structure of the story, even as Rey's story confronts the possibility of the end of the story form and his end.

———————————

Adorno suggested that the horrors of Auschwitz created a crisis for poetic production because the concept of cultural progress was responsible for the barbarism of genocidal extermination. Cultural criticism cannot comprehend the depth of this crisis because "absolute reification . . . is now preparing to absorb the mind [Geist] entirely."[27] In a subsequent reformulation, he notes that poetry is an important expression of suffering and speaks instead of a crisis of living, the torture of "mere survival [Weiterleben]." "Perennial suffering has as much right to expression as a tortured man has to scream; hence it may be wrong to say that after Auschwitz you could no longer write poems. But it is not wrong to raise the less cultural question whether after Auschwitz you can still go on living—especially whether one who escaped by accident, one who by rights should have been killed, may go on living."[28] But Adorno was wrong in his assessment of literature and survival. The postcolonial world literature I have discussed attests to literature's continuing pertinence, not only as an expression of humanity's ideals or suffering, but as an active force for the emergence of new subjects in the world. In opposition to the calculative appropriation of time that sustains contemporary global capitalism, the novels I have considered propose revolutionary time and worldly ethics as alternative temporalities. Global capitalism's web of instrumentalities is more pervasive and tenacious than the reifying processes Adorno diagnosed. These instrumentalities do not only form consciousness but also fabricate the materiality of bodies. For this reason, the sheer fact of existence is a fundamental resource for the postcolonial remaking of the world. Sheer survival is based on the inhuman force that gives time and opens a world and lets us be *with* others, such that, in Arendt's words, we are "neither for nor against them—that is, in sheer human togetherness."[29] Plural human togetherness precedes and enables any form of subjective intercourse, for example, cosmopolitan sociality. The inhuman condition of human togetherness disrupts capitalist instrumentality and creates openings for other worlds precisely because it cannot be appropriated by rational calculation. There is a special connection between the opening of worlds and the literary, because such fabulation is the very essence, the ontological condition of possibility of literature. In the final analysis, the question of literature's genesis—why is there still this thing called literature in our age of advanced teletechnomediation?—cannot be answered sociologically in terms of market forces. It is instead a simulacrum of Heidegger's question "Why something at all and not nothing?" The power of postcolonial world literature is fragile because it draws on the incalculable force of worlding that can also undermine progressive projects of world-making. This force is real and immanent to the global capitalist system. It always remains and cannot be destroyed without annihilating existence itself.

Introduction

1 William Kentridge, "Refuse the Hour," lecture delivered during the performance *Refuse the Hour*, 2012, insert in William Kentridge, *The Refusal of Time* (Paris: Éditions Xavier Barral, 2012), xiii–xiv.

2 Kentridge, "Refuse the Hour," xiv.

3 Peter Galison and William Kentridge, "Give Us Back Our Sun," in Kentridge, *The Refusal of Time*, 157.

4 Immanuel Kant, "Idea of a Universal History with a Cosmopolitan Purpose," in *Political Writings*, ed. Hans Reiss and trans. H. B. Nisbet (Cambridge: Cambridge University Press, 1991), 51–52, translation modified; *Idee zu einer allgemeinen Geschichte in weltbürgerlicher Absicht*, in *Schriften zur Anthropologie, Geschichtsphilosophie, Politik und Pädagogik 1*, ed. Wilhelm Weischedel (Frankfurt am Main: Suhrkamp, 1968), 47–48.

5 For a summary of the various possible and missed connections between world literature and cosmopolitanism in existing theories of world literature, see César Domínguez, "World Literature and Cosmopolitanism," in *The Routledge Companion to World Literature*, ed. Theo D'haen, David Damrosch, and Djelal Kadir (New York: Routledge, 2011): 242–52.

6 Thomas G. Pavel, *Fictional Worlds* (Cambridge, MA: Harvard University Press, 1986), 10. For a similar approach to world literature, see Eric Hayot, *On Literary Worlds* (Oxford: Oxford University Press, 2012).

7 Pavel, *Fictional Worlds*, 46, 50.

8 See Failed States Index of the Fund for Peace, http://ffp.statesindex.org. Somalia, the setting of Nuruddin Farah's *Gifts*, has occupied first place on the index in the past six years.

9 See Helen Stacy, "The Legal System of International Human Rights," in David Palumbo-Liu, Bruce Robbins, and Nirvana Tanoukhi (eds.), *Immanuel Wallerstein and the Problem of the World: System, Scale, Culture* (Durham, NC: Duke University Press, 2011), 187–201. See also Martti Koskenniemi, *The Gentle Civilizer of Nations*, (Cambridge: Cambridge University Press, 2001) and Anthony Anghie, *Imperialism, Sovereignty and the Making of International Law* (Cambridge: Cambridge University Press, 2007).

10 Engseng Ho, "Inter-Asia Then and Now," plenary lecture, ssrc Conference on Inter-Asian Connections, University of Hong Kong, June 8, 2012. Unpublished manuscript on file with the author.

11 Anna Lowenhaupt Tsing, *Friction: An Ethnography of Global Connection* (Princeton, NJ: Princeton University Press, 2005).

12 See, for example, "What Counts as World Literature?," edited by Caroline Levine and B. Venkat Mani, special issue, *Modern Language Quarterly* 74.2 (June 2013).

13 Amihud Gilead, "Teleological Time: A Variation of a Kantian Theme," *Review of Metaphysics* 38 (March 1985): 529–62.

14 I have discussed the extended analogy between organic life and freedom in greater detail in Pheng Cheah, *Spectral Nationality: Passages of Freedom from Kant to Postcolonial Literatures of Liberation* (New York: Columbia University Press, 2003).

15 For Hegel and Marx, what is transcended is, respectively, the particularity of finite national spirits and the limitations of time on the development of productive forces.

16 Gayatri Chakravorty Spivak, "Three Women's Texts and a Critique of Imperialism," in "'Race,' Writing, and Difference," special issue, *Critical Inquiry* 12.1 (autumn 1985): 243–61, especially 243–45. For an argument that Spivak may have overstated the impact of the epistemic violence of imperialist and colonial worlding in a way that precludes anticolonial resistance, see Ania Loomba, "Overworlding the 'Third World,'" in "Neocolonialism," ed. Robert Young, special issue, *Oxford Literary Review* 13 (1991): 164–91.

17 Spivak, "Three Women's Texts," 260n1.

18 Gayatri Chakravorty Spivak, "The Rani of Sirmur: An Essay in Reading the Archives," *History and Theory* 24.3 (October 1985): 253.

19 Boaventura de Sousa Santos, "A Critique of Lazy Reason: Against the Waste of Experience," in *The Modern World-System in the Longue Durée*, ed. Immanuel Wallerstein (London: Paradigm, 2004), 169.

20 Although the students are not identified by name in the evaluations, they are asked to identify their department and major field.

Chapter 1. The New World Literature

1 Charles Bernheimer, ed., *Comparative Literature in the Age of Multiculturalism* (Baltimore: Johns Hopkins University Press, 1995), and Haun Saussy, ed., *Comparative Literature in an Age of Globalization* (Baltimore: Johns Hopkins University Press, 2006).

2 See Mary Louise Pratt's contribution in the Bernheimer volume, "Comparative Literature and Global Citizenship," 58–65. Pratt argues for the importance of "new forms of cultural citizenship in a globalizing world" (62).

3 For a recent polemical statement of this critique of world literature in English translation, see Gayatri Chakravorty Spivak, *Death of a Discipline* (New York: Columbia University Press, 2003).

4 Erich Auerbach, "Philology and *Weltliteratur*," trans. Marie and Edward Said, *Centennial Review* 13.1 (1969): 1–17; "Philologie der Weltliteratur," in *Weltliteratur. Festgabe für Fritz Stich zum 70. Geburtstag*, ed. Walter Muschg and Emil Staiger

(Bern: Francke Verlag, 1972), 39–50. Subsequent references refer to the translation first, followed by the German text. Translation modified where appropriate.

5   Auerbach, "Philology and *Weltliteratur*," 2; 39, translation modified.

6   Auerbach, "Philology and *Weltliteratur*," 4; 40.

7   Auerbach, "Philology and *Weltliteratur*," 4–5; 41, translation modified.

8   Auerbach, "Philology and *Weltliteratur*," 2; 39.

9   Auerbach, "Philology and *Weltliteratur*," 3; 39, translation modified.

10 In comparison, critical theories of world cinema and world music are more alert to the dangers of the commodification of difference and hold less naïve views about the market metaphor. For an incisive critique of the relation between world cinema and industrialized global culture that draws an analogy between world cinema and world music, see Martin Roberts, "'Baraka': World Cinema and the Global Culture Industry," *Cinema Journal* 37.3 (spring 1998): 62–82. On world music as a commercial marketing tool, see Steven Feld, "A Sweet Lullaby for World Music," *Public Culture* 12.1 (2000): 145–71.

11 See Patricia Cohen, "In Tough Times, the Humanities Must Justify Their Worth," *New York Times*, February 25, 2009.

12 For a bourgeois liberal account of globalization from the discipline of economics, see Robert Solomon, *The Transformation of the World Economy*, 2nd ed. (New York: St. Martin's Press, 1999), and *Money on the Move: The Revolution in International Finance since 1980* (Princeton, NJ: Princeton University Press, 1999). For a more tempered view that discusses the negative consequences of the globalization of money flows, see Barry Eichengreen, *Globalizing Capital: A History of the International Monetary System*, updated ed. (Princeton, NJ: Princeton University Press, 1998).

13 David Damrosch, *What Is World Literature?* (Princeton, NJ: Princeton University Press, 2003), 4.

14 Damrosch, *What Is World Literature?*, 6, emphasis added.

15 Damrosch, *What Is World Literature?*, 289.

16 Damrosch, *What Is World Literature?*, 4.

17 Damrosch, *What Is World Literature?*, 298.

18 Damrosch, *What Is World Literature?*, 4.

19 Franco Moretti, "World-Systems Analysis, Evolutionary Theory, *Weltliteratur*," in *Immanuel Wallerstein and the Problem of the World: System, Scale, Culture*, ed. David Palumbo-Liu, Bruce Robbins, and Nirvana Tanoukhi (Durham, NC: Duke University Press, 2011), 75.

20 John Pizer, "Goethe's 'World Literature' Paradigm and Contemporary Cultural Globalization," *Comparative Literature* 52.3 (summer 2000): 213. The following quote comes from page 225.

21 See David Harvey, *The Condition of Postmodernity* (Cambridge: Blackwell, 1990).

22 Pascale Casanova, *The World Republic of Letters*, trans. M. B. DeBevoise (Cambridge, MA: Harvard University Press, 2004), 3–4: "This space is not an abstract and theoretical construction, but an actual—albeit unseen—world made up by lands of literature; a world in which what is judged worthy of being considered

literary is brought into existence; a world in which the ways and means of literary art are argued over and decided."

23 Pascale Casanova, "Literature as a World," *New Left Review* 31 (January-February 2005): 73.

24 Casanova, *World Republic of Letters*, 12.

25 Casanova, *World Republic of Letters*, 40. Casanova's understanding of globalization does not account for how it creates hierarchies and involves multidirectional struggles.

26 Casanova, "Literature as a World," 72.

27 Literature as a world is "a parallel territory, relatively autonomous from the political domain, and dedicated as a result to questions, debates, inventions of a specifically literary nature. Here, struggles of all sorts . . . come to be refracted, diluted, deformed or transformed according to a literary logic, and in literary forms" (Casanova, "Literature as a World," 72).

28 Casanova, "Literature as a World," 71.

29 Casanova, *World Republic of Letters*, 81.

30 Casanova, *World Republic of Letters*, 172. Marketized world literature is "a short-term boost to publishers' profits in the most market-oriented and powerful centers through the marketing of products intended for rapid, 'de-nationalized' circulation" (74).

31 Although Casanova claims to be influenced by Bourdieu, the concept of relative autonomy is distinctly Althusserian. The world republic of letters is determined in the last instance in the same way that Althusser spoke of "the determination in the last instance by the economic." See Louis Althusser, "Contradiction and Overdetermination," in *For Marx*, trans. Ben Brewster (London: Verso, 1990), 113. For Althusser, the superstructure has the weak effectivity of the "specification" of a contradiction and "overdetermines" it, using a term borrowed from Freud's analysis of dreamwork.

32 Franco Moretti, "Graphs, Maps, Trees: Abstract Models for Literary History—2," *New Left Review* 26 (March-April 2004): 79–103. The quotation, slightly modified, is from p. 103. Moretti's description of literary sociology is as follows: "Deducing from the *form* of an object the *forces* that have been at work: this is the most elegant definition ever of what literary sociology should be" (97).

33 Franco Moretti, "Graphs, Maps, Trees: Abstract Models for Literary History—3," *New Left Review* 28 (July-August 2004): 63.

34 In the case of the novel, it shows, Moretti argues, that the autonomous rise of the novel in European nations is a myth or at least an exception rather than the rule. See Franco Moretti, "Conjectures on World Literature," *New Left Review* 1 (January-February 2000): 58–61. Moretti's model is one of qualified or mitigated Eurocentrism. On the one hand, the influence still flows from western Europe, and its genres are prototypes. On the other hand, the western European path of the development of literary forms is no longer modular, and that of peripheral cultures becomes so.

35 Moretti, "Conjectures on World Literature," 64.

36 There is some terminological imprecision in Moretti's characterization of social relations in terms of forces. Marx conceived of social relations as forms by which productive forces become regulated and harnessed. Moretti's use of this vocabulary clearly illustrates the superstructural character of literary forms in his argument. For Marx, literary forms are the forms of forms, so to speak. For Moretti, they are the forms of forces.

37 Franco Moretti, "The End of the Beginning: Reply to Christopher Prendergast," *New Left Review* 41 (September-October 2006): 73. In this vein, he suggests that the form of the gothic novel was more useful than the amorous epistolary fiction to capture the traumas of the revolutionary years. Similarly, the rise of free indirect style is a refraction of the problem of modern socialization. It grants the individual some freedom while permeating it with the impersonal stance of the narrator, thereby transposing the objective into the subjective. The argument about the gothic novel is made in "Graphs, Maps, Trees: Abstract Models for Literary History—1," *New Left Review* 24 (November-December 2003): 82. The argument about free indirect style is in "Graphs, Maps, Trees: Abstract Models for Literary History—3," 56.

38 This is a simplistic account of pleasure and desire that reduces desire to consumption for pleasure. It does not take into account the complexity of psychical forces and their link to signification, or the complex morphology of needs and their imaginary, where one might broach the question of an inhuman material force. On Nietzsche's understanding of the reactive character of consciousness as a dominated force vis-à-vis the body's superior force, see Gilles Deleuze, *Nietzsche and Philosophy*, trans. Hugh Tomlinson (New York: Columbia University Press, 1983), 39–44. One can make the same argument about Marx's base-superstructure model, which informs Moretti's account of literature as an abstract of social forces.

39 See Henri Lefebvre, *The Production of Space*, trans. David Nicholson-Smith (Oxford: Blackwell, 1991), 39.

40 Moretti, "World-Systems Analysis, Evolutionary Theory, *Weltliteratur*," 76.

41 See Gerhart Hoffmeister, "Reception in Germany and Abroad," in *The Cambridge Companion to Goethe*, ed. Lesley Sharpe (Cambridge: Cambridge University Press, 2002), and Fritz Strich, *Goethe and World Literature*, trans. C. A. M. Sym (New York: Hafner, 1949).

42 Johann Wolfgang Goethe, "*Le Tasse*, drame historique en cinq actes, par Monsieur Alexandre Duval," in *Über Kunst und Alterthum*, VI, 1 (1827), in *Sämtliche Werke, I. Abteilung, Band 22, Ästhetische Schriften 1824–1832, Über Kunst und Altertum V–VI*, ed. Anne Bohnenkamp (Frankfurt am Main: Deutscher Klassiker, 1999), 356–57; "Some Passages Pertaining to the Concept of World Literature," in *Comparative Literature: The Early Years. An Anthology of Essays*, ed. Hans-Joachim Schulz and Phillip H. Rhein (Chapel Hill: University of North Carolina Press, 1973), 5. Translation modified. Subsequent references will be to this edition with the translation following the German text.

43 Johann Wolfgang Goethe, "On the *Edinburgh Reviews*," in *Über Kunst und Alterthum*, VI, 2 (1828), in *Sämtliche Werke, Band 22, Ästhetische Schriften 1824–1832, Über Kunst und Altertum V–VI*, ed. Anne Bohnenkamp (Frankfurt am Main: Deutscher Klassiker, 1999), 491; "Some Passages," 8.

44 Letter to Carlyle, July 20, 1827, in *Sämtliche Werke, II. Abteilung, Band 10 (37), Die Letzten Jahre. Briefe, Tagebücher und Gespräche von 1823 bis zu Goethes Tod*, Teil 1, *Von 1823 bis zum Tode Carl Augusts 1828*, ed. Horst Fleig (Frankfurt am Main: Deutscher Klassiker, 1993), 497; *Correspondence between Goethe and Carlyle*, ed. Charles Eliot Norton (London: Macmillan, 1887), 24–25, translation modified.

45 This and the following quote are from Goethe, Letter to Carlyle, 498; 25–26.

46 The quotes are from, respectively, Johann Wolfgang Goethe, "Bezüge nach Aussen" [Relations to foreign countries], in *Über Kunst und Alterthum*, VI, 2 (1828), in *Sämtliche Werke, I. Abteilung, Band 22, Ästhetische Schriften 1824–1832, Über Kunst und Altertum V–VI*, ed. Anne Bohnenkamp (Frankfurt am Main: Deutscher Klassiker, 1999), 427–28, and "Aus dem Faszikel zu Carlyles *Leben Schillers*," in *Sämtliche Werke, Band 22, Ästhetische Schriften 1824–1832, Über Kunst und Altertum V–VI*, ed. Anne Bohnenkamp (Frankfurt am Main: Deutscher Klassiker, 1999), 866–67. Translations from "Some Passages," 7–8; 10.

47 "Aus dem Faszikel zu Carlyles *Leben Schillers*," 866; 10.

48 "Aus dem Faszikel zu Carlyles *Leben Schillers*," 867; 10.

49 See Jürgen Habermas, *The Inclusion of the Other: Studies in Political Theory*, ed. Ciaran Cronin and Pablo De Greiff (Cambridge, MA: MIT Press, 1998), and *The Postnational Constellation: Political Essays*, trans. and ed. Max Pensky (Cambridge, MA: MIT Press, 2001). For Habermas, all system imperatives are regulated by the constitutive presupposition of communication, which is expressed as norms.

50 See Jacques Derrida, "Globalization, Peace and Cosmopolitanism," in *Negotiations: Interventions and Interviews, 1971–2001* (Palo Alto, CA: Stanford University Press, 2002), and "Une Europe de l'espoir," *Le Monde diplomatique*, November 2004: 3; http://www.monde-diplomatique.fr/2004/11/DERRIDA/11677.

51 Johann Peter Eckermann, *Gespräche mit Goethe in den letzten Jahren seines Lebens* (Berlin: Aufbau, 1982), 198; Johann Wolfgang von Goethe, *Conversations with Eckermann 1823–1832*, trans. John Oxenford (San Francisco: Northpoint Press, 1984), 133.

52 Johann Wolfgang Goethe, "*Le Tasse*," 357; 5.

53 Adam Smith, *An Inquiry into the Nature and Causes of the Wealth of Nations* (Chicago: University of Chicago Press, 1976), vol. 1, 519.

54 Smith, *An Inquiry*, vol. 1, 514.

55 Smith, *An Inquiry*, vol. 1, 519.

56 Immanuel Kant, *Toward Perpetual Peace: A Philosophical Project*, in *Practical Philosophy*, trans. and ed. Mary Gregor (Cambridge: Cambridge University Press, 1996), 333; *Zum ewigen Frieden. Ein philosophischer Entwurf*, in *Schriften zur Anthropologie, Geschichtsphilosophie, Politik und Pädagogik 1*, in *Werkausgabe XI*, ed. W. Weischedel (Frankfurt am Main: Suhrkamp, 1968), 222.

57 Immanuel Kant, *Critique of the Power of Judgment*, trans. Paul Guyer and Eric Matthews (Cambridge: Cambridge University Press, 2000), § 83, 301; *Kritik der Urteilskraft*, in *Werkausgabe* X, ed. Wilhelm Weischedel (Frankfurt am Main: Suhrkamp, 1968), 392.

58 Kant, *Critique of the Power of Judgment*, § 60, 229; *Kritik der Urteilskraft*, 300.

59 Kant, *Critique of the Power of Judgment*, § 40, 173–74; *Kritik der Urteilskraft*, 225. For a discussion on the tension between *sensus communis* and the preparation of sociability through taste, see Jean-François Lyotard, "Sensus Communis: The Subject in *Statu Nascendi*," in *Who Comes After the Subject?*, ed. Eduardo Cadava, Peter Connor, and Jean-Luc Nancy (New York: Routledge, 1991), 217–35.

Chapter 2. The World According to Hegel

1 Spirit is self-conscious reason and assumes three shapes: subjective spirit (further distinguished into soul, consciousness, and spirit), objective spirit (further distinguished into right, morality, and ethical life [*Sittlichkeit*]), and absolute spirit (further distinguished into art, religion, and philosophy). The first two forms of spirit are finite, whereas absolute spirit is infinite. See G. W. F. Hegel, *Hegel's Philosophy of Mind. Part Three of the Philosophical Sciences (1830)*, trans. William Wallace and A. V. Miller (Oxford: Clarendon, 1971); *Enzyklopädie der philosophischen Wissenschaften im Grundrisse 1830, Dritter teil, Die Philosophie des Geistes, Werke* 10, ed. Eva Moldenhauer and Karl Markus Michel (Frankfurt am Main: Suhrkamp, 1986), hereafter PS, with page references to the translation followed by page references to the German text. Translations modified where appropriate.

2 The three stages of ethical life are the family, civil society and the state. See G. W. F. Hegel, *Elements of the Philosophy of Right*, ed. Allen W. Wood, trans. H. B. Nisbet (Cambridge: Cambridge University Press, 1991); *Grundlinien der Philosophie des Rechts, Werke* 7, ed. Eva Moldenhauer and Karl Markus Michel (Frankfurt am Main: Suhrkamp, 1986), hereafter PR, with page references to the translation followed by page references to the German text. Translations modified where appropriate.

3 PR, § 340, 371; 503.

4 G. W. F. Hegel, *Lectures on the Philosophy of World History. Introduction: Reason in History*, trans. H. B Nisbet (Cambridge: Cambridge University Press, 1980), 33; *Vorlesungen über die Philosophie der Weltgeschichte*, vol. 1, *Die Vernunft in der Geschichte* (Hamburg: Felix Meiner, 1955), 36, hereafter LPWH, with page references to the translation followed by page references to the German text. Translations modified where appropriate.

5 LPWH, 68–69; 79–80.

6 LPWH, 33; 36.

7 LPWH, 33; 36.

8 LPWH, 28; 29.

9 LPWH, 46; 53, translation modified. Nisbet has translated the clause as "this ultimate end is the intention which underlies the world."

10 *LPWH*, 127; 153, translation modified.

11 *LPWH*, 127; 153. See also G. W. F. Hegel, *Hegel's Philosophy of Nature. Part Two of the Encyclopaedia of the Philosophical Sciences (1830)*, trans. A. V. Miller (London: Clarendon Press, 1970), § 258R, 35: "Time itself is the *becoming*, this coming-to-be and passing away, *the actually existent abstraction, Chronos*, from whom everything is born and by whom its offspring is destroyed," and § 258Z, 35–36: "Time is only this abstraction of destruction. It is because things are finite that they are in time; it is not because they are in time that they perish."

12 G. W. F. Hegel, *Aesthetics: Lecture on Fine Arts*, vol. 1, trans. T. M. Knox (Oxford: Clarendon Press, 1998), 459. Hegel uses the phrase, "falls a victim to the unhistorical power of time," to describe nations that fail to achieve a stable existence because they have not formed states and also explains their instability through an analogy with Chronos.

13 G. W. F. Hegel, *Hegel and the Human Spirit: A Translation of the Jena Lectures on the Philosophy of Spirit (1805–6) with commentary*, trans. Leo Rauch (Detroit: Wayne State University Press, 1983), 70; *Jenaer Realphilosophie. Vorlesungmanuskripte zur Philosophie der Natur und des Geistes von 1805–1806* (Hamburg: Felix Meiner, 1969), 186.

14 *LPWH*, 128; 154, translation modified.

15 *LPWH*, 33; 36, translation modified.

16 See *LPWH*, 35–36; 39–40.

17 *LPWH*, 30–31; 32–33, translation modified.

18 *LPWH*, 36; 40, translation modified.

19 *PS*, § 548; 277; 347, translation modified.

20 *PR*, § 340, 371; 503.

21 See *LPWH*, 52–53; 60.

22 *LPWH*, 64; 74–75, translation modified.

23 *LPWH*, 42; 48.

24 *LPWH*, 29; 30.

25 See *PR*, § 342, 372; 504: "World history is the necessary development, from the concept of the freedom of spirit alone, of the moments of reason and hence of spirit's self-consciousness and freedom. It is the exposition and *actualization of universal spirit.*"

26 *PR*, § 344, 373; 505.

27 *PR*, § 348, 375; 506.

28 *PR*, § 348, 375; 506.

29 *PR*, § 375; 507.

30 *PR*, § 347, 374; 506.

31 *LPWH*, 43; 48–49, translation modified.

32 *LPWH*, 101; 120.

33 *LPWH*, 101; 121.

34 *LPWH*, 58; 67.

35 *LPWH*, 143; 174.

36 Hegel, *Aesthetics: Lecture on Fine Arts*, 77.

37 Ranajit Guha, *History at the Limit of World-History* (New York: Columbia University Press, 2002), 5.

Chapter 3. The World as Market

1 Karl Marx and Friedrich Engels, *Manifesto of the Communist Party*, in *The Revolutions of 1848. Political Writings*, vol. 1, ed. David Fernbach (Harmondsworth, England: Penguin, 1973), 71; *Manifest der Kommunistichen Partei* (1848), in *Marx/Engels Gesamtausgabe*, vol. 1:6, ed. V. Adoratskij (Berlin: Marx-Engels Verlag, 1932), 529–30, translation modified, hereafter MKP, with page references to the translation followed by page references to the German text. Translations modified where appropriate.

2 Karl Marx and Friedrich Engels, *The German Ideology*, ed. C. J. Arthur (New York: International, 1970), 55; *Die Deutsche Ideologie, Marx/Engels Gesamtausgabe*, vol. 1:5, ed. V. Adoratskij (Berlin: Marx-Engels Verlag, 1932), 26, hereafter DI, with page references to the translation followed by page references to the German text. Translations modified where appropriate.

3 *DI*, 58; 35.

4 *DI*, 59; 28.

5 *DI*, 78; 49–50.

6 Immanuel Kant, *Anthropology from a Pragmatic Point of View*, in Immanuel Kant, *Anthropology, History and Education*, ed. Günter Zöller and Robert Louden (Cambridge: Cambridge University Press, 2011), 420; *Anthropologie in pragmatischer Hinsicht*, in *Werkausgabe* XII, ed. Wilhelm Weischedel (Frankfurt am Main: Suhrkamp, 1968), 678.

7 Kant, *Anthropology from a Pragmatic Point of View*, 241–42; 411.

8 G. W. F. Hegel, *Lectures on the Philosophy of World History. Introduction: Reason in History*, trans. H. B. Nisbet (Cambridge: Cambridge University Press, 1980), 57; *Vorlesungen über die Philosophie der Weltgeschichte*, vol. 1, *Die Vernunft in der Geschichte* (Hamburg: Felix Meiner, 1955), 66.

9 Hegel, *Lectures on the Philosophy of World History*, 57; 66.

10 This distinction is easy to miss. In the passage quoted earlier, *Weltteilen* is translated as "every quarter of the globe," when it should be "every part of the world," because Marx is describing how capitalist relations of production turn the globe into a world, a system of needs, in which different quarters of the globe are made into parts of an organized whole.

11 Karl Marx, *Capital: A Critique of Political Economy, Volume 1*, trans. Ben Fowkes (Harmondsworth, England: Penguin, 1976), 247; *Das Kapital: Kritik der politischen Ökonomie, Erster Band* (Berlin: Dietz, 1962), 161, hereafter C1, with page references to the translation followed by page references to the German text. Translation modified where appropriate.

12 Karl Marx, *Capital: A Critique of Political Economy, Volume 3*, trans. David Fernbach (Harmondsworth, England: Penguin, 1981), 205; *Das Kapital: Kritik der politischen Ökonomie, Dritter Band* (Berlin: Dietz, 1964), 120, hereafter C3, with

page references to the translation followed by page references to the German text. Translation modified where appropriate.

13　*C1*, 915; 779.

14　*C1*, 155; 77.

15　*C1*, 159; 80–81.

16　*C1*, 159–60; 81.

17　*C1*, 166; 87.

18　See *C1*, 166–67; 87–88.

19　My brief account of reification is a paraphrase of George Markus, "Alienation and Reification in Marx and Lukacs," *Thesis Eleven* 5/6 (1982): 150–52.

20　See Markus, "Alienation," 152.

21　*C3*, 969–70; 839.

22　*C3*, 451; 345–46.

23　*C3*, 444–45; 349.

24　Karl Marx, *Grundrisse: Foundations of the Critique of Political Economy*, trans. Martin Nicolaus (Harmondsworth, England: Penguin, 1973), 516–17; *Grundrisse der Kritik der politischen Ökonomie* (Berlin: Dietz, 1953), 415–16, hereafter *G*, with page references to the translation followed by page references to the German text. Translation modified where appropriate.

25　Marx uses the terms *Zirkulation* and *Umlauf* interchangeably, and each has a broad and narrow meaning.

26　*G*, 517; 416.

27　*G*, 518; 417.

28　*G*, 521; 420.

29　*G*, 521–22; 420.

30　*G*, 534–35; 433: "Quite different is the time which generally passes before the commodity makes its transition into money; or the time during which it remains a commodity, only a potential but not actual value."

31　*G*, 539–40; 438.

32　*G*, 407–8; 311.

33　*G*, 409–10; 312–13.

34　*G*, 410; 313–14.

35　*G*, 540; 438.

36　*C3*, 358–59; 260.

37　*DI*, 50; 19.

38　*G*, 84; 6.

39　*C1*, 443; 345.

40　*C1*, 444; 346.

41　*C1*, 447; 349.

42　*C1*, 448; 350.

43　*C1*, 449–50; 351.

44　*DI*, 56; 24.

45　*DI*, 55; 26.

46 *DI*, 56; 25.

47 *DI*, 56–57; 25.

48 David Harvey, *The Condition of Postmodernity* (Cambridge: Blackwell, 1990), 300.

49 Immanuel Wallerstein, *The Modern World-System: Capitalist Agriculture and the Origins of the European World-Economy in the Sixteenth Century* (New York: Academic Press, 1974), 38.

50 Wallerstein, *Modern World-System*, 162.

51 Wallerstein, *Modern World-System*, 15, my emphasis.

52 Immanuel Wallerstein, "The Rise and Future Demise of the World Capitalist System: Concepts for Comparative Analysis," in *The Capitalist World-Economy: Essays by Immanuel Wallerstein* (Cambridge: Cambridge University Press, 1979), 15.

53 Immanuel Wallerstein, *The Modern World-System II: Mercantilism and the Consolidation of the European World-Economy 1600–1750* (New York: Academic Press, 1980), 129.

54 Wallerstein, *Modern World-System*, 10.

55 Immanuel Wallerstein, *The Modern World-System III: The Second Era of Great Expansion of the Capitalist World-Economy, 1730–1840s* (New York, Academic Press: 1989), 129, emphasis added. Reasons for the incorporation of the entire globe include the access to greater quantities of raw materials and new raw materials unavailable in Europe, the search for new markets, and new sources of labor and sites for the production of lower-ranking commodities that are nevertheless essential for daily use in the capitalist system.

56 Wallerstein, *Modern World-System III*, 130.

57 Wallerstein, "Rise and Future Demise of the World Capitalist System," 27.

58 Wallerstein, *Modern World-System*, 308.

59 Wallerstein, *Modern World-System*, 339.

60 Wallerstein, "Dependence in an Interdependent World: The Limited Possibilities of Transformation within a Capitalist World-Economy," in *Capitalist World-Economy*, 73.

61 This approach is found in modified form in Fredric Jameson's aesthetic of cognitive mapping.

62 Georg Lukács, *Studies in European Realism*, trans. Edith Bone (New York: Grosset and Dunlap, 1964), 7.

63 Lukács, *Studies in European Realism*, 5.

64 Herbert Marcuse, *One-Dimensional Man: Studies in the Ideology of Advanced Industrial Society*, 2nd ed. (Boston: Beacon Press, 1991), 63.

65 Theodor Adorno, *Aesthetic Theory*, trans. Robert Hullot-Kentor (Minneapolis: University of Minnesota Press, 1997), 225–26.

66 Henri Lefebvre, *The Production of Space*, trans. Donald Nicholson-Smith (Oxford: Blackwell, 1991), 21, hereafter *PoS*.

67 *PoS*, 21–22. Lefebvre's examples are Marx, Bergson, and Husserl. David Harvey draws on Lefebvre's argument about Hegel's freezing of time in statized space when he claims that "Marx . . . had restored historical time (and class relations)

to primacy of place in social theory, in part as a reaction to Hegel's spatialized conception of the 'ethical state' as the end-point of a teleological history" (*Condition of Postmodernity*, 273).

68 *PoS*, 51.

69 *PoS*, 341.

70 See *PoS*, 33, 38–43.

71 *PoS*, 42.

72 *PoS*, 42.

73 *PoS*, 42.

74 Lefebvre's actual wording is: "the paradigmatic (or 'significant') opposition between use and exchange, between global networks and the determinate locations of production and consumption, is transformed here into a dialectical contradiction, and in the process it becomes spatial" (*PoS*, 341).

75 *PoS*, 39.

76 The quoted phrase is from *PoS*, 41.

77 "The world of images and signs exercises a fascination, skirts or submerges problems, and diverts attention from the 'real'—i.e. from the possible. While occupying space, it also signifies space, substituting a mental and therefore abstract space for spatial practice—without, however, doing anything really to unify those spaces that it seems to combine in the abstraction of signs and images" (*PoS*, 389).

78 *PoS*, 42.

79 *PoS*, 422.

80 *PoS*, 54.

81 *PoS*, 59.

82 The role Lefebvre attributes to art and the imagination in transforming social space is not dissimilar to the important role of the aesthetic in instituting new forms of experience in Jacques Rancière's account of the distribution of the sensible. See Rancière, *The Politics of Aesthetics: The Distribution of the Sensible*, trans. Gabriel Rockhill (London: Continuum, 2004).

83 David Harvey, *The Limits to Capital* (Chicago: University of Chicago Press, 1982), 386.

84 Harvey, *Limits to Capital*, 387.

85 David Harvey, *Spaces of Global Capitalism* (London: Verso, 2006), 77, hereafter *SoGC*.

86 *SoGC*, 81.

87 *SoGC*, 84.

88 *SoGC*, 132.

89 This and the following quote are from *SoGC*, 139.

90 *PoS*, 39.

Chapter 4. Worlding

1 Martin Heidegger, *The Fundamental Concepts of Metaphysics: World, Finitude, Solitude*, trans. William McNeill and Nicholas Walker (Bloomington: Indiana University Press, 1995), 347, translation modified; *Die Grundbegriffe der Metaphysik: Welt—*

Endlichkeit—Einsamkeit, Gesamtausgabe, II. Abteilung: Vorlesungen 1923–1944, Band 29/30, Freiburger Vorlesung Wintersemester 1929/30, ed. Friedrich-Wilhelm von Hermann (Frankfurt am Main: Vittorio Klostermann, 1983), 504. Emphasis in the original. Hereafter *FCM*, with page numbers of the translation followed by the German text.

2 Martin Heidegger, *Basic Problems of Phenomenology*, trans. Albert Hofstadter, rev. ed. (Bloomington: Indiana University Press, 1988), 166; *Die Grundprobleme der Phänomenologie, Gesamtausgabe, II. Abteilung: Vorlesungen 1923–1944,* Band 24, Marburger Vorlesung Sommersemester 1927, ed. Friedrich-Wilhelm von Hermann (Frankfurt am Main: Vittorio Klostermann, 1975), 236. Emphasis in the original. Hereafter *BPP*, with page numbers of the translation followed by the German text.

3 My discussion of Heidegger's account of the world focuses primarily on *Being and Time* and the lecture courses he delivered at the University of Marburg between 1925 and 1928, before and after the writing of *Being and Time*, with occasional references to Heidegger's later writings after the so-called *Kehre*. The ideas from the earlier part of his corpus are undoubtedly those that influenced Hannah Arendt's thought because they were developed and publicly delivered during her time as his student at Marburg from 1924 to 1925.

4 Martin Heidegger, *Being and Time*, trans. Joan Stambaugh (Albany: State University of New York Press, 1996), 60; *Sein und Zeit, Gesamtausgabe, I. Abteilung: Veröffentlichte Schriften 1914–1970*, Band 2, ed. Friedrich-Wilhelm von Hermann (Frankfurt am Main: Vittorio Klostermann, 1977), 64, hereafter *BT*, with page numbers of the translation followed by those from the 1953 Max Niemeyer edition of the German text. See also Martin Heidegger, *The Metaphysical Foundations of Logic*, trans. Michael Heim (Bloomington: Indiana University Press, 1984), 180; *Metaphysische Anfangsgründe der Logik im Ausgang von Leibniz, Gesamtausgabe, II. Abteilung: Vorlesungen 1923–1944*, Band 26, Marburger Vorlesung Sommersemester 1928, ed. Klaus Held (Frankfurt am Main: Vittorio Klostermann, 1978), 231. Hereafter *MFL*, with page numbers of the translation followed by the German text.

5 In order to maintain consistency across the English translations of different texts by Heidegger, I will translate *Besorgen* as "taking care," *Sorge*, which refers to Dasein's relations to other beings that are not Dasein, as "care" and *Fürsorge*, which refers to Dasein's relations to other Dasein, as "concern." The English translations of the Marburg lectures render *Besorgen* as "concern," whereas English translations of *Sein und Zeit* render *Fürsorge* as "concern."

6 Martin Heidegger, *History of the Concept of Time. Prolegomena*, trans. Theodore Kisiel (Bloomington: Indiana University Press, 1985), 171; *Prolegomena zur Geschichte des Zeitbegriffs, Gesamtausgabe, II. Abteilung: Vorlesungen 1923–1944*, Band 20, Marburger Vorlesung Sommersemester 1925, ed. Petra Jaeger (Frankfurt am Main: Vittorio Klostermann, 1979), 230. Hereafter *HCT*, with page numbers of the translation followed by the German text.

7 *HCT*, 194; 263.

8 *HCT*, 176–77; 238.

9 "We shall designate the phenomenal structure of the worldhood of space [der Weltlichkeit des Raumes] as the *aroundness* [*das Umhafte*] of the world as environment [Umwelt; the world *around* us]" (*HCT*, 224; 308).

10 I will translate *Zuhandene* as "handy" and *Vorhandene* as "extant and at hand," or "objective presence." *Vorhandene* has a decidedly negative connotation from *Being and Time* onward and is identified with objective being, whereas in *History of the Concept of Time*, Heidegger at times distinguishes the extant from objective nature. Stambaugh's translation of *Being and Time* renders *Zuhandene* as "at hand" and *Vorhandene* as "objective presence." I have modified "at hand" to "handy" for the sake of consistency.

11 *HCT*, 191; 259–60.

12 *HCT*, 192; 261.

13 *HCT*, 196; 267.

14 *HCT*, 228; 313–14.

15 *HCT*, 229–30; 315–16.

16 *HCT*, 183; 248.

17 *BT*, 78; 84.

18 See *BT*, 109; 116, *HCT*, 238; 327.

19 See also Heidegger's more extended discussion in "On the Essence of Ground," trans. William McNeill, in *Pathmarks*, ed. William McNeill (Cambridge: Cambridge University Press, 1998), 97–135; "Vom Wesen des Grundes," *Wegmarken, Gesamtausgabe, I. Abteilung: Veröffentlichte Schriften 1914–1970*, Band 9, ed. Friedrich-Wilhelm von Hermann (Frankfurt am Main: Vittorio Klostermann, 1976), 123–75, hereafter "oeg," with page numbers of the translation followed by the German text. The relevant pages on the idea of the world are 111–21; 142–56. This piece was written in 1928, the same year as *MFL*, and published in a Festschrift for Husserl in 1929. It discusses many of the same thinkers, especially Heraclitus, Augustine, and Kant, in greater detail, at times, with a different emphasis.

20 "κόσμος now comes to be used directly as a term for a determinate fundamental kind of human existence." In the same vein, in the Gospel of John, "world designates the fundamental form of human Dasein removed from God, the *character of being human* pure and simple" ("oeg," 112–13; 143–44).

21 Heidegger disingenuously exaggerates the sharpness of the break of modern from Christian metaphysics. They share the same understanding of the world as a condition that needs to be transcended.

22 The thought of radical finitude is not an atheism. The question of the existence of God is left suspended, and existence is understood on the basis of temporality instead of an atemporal being.

23 See *BT*, 334; 365.

24 Compare "oeg," 121; 156: "World belongs to a *relational* structure distinctive of Dasein as such, a structure that we called being-in-the-world."

25 Compare: "Only so long as Dasein is, is existent, is world given" (*BPP*, 296; 420). "World exists—that is, it is—only if Dasein exists, only if there is Dasein" (*BPP*, 297; 422). "Existing, Dasein is its world" (*BT*, 333; 364).

26 Martin Heidegger, "Letter on 'Humanism,'" trans. Frank A. Capuzzi, in *Pathmarks*, ed. William McNeill (Cambridge: Cambridge University Press, 1998), 266; "Brief über den 'Humanismus,'" in *Wegmarken, Gesamtausgabe, I. Abteilung: Veröffentlichte Schriften 1914–1970*, Band 9, ed. Friedrich-Wilhelm von Hermann (Frankfurt am Main: Vittorio Klostermann, 1976), 349–50, translation modified, hereafter "LH," with page numbers of the translation followed by the German text. Hence, any possible relation to God needs be thought on the basis of the temporal world and not the other way around.

27 *BT*, 335; 366, *BPP*, 299; 424.

28 *Being and Time* and the Marburg lecture courses delivered between 1925 and 1928 take the existential approach. The comparative approach is developed in *The Fundamental Concepts of Metaphysics*, a lecture course delivered at the University of Freiburg in the winter semester of 1929–1930.

29 "OEG," 126; 164, emphasis in the original.

30 "OEG," 126; 164.

31 Martin Heidegger, "The Age of the World Picture," in *Off the Beaten Track*, ed. and trans. Julian Young and Kenneth Haynes (Cambridge: Cambridge University Press, 2002), 68, translation modified; *Die Zeit des Weltbildes*, in *Holzwege, Gesamtausgabe, I. Abteilung: Veröffentlichte Schriften 1914–1970*, Band 5, ed. Friedrich-Wilhelm von Hermann (Frankfurt am Main: Vittorio Klostermann, 1977), 90, hereafter "AWP," with page numbers of the translation followed by the German text.

32 Martin Heidegger, "Memorial Address," in *Discourse on Thinking*, trans. John M. Anderson and E. Hans Freund (New York: Harper and Row, 1966), 48, translation modified; *Gelassenheit* (Tübingen: Neske, 1959), 17.

33 See *BPP*, 297; 421.

34 See *HCT*, 243; 335.

35 For an account of the relation between Heidegger's earlier and later accounts of the world that focuses specifically on art, see Françoise Dastur, "Heidegger's Freiburg Version of the Origin of the Work of Art," in *Heidegger toward the Turn: Essays on the Work of the 1930s*, ed. James Risser (Albany: State University of New York Press, 1999), 119–42. I have argued for greater continuity between the early and late Heidegger's concepts of world than Dastur allows.

36 Martin Heidegger, "The Origin of the Work of Art," in Young and Haynes, *Off the Beaten Track*, 23; *Der Ursprung des Kunstwerkes*, in *Holzwege, Gesamtausgabe, I. Abteilung: Veröffentlichte Schriften 1914–1970*, Band 5, ed. Friedrich-Wilhelm von Hermann (Frankfurt am Main: Vittorio Klostermann, 1977), 30–31, hereafter "OWA," with page numbers of the translation followed by the German text.

Chapter 5. The In-Between World

1 Hannah Arendt, "Concern with Politics in Recent European Philosophical Thought," in *Essays in Understanding 1930–1954: Formation, Exile, and Totalitarianism*, ed. Jerome Kohn (New York: Schocken, 1994) (hereafter "CP"), 446n5. This passage is from an earlier draft of the essay and was added as a note.

2 In "Martin Heidegger at Eighty," Arendt phrases the same criticism about the philosopher's denigration of the political realm more mildly in terms of the thinker's withdrawal from everyday life in Heidegger's later writings. Because the ordinary world is characterized by the withdrawal and oblivion of being, "annulment of this 'withdrawal' . . . is always paid for by a withdrawal from the world of human affairs, and this remoteness is never more manifest than when thinking ponders exactly these affairs, training them into its own sequestered stillness." Hannah Arendt, "Martin Heidegger at Eighty," trans. Albert Hofstadter, *New York Review of Books*, October 21, 1971, http://www.nybooks.com/articles/archives/1971/oct/21/martin-heidegger-at-eighty/, accessed March 22, 2013.

3 Seyla Benhabib suggests that Dasein is characterized by existential solipsism and Heidegger's analysis of Dasein is guilty of methodological solipsism. See *The Reluctant Modernism of Hannah Arendt* (London: Sage, 1996), 107. In his erudite philosophical study, *The Thracian Maid and the Professional Thinker: Arendt and Heidegger*, trans. Michael Gendre (Albany: State University of New York Press, 1997), Jacques Taminiaux suggests that Heidegger's reinterpretation of Aristotelian praxis as being-in-the-world entails a "fundamental solipsism" because the world is disclosed "only by the encounter with nothingness experienced through anxiety by a radically isolated self" (14, 34). Individuation through being-toward-death involves "a face to face with oneself in the solitude of one's own conscience, in a fundamental absence of relations" (34). Hence, it is a turn away from the world that "leads to the radical isolation of being *Selbst* whose activity . . . is strictly limited to the solitary and silent seeing of *Dasein*'s ownmost can-be" (87). Even Dana Villa, who shows more appreciation for Heidegger's account of the world in *Arendt and Heidegger: The Fate of the Political* (Princeton, NJ: Princeton University Press, 1996), suggests that Heidegger's "notion of authentic *Existenz* was surprisingly devoid of a robust interactive dimension" and that the view of authentic *Dasein* from Division II of *Being and Time* has a "largely individualistic character." See Dana Villa, "Arendt, Heidegger, and the Tradition," *Social Research* 74.4 (winter 2007): 995, 996.

4 Hannah Arendt, "What Is Existential Philosophy?," in *Essays in Understanding 1930–1954: Formation, Exile, and Totalitarianism*, ed. Jerome Kohn (New York: Schocken, 1994), 181, hereafter "WEP."

5 Benhabib's reconstruction of Heidegger's account of being-in-the-world is limited to his analysis of the *Umwelt* and the work-world (see *Reluctant Modernism*, 51–52, 105). Taminiaux is silent on the world's grounding in temporality and its connection to *Mitsein* as original community and Heidegger's critique of solipsism (*Thracian Maid*, 13–14).

6 For example, Benhabib suggests that the categories of Heidegger's thought symptomatically reflect the disintegrating conditions of his time, which may have led him to support National Socialism (Benhabib, *Reluctant Modernism*, 55).

7 See Benhabib, *Reluctant Modernism*, 105–6, and Villa, *Arendt and Heidegger*, 122, 136, and "Arendt, Heidegger and the Tradition," 984, 995.

8 Martin Heidegger, *Being and Time*, trans. Joan Stambaugh (Albany: State University of New York Press, 1996), 274; *Sein und Zeit, Gesamtausgabe, I. Abteilung: Veröffentlichte Schriften, 1914–1970*, Band 2, ed. Friedrich–Wilhelm von Hermann (Frankfurt am Main: Vittorio Klostermann, 1977), 298. On the possibility of authentic modes of collective existence, see Villa, *Arendt and Heidegger*, 134, 212.

9 Hannah Arendt, "On Humanity in Dark Times: Thoughts about Lessing," in *Men in Dark Times* (San Diego, CA: Harcourt Brace, 1983), 4.

10 See Hannah Arendt, *The Human Condition* (Chicago: University of Chicago Press, 1958), 8, hereafter HC.

11 Hannah Arendt, "The Concept of History: Ancient and Modern," in *Between Past and Future: Six Exercises in Political Thought* (New York: Viking Press, 1961), 61, emphasis added.

12 Hannah Arendt, "The Crisis in Education," in *Between Past and Future*, 174, emphasis in the original.

13 Arendt, "Crisis in Education," 196.

14 The second edition of *The Origins of Totalitarianism* (1958) (San Diego, CA: Harcourt Brace, 1973), 479, ends with the same hopeful refrain.

15 Hannah Arendt, "What Is Freedom?," in *Between Past and Future*, 167.

16 Arendt, "What Is Freedom?," 169–70.

17 Hannah Arendt, *Was ist Politik? Fragmente aus dem Nachlaß*, ed. Ursula Ludz (Munich: Piper, 2003), 32; "Introduction *into* Politics," in *The Promise of Politics*, ed. Jerome Kohn (New York: Schocken, 2005), 111–12.

18 Arendt, *Was ist Politik?*, 33–34; "Introduction *into* Politics," 112–13, translation modified.

19 Arendt, *Was ist Politik?*, 50; "Introduction *into* Politics," 127.

20 Hannah Arendt, *Love and Saint Augustine*, ed. Joanna Vecchiarelli Scott and Judith Chelius Stark (Chicago: University of Chicago Press, 1996), 66n80, hereafter LSA.

21 Hannah Arendt, "Labor, Work, Action," in *Amor Mundi: Explorations in the Faith and Thought of Hannah Arendt*, ed. James W. Bernauer (Boston: Martinus Nijhoff, 1987), 34. Compare HC, 136.

22 Arendt, "Labor, Work, Action," 35.

23 Hannah Arendt, "Culture and Politics," in *Reflections on Literature and Culture*, ed. Susannah Young-ah Gottlieb (Palo Alto, CA: Stanford University Press, 2007), 189–90.

24 For an interesting account of narrative as the first dimension of human life, that is, life as a political being, see Julia Kristeva, *Hannah Arendt*, trans. Ross Guberman (New York: Columbia University Press, 2001), 69–99.

25 Arendt, "On Humanity in Dark Times," 21.

26 "Insofar as any 'mastering' of the past is possible, it consists in relating what has happened. . . . As long as the meaning of the events remains alive . . . 'mastering of the past' can take the form of ever-recurrent narration." Arendt, "On Humanity in Dark Times," 21.

27 Arendt, "On Humanity in Dark Times," 21.

28 Arendt, "Culture and Politics," 190.

29 Arendt, "On Humanity in Dark Times," 21–22.

30 For a fuller discussion of Arendt's account of world alienation, see Villa, *Arendt and Heidegger*, 188–201.

31 Arendt, *Origins of Totalitarianism*, 298.

32 Arendt, *Origins of Totalitarianism*, 297.

33 Arendt, *Origins of Totalitarianism*, 302.

34 Arendt, *Was ist Politik?*, 90; "Introduction *into* Politics," 162, translation modified.

35 Arendt, *Was ist Politik?*, 122–23; "Introduction *into* Politics," 190–91, translation modified.

36 Arendt, "Epilogue," in *Promise of Politics*, 201.

Chapter 6. The Arriving World

1 Jacques Derrida, "Deconstruction and the Other," in *Dialogues with Contemporary Continental Thinkers: The Phenomenological Heritage*, ed. Richard Kearney (Manchester, UK: Manchester University Press, 1984), 109, 110: "Heidegger is probably the most constant influence. . . . My relationship with Heidegger is much more enigmatic and extensive: here my interest was not just *methodological* but *existential*. The themes of Heidegger's questioning always struck me as necessary." "I owe a considerable debt to Heidegger's 'path of thought.'"

2 Other instances of Heidegger's privileging of presence include his search for the meaning of being and his characterization of being as presencing (*anwesen*), his distinction between authentic and inauthentic modes of temporality, his characterization of authentic temporality as original and inauthentic temporality as a fall from original temporality as a result of Dasein's absorption by the objects of care, and his view that having an understanding of the meaning of being, being-toward-death, and having a world are proper to Dasein.

3 Martin Heidegger, *Being and Time*, trans. Joan Stambaugh (Albany: State University of New York Press, 1996), 380–81; *Sein und Zeit, Gesamtausgabe, I. Abteilung: Veröffentlichte Schriften, 1914–1970*, Band 2, ed. Friedrich–Wilhelm von Hermann (Frankfurt am Main: Vittorio Klostermann, 1977), 414, hereafter BT, with page numbers of the translation followed by those from the 1953 Max Niemeyer edition of the German text.

4 Jacques Derrida, "*Ousia* and *Grammē*: Note on a Note from *Being and Time*," in *Margins of Philosophy*, trans. Alan Bass (Chicago: University of Chicago Press, 1982), 55.

5 Derrida, "*Ousia* and *Grammē*," 55.

6 Jacques Derrida, "Différance," in *Margins of Philosophy*, trans. Alan Bass (Chicago: University of Chicago Press, 1982), 13.

7 Derrida, "*Ousia* and *Grammē*," 56.

8 Derrida, "*Ousia* and *Grammē*," 60: "Time is that which is thought on the basis of being as presence, and if something—which bears a relation to time, but is not time—is to be thought beyond the determination of being as presence, it cannot be a question of something that still could be called time."

9 The aporetic relation of death to life is, however, in Derrida's view, one of the figures, even a privileged figure, for radical finitude. See Jacques Derrida, *Aporias: Dying-Awaiting (One Another at) "the Limits of Truth,"* trans. Thomas Dutoit (Palo Alto, CA: Stanford University Press, 1993).

10 Jacques Derrida, *Given Time—I. Counterfeit Money*, trans. Peggy Kamuf (Chicago: University of Chicago Press, 1992), 13–14, hereafter *GT*.

11 Jacques Derrida, *Speech and Phenomena and Other Essays on Husserl's Theory of Signs*, trans. David B. Allison (Evanston, IL: Northwestern University Press, 1973), 86.

12 Derrida, "Différance," 11.

13 Derrida, "Différance," 12.

14 Derrida, "Différance," 26fn26.

15 Jacques Derrida, "Tympan," in *Margins of Philosophy*, xxiii.

16 Jacques Derrida, *Positions*, trans. Alan Bass (Chicago: University of Chicago Press, 1981), 59.

17 Derrida, "Différance," 26fn26.

18 Jacques Derrida, *Rogues: Two Essays on Reason*, trans. Pascale-Anne Brault and Michael Naas (Palo Alto, CA: Stanford University Press, 2005), 152; *Voyous: Deux essais sur la raison* (Paris: Galilée, 2003), 210, hereafter *R*, with page numbers from the translation followed by the French text.

19 *R*, 84; 123.

20 Jacques Derrida, *Politics of Friendship*, trans. George Collins (New York: Verso, 1997), 68–69.

21 *R*, 152; 210.

22 Jacques Derrida, "The Deconstruction of Actuality," in *Negotiations: Interventions and Interviews 1971–2001*, ed. and trans. Elizabeth Rottenberg (Palo Alto, CA: Stanford University Press, 2002), 95.

23 Derrida, *Aporias*, 34.

24 Accordingly, Arendt suggests that the power to promise provides a degree of sovereignty that stabilizes the unpredictability of action (*HC*, 245).

25 Jacques Derrida, *Of Grammatology*, trans. Gayatri Chakravorty Spivak (Baltimore: Johns Hopkins University Press, 1976), 50; *De la Grammatologie* (Paris: Minuit, 1967), 73.

26 For a similar postphenomenological account of the world that distinguishes the world from the globe and sees the world as that which takes place in the im-possible qua structure of the pure event, see Jean-Luc Nancy, *The Creation of the World, or*

Globalization, trans. Raffoul and David Pettigrew (Albany: State University of New York Press, 2007), and *The Sense of the World*, trans. Jeffrey S. Librett (Minneapolis: University of Minnesota Press, 1997). Nancy, however, characterizes the world as an absolute immanence that exists for itself and only refers to itself.

27 In "The University without Condition," in *Without Alibi*, trans. Peggy Kamuf (Palo Alto, CA: Stanford University Press, 2002), 223, Derrida speaks of "the *mondialisation du monde*."

28 Jacques Derrida, "Une Europe de l'espoir," *Le Monde diplomatique* (November 2004): 3, http://archives.mondediplo.com/article11677.html, accessed May 8, 2013; "A Europe of Hope," trans. Pleshette DeArmitt, Justine Malle, and Kas Saghafi, *Epoché* 10.2 (spring 2006): 409, translation modified.

29 Jacques Derrida, "Globalization, Peace, and Cosmopolitanism," in *Negotiations: Interventions and Interviews 1971–2001*, ed. and trans. Elizabeth Rottenberg (Palo Alto, CA: Stanford University Press, 2002), 374–75.

30 Derrida, "University without Condition," 224.

31 Derrida, "University without Condition," 203. Compare Derrida, "Globalization, Peace, and Cosmopolitanism," 375.

32 *R*, 18; 38–39: "In a modern sense, which would no longer be that of the Stoics or Saint Paul, the thought of a cosmopolitical democracy perhaps presupposes a theocosmogony, a cosmology, and a vision of the world determined by the spherical roundness of the globe."

33 *R*, xiv; 14.

34 *R*, 155; 213. The quotations in the next paragraph are from the same page.

35 Jacques Derrida, "Rams: Uninterrupted Dialogue—Between Two Infinities, the Poem," in *Sovereignties in Question: The Poetics of Paul Celan*, ed. Thomas Dutoit and Outi Pasanen (New York: Fordham University Press, 2005). See also Jacques Derrida, *The Beast and the Sovereign*, vol. 2, trans. Geoffrey Bennington (Chicago: University of Chicago Press, 2011), 104–5, 169–70, 266–68.

36 On death as the border where I always anachronistically wait for and mourn the other, see Derrida, *Aporias*, 65–66.

37 Derrida, "Rams," 140.

38 Derrida, "Rams," 163.

39 Derrida, "Globalization, Peace, and Cosmopolitanism," 375–76.

40 Derrida, "Globalization, Peace, and Cosmopolitanism," 376.

41 Derrida, "Globalization, Peace, and Cosmopolitanism," 375.

42 Jacques Derrida, *Specters of Marx—The State of the Debt, the Work of Mourning and the New International*, with an introduction by Bernd Magnus and Stephen Cullenberg, trans. Peggy Kamuf (New York: Routledge, 1994), 107.

43 Derrida's idea of a new international democracy develops his long-standing critique of fraternity as the basis of politics. See Derrida, *Politics of Friendship*, especially the reading of Michelet on 237–38.

44 Jacques Derrida, "Autoimmunity: Real and Symbolic Suicides: A Dialogue with Jacques Derrida," in *Philosophy in a Time of Terror: Dialogues with Jürgen Haber-*

mas and Jacques Derrida, ed. Giovanna Borradori (Chicago: University of Chicago Press, 2003), 130.

45 Jacques Derrida, "As If It Were Possible, 'Within Such Limits' . . . ," in *Negotiations*, 367, translation modified.

46 Jacques Derrida, "Not Utopia, the Im-possible," in *Paper Machine*, trans. Rachel Bowlby (Palo Alto, CA: Stanford University Press, 2005), 131.

47 On the aporetic character of *vouloir dire*, see Derrida's performative treatment of the phrase "Pardon de ne pas vouloir dire" (Pardon for not meaning/for not intending to say) in *Literature in Secret: An Impossible Filiation*, in *The Gift of Death and Literature in Secret*, trans. David Wills (Chicago: University of Chicago Press, 2008).

48 The formulation of writing as the radical absence of the subject that constitutes subjectivity can be found as early as 1962 in Derrida's characterization of writing as "a kind of autonomous transcendental field from which every present subject can be absent," a "subjectless transcendental field" that is the condition for transcendental subjectivity. See Jacques Derrida, *Edmund Husserl's Origin of Geometry: An Introduction*, trans. John P. Leavey (Lincoln: University of Nebraska Press, 1989), 88. Derrida already links writing to an undecipherable archaeological secret here.

49 Jacques Derrida, "Passions: 'An Oblique Offering,'" in *On the Name*, ed. Thomas Dutoit, trans. David Wood, John P. Leavey Jr. and Ian McLeod (Palo Alto, CA: Stanford University Press, 1995), 29.

50 Jacques Derrida, "Signature Event Context," in *Margins of Philosophy*, 318.

51 Derrida's interest in literature as a nonintentional force was announced at the beginning of his scholarly career. In 1957, he had planned to write a thesis examining literature within the framework of Husserlian phenomenology titled "The Ideality of the Literary Object." See Jacques Derrida, "Punctuations: The Time of a Thesis," in *Eyes of the University: Right to Philosophy 2*, trans. Jan Plug et al. (Palo Alto, CA: Stanford University Press, 2004), 116.

52 Derrida, "Passions," 143–44n14.

53 Derrida, *Literature in Secret*, 131.

54 Derrida, *Literature in Secret*, 130–31.

55 In his earlier critique of Austin's exclusion of "nonserious" literary language from the sphere of performative language and his argument that citation on a stage, in a poem, or in a work of fiction is in fact "the determined modification of a general citationality," Derrida proposed a similar generalization of literature into the condition of possibility of presence. See Derrida, "Signature Event Context," 325.

56 Compare Jacques Derrida, "Living On: Borderlines," in Harold Bloom et al., *Deconstruction and Criticism* (London: Routledge Kegan Paul, 1979), 136: "[The] domain [of 'living, living on'] is indeed in a narrative formed out of traces, writing, distance, teleo-graphy."

57 Derrida, "Living On," 145–46.

58 Derrida, "Living On," 146.

59 Derrida, "Living On," 87.

60 This is why Derrida is interested in a set of writers different from those that occu-pied Heidegger: Mallarmé, Blanchot, Baudelaire, Celan, etc. instead of Hölderlin and Rilke.

61 In a comment on Paul de Man's account of the narrative structure of allegory, Derrida notes that the reference to the other "precludes any totalizing summary—the exhaustive narrative or the total absorption of a memory." *Memoires: for Paul de Man*, trans. by Cecile Lindsay, Jonathan Culler, Eduardo Cadava, and Peggy Kamuf, rev. ed. (New York: Columbia University Press, 1989), 11.

Chapter 7. Postcolonial Openings

1 Immanuel Wallerstein, *The Modern World-System: Capitalist Agriculture and the Origins of the European World-Economy in the Sixteenth Century* (New York: Academic Press, 1974), 129, 301–2. "First unity of the world" is Fernand Braudel's phrase.

2 Wallerstein, *Modern World-System*, 339.

3 Immanuel Wallerstein, *The Modern World-System II: Mercantilism and the Consolidation of the European World-Economy 1600–1750* (New York: Academic Press, 1980), 65.

4 Hannah Arendt, *On Revolution* (New York: Viking Press, 1965), 53–61.

5 Hannah Arendt, *Was ist Politik? Fragmente aus dem Nachlaß*, ed. Ursula Ludz (Munich: Piper, 2003), 105–6, translation modified; "Introduction *into* Politics," in *The Promise of Politics*, ed. Jerome Kohn (New York: Schocken, 2005), 175–76.

6 Frantz Fanon, *Black Skin, White Masks*, trans. Richard Philcox (New York: Grove Press, 2008), 201.

7 I have discussed the organismic metaphor for freedom or political organicism in *Spectral Nationality: Passages of Freedom from Kant to Postcolonial Literatures of Liberation* (New York: Columbia University Press, 2003). In particular, see chapter 4 for an extended discussion of the writings of Fanon and Amilcar Cabral as exemplars of the philosophy of socialist decolonization.

8 Fanon, *Black Skin, White Masks*, 199.

9 Frantz Fanon, *The Wretched of the Earth*, trans. Richard Philcox (New York: Grove Press, 2004), 9.

10 Karl Marx and Friedrich Engels, *Die Deutsche Ideologie*, in *Marx/Engels Gesamtausgabe*, ed. V. Adoratskij (Berlin: Marx-Engels Verlag, 1932), vol. 1:5 in *Marx/Engels Gesamtausgabe*, ed. V. Adoratskij (Berlin: Marx-Engels Verlag, 1932), 57; *The German Ideology: Part One, with Selections from Parts Two and Three*, ed. C. J. Arthur (New York: International, 1970), 92.

11 Fanon, *Wretched of the Earth*, 82–83.

12 Fanon, *Wretched of the Earth*, 167.

13 Fanon, *Wretched of the Earth*, 173.

14 C. L. R. James, *Nkrumah and the Ghana Revolution* (London: Allison and Busby, 1977), 62.

15 Kwame Nkrumah, *Consciencism: Philosophy and Ideology for Decolonization and Development with Particular Reference to the African Revolution* (London: Heinemann, 1964), 63. Jomo Kenyatta, the founding father of the Kenyan nation, likewise spoke of the urgency of building a nation that is deeply rooted in African ideas and noted that this will require "rewriting school textbooks, evolving new architecture, and songs based on African traditional forms and culture." *Haarambee! The Prime Minister of Kenya's Speeches 1963–1964* (Nairobi: Oxford University Press, 1964), 33.

16 Nkrumah, *Consciencism*, 70.

17 On pan-Africanism as the development of nationalism within a continental framework, see Kwame Nkrumah, *Handbook of Revolutionary Warfare: A Guide to the Armed Phase of the African Revolution* (New York: International, 1968), 27, and *Address to the Nationalists' Conference*, Accra, June 4, 1962.

18 Quoted in "Introduction," *Bandung. Texts of Selected Speeches and Final Communique of the Asian-African Conference* (New York: Far East Reporter, 1955), 5. On the normative significance of Bandung as the precursor of the Non-Aligned Movement, see Amitav Acharya and See Seng Tan, "Introduction: The Normative Relevance of the Bandung Conference for Contemporary Asian and International Order," in *Bandung Revisited: The Legacy of the 1955 Asian-African Conference for International Order*, ed. See Seng Tan and Amitav Acharya (Singapore: National University of Singapore Press, 2008), 1–16, and Alim-Khan, *The Non-Aligned Movement: Achievements, Problems, Prospects* (Moscow: Novosti, 1985).

19 "Speech by President Sukarno of Indonesia at the Opening of the Conference," in *Asia-Africa Speaks from Bandung* (Ministry of Foreign Affairs, Indonesia, 1955), 21.

20 "Speech by President Sukarno," 20.

21 See "Final Communique of the Asian-African Conference," in *Asia-Africa Speaks*, 161–69. On Bandung's legacy for the evolution of international human rights, see Roland Burke, *Decolonization and the Evolution of International Human Rights* (Philadelphia: University of Pennsylvania Press, 2014), chapter 1.

22 Kwame Nkrumah, *I Speak of Freedom: A Statement of African Ideology* (New York: Praeger, 1961), 128.

23 Jürgen Habermas, "Conceptions of Modernity: A Look Back at Two Traditions," in *The Postnational Constellation: Political Essays*, trans. Max Pensky (Cambridge, MA: MIT Press, 2001), 132.

24 See Pheng Cheah, "Universal Areas: Asian Studies in a World in Motion," *Traces* 1.1 (2001): 37–70. This strand of thought has been used by some Asian governments to circumvent international public criticism of their poor human rights records.

25 See Zhao Tingyang, "A Political World Philosophy in Terms of All-under-Heaven (Tian-xia)," *Diogenes* 221 (2009): 5–18, and "Rethinking Empire from a Chinese Concept 'All-under-Heaven' (Tian-xia)," *Social Identities: Journal for the Study of Race, Nation and Culture* 12.1 (2006): 29–41.

26 Partha Chatterjee, *The Nation and Its Fragments: Colonial and Postcolonial Histories* (Princeton, NJ: Princeton University Press, 1993), 5–6, my emphasis.

27 Chatterjee, *Nation and Its Fragments*, 234–39.

28 Dipesh Chakrabarty, *Provincializing Europe: Postcolonial Thought and Historical Difference* (Princeton, NJ: Princeton University Press, 2000), 7–8.

29 Chakrabarty, *Provincializing Europe*, 15. Compare 16: "The human exists in a frame of a single and secular historical time that envelops other kinds of time."

30 Chakrabarty, *Provincializing Europe*, 12–13.

31 These phrases are from Chakrabarty, *Provincializing Europe*, 95, 239.

32 Charles Taylor has correctly suggested that theories of alternative modernities are cultural theories of modernity because cultural specificity is seen as important in understanding the spread of modernity. See "Two Theories of Modernity," *Public Culture* 11.1 (1999): 162.

33 Taylor, "Two Theories of Modernity," 94.

34 Habermas, *Postnational Constellation*, 124.

35 Chakrabarty, *Provincializing Europe*, 95.

36 See Cheah, *Spectral Nationality*, 191–200.

37 Moyna, a character in Amitav Ghosh's *The Hungry Tide*, which I will discuss in chapter 9, personifies the subaltern desire for modernization.

38 Nestor Garcia Canclini, *Hybrid Cultures: Strategies for Entering and Leaving Modernity*, trans. Christopher L. Chiappari and Silvia Lopez (Minneapolis: University of Minnesota Press, 1995), 2.

39 Canclini, *Hybrid Cultures*, 44.

40 Canclini, *Hybrid Cultures*, 46.

41 Canclini, *Hybrid Cultures*, 3.

42 Canclini, *Hybrid Cultures*, xli.

43 Canclini, *Hybrid Cultures*, xxxii.

44 Canclini, *Hybrid Cultures*, 54.

45 Gayatri Chakravorty Spivak, "Can the Subaltern Speak?," in *Marxism and the Interpretation of Culture*, ed. Cary Nelson and Lawrence Grossberg (Urbana: University of Illinois Press, 1988), 271–313.

46 Partha Chatterjee, *Lineages of Political Society: Studies in Postcolonial Democracy* (New York: Columbia University Press, 2011), 23.

47 See Benedict Anderson, *Imagined Communities: Reflections on the Origin and Spread of Nationalism*, 2nd ed. (London: Verso, 1991), and "El Malhadado País," in *The Spectre of Comparisons: Nationalism, Southeast Asia and the World* (London: Verso, 1998). I have discussed Anderson's account of the link between nation and novel in greater detail in "Grounds of Comparison," in *Grounds of Comparison: Around the Work of Benedict Anderson*, ed. Pheng Cheah and Jonathan Culler (New York: Routledge, 2003).

48 I have discussed the importance of the bildungsroman as the privileged genre of the early nationalist novel in decolonizing space in "Novel Nation," chapter 5 of *Spectral Nationality*.

49 Salman Rushdie, *Imaginary Homelands: Essays and Criticism, 1981–1991* (London: Granta, 1992), 301–2.

50 Salman Rushdie, *Midnight's Children* (Harmondsworth, England: Penguin, 1991), 517.

Chapter 8. Projecting a Future World from the Memory of Precolonial Time

1 Michelle Cliff, *Abeng* (Trumansburg, NY: Crossing Press, 1984), 127, hereafter *A*, with page numbers in parentheses.

2 Rex Nettleford, *Caribbean Cultural Identity: The Case of Jamaica. An Essay in Cultural Dynamics* (Los Angeles: Center for Afro-American Studies and UCLA Latin American Center Publications, 1979), xxiii, emphasis in the original. Nettleford is the former vice-chancellor of the University of the West Indies and the founder of the National Dance Theatre Company of Jamaica.

3 Nettleford, *Caribbean Cultural Identity*, 60.

4 Nettleford, *Caribbean Cultural Identity*, 52.

5 Nettleford, *Caribbean Cultural Identity*, 49.

6 Michelle Cliff, *No Telephone to Heaven* (London: Methuen, 1987), 16, hereafter *NTTH*, with page numbers in parentheses.

7 Edward W. Said, *Culture and Imperialism* (London: Chatto and Windus, 1993), 69–70.

8 Said, *Culture and Imperialism*, 116.

9 Said, *Culture and Imperialism*, 115.

10 Karl Marx, *Capital: A Critique of Political Economy, Volume 1*, trans. Ben Fowkes (Harmondsworth, England: Penguin, 1976), 436–37; *Das Kapital: Kritik der politischen Ökonomie. Erster Band* (Berlin: Dietz, 1962), 338.

11 Éric Alliez, *Capital Times: Tales from the Conquest of Time*, trans. Georges Van Den Abbeele (Minneapolis: University of Minnesota Press, 1996), 13.

12 Immanuel Wallerstein, *The Modern World-System: Capitalist Agriculture and the Origins of the European World-Economy in the Sixteenth Century* (New York: Academic Press, 1974), 43. The Portuguese colonization of the Atlantic islands (Madeira, the Canary and Cape Verde Islands) for the purposes of sugar production occurred in the mid-fifteenth century.

13 Sidney Mintz, *Sweetness and Power: The Place of Sugar in Modern History* (New York: Viking Penguin, 1985), xxix.

14 Adam Smith, *An Inquiry into the Nature and Causes of the Wealth of Nations* (Chicago: University of Chicago Press, 1976), bk. 1, ch. 11, 175, 176, and bk. 3, ch. 2, 412.

15 John Stuart Mill, *Principles of Political Economy*, ed. J. M. Robson, vol. 3 (Toronto: University of Toronto Press, 1965), 693.

16 Mintz, *Sweetness and Power*, 47.

17 Mintz, *Sweetness and Power*, 47.

18 Mintz, *Sweetness and Power*, 51–52.

19 Frank Fonda Taylor, *To Hell with Paradise: A History of the Jamaican Tourist Industry* (Pittsburgh: University of Pittsburgh Press, 1993), 30.

20 Taylor, *To Hell with Paradise*, 53.

21 Taylor, *To Hell with Paradise*, 53.

22 Frantz Fanon, *The Wretched of the Earth*, trans. Richard Philcox (New York: Grove, 2004), 101–2.

23 Polly Patullo, *Last Resorts: The Cost of Tourism in the Caribbean* (London: Cassell, 1996), 6.

24 Edward Seaga, "Tourism as the Driver of Change in the Jamaican Economy," in *Tourism: The Driver of Change in the Jamaican Economy?*, ed. Kenneth O. Hall and Rheima Holding (Kingston, Jamaica: Ian Randle, 2006), xxvii–viii. For a critical evaluation of heritage tourism, see Grant H. Cornwell and Eve W. Stoddard, "From Sugar to Heritage Tourism in the Caribbean: Economic Strategies and National Identities," in *Caribbean Tourism: Alternatives for Community Development*, ed. Chandana Jayawardena (Kingston, Jamaica: Ian Randle, 2007), 205–21.

25 Patullo, *Last Resorts*, 15. Patullo notes that Caribbean governments were "forced to sell hotels by the privatization agenda of the International Monetary Fund. Under IMF tutelage, Jamaica, which owned 12 hotels at one stage, began to divest through the 1980s, and by the mid-1990s all but one hotel . . . had been sold" (23).

26 George Gmelch, *Behind the Smile: The Working Lives of Caribbean Tourism*, 2nd ed. (Bloomington: Indiana University Press, 2012), 38.

27 Gmelch, *Behind the Smile*, 37–38. The local population fills menial jobs in the tourist industry, whereas foreigners are given higher paying positions because they are deemed to have greater expertise.

28 Taylor, *To Hell with Paradise*, 175.

29 Hilary Beckles, quoted in Patullo, *Last Resorts*, 65.

30 Kamala Kempadoo, *Sexing the Caribbean: Gender, Race, and Sexual Labor* (New York: Routledge, 2004), 138–39.

31 Sidney W. Mintz, "From Plantations to Peasantries," in *Caribbean Contours*, ed. Sidney W. Mintz and Sally Price (Baltimore: Johns Hopkins University Press, 1985), 131.

32 Mintz, "From Plantations to Peasantries," 151.

33 Ian Gregory Strachan, *Paradise and Plantation: Tourism and Culture in the Anglophone Caribbean* (Charlottesville: University of Virginia Press, 2002), 81, 83.

34 Derek Walcott, "The Antilles: Fragments of Epic Memory," Nobel Lecture, December 7, 1992, http://www.nobelprize.org/nobel_prizes/literature/laureates/1992/walcott-lecture.html.

35 Michelle Cliff, "Sites of Memory," in *If I Could Write This in Fire* (Minneapolis: University of Minnesota Press, 2008), 58.

36 The first quote is from *A*, 27. The second quote is from Meryl F. Schwartz, "An Interview with Michelle Cliff," *Contemporary Literature* 34.4 (winter 1993): 612.

37 On the economic necessity of replacing indentured labor with slave labor for the cultivation of sugar cane in the Caribbean, see Immanuel Wallerstein, *The Modern World-System II: Mercantilism and the Consolidation of the European World-Economy 1600–1750* (New York: Academic Press, 1980), 171–75.

38 Jürgen Habermas, *The Structural Transformation of the Public Sphere*, trans. Thomas Burger and Frederick Lawrence (Cambridge, MA: MIT Press, 1989).

39 The Latin *cultura* (cultivation, culture) is etymologically related to *colonus* (colonist, farmer) and *colonia* (colony) through *colo* (till, cultivate).

40 Michelle Cliff, "Caliban's Daughter: The Tempest and the Teapot," *Frontiers: A Journal of Women Studies* 12.2 (1991): 40.

41 Cliff, "Caliban's Daughter," 37.

42 She calls herself Sycorax's granddaughter and notes that Bertha's savagery originates in the forest and is transfused from her mother's bloodline (Cliff, "Caliban's Daughter," 37, 41).

43 Aristotle, *Physics*, trans. Robin Waterfield (Oxford: Oxford University Press, 1996), IV.4.210.b32, 85.

44 Aristotle, *Physics*, IV.4.212.a21, 88.

45 See Jacques Derrida, *Specters of Marx: The State of the Debt, the Work of Mourning and the New International*, trans. Peggy Kamuf (New York: Routledge, 1994), 82–83.

46 See Pheng Cheah, *Spectral Nationality: Passages of Freedom from Kant to Postcolonial Literatures of Liberation* (New York: Columbia University Press, 2003), chapter 5.

47 Strachan, *Paradise and Plantation*, 193.

48 Belinda Edmonson, "Race, Privilege, and the Politics of (Re)writing History: An Analysis of the Novels of Michelle Cliff," *Callaloo* 16.1 (winter 1993), 185, 190.

49 Cliff, "Caliban's Daughter," 45.

50 V. S. Naipaul, *A Way in the World* (New York: Vintage, 1994), 377.

51 Naipaul, *A Way in the World*, 378.

52 Cliff, "Caliban's Daughter," 45–46.

53 William Wordsworth, "A Slumber Did My Spirit Seal," in William Wordsworth and Samuel Taylor Coleridge, *Lyrical Ballads*, ed. R. L. Brett and A. R. Jones (New York: Methuen, 1968), 154.

Chapter 9. World Heritage Preservation and the Expropriation of Subaltern Worlds

1 *The Circle of Reason* received the Prix Medicis étrangère (1990), *The Shadow Lines* was awarded the Sahitya Akademi Prize (1990), *The Calcutta Chromosome* was awarded the Arthur C. Clarke Award in 1996, Ghosh declined the Commonwealth Writers' Prize for *The Glass Palace* in 2000, he won the Dan David Prize for literary achievement in 2010, and *Sea of Poppies* received the Tagore Literature Award in 2012.

2 Chitra Sankaran, "Diasporic Predicaments: An Interview with Amitav Ghosh," in *History, Narrative, and Testimony in Amitav Ghosh's Fiction*, ed. Chitra Sankaran (Albany: State University of New York Press, 2012), 8.

3 The UNESCO World Heritage List inscription of the Sundarbans National Park accords it "Outstanding Universal Value" because it is "the largest mangrove forest in the world and the only one inhabited by the tiger" and its mangrove ecosystem

is unique for "its immensely rich mangrove flora and mangrove-associated fauna." Its threatened animal species include the Irrawaddy and Ganges River dolphins, the king cobra, and the river terrapin. See http://whc.unesco.org/en/list/452, accessed June 29, 2013.

4 Amitav Ghosh, *The Hungry Tide* (Boston: Houghton Mifflin Harcourt, 2005), 59, hereafter HT, with page numbers cited parenthetically.

5 Ghosh observes that the Sundarbans is an "area of darkness" and that he wrote the novel "to shine a light" on this little-known area. The hundreds of tiger-inflicted deaths in the Sundarbans every year go unnoticed because its inhabitants do not "have a voice" and "can't make themselves heard and understood" by virtue of their extreme poverty. Amitav Ghosh, "The Chronicle Interview: Amitav Ghosh, *The Hungry Tide*," *U.N. Chronicle* 13.4 (2005): 49, 52.

6 I have followed Ghosh's novel for the English spellings of the names of people and deities in the story of Bon Bibi and for place names. I have used "Morichjhãpi" instead of "Marichjhapi" or "Morichjhanpi" and "Dukhey" instead of "Dukhe."

7 Passages from Nirmal's diary are italicized in the novel and typographically set apart from the narrative of contemporary events unfolding in the "present" of the novel.

8 Rilke's poetry informs the organization of the novel's structure and its thematic content. The titles of some episodes come from Rilke. See, for example, "Transformation" (HT, 184), "Destiny" (HT, 193), and "A Post Office on Sunday" (HT, 232).

9 See Rainer Maria Rilke, *Duino Elegies and The Sonnets to Orpheus*, trans. A. Poulin, Jr. (Boston: Houghton Mifflin, 1977), First Elegy, 4–5. This is an English-German edition and reproduces the German text from Rilke's *Sämtliche Werke*, vol. 1 (Frankfurt am Main: Insel, 1955).

10 Rilke, *Duino Elegies*, 50–51.

11 Hannah Arendt and Günther Stern, "Rilke's *Duino Elegies*," in *Reflections on Literature and Culture*, ed. Susannah Young-ah Gottlieb (Palo Alto, CA: Stanford University Press, 2007), 22.

12 On the Sahara India Pariwar business group's ecotourism plans for the Sundarbans, see Amitav Ghosh, "Folly in the Sundarbans," (November 2004), http://www.amitavghosh.com/essays/folly.html, accessed July 5, 2013. On the other issues, see Ghosh, "Chronicle Interview," 51.

13 See, for instance, Upamanyu Pablo Mukherjee, *Postcolonial Environments: Nature, Culture and the Contemporary Indian Novel in English* (Basingstoke, England: Palgrave Macmillan, 2010), chapter 5; Alexa Weik, "The Home, the Tide and the World: Eco-cosmopolitan Encounters in Amitav Ghosh's *The Hungry Tide*," *Journal of Commonwealth and Postcolonial Studies* 13.2–14.1 (2006–2007): 120–41; Divya Anand, "Locating the Politics of the Environment and the Exploited in Amitav Ghosh's *The Hungry Tide*," in *Essays in Ecocriticism*, ed. Nirmal Selvamony, Nirmaldasan, and Rayson K. Alex (New Delhi: Sarup and Sons, 2007), 156–71, and "Words on Water: Nature and Agency in Amitav Ghosh's *The Hungry Tide*," *Concentric: Literary and Cultural Studies* 34.1 (March 2008): 21–44.

14 The following discussion of deep ecological biocentrism is a paraphrase of Ramachandra Guha, "Radical American Environmentalism and Wilderness Preservation: A Third World Critique," chapter 5 of Ramachandra Guha and Juan Martinez-Alier, *Varieties of Environmentalism: Essays North and South* (London: Earthscan, 1997), pp. 93–94.

15 Guha, "Radical American Environmentalism," 94.

16 This is how Piya interprets Fokir's local knowledge of dolphin migration patterns (*HT*, 95). She describes local fishermen who catch fish alongside dolphins as a "remarkable instance of symbiosis between human beings and a population of wild animals" (*HT*, 140) and compares the bodily motions of the sleeping Fokir and his son, Tutul, to dolphins (*HT*, 115).

17 Ghosh, "Chronicle Interview," 51–52.

18 Guha, "Radical American Environmentalism," 95–96.

19 I am paraphrasing Ramachandra Guha, "The Environmentalism of the Poor," chapter 1 of Guha and Martinez-Alier, *Varieties of Environmentalism*, 16–17.

20 This symbolic expropriation has its roots in the images of the Sundarbans as uninhabited "wastelands" deployed by the colonial authorities between 1770 and 1830 in order to expropriate the Sundarbans as state property and a source of timber. See Annu Jalais, *Forest of Tigers: People, Politics and Environment in the Sundarbans* (London: Routledge, 2011), 182–87, and Ranjan Chakrabarti, "Local People and the Global Tiger: An Environmental History of the Sundarbans," *Global Environment* 3 (2009): 72–95, esp. 78–87.

21 Waves of refugees arrived in the wake of riots in 1946 and 1950, and whenever relations between Pakistan and India worsened and there was communal violence. The rest of this paragraph summarizes Joya Chatterji's detailed study *The Spoils of Partition: Bengal and India, 1947–1967* (Cambridge: Cambridge University Press, 2007), chapter 3, esp. 111–38. See also Joya Chatterji, "'Dispersal' and the Failure of Rehabilitation: Refugee Camp-Dwellers and Squatters in West Bengal," *Modern Asian Studies* 41.5 (2007): 995–1032, and Tai Yong Tan and Gyanesh Kudaisya, "Divided Landscapes, Fragmented Identities: East Bengal Refugees and their Rehabilitation in India, 1947–79," chapter 6 of *The Aftermath of Partition in South Asia* (London: Routledge, 2000).

22 See Chatterji, *Spoils of Partition*, 138.

23 See *HT*, 136–37.

24 Ross Mallick, *Development Policy of a Communist Government: West Bengal since 1977* (Cambridge: Cambridge University Press, 1993), 101. The first part of this paragraph draws on Mallick's book. The massacre was a heinous crime on the part of West Bengal's Communist government because it was elected to power by support from mistreated refugees who were promised resettlement in the Sundarbans. It illustrates the Communist government's inability to represent the interests of the poor and exploited.

25 Ross Mallick, "Refugee Resettlement in Forest Reserves: West Bengal Policy Reversal and the Marichjhapi Massacre," *Journal of Asian Studies* 58.1 (February 1999): 117.

26 Jalais's book should be regarded as a requisite companion volume to Ghosh's novel because it provides a deeper social scientific and cultural analysis of the context needed for a more adequate reading of the novel.

27 The first quote comes from the World Wildlife Fund, http://worldwildlife.org /species/tiger, accessed July 10, 2013. The second quote comes from Jalais, *Forest of Tigers*, 8–9.

28 Jalais, *Forest of Tigers*, 68. The rest of my discussion of Bonbibi draws on Jalais's study, esp. pp. 68–89.

29 Jalais, *Forest of Tigers*, 70.

30 Jalais, *Forest of Tigers*, 69.

31 Jalais, *Forest of Tigers*, 81.

32 Jalais, *Forest of Tigers*, 203–4.

33 Guha, "Environmentalism of the Poor," 5.

34 Neel Ahuja's brief discussion of *The Hungry Tide* in "Species in a Planetary Frame: Eco-cosmopolitanism, Nationalism, and *The Cove*," *Tamkang Review* 42.2 (June 2012): 13–32, makes a similar point but misses the heavy irony of Nirmal's deep ecological vision.

35 Rilke, *Duino Elegies*, 50–51.

36 See also *HT*, 141–41 and 158–59.

37 The lines are quoted in *HT*, 298, and are from Rilke, *Duino Elegies*, 22–23. I have modified the translation.

38 Rilke, *Duino Elegies*, 22–23.

39 T. Vijay Kumar, "'Postcolonial' Describes You as a Negative": An Interview with Amitav Ghosh," *Interventions* 9.1 (2007): 103.

40 Ghosh, "Chronicle Interview," 48. The following quotation also comes from p. 48.

41 Ghosh, "Chronicle Interview," 51. The next quotation also comes from p. 51.

42 Ghosh's example is the childhood associations and meaningful memories that are stimulated by Piya's encounter with Bengali words; Ghosh, "Chronicle Interview," 51.

43 Ghosh, "Chronicle Interview," 48.

44 Mukherjee, *Postcolonial Environments*, 122.

45 Mukherjee, *Postcolonial Environments*, 121. Mukherjee provides a useful account of the Jatra form and its formal aspects on pp. 123–29.

46 Ngũgĩ wa Thiong'o, *Decolonising the Mind: The Politics of Language in African Literature* (Portsmouth, NH: Heinemann, 1986).

47 On the sources of the legend, see Annu Jalais, "*Bonbibi*: Bridging Worlds," *Indian Folklife*, no. 28 (January 2008): 6–8.

48 See *HT*, 265.

Chapter 10. Resisting Humanitarianization

1 On Somalia as a failed state, see Terrence Lyons and Ahmed I. Samatar, *Somalia: State Collapse, Multilateral Intervention and Strategies for Political Reconstruction*, Brookings Occasional Papers (Washington D.C.: Brookings Institution, 1995).

2 Jonathan Benthall, *Disasters, Relief and the Media* (London: Tauris, 1993), 174–76.

3 On humanitarian intervention in Somalia as philanthropic imperialism and humanitarian impunity, see Alex de Waal, *Famine Crimes: Politics and the Disaster Relief Industry in Africa* (London: African Rights and the International African Institute and James Currey, 1997), 179–91, and Alex de Waal and Rakiya Omaar, "Can Military Intervention be 'Humanitarian'?," *Middle East Report* 187, vol. 24 (March-April 1994), http://www.merip.org/mer/mer187/can-military-intervention-be-humanitarian (accessed November 14, 2013).

4 Eric Schmitt, "Somali War Casualties May Be 10,000," *New York Times*, December 8, 1993. In comparison, eighty-three UN peacekeepers were killed.

5 Nuruddin Farah, *Gifts* (New York: Penguin, 2000), hereafter *G*, with page numbers cited parenthetically. First published in Swedish translation in 1990; an English edition of the novel appeared in Zimbabwe in 1992. The US edition appeared in 1999. The novel is set in the late 1980s. A fictive newspaper report mentions gifts of milk from the European Community that have been contaminated by the Chernobyl nuclear plant accident of April 26, 1986 (*G*, 23).

6 Nuruddin Farah, "Another Little Piece of My Heart," *New York Times*, August 2, 2004.

7 Nuruddin Farah, "Celebrating Differences: The 1998 Neustadt Lecture," *World Literature Today* 72.4 (autumn 1998): 710.

8 Farah, "Celebrating Differences," 712.

9 The first quote is from Reed Way Dasenbrock, "Nuruddin Farah: A Tale of Two Trilogies," *World Literature Today* 72.4 (autumn 1998): 752. The second description is from Simon Gikandi, "Nuruddin Farah and Postcolonial Textuality," *World Literature Today* 72.4 (autumn 1998): 758.

10 Gikandi, "Nuruddin Farah and Postcolonial Textuality," 758.

11 Nuruddin Farah, "Why I Write," *Third World Quarterly* 10.4 (October 1988): 1597.

12 Farah, "Why I Write," 1599.

13 See, for instance, Luc Boltanski, *Distant Suffering: Morality, Media and Politics*, trans. Graham Burchell (Cambridge: Cambridge University Press, 1999), Didier Fassin, *Humanitarian Reason: A Moral History of the Present*, trans. Rachel Gomme (Berkeley: University of California Press, 2012), Peter Redfield, *Life in Crisis: The Ethical Journey of Doctors without Borders* (Berkeley: University of California Press, 2013). For a related critique of development aid, see R. L. Stirrat and Heiko Henkel, "The Development Gift: The Problem of Reciprocity in the NGO World," *Annals of the American Academy of Political and Social Science* 554 (November 1997): 66–80.

14 See Mark Duffield, "The Political Economy of Internal War: Asset Transfer, Complex Emergencies and International Aid," in *War and Hunger: Rethinking International Responses to Complex Emergencies*, ed. Joanna Macrae, Anthony Zwi, Mark Duffield, and Hugo Slim (London: Zed, 1994), 50–69, and de Waal, *Famine Crimes*, 53.

15 Duffield, "The Political Economy of Internal War," 58.

16 De Waal, *Famine Crimes*, 66.

17 De Waal, *Famine Crimes*, 67.

18 De Waal, *Famine Crimes*, 66. De Waal astutely makes the productive distinction between "soft" and "hard" humanitarian interests, where the former refers to the noble ideals that are the stated aims of humanitarian organizations, while the latter refers to institutional demands.

19 Alex de Waal and Rakiya Omaar, "Doing Harm by Doing Good? The International Relief Effort in Somalia," *Current History* 92.574 (May 1, 1993): 202.

20 De Waal and Omaar, "Can Military Intervention be 'Humanitarian'?"

21 On the informal economy, see Alex de Waal, "The Shadow Economy," *Africa Report* 38.2 (March 1993): 24–28.

22 Mark Duffield, Joanna Macrae, and Anthony Zwi, "Conclusion," in *War and Hunger*, 225.

23 Duffield et al., "Conclusion," 227.

24 The right of humanitarian intervention refers to the right of external powers to intervene in the domestic affairs of a sovereign nation-state by using force or the threat of force for humanitarian reasons such as the protection of that nation-state's citizens in situations such as genocide, civil war or famine, where the actions of the government of that nation-state has caused suffering or the nation-state is unable to prevent such suffering because it is in a state of anarchy. Article 2(4) of the United Nations Charter prohibits military intervention in the territory of another state. However, in the post-Cold War era, the UN Security Council has authorized humanitarian intervention, for example, in Iraq (Resolution 688, 5 April 1991), Liberia (Resolution 788, 19 November 1992) and Somalia (Resolution 794, 3 December 1992). For discussions of the validity of the right of humanitarian intervention in public international law, see Christopher Greenwood, "Is There a Right of Humanitarian Intervention?" *The World Today* 49.2 (February 1993): 34–40, and Ian Hurd, "Is Humanitarian Intervention Legal?" *Ethics and International Affairs* 25.3 (2011): 293–313. On the disregard of victims by humanitarian organizations, see Katerina Tomasevski, "Human Rights and Wars of Starvation," *War and Hunger*, 86. Tomasevski notes that international human rights law does not treat victims as a subject of rights or a party to international legal procedures. They have no legal standing even in situations of mass victimization.

25 De Waal, *Famine Crimes*, 189.

26 See Alex de Waal, "On the Perception of Poverty and Famines," *International Journal of Moral and Social Studies* 2.3 (1987): 251–62.

27 De Waal, *Famine Crimes*, 82.

28 Benthall, *Disasters, Relief and the Media*, 178.

29 Benthall, *Disasters, Relief and the Media*, 180.

30 Benthall, *Disasters, Relief and the Media*, 189.

31 Rakiya Omaar, "Disaster Pornography from Somalia," *Los Angeles Times*, December 10, 1992, and Robert Block, "Somalia: White House 'Steamrollered' into Intervention," *Independent*, December 10, 1992.

32 Omaar, "Disaster Pornography." Omaar was dismissed from Africa Watch for opposing US intervention.

33 Alex de Waal and Rakiya Omaar, "The Lessons of Famine," *Africa Report* 37.6 (November 1, 1992): 62.

34 De Waal, *Famine Crimes*, 83.

35 See Francis Ngaboh-Smart, "Dimensions of Gift Giving in Nuruddin Farah's *Gifts*," *Research in African Literatures* 27.4 (winter 1996): 144–56.

36 Duniya's dying father gave her in marriage to Zubair, a much older blind man, with the sanction of her older half-brother, Shiriye, who had accepted Zubair's gift of bride-wealth. She then married her former landlord, Taariq. Her youngest daughter with Taariq is raised in the household of his brother, Qaasim. Duniya is beholden to Qaasim because she lives in one of his properties for a token rent. She is also assisted by her other brother, Abshir, who makes monthly gifts of US currency to her and has promised to pay for her children's education. Now divorced, she has embarked on a relationship with Bosaaso.

37 Marcel Mauss, *The Gift: The Form and Reason for Exchange in Archaic Societies*, trans. W. D. Halls (New York: Norton, 1990), 65.

38 Mauss, *The Gift*, 69, 83.

39 See Alison Mitchell, "A New Question in Somalia: When Does Free Food Hurt?," *New York Times*, January 13, 1993.

40 For studies of non-Western cultural traditions of philanthropy and relief aid that respond to critiques of humanitarianism, see Jonathan Benthall and Jerome Bellion-Jourdan, *The Charitable Crescent: Politics of Aid in the Muslim World* (London: Tauris, 2003), Jonathan Benthall, "The Palestinian Zakat Committees 1993–2007 and Their Contested Interpretations," *PSIO Occasional Paper* 1 (Geneva: Graduate Institute of International and Development Studies: 2008), "Islamic Charities, Faith-Based Organizations and the International Aid System," in *Understanding Islamic Charities*, ed. J. Alterman and K. van Hippel (Washington D.C.: Center for Strategic and International Studies Press, 2007); Erica Bornstein, *Disquieting Gifts: Humanitarianism in New Delhi* (Palo Alto, CA: Stanford University Press, 2012), Amy Singer, *Charity in Islamic Societies* (Cambridge: Cambridge University Press, 2008), and "The Persistence of Philanthropy," *Comparative Studies of South Asia, Africa and the Middle East* 31.3 (2011): 557–68. For a study of Somalian philanthropic traditions, see Cindy Horst, "A Monopoly on Assistance: International Aid to Refugee Camps and the Neglected Role of the Somali Diaspora," *Afrika Spectrum* 43.1 (2008): 121–31.

41 Stirrat and Henkel, "Development Gift," 79.

42 Horst, "Monopoly on Assistance," 123.

43 Horst, "Monopoly on Assistance," 128.

44 De Waal, *Famine Crimes*, 168. See also de Waal and Omaar, "Lessons of Famine," 63–64.

45 Duniya loses her footing as Bosaaso becomes part of her inner world. Farah conveys this rapid transformation with imagery of conception. See *G*, 12.

46 See, for example, Taariq's newspaper story about the magic cow (*G*, 56–59) and Nasiiba's fraternal twin, Mataan's story about the brass pot (*G*, 74).

47 Critics have suggested that the novel's characters attempt to create identities for themselves that are not restricted by the traditional familial and societal roles they are expected to play and that storytelling is therefore a political act of anti-authoritarian self-invention. See Patricia Alden and Louis Tremaine, "Reinventing Family in the Second Trilogy of Nuruddin Farah," *World Literature Today* 72.4 (autumn 1998): 759–66, and Jacqueline Bardolph, "Brothers and Sisters in Nuruddin Farah's Two Trilogies," *World Literature Today* 72.4 (autumn 1998): 727–32.

48 This and the following quotation are from Frantz Fanon, *The Wretched of the Earth*, trans. Richard Philcox (New York: Grove Press, 2004), 174.

49 Samir Amin, *Obsolescent Capitalism: Contemporary Politics and Global Disorder*, trans. Patrick Camiller (London: Zed, 2003), 122.

Epilogue. Without Conclusion

1 Rabindranath Tagore, "World Literature," in *Rabindranath Tagore: Selected Writings on Literature and Language*, ed. Sukanta Chaudhuri (New Delhi: Oxford University Press, 2001), 147–49.

2 Gerard Genette, *Narrative Discourse*, trans. Jane E. Lewin (Ithaca, NY: Cornell University Press, 1980), 34.

3 Genette, *Narrative Discourse*, 87.

4 Genette, *Narrative Discourse*, 87–88.

5 Franco Moretti, *The Way of the World: The Bildungsroman in European Culture* (London: Verso, 1987), 7.

6 Salman Rushdie, *Midnight's Children* (Harmondsworth, England: Penguin, 1991), 534.

7 See Jean-François Lyotard, *The Postmodern Condition: A Report on Knowledge*, trans. Geoff Bennington and Brian Massumi (Minneapolis: University of Minnesota Press, 1984), 37–41. "Little narrative" (*petit récit*) is from p. 60. On the "little stories" (*petites histoires*) of the Cashinahua Indians, see Jean-François Lyotard, *The Differend: Phrases in Dispute*, trans. Georges Van Den Abbeele (Minneapolis: University of Minnesota Press, 1988), 152–55.

8 See Benedict Anderson, "Cacique Democracy in the Philippines," in *The Spectre of Comparisons: Nationalism, Southeast Asia and the World* (London: Verso, 1998), esp. 194–98. This group achieved economic ascendancy by profiting from the regional Anglo-Pacific trade system dominated by British and American traders.

9 Anderson, "Cacique Democracy," 201.

10 Paul D. Hutchcroft, *Booty Capitalism: The Politics of Banking in the Philippines* (Ithaca, NY: Cornell University Press, 1998), 27.

11 Anderson, "Cacique Democracy," 203.

12 Anderson, "Cacique Democracy," 205.

13 David C. Kang, *Crony Capitalism: Corruption and Development in South Korea and the Philippines* (Cambridge: Cambridge University Press, 2002), 31.

14 Anderson, "Cacique Democracy," 208.

15 For a fuller discussion of the Philippine patrimonial state, see Hutchcroft, *Booty Capitalism*, 13–44.

16 Hutchcroft, *Booty Capitalism*, 35.

17 Hutchcroft, *Booty Capitalism*, 40.

18 Ninotchka Rosca, *State of War* (New York: Norton, 1988), 192, 336–37, hereafter sw, with page numbers cited in parentheses.

19 Walter Benjamin, "The Storyteller: Reflections on the Work of Nikolai Leskov," in *Illuminations*, ed. Hannah Arendt and trans. Harry Zohn (New York: Schocken, 1969), 86; *Der Erzähler: Betrachtungen zum Werk Nikolai Lesskows*, in *Erzählen. Schriften zur Theorie der Narration und zur literarischen Prosa*, ed. Alexander Honold (Frankfurt am Main: Suhrkamp, 2007), 106, hereafter "S," with page references to the translation followed by the German text. Benedict Anderson also uses Benjamin's essay to read Mario Vargas Llosa's novel *El Hablador* as "a novel about 'stories' and also about a narrator 'in love with' an *Erzähler*, as well as a novelist in love with the idea of the *Erzähler*" ("El Malhadado País," in *The Spectre of Comparisons*, 352). Anderson explains Vargas Llosa's fascination with the story form in terms of the history and sociological composition of the Americas. In contradistinction, my argument concerns the connection between the story and the giving of time.

20 Timothy Mo, *Renegade or Halo²* (London: Paddleless Press, 1999), 40, hereafter *Re*, with page numbers in parentheses.

21 Benedict Anderson has analyzed the importance of this phrase, which he translates as "the spectre of comparisons," arguing that this comparative consciousness yields a non-Eurocentric method of comparison. See *The Spectre of Comparisons*, 2. For a more sustained discussion of Rizal's passage, see Pheng Cheah, "Grounds of Comparison," in *Grounds of Comparison: Around the Work of Benedict Anderson*, ed. Pheng Cheah and Jonathan Culler (New York: Routledge, 2003), 1–20, and "The Material World of Comparison," in *Comparison: Theories, Approaches, Uses*, ed. Rita Felski and Susan Stanford Friedman (Baltimore: Johns Hopkins University Press, 2013), 168–90.

22 Rey can be seen as a contemporary version of the Manila man, a native of the Spanish Philippines who worked as an international seafarer and undertook mercenary activities. See Filomeno V. Aguilar Jr., "Filibustero, Rizal, and the Manilamen of the Nineteenth Century," *Philippine Studies* 59.4 (2011): 429–69. The Manila man is arguably a precursor of the Overseas Filipino Worker. I thank Caroline Hau for this point.

23 On *Renegade* as a picaresque novel, see Brian Finney, "Migrancy and the Picaresque in Timothy Mo's *Renegade or Halo²*," *Critique* 49.1 (fall 2007): 61–76.

24 See *Re*, 493: "Rodrigo was also a Cuban who didn't like Cubans. In short, he was a renegade."

25 *Halo-halo* is the Tagalog term for "hodge-podge." Similar desserts are found in other Southeast Asian countries, such as *ais campur, ais kacang*, or *air batu campur* (ABC) in Malaysia, Singapore, and Indonesia.

26 Simeon Dumdum, Timothy Mo, and Resil Mojares, "In Conversation: Cebuano Writers on Philippine Literature and English," *World Englishes* 23.1 (2004): 198.

27 Theodor W. Adorno, "Cultural Criticism and Society," in *Prisms*, trans. Samuel and Sherry Weber (Cambridge, MA: MIT Press, 1981), 34; "Kulturkritik und Gesellschaft," in *Prismen, Kulturkritik und Gesellschaft I, Gesammelte Schriften,* Band 10.1, ed. Rolf Tiedemann (Frankfurt am Main: Suhrkamp, 1955), 30.

28 Theodor W. Adorno, *Negative Dialectics*, trans. E. B. Ashton (New York: Continuum, 1973), 362–63; *Negative Dialektik* (Frankfurt am Main: Suhrkamp, 1966), 353.

29 Hannah Arendt, *The Human Condition* (Chicago: University of Chicago Press, 1958), 180.

SELECT BIBLIOGRAPHY

Works by Hannah Arendt

"The Concept of History: Ancient and Modern." In *Between Past and Future: Six Exercises in Political Thought*, 41–90. New York: Viking Press, 1961.

"Concern with Politics in Recent European Philosophical Thought." In *Essays in Understanding 1930–1954: Formation, Exile, and Totalitarianism*, ed. Jerome Kohn, 428–47. New York: Schocken, 1994.

"The Crisis in Education." In *Between Past and Future: Six Exercises in Political Thought*, 173–96. New York: Viking Press, 1961.

"Culture and Politics." In *Reflections on Literature and Culture*, ed. Susannah Young-ah Gottlieb, 179–202. Palo Alto: Stanford University Press, 2007.

"Epilogue." In *The Promise of Politics*, ed. Jerome Kohn, 201–4. New York: Schocken, 2005.

The Human Condition. Chicago: University of Chicago Press, 1958.

"Introduction *into* Politics." In *The Promise of Politics*, ed. Jerome Kohn, 93–200. New York: Schocken, 2005.

"Labor, Work, Action." In *Amor Mundi: Explorations in the Faith and Thought of Hannah Arendt*, ed. James W. Bernauer, 29–42. Boston: Nijhoff, 1987.

Love and Saint Augustine, ed. Joanna Vecchiarelli Scott and Judith Chelius Stark. Chicago: University of Chicago Press, 1996.

"Martin Heidegger at Eighty." Trans. Albert Hofstadter. *New York Review of Books*, October 21, 1971, http://www.nybooks.com/articles/archives/1971/oct/21/martin -heidegger-at-eighty/.

"On Humanity in Dark Times: Thoughts about Lessing." Trans. Clara and Richard Winston. In *Men in Dark Times*, 3–31. San Diego: Harcourt Brace, 1983.

On Revolution. New York: Viking Press, 1965.

The Origins of Totalitarianism. 2nd ed. San Diego: Harcourt Brace, 1973.

The Promise of Politics. Ed. Jerome Kohn. New York: Schocken, 2005.

Was ist Politik? Fragmente aus dem Nachlaß. Ed. Ursula Ludz. Munich: Piper, 2003.

"What Is Existential Philosophy?" In *Essays in Understanding, 1930–1954: Formation, Exile, and Totalitarianism*, ed. Jerome Kohn, 163–87. New York: Schocken, 1994.

"What Is Freedom?" In *Between Past and Future: Six Exercises in Political Thought*, 143–71.

Arendt, Hannah, and Günther Stern. "Rilke's *Duino Elegies.*" In *Reflections on Literature and Culture*, ed. Susannah Young-ah Gottlieb, 1–23. Palo Alto: Stanford University Press, 2007.

Works by Jacques Derrida

Aporias: Dying-Awaiting (One Another at) "the Limits of Truth." Trans. Thomas Dutoit. Palo Alto: Stanford University Press, 1993.

"As If It Were Possible, 'Within Such Limits' . . ." In *Negotiations: Interventions and Interviews 1971–2001*, ed. and trans. Elizabeth Rottenberg, 343–70. Palo Alto: Stanford University Press, 2002.

"Autoimmunity: Real and Symbolic Suicides: A Dialogue with Jacques Derrida." In *Philosophy in a Time of Terror: Dialogues with Jürgen Habermas and Jacques Derrida*, ed. Giovanna Borradori, 85–136. Chicago: University of Chicago Press, 2003.

The Beast and the Sovereign. Vol. 2. Trans. Geoffrey Bennington. Chicago: University of Chicago Press, 2011.

"Deconstruction and the Other." In *Dialogues with Contemporary Continental Thinkers: The Phenomenological Heritage*, ed. Richard Kearney, 107–26. Manchester: Manchester University Press, 1984.

"The Deconstruction of Actuality." In *Negotiations: Interventions and Interviews 1971–2001*, ed. and trans. Elizabeth Rottenberg, 85–116. Palo Alto: Stanford University Press, 2002.

"Différance." In *Margins of Philosophy*, trans. Alan Bass, 1–27. Chicago: University of Chicago Press, 1982.

Edmund Husserl's Origin of Geometry: An Introduction. Trans. John P. Leavey. Lincoln: University of Nebraska Press, 1989.

"A Europe of Hope." Trans. Pleshette DeArmitt, Justine Malle and Kas Saghafi, *Epoché* 10.2 (spring 2006): 407–12.

"Une Europe de l'espoir." *Le Monde diplomatique.* November 2004. http://archives.mondediplo.com/article11677.html.

The Gift of Death and Literature in Secret. Trans. David Wills. Chicago: University of Chicago Press, 2008.

Given Time—I. Counterfeit Money. Trans. Peggy Kamuf. Chicago: University of Chicago Press, 1992.

"Globalization, Peace, and Cosmopolitanism." In *Negotiations: Interventions and Interviews 1971–2001*, ed. and trans. Elizabeth Rottenberg, 371–86. Palo Alto: Stanford University Press, 2002.

Of Grammatology. Trans. Gayatri Chakravorty Spivak. Baltimore: Johns Hopkins University Press, 1976.

De la Grammatologie. Paris: Minuit, 1967.

"Living On: Borderlines." In Harold Bloom et al., *Deconstruction and Criticism*, 75–176. London: Routledge Kegan Paul, 1979.

Memoires for Paul de Man. Trans. by Cecile Lindsay, Jonathan Culler, Eduardo Cadava, and Peggy Kamuf. Rev. ed. New York: Columbia University Press, 1989.

"Not Utopia, the Im-possible." In *Paper Machine*, trans. Rachel Bowlby, 121–35. Palo Alto: Stanford University Press, 2005.

"*Ousia* and *Grammē*: Note on a Note from *Being and Time*." In *Margins of Philosophy*, trans. Alan Bass, 29–67. Chicago: University of Chicago Press, 1982.

"Passions: 'An Oblique Offering.'" In *On the Name*, ed. Thomas Dutoit, trans. David Wood, John P. Leavey Jr., and Ian McLeod, 3–34. Palo Alto: Stanford University Press, 1995.

Politics of Friendship. Trans. George Collins. New York: Verso, 1997.

Positions. Trans. Alan Bass. Chicago: University of Chicago Press, 1981.

"Punctuations: The Time of a Thesis." In *Eyes of the University: Right to Philosophy 2*, trans. Jan Plug et al., 113–28. Palo Alto: Stanford University Press, 2004.

"Rams: Uninterrupted Dialogue—Between Two Infinities, the Poem." In *Sovereignties in Question: The Poetics of Paul Celan*, ed. Thomas Dutoit and Outi Pasanen, 135–63. New York: Fordham University Press, 2005.

Rogues: Two Essays on Reason. Trans. Pascale-Anne Brault and Michael Naas. Palo Alto: Stanford University Press, 2005.

"Signature Event Context." In *Margins of Philosophy*, trans. Alan Bass, 307–30. Chicago: University of Chicago Press, 1982.

Specters of Marx—The State of the Debt, the Work of Mourning and the New International. With an introduction by Bernd Magnus and Stephen Cullenberg. Trans. Peggy Kamuf. New York: Routledge, 1994.

Speech and Phenomena and Other Essays on Husserl's Theory of Signs. Trans. David B. Allison. Evanston, IL: Northwestern University Press, 1973.

"Tympan." In *Margins of Philosophy*, trans. Alan Bass, ix–xxix. Chicago: University of Chicago Press, 1982.

"The University without Condition." In *Without Alibi*, trans. Peggy Kamuf, 202–37. Palo Alto: Stanford University Press, 2002.

Voyous: Deux essais sur la raison. Paris: Galilée, 2003.

Works by Johann Wolfgang Goethe

"Aus dem Faszikel zu Carlyles *Leben Schillers*." In *Sämtliche Werke, I. Abteilung, Band 22, Ästhetische Schriften 1824–1832, Über Kunst und Altertum V–VI*, ed. Anne Bohnenkamp, 865–68. Frankfurt am Main: Deutscher Klassiker, 1999.

"Bezüge nach Aussen." In *Über Kunst und Alterthum*, VI, 2 (1828), in *Sämtliche Werke, I. Abteilung, Band 22*, ed. Anne Bohnenkamp, 427–28. Frankfurt am Main: Deutscher Klassiker, 1999.

Conversations with Eckermann 1823–1832. Trans. John Oxenford. San Francisco: Northpoint Press, 1984.

Correspondence between Goethe and Carlyle. Ed. Charles Eliot Norton. London: Macmillan, 1887.

"*Le Tasse*, drame historique en cinq actes, par Monsieur Alexandre Duval." In *Über Kunst und Alterthum*, VI, 1 (1827), in *Sämtliche Werke, I. Abteilung, Band 22*, ed. Anne Bohnenkamp, 353–57.

Letter to Carlyle, July 20, 1827. In *Sämtliche Werke, II. Abteilung, Band 10 (37), Die Letzten Jahre. Briefe, Tagebücher und Gespräche von 1823 bis zu Goethes Tod*, Teil 1 Von 1823 bis zum Tode Carl Augusts 1828, ed. Horst Fleig, 496–99. Frankfurt am Main: Deutscher Klassiker, 1993.

"On the *Edinburgh Reviews*." In *Über Kunst und Alterthum*, VI, 2 (1828), in *Sämtliche Werke, I, Abteilung, Band 22*, ed. Anne Bohnenkamp, 491–93. Frankfurt am Main: Deutscher Klassiker, 1999.

"Some Passages Pertaining to the Concept of World Literature." In *Comparative Literature: The Early Years. An Anthology of Essays*, ed. Hans-Joachim Schulz and Phillip H. Rhein, 5–11. Chapel Hill: University of North Carolina Press, 1973.

Eckermann, Johann Peter. *Gespräche mit Goethe in den letzten Jahren seines Lebens.* Berlin: Aufbau, 1982.

Works by Martin Heidegger

"The Age of the World Picture." In *Off The Beaten Track*, ed. and trans. Julian Young and Kenneth Haynes, 57–85. Cambridge: Cambridge University Press, 2002.

Basic Problems of Phenomenology. Trans. Albert Hofstadter. Rev. ed. Bloomington: Indiana University Press, 1988.

Being and Time. Trans. Joan Stambaugh. Albany: State University of New York Press, 1996.

"Brief über den 'Humanismus.'" In *Wegmarken, Gesamtausgabe, I. Abteilung: Veröffentlichte Schriften 1914–1970, Band 9*, ed. Friedrich-Wilhelm von Hermann, 313–64. Frankfurt am Main: Vittorio Klostermann, 1976.

The Fundamental Concepts of Metaphysics: World, Finitude, Solitude. Trans. William McNeill and Nicholas Walker. Bloomington: Indiana University Press, 1995.

Gelassenheit. In *Gelassenheit*, 9–28. Tübingen: Neske, 1959.

Die Grundbegriffe der Metaphysik: Welt—Endlichkeit—Einsamkeit, Gesamtausgabe, II. Abteilung: Vorlesungen 1923–1944, Band 29/30, Freiburger Vorlesung Wintersemester 1929/30. Ed. Friedrich-Wilhelm von Hermann. Frankfurt am Main: Vittorio Klostermann, 1983.

Die Grundprobleme der Phänomenologie, Gesamtausgabe, II. Abteilung: Vorlesungen 1923–1944, Band 24, Marburger Vorlesung Sommersemester 1927, ed. Friedrich-Wilhelm von Hermann. Frankfurt am Main: Vittorio Klostermann, 1975.

History of the Concept of Time. Prolegomena. Trans. Theodore Kisiel. Bloomington: Indiana University Press, 1985.

"Letter on 'Humanism'" Trans. Frank A. Capuzzi. In *Pathmarks*, ed. William McNeill, 239–76. Cambridge: Cambridge University Press, 1998.

"Memorial Address." In *Discourse on Thinking*, trans. John M. Anderson and E. Hans Freund, 43–57. New York: Harper and Row, 1966.

The Metaphysical Foundations of Logic. Trans. Michael Heim. Bloomington: Indiana University Press, 1984.

Metaphysische Anfangsgründe der Logik im Ausgang von Leibniz, Gesamtausgabe, II. Abteilung: Vorlesungen 1923–1944, Band 26, Marburger Vorlesung Sommersemester 1928. Ed. Klaus Held. Frankfurt am Main: Vittorio Klostermann, 1978.

"On the Essence of Ground." Trans. William McNeill. In *Pathmarks*, ed. William McNeill, 97–135. Cambridge: Cambridge University Press, 1998.

"The Origin of the Work of Art." In *Off the Beaten Track*, ed. and trans. Julian Young and Kenneth Haynes, 1–56. Cambridge: Cambridge University Press, 2002.

Prolegomena zur Geschichte des Zeitbegriffs, Gesamtausgabe, II. Abteilung: Vorlesungen 1923–1944, Band 20, Marburger Vorlesung Sommersemester 1925. Ed. Petra Jaeger. Frankfurt am Main: Vittorio Klostermann, 1979.

Sein und Zeit, Gesamtausgabe, I. Abteilung: Veröffentlichte Schriften 1914–1970, Band 2, Ed. Friedrich-Wilhelm von Hermann. Frankfurt am Main: Vittorio Klostermann, 1977.

Der Ursprung des Kunstwerkes. In *Holzwege, Gesamtausgabe, I. Abteilung: Veröffentlichte Schriften 1914–1970*, Band 5, ed. Friedrich-Wilhelm von Hermann, 1–74. Frankfurt am Main: Vittorio Klostermann, 1977.

"Vom Wesen des Grundes." In *Wegmarken, Gesamtausgabe, I. Abteilung: Veröffentlichte Schriften 1914–1970*, Band 9, ed. Friedrich-Wilhelm von Hermann, 123–75. Frankfurt am Main: Vittorio Klostermann, 1976.

Die Zeit des Weltbildes. In *Holzwege, Gesamtausgabe, I. Abteilung: Veröffentlichte Schriften 1914–1970*, Band 5, ed. Friedrich-Wilhelm von Hermann, 75–114. Frankfurt am Main: Vittorio Klostermann, 1977.

Works by Georg Wilhelm Friedrich Hegel

Aesthetics: Lecture on Fine Arts. Vol. 1. Trans. T. M. Knox. Oxford: Clarendon Press, 1998.

Elements of the Philosophy of Right. Ed. Allen W. Wood. Trans. H. B. Nisbet. Cambridge: Cambridge University Press, 1991.

Enzyklopädie der philosophischen Wissenschaften im Grundrisse 1830. Dritter teil. Die Philosophie des Geistes. Werke 10. Ed. Eva Moldenhauer and Karl Markus Michel. Frankfurt am Main: Suhrkamp, 1986.

Grundlinien der Philosophie des Rechts. Werke 7. Ed. Eva Moldenhauer and Karl Markus Michel. Frankfurt am Main: Suhrkamp, 1986.

Hegel's Philosophy of Mind. Part Three of the Encyclopaedia of the Philosophical Sciences (1830). Trans. William Wallace and A. V. Miller. Oxford: Clarendon, 1971.

Hegel's Philosophy of Nature. Part Two of the Encyclopaedia of the Philosophical Sciences (1830). Trans. A. V. Miller. Oxford: Clarendon, 1970.

Hegel and the Human Spirit: A Translation of the Jena Lectures on the Philosophy of Spirit (1805–6) with Commentary. Trans. Leo Rauch. Detroit: Wayne State University Press, 1983.

Jenaer Realphilosophie. Vorlesungmanuskripte zur Philosophie der Natur und des Geistes von 1805–1806. Hamburg: Felix Meiner, 1969.

Lectures on the Philosophy of World History. Introduction: Reason in History. Trans. H. B. Nisbet. Cambridge: Cambridge University Press, 1980.

Vorlesungen über die Philosophie der Weltgeschichte. Vol. 1. *Die Vernunft in der Geschichte*. Hamburg: Felix Meiner, 1955.

Works by Karl Marx

Capital: A Critique of Political Economy. Volume 1. Trans. Ben Fowkes. Harmondsworth, England: Penguin, 1976.

Capital: A Critique of Political Economy. Volume 3. Trans. David Fernbach. Harmondsworth, England: Penguin, 1981.

Grundrisse der Kritik der politischen Ökonomie. Berlin: Dietz, 1953.

Grundrisse: Foundations of the Critique of Political Economy. Trans. Martin Nicolaus. Harmondsworth, England: Penguin, 1973.

Das Kapital: Kritik der politischen Ökonomie. Erster Band. Berlin: Dietz, 1962.

Das Kapital: Kritik der politischen Ökonomie. Dritter Band. Berlin: Dietz, 1964.

Marx, Karl, and Friedrich Engels. *Die Deutsche Ideologie. Marx/Engels Gesamtausgabe*, vol. 1:5, ed. V. Adoratskij. Berlin: Marx-Engels Verlag, 1932.

Marx, Karl, and Friedrich Engels. *The German Ideology: Part One, with Selections from Parts Two and Three*. Ed. C. J. Arthur. New York: International, 1970.

Marx, Karl, and Friedrich Engels. *Manifest der Kommunistichen Partei* (1848). In *Marx/Engels Gesamtausgabe*, vol. 1:6, ed. V. Adoratskij, 523–57. Berlin: Marx-Engels Verlag, 1932.

Marx, Karl, and Friedrich Engels. *Manifesto of the Communist Party*. In *The Revolutions of 1848. Political Writings*, vol. 1, ed. David Fernbach, 62–98. Harmondsworth, England: Penguin, 1973.

Primary Literary Works and Interviews

Cliff, Michelle. *Abeng*. Trumansburg, NY: Crossing Press, 1984.

Cliff, Michelle. "Caliban's Daughter: The Tempest and the Teapot." *Frontiers: A Journal of Women Studies* 12.2 (1991): 36–51.

Cliff, Michelle. *No Telephone to Heaven*. London: Methuen, 1987.

Cliff, Michelle. "Sites of Memory." In *If I Could Write This in Fire*, 49–64. Minneapolis: University of Minnesota Press, 2008.

Dumdum, Simeon, Timothy Mo, and Resil Mojares. "In Conversation: Cebuano Writers on Philippine Literature and English." *World Englishes* 23.1 (2004): 191–98.

Farah, Nuruddin. "Another Little Piece of My Heart." *New York Times*, August 2, 2004.

Farah, Nuruddin. "Celebrating Differences: The 1998 Neustadt Lecture." *World Literature Today* 72.4 (autumn 1998): 709–12.

Farah, Nuruddin. *Gifts*. New York: Penguin, 2000.

Farah, Nuruddin. "Why I Write." *Third World Quarterly* 10.4 (October 1988): 1591–99.

Ghosh, Amitav. "The Chronicle Interview: Amitav Ghosh, *The Hungry Tide*." *U.N. Chronicle* 13.4 (2005): 48–52.

Ghosh, Amitav. "Folly in the Sundarbans." November 2004. http://www .amitavghosh.com/essays/folly.html, accessed July 5, 2013.

Ghosh, Amitav. *The Hungry Tide*. Boston: Houghton Mifflin Harcourt, 2005.

Kumar, T. Vijay. "'Postcolonial' Describes You as a Negative": An Interview with Amitav Ghosh." *Interventions* 9.1 (2007): 99–105.

Mo, Timothy. *Renegade or Halo²*. London: Paddleless Press, 1999.

Naipaul, V. S. *A Way in the World*. New York: Vintage, 1994.

Rilke, Rainer Maria. *Duino Elegies and The Sonnets to Orpheus*. Trans. A. Poulin, Jr. Boston: Houghton Mifflin, 1977.

Rosca, Ninotchka. *State of War*. New York: Norton, 1988.

Rushdie, Salman. *Imaginary Homelands: Essays and Criticism, 1981–1991*. London: Granta, 1992.

Rushdie, Salman. *Midnight's Children*. Harmondsworth, England: Penguin, 1991.

Sankaran, Chitra. "Diasporic Predicaments: An Interview with Amitav Ghosh." In *History, Narrative, and Testimony in Amitav Ghosh's Fiction*, ed. Chitra Sankaran, 1–15. Albany: State University of New York Press, 2012.

Schwartz, Meryl F. "An Interview with Michelle Cliff." *Contemporary Literature* 34.4 (winter 1993): 596–619.

Tagore, Rabindranath. "World Literature." In *Rabindranath Tagore: Selected Writings on Literature and Language*, ed. Sukanta Chaudhuri, 138–50. New Delhi: Oxford University Press, 2001.

Walcott, Derek. "The Antilles: Fragments of Epic Memory." Nobel Lecture. December 7, 1992. http://www.nobelprize.org/nobel_prizes/literature/laureates/1992 /walcott-lecture.html.

Wordsworth, William. "A Slumber Did My Spirit Seal." In William Wordsworth and Samuel Taylor Coleridge, *Lyrical Ballads*, ed. R. L. Brett and A. R. Jones, 154. New York: Methuen, 1968.

Other Works

Adorno, Theodor W. *Aesthetic Theory*. Trans. Robert Hullot-Kentor. Minneapolis: University of Minnesota Press, 1997.

Adorno, Theodor W. "Cultural Criticism and Society." In *Prisms*, trans. Samuel and Sherry Weber, 17–34. Cambridge, MA: MIT Press, 1981.

Adorno, Theodor W. "Kulturkritik und Gesellschaft." In *Prismen, Kulturkritik und Gesellschaft I, Gesammelte Schriften*, Band 10.1, ed. Rolf Tiedemann, 11–30. Frankfurt am Main: Suhrkamp, 1955.

Adorno, Theodor W. *Negative Dialectics*. Trans. E. B. Ashton. New York: Continuum, 1973.

Adorno, Theodor W. *Negative Dialektik*. Frankfurt am Main: Suhrkamp, 1966.

Alden, Patricia, and Louis Tremaine. "Reinventing Family in the Second Trilogy of Nuruddin Farah." *World Literature Today* 72.4 (autumn 1998): 759–66.

Alim-Khan. *The Non-Aligned Movement: Achievements, Problems, Prospects.* Moscow: Novosti, 1985.

Alliez, Éric. *Capital Times: Tales from the Conquest of Time.* Trans. Georges Van Den Abbeele. Minneapolis: University of Minnesota Press, 1996.

Amin, Samir. *Obsolescent Capitalism: Contemporary Politics and Global Disorder.* Trans. Patrick Camiller. London: Zed, 2003.

Anderson, Benedict. *Imagined Communities: Reflections on the Origin and Spread of Nationalism.* 2nd ed. London: Verso, 1991.

Anderson, Benedict. *The Spectre of Comparisons: Nationalism, Southeast Asia and the World.* London: Verso, 1998.

Aristotle. *Physics.* Trans. Robin Waterfield. Oxford: Oxford University Press, 1996.

Asia-Africa Speaks from Bandung. Ministry of Foreign Affairs, Indonesia, 1955.

Auerbach, Erich. "Philology and *Weltliteratur.*" Trans. Marie and Edward Said. *Centennial Review* 13.1 (1969): 1–17.

Auerbach, Erich. "Philologie der Weltliteratur." In *Weltliteratur. Festgabe für Fritz Stich zum 70. Geburtstag*, ed. Walter Muschg and Emil Staiger, 39–50. Bern: Francke Verlag, 1972.

Bandung. Texts of Selected Speeches and Final Communique of the Asian-African Conference. New York: Far East Reporter, 1955.

Bardolph, Jacqueline. "Brothers and Sisters in Nuruddin Farah's Two Trilogies." *World Literature Today* 72.4 (autumn 1998): 727–32.

Benhabib, Seyla. *The Reluctant Modernism of Hannah Arendt.* London: Sage, 1996.

Benjamin, Walter. *Der Erzähler: Bertrachtungen zum Werk Nikolai Lesskows.* In *Erzählen. Schriften zur Theorie der Narration und zur literarischen Prosa*, ed. Alexander Honold, 103–28. Frankfurt am Main: Suhrkamp, 2007.

Benjamin, Walter. "The Storyteller: Reflections on the Work of Nikolai Leskov." In *Illuminations*, ed. Hannah Arendt and trans. Harry Zohn, 83–109. New York: Schocken, 1969.

Benthall, Jonathan. *Disasters, Relief and the Media.* London: Tauris, 1993.

Benthall, Jonathan, and Jerome Bellion-Jourdan. *The Charitable Crescent: Politics of Aid in the Muslim World.* London: Tauris, 2003.

Bernheimer, Charles, ed. *Comparative Literature in the Age of Multiculturalism.* Baltimore: Johns Hopkins University Press, 1995.

Boltanski, Luc. *Distant Suffering: Morality, Media and Politics*. Trans. Graham Burchell. Cambridge: Cambridge University Press, 1999.

Burke, Roland. *Decolonization and the Evolution of International Human Rights*. Philadelphia: University of Pennsylvania Press, 2014.

Canclini, Nestor Garcia. *Hybrid Cultures: Strategies for Entering and Leaving Modernity*. Trans. Christopher L. Chiappari and Silvia Lopez. University of Minnesota Press, 1995.

Casanova, Pascale. "Literature as a World." *New Left Review* 31 (January-February 2005): 71–90.

Casanova, Pascale. *The World Republic of Letters*. Trans. M. B. DeBevoise. Cambridge: Harvard University Press, 2004.

Chakrabarty, Dipesh. *Provincializing Europe: Postcolonial Thought and Historical Difference*. Princeton, NJ: Princeton University Press, 2000.

Chatterjee, Partha. *Lineages of Political Society: Studies in Postcolonial Democracy*. New York: Columbia University Press, 2011.

Chatterjee, Partha. *The Nation and Its Fragments: Colonial and Postcolonial Histories*. Princeton, NJ: Princeton University Press, 1993.

Chatterji, Joya. "'Dispersal' and the Failure of Rehabilitation: Refugee Camp-Dwellers and Squatters in West Bengal." *Modern Asian Studies* 41.5 (2007): 995–1032.

Chatterji, Joya. *The Spoils of Partition: Bengal and India, 1947–1967*. Cambridge: Cambridge University Press, 2007.

Cheah, Pheng. "Grounds of Comparison." In *Grounds of Comparison: Around the Work of Benedict Anderson*, ed. Pheng Cheah and Jonathan Culler, 1–20. New York: Routledge, 2003.

Cheah, Pheng. "The Material World of Comparison." In *Comparison: Theories, Approaches, Uses*, ed. Rita Felski and Susan Stanford Friedman, 168–90. Baltimore: Johns Hopkins University Press, 2013.

Cheah, Pheng. *Spectral Nationality: Passages of Freedom from Kant to Postcolonial Literatures of Liberation*. New York: Columbia University Press, 2003.

Cheah, Pheng. "Universal Areas: Asian Studies in a World in Motion." *Traces* 1.1 (2001): 37–70.

Cornwell, Grant H., and Eve W. Stoddard. "From Sugar to Heritage Tourism in the Caribbean: Economic Strategies and National Identities." In *Caribbean Tourism: Alternatives for Community Development*, ed. Chandana Jayawardena, 205–21. Kingston, Jamaica: Ian Randle, 2007.

Damrosch, David. *What Is World Literature?* Princeton, NJ: Princeton University Press, 2003.

Dasenbrock, Reed Way. "Nuruddin Farah: A Tale of Two Trilogies." *World Literature Today* 72.4 (autumn 1998): 747–52.

Dastur, Françoise. "Heidegger's Freiburg Version of the Origin of the Work of Art." In *Heidegger Toward the Turn: Essays on the Work of the 1930s*, ed. James Risser, 119–42. Albany: State University of New York Press, 1999.

de Waal, Alex. *Famine Crimes: Politics and the Disaster Relief Industry in Africa*. London: African Rights and the International African Institute and James Currey, 1997.

de Waal, Alex. "On the Perception of Poverty and Famines." *International Journal of Moral and Social Studies* 2.3 (1987): 251–62.

de Waal, Alex. "The Shadow Economy." *Africa Report* 38.2 (March 1993): 24–28.

de Waal, Alex, and Rakiya Omaar. "Can Military Intervention Be 'Humanitarian'?" *Middle East Report* 187.24 (March–April 1994). http://www.merip.org/mer /mer187/can-military-intervention-be-humanitarian.

de Waal, Alex, and Rakiya Omaar. "Doing Harm by Doing Good? The International Relief Effort in Somalia." *Current History* 92.574 (May 1, 1993): 198–202.

de Waal, Alex, and Rakiya Omaar. "The Lessons of Famine." *Africa Report* 37.6 (November 1, 1992): 62–64.

Duffield, Mark. "The Political Economy of Internal War: Asset Transfer, Complex Emergencies and International Aid." In *War and Hunger: Rethinking International Responses to Complex Emergencies*, ed. Joanna Macrae, Anthony Zwi, Mark Duffield and Hugo Slim, 50–69. London: Zed, 1994.

Edmonson, Belinda. "Race, Privilege, and the Politics of (Re)writing History: An Analysis of the Novels of Michelle Cliff." *Callaloo* 16.1 (winter 1993): 180–91.

Fanon, Frantz. *Black Skin, White Masks*. Trans. Richard Philcox. New York: Grove Press, 2008.

Fanon, Frantz. *The Wretched of the Earth*. Trans. Richard Philcox. New York: Grove Press, 2004.

Fassin, Didier. *Humanitarian Reason: A Moral History of the Present*. Trans. Rachel Gomme. Berkeley: University of California Press, 2012.

Finney, Brian. "Migrancy and the Picaresque in Timothy Mo's *Renegade or Halo²*." *Critique* 49.1 (fall 2007): 61–76.

Genette, Gerard. *Narrative Discourse*. Trans. Jane E. Lewin. Ithaca, NY: Cornell University Press, 1980.

Gikandi, Simon. "Nuruddin Farah and Postcolonial Textuality." *World Literature Today* 72.4 (autumn 1998): 753–58.

Gilead, Amihud. "Teleological Time: A Variation of a Kantian Theme." *Review of Metaphysics* 38 (March 1985): 529–62.

Gmelch, George. *Behind the Smile: The Working Lives of Caribbean Tourism*. 2nd ed. Bloomington: Indiana University Press, 2012.

Guha, Ramachandra, and Juan Martinez-Alier. *Varieties of Environmentalism: Essays North and South*. London: Earthscan, 1997.

Guha, Ranajit. *History at the Limit of World-History*. New York: Columbia University Press, 2002.

Habermas, Jürgen. "Conceptions of Modernity: A Look Back at Two Traditions." In *The Postnational Constellation: Political Essays*, trans. Max Pensky, 130–56. Cambridge, MA: MIT Press, 2001.

Habermas, Jürgen. *The Inclusion of the Other: Studies in Political Theory*. Ed. Ciaran Cronin and Pablo De Greiff. Cambridge, MA: MIT Press, 1998.

Habermas, Jürgen. *The Postnational Constellation: Political Essays*. Trans. Max Pensky. Cambridge, MA: MIT Press, 2001.

Habermas, Jürgen. *The Structural Transformation of the Public Sphere*. Trans. Thomas Burger and Frederick Lawrence. Cambridge, MA: MIT Press, 1989.

Harvey, David. *The Condition of Postmodernity*. Cambridge: Blackwell, 1990.

Harvey, David. *The Limits to Capital*. Chicago: University of Chicago Press, 1982.

Harvey, David. *Spaces of Global Capitalism*. London: Verso, 2006.

Horst, Cindy. "A Monopoly on Assistance: International Aid to Refugee Camps and the Neglected Role of the Somali Diaspora." *Afrika Spectrum* 43.1 (2008): 121–31.

Hutchcroft, Paul D. *Booty Capitalism: The Politics of Banking in the Philippines*. Ithaca, NY: Cornell University Press, 1998.

Jalais, Annu. "*Bonbibi*: Bridging Worlds." *Indian Folklife*, no. 28 (January 2008): 6–8.

Jalais, Annu. *Forest of Tigers: People, Politics and Environment in the Sundarbans*. London: Routledge, 2011.

James, C. L. R. *Nkrumah and the Ghana Revolution*. London: Allison and Busby, 1977.

Kang, David C. *Crony Capitalism: Corruption and Development in South Korea and the Philippines*. Cambridge: Cambridge University Press, 2002.

Kant, Immanuel. *Anthropology from a Pragmatic Point of View*. In *Anthropology, History and Education*, ed. Günter Zöller and Robert Louden, 231–429. Cambridge: Cambridge University Press, 2011.

Kant, Immanuel. *Anthropologie in pragmatischer Hinsicht*. In *Schriften zur Anthropologie, Geschichtsphilosophie, Politik und Pädagogik 2*, in *Werkausgabe* XII, ed. Wilhelm Weischedel, 397–690. Frankfurt am Main: Suhrkamp, 1968.

Kant, Immanuel. *Critique of the Power of Judgment*. Trans. Paul Guyer and Eric Matthews. Cambridge: Cambridge University Press, 2000.

Kant, Immanuel. "Idea of a Universal History with a Cosmopolitan Purpose." In *Political Writings*, ed. Hans Reiss and trans. H. B. Nisbet, 41–53. Cambridge: Cambridge University Press, 1991.

Kant, Immanuel. *Idee zu einer allgemeinen Geschichte in weltbürgerlicher Absicht*. In *Schriften zur Anthropologie, Geschichtsphilosophie, Politik und Pädagogik 1*, in *Werkausgabe* XI, ed. Wilhelm Weischedel, 31–50. Frankfurt am Main: Suhrkamp, 1968.

Kant, Immanuel. *Kritik der Urteilskraft*. *Werkausgabe* X, ed. Wilhelm Weischedel. Frankfurt am Main: Suhrkamp, 1968.

Kant, Immanuel. *Toward Perpetual Peace: A Philosophical Project*. In *Practical Philosophy*, trans. and ed. Mary Gregor, 317–51. Cambridge: Cambridge University Press, 1996.

Kant, Immanuel. *Zum ewigen Frieden. Ein philosophischer Entwurf*. In *Schriften zur Anthropologie, Geschichtsphilosophie, Politik und Pädagogik 1*, *Werkausgabe*, XI, ed. Wilhelm Weischedel, 191–251. Frankfurt am Main: Suhrkamp, 1968.

Kempadoo, Kamala. *Sexing the Caribbean: Gender, Race, and Sexual Labor*. New York: Routledge, 2004.

Kenyatta, Jomo. *Haarambee! The Prime Minister of Kenya's Speeches 1963–1964.* Nairobi: Oxford University Press, 1964.

Kristeva, Julia. *Hannah Arendt.* Trans. Ross Guberman. New York: Columbia University Press, 2001.

Lefebvre, Henri. *The Production of Space.* Trans. David Nicholson-Smith. Oxford: Blackwell, 1991.

Lukács, Georg. *Studies in European Realism.* Trans. Edith Bone. New York: Grosset and Dunlap, 1964.

Lyotard, Jean-François. *The Differend: Phrases in Dispute.* Trans. Georges Van Den Abbeele. Minneapolis: University of Minnesota Press, 1988.

Lyotard, Jean-François. *The Postmodern Condition: A Report on Knowledge.* Trans. Geoff Bennington and Brian Massumi. Minneapolis: University of Minnesota Press, 1984.

Mallick, Ross. *Development Policy of a Communist Government: West Bengal since 1977.* Cambridge: Cambridge University Press, 1993.

Mallick, Ross. "Refugee Resettlement in Forest Reserves: West Bengal Policy Reversal and the Marichjhapi Massacre." *Journal of Asian Studies* 58.1 (February 1999): 104–25.

Marcuse, Herbert. *One-Dimensional Man: Studies in the Ideology of Advanced Industrial Society.* 2nd ed. Boston: Beacon Press, 1991.

Mauss, Marcel. *The Gift: The Form and Reason for Exchange in Archaic Societies.* Trans. W. D. Halls. New York: Norton, 1990.

Mill, John Stuart. *Principles of Political Economy.* Ed. J. M. Robson. Toronto: University of Toronto Press, 1965.

Mintz, Sidney W. "From Plantations to Peasantries." In *Caribbean Contours,* ed. Sidney W. Mintz and Sally Price, 127–53. Baltimore: Johns Hopkins University Press, 1985.

Mintz, Sidney W. *Sweetness and Power: The Place of Sugar in Modern History.* New York: Viking Penguin, 1985.

Moretti, Franco. "Conjectures on World Literature." *New Left Review* 1 (January-February 2000): 54–68.

Moretti, Franco. "The End of the Beginning: Reply to Christopher Prendergast." *New Left Review* 41 (September-October 2006): 71–86.

Moretti, Franco. "Graphs, Maps, Trees: Abstract Models for Literary History—1." *New Left Review* 24 (November-December 2003): 67–93.

Moretti, Franco. "Graphs, Maps, Trees: Abstract Models for Literary History—2." *New Left Review* 26 (March-April 2004): 79–103.

Moretti, Franco. "Graphs, Maps, Trees: Abstract Models for Literary History—3." *New Left Review* 28 (July-August 2004): 43–63.

Moretti, Franco. *The Way of the World: The Bildungsroman in European Culture.* London: Verso, 1987.

Moretti, Franco. "World-Systems Analysis, Evolutionary Theory, *Weltliteratur*." In *Immanuel Wallerstein and the Problem of the World: System, Scale, Culture,* ed.

David Palumbo-Liu, Bruce Robbins, and Nirvana Tanoukhi, 67–77. Durham, NC: Duke University Press, 2011.

Mukherjee, Upamanyu Pablo. *Postcolonial Environments: Nature, Culture and the Contemporary Indian Novel in English*. Basingstoke, England: Palgrave Macmillan, 2010.

Nancy, Jean-Luc. *The Creation of the World, or Globalization*. Trans. François Raffoul and David Pettigrew. Albany: State University of New York Press, 2007.

Nancy, Jean-Luc. *The Sense of the World*. Trans. Jeffrey S. Librett. Minneapolis: University of Minnesota Press, 1997.

Nettleford, Rex. *Caribbean Cultural Identity: The Case of Jamaica. An Essay in Cultural Dynamics*. Los Angeles: Center for Afro-American Studies and UCLA Latin American Center Publications, 1979.

Ngaboh-Smart, Francis. "Dimensions of Gift Giving in Nuruddin Farah's *Gifts*," *Research in African Literatures* 27.4 (winter 1996): 144–56.

Ngũgĩ, wa Thiong'o. *Decolonising the Mind: The Politics of Language in African Literature*. Portsmouth, NH: Heinemann, 1986.

Kwame Nkrumah. *Address to the Nationalists' Conference*. Accra, June 4, 1962.

Kwame Nkrumah. *Consciencism: Philosophy and Ideology for Decolonization and Development with Particular Reference to the African Revolution*. London: Heinemann, 1964.

Kwame Nkrumah. *Handbook of Revolutionary Warfare: A Guide to the Armed Phase of the African Revolution*. New York: International, 1968.

Kwame Nkrumah. *I Speak of Freedom: A Statement of African Ideology*. New York: Praeger, 1961.

Omaar, Rakiya. "Disaster Pornography from Somalia." *Los Angeles Times*, December 10, 1992.

Patullo, Polly. *Last Resorts: The Cost of Tourism in the Caribbean*. London: Cassell, 1996.

Pavel, Thomas G. *Fictional Worlds*. Cambridge, MA: Harvard University Press, 1986.

Pratt, Mary Louise. "Comparative Literature and Global Citizenship." In *Comparative Literature in the Age of Multiculturalism*, ed. Charles Bernheimer, 58–65. Baltimore, MD: Johns Hopkins University Press, 1995.

Said, Edward W. *Culture and Imperialism*. London: Chatto and Windus, 1993.

Saussy, Haun, ed. *Comparative Literature in an Age of Globalization*. Baltimore: Johns Hopkins University Press, 2006.

Singer, Amy. *Charity in Islamic Societies*. Cambridge: Cambridge University Press, 2008.

Smith, Adam. *An Inquiry into the Nature and Causes of the Wealth of Nations*. 2 vols. Chicago: University of Chicago Press, 1976.

Spivak, Gayatri Chakravorty. "Can the Subaltern Speak?" In *Marxism and the Interpretation of Culture*, ed. Cary Nelson and Lawrence Grossberg, 271–313. Urbana: University of Illinois Press, 1988.

Spivak, Gayatri Chakravorty. "The Rani of Sirmur: An Essay in Reading the Archives." *History and Theory* 24.3 (October 1985): 247–72.

Spivak, Gayatri Chakravorty. "Three Women's Texts and a Critique of Imperialism." In "'Race,' Writing, and Difference," special issue, *Critical Inquiry* 12.1 (autumn 1985): 243–61.

Stirrat, R. L., and Heiko Henkel. "The Development Gift: The Problem of Reciprocity in the NGO World." *Annals of the American Academy of Political and Social Science* 554 (November 1997): 66–80.

Strachan, Ian Gregory. *Paradise and Plantation: Tourism and Culture in the Anglophone Caribbean*. Charlottesville: University of Virginia Press, 2002.

Taminiaux, Jacques. *The Thracian Maid and the Professional Thinker: Arendt and Heidegger*. Trans. Michael Gendre. Albany: State University of New York Press, 1997.

Tan, See Seng, and Amitav Acharya, eds. *Bandung Revisited: The Legacy of the 1955 Asian-African Conference for International Order*. Singapore: National University of Singapore Press, 2008.

Taylor, Charles. "Two Theories of Modernity." *Public Culture* 11.1 (1999): 153–74.

Taylor, Frank Fonda. *To Hell with Paradise: A History of the Jamaican Tourist Industry*. Pittsburgh: University of Pittsburgh Press, 1993.

Villa, Dana. *Arendt and Heidegger: The Fate of the Political*. Princeton, NJ: Princeton University Press, 1996.

Villa, Dana. "Arendt, Heidegger, and the Tradition." *Social Research* 74.4 (winter 2007): 983–1002.

Wallerstein, Immanuel. "Dependence in an Interdependent World: The Limited Possibilities of Transformation within a Capitalist World-Economy." In *The Capitalist World-Economy: Essays by Immanuel Wallerstein*, 66–94. Cambridge: Cambridge University Press, 1979.

Wallerstein, Immanuel. *The Modern World-System: Capitalist Agriculture and the Origins of the European World-Economy in the Sixteenth Century*. New York: Academic Press, 1974.

Wallerstein, Immanuel. *The Modern World-System II: Mercantilism and the Consolidation of the European World-Economy 1600–1750*. New York: Academic Press, 1980.

Wallerstein, Immanuel. *The Modern World-System III: The Second Era of Great Expansion of the Capitalist World-Economy, 1730–1840s*. New York: Academic Press, 1989.

Wallerstein, Immanuel. "The Rise and Future Demise of the World Capitalist System: Concepts for Comparative Analysis." In *The Capitalist World-Economy: Essays by Immanuel Wallerstein*, 1–36. Cambridge: Cambridge University Press, 1979.

Asia: anticolonial nationalism in, 201–2, 239; decolonization in, 198; historicism and heterotemporality in, 202–10; modernity and community in, 200–210; transregional networks in, 4–5
Asian Development Bank, 257
Auerbach, Erich, 24–27, 31, 42, 45, 48, 82
Aufhebung, of commodities, 67–68
Aufzeichnungen des Malte Laurids Brigge (Rilke), 126–30
Augustine (St.), Arendt's dissertation on, 140
authenticity, Heidegger on, 124–25
authorial meaning, Derrida's discussion of, 181–86
authoritarianism: humanitarianism and, 284–89; literature's resistance to, 282–89
autonomy: of aesthetic, 81–82; in world literature, 31–33, 78, 336n31

Bandung Conference of 1955, 198
Barre, Siad, 278–79, 282
Barthes, Roland, 183
Battle of Mogadishu, 278
Being and Time (Heidegger), 98–100, 102, 105, 345n3, 346n10, 347n28; Arendt's discussion of, 135; Derrida's discussion of, 162–65
being-with-others: Arendt's analysis of, 133–36; cosmopolitanism and, 125; Heidegger's concept of, 103–7
Bell Trade Act, 315
Benhabib, Seyla, 348n3, 348n5, 349n6
Benjamin, Walter, 321–24, 326, 367n19
Benthall, Jonathan, 278–79, 286–89
Bernheimer Report, 23
Bildung: capital time and, 239; Cliff's writing and, 220–21, 236–45; in Farah's *Gifts,* 305–9; Heidegger's worldliness and, 116–17; Marxist theory and, 63–65; in postcolonial

world literature, 212–15; precolonial past and, 227–33
bildungsroman: colonial ideology and, 220, 227, 236; cultural modernization and, 212; nationalism and, 239; protagonist of, 29; spirit or proletariat in, 152; transformation principle and, 313
biological life: subaltern modernity and, 206–10; violence of decolonization and, 193–98
biopolitics: environmentalism and, 254–59; subaltern modernity and, 206
Black Skin, White Masks (Fanon), 195–96
Bon Bibi myth, 292; in Ghosh's *Hungry Tide,* 258–59, 270–71
Bourdieu, Pierre, 31, 336n31

Canclini, Nestor Garcia, 202, 206–10
capitalist globalization, 2; alienation of, 65–77; Asian ideal of community and, 201–10; breaking down of barriers by, 72–77; circulation time of capital, 68–77, 353n55; delegitimation of humanities and, 27–28; Derrida on, 161, 174–80; environmentalism and, 253–59; Farah's *Gifts* and resistance to, 303–9; in Ghosh's fiction, 246–48; inversion of spiritualist models and, 60–91; Latin American modernity and, 207–10; literary studies and, 23–45; local traditions of reciprocity and giving and, 292–95; market metaphor and force of, 28–38; in Philippines, 315–31; postcoloniality and, 198–210, 210–15; retemporalization of world and, 65–77; spatialization and, 62–65; subalternity and, 203–10; sugar and tourism capital, 220–27; temporality of, 220–27, 239–45; worldliness

human other, 162–67; on world as text, 167–73

Descartes, René, 98–99

de Sousa Santos, Boaventura, 12

developmentalism, Eurocentric teleology of, 211–15

De Waal, Alex, 283, 285–86

dialectics of place, in Cliff's fiction, 233–39

différance, Derrida on, 168–73

"Différance" (Derrida), 164–67

discourse, Heidegger on, 127–28

dispossession, global capitalism and, 64–65

domination, Hegel's justification of, 51–55

drama, Arendt's discussion of, 152–54

Duino Elegies (Rilke), 18, 249–53, 263–67

Dussel, Enrique, 200

ecotourism, 253–59, 361n20

El Hablador (Vargas Llosa), 367n19

emergence, local traditions of, 289–95

Enlightenment philosophy, precolonial past and, 229–33

environmentalism: deep communication concerning, 267–70; hostility of nature in Ghosh's fiction and, 248–53; local movements for, 259–67; religious beliefs and, 254–59, 270; unworlding and, 253–59

equality. *See* inequality

Eurocentrism: canonical literature and, 23, 234–39; Derrida on, 178–80; developmentalism and, 211–15; in Ghosh's fiction, 267–70; hierarchy of cultural forms and, 56–59; humanitarianism and, 283–89; modernity and time and, 200–210; normative definitions based on, 43–45; postcolonial world literature and, 14–19, 192–93, 217–20, 227–33; in storytell-

ing, 313; temporality of capital and, 221–27, 239–45

exclusion, world literature and question of, 192–93

existence, Arendt's discussion of, 136–44

expropriation: ecotourism and, 253–59, 361n20; humanitarian aid and, 291–95

Failed States Index, cartography of, 4

faith, mythology and, 302–9

Fanon, Frantz, 195–97, 223–24

Farah, Nuruddin, 12–16, 215, 279–309; aporia of postcoloniality in fiction of, 300–309; on humanitarian aid in Somalia, 282–89

feminist-maternal ontopology, postcolonial dialectics and, 233–39

folk culture: in Cliff's novels, 239–45; in Ghosh's fiction, 253, 257–59, 267–70; heterotemporality of, 13; in Somalia, 18, 281, 286, 298–300

force: Heidegger on, 117–20, 126–30; worldliness and, 95, 191–93. *See* normative force

foreign aid, dehumanization by, 287–89

Forest Act (India), 256–57

forests: in Cliff's fiction, 233–39; in Ghosh's *Hungry Tide,* 247–53; Indian environmentalism and biopolitics and, 255–59

formal semantics, world literature and, 4–5

form of literature: deep communication and, 269–70; world literature and, 34–38

Frankfurt School, 82, 87

freedom: Arendt's discussion of, 140–44; Derrida on, 171–72; Kant on, 171; violence of decolonization and, 193–98, 239–45

Friends of the Earth, 255–56

Fund for Peace, 4

Gelassenheit (Heidegger), 121–22
gender, landscape and, 235–39
genocide: Arendt on, 194–98; culture
    and, 195–98, 330–31
geographical turn: in Cliff's novels,
    244–45; dialectics of place and,
    233–39; in postcolonial criticism,
    218–20
geological time: in Cliff's novels,
    244–45; in Ghosh's fiction, 250–53;
    precolonial past and, 232–33
German idealism: teleological time and,
    7; world literature and, 43–45
German language, world literature in,
    40–45
Ghosh, Amitav, 12–15, 215, 246–77,
    356n37, 359n1; on deep time and
    communication, 267–70; on envi-
    ronmental decline, 253–59; on litera-
    ture as poetry, 271
Gifts (Farah), 12–13, 18, 215, 279–309;
    aporia of postcoloniality in,
    300–309; critique of humanitarian-
    ism in, 282, 287–89; local traditions
    of giving and reciprocity in, 289–95;
    storytelling in, 296–300
Gikandi, Simon, 281
Gilead, Amihud, 6–7
Given Time (Derrida), 166–67, 183–85
global hierarchy: of cultural forms,
    55–59; justification of violence and,
    51–55; temporal calculation and, 1–2
globalization. See capitalist
    globalization
global warming, capitalism and,
    253–59
Goethe, Johanne Wolfgang: Euro-
    centrism of, 43–45, 192–93; Hegel
    and, 46, 52–55; physico-geographic
    world and, 63, 65, 81; on spiritual
    intercourse, 194–95, 211, 271, 280–81;
    Weltliteratur concept of, 6, 10,
    24–26, 37–45, 77–78, 191–92

gothic novel, Moretti's comments on,
    337n37
governmentality: anticolonialism and,
    242–45; in Ghosh's fiction, 250–53;
    humanitarian aid and undermining
    of, 291–95; subalternity and moder-
    nity and, 204–10
Gramsci, Antonio, 89
Great Expectations (Dickens), 18, 228
Greek classicism: in Arendt's work,
    143–44; framing of world litera-
    ture and, 42–45; in Hegel's cultural
    hierarchy, 57–58
Greenwich Mean Time: anticolonial
    nationalism and, 202; global subor-
    dination to, 1
Grosse, glühende Wölbung (Vast, Glow-
    ing Vault) (Celan), 177–78
Guha, Ramachandra, 254–56, 259–60
Guha, Ranajit, 203
Gulliver's Travels (Swift), 326

Habermas, Jürgen, 42, 200, 204,
    338n49
Hakluyt, Richard, 326
Hamilton, Daniel (Sir), 262–65
Harvey, David, 30–31, 77–91
Hegel, G. W. F.: on hierarchy of cultural
    forms, 55–59, 78; on modernity, 83,
    201, 205; postcolonial literature and,
    211, 279–80; spiritualist model of, 45,
    61; world literature and work of, 7–8,
    10, 46–59, 63, 81, 191
Heidegger, Martin, 95; anthropolo-
    gism in, 96, 101–2, 135, 162; Arendt's
    revision of, 96, 125, 130–60, 345n3,
    348n2; being-with-others concept
    and, 103–7; cosmopolitanism cri-
    tiqued by, 122–25; critique of anthro-
    pologism in, 169–70; deconstruction
    and, 161–62; Derrida and, 96, 161–87,
    350n1; force of worlding and tran-
    scendence in, 113–20; Husserl and,

Jalais, Annu, 257–59, 361n26
Jamaica: anticolonial activism in, 239–45; dialectics of place in, 233–39; postcolonial literature in, 215, 220–45; precolonial past in, 227–33; sugar and tourism capital in, 221–27, 358n25; worldlessness in, 217–20
James, C. L. R., 197
Jameson, Fredric, 210
Jane Eyre (Brontë), 18, 217, 228, 235
judicial court, Hegel's metaphor of, 47, 51–55

Kant, Immanuel, 2–3; *Bildung* and, 63; on commerce and world literature, 44–45; on freedom and reason, 171; Hegel and, 46; Third Critique of, 6–7; worlding and work of, 10, 280
Kentridge, William, 1–2
Kenyatta, Jomo, 354n15

labor: Arendt on, 136–47; Heidegger on, 124–25; material world of production and, 81; social characteristics of, 66–77; subalternity and, 203–10
Latin America, modernity and capitalism in, 206–10
Lefebvre, Henri, 36–37, 83–91, 234, 343n67, 344n82
"Letter on 'Humanism'" (Heidegger), 113–20, 122
literary production, market exchange and, 34–38
literary studies: delegitimation of, 27–28; globalization and, 23–45; subject-formation in, 85–86
local community: environmental movements in, 259–67; giving and reciprocity in, 289–95
logos, Aristotle's concept of, 127–30
Lukács, Georg, 81–82, 88
Lyotard, Jean-François, 313–14

Magellan, Ferdinand, 316–18, 325
magical realism, 213
Mallick, Ross, 246, 257
Manifesto of the Communist Party (Marx), 60–61
Marcuse, Herbert, 82
market exchange: Arendt on, 149–54; gift economy *vs.*, 303–9; globalization and, 60–91; humanitarian aid and, 283–89; Lefebvre's theory of space and, 83–84; retemporalization of world and, 65–77; slavery and, 216–17; subalternity and modernity and, 203–10; world literature and, 28–38, 43–45, 336n30
Maroon slave rebellion, 234–35
Marquez, Gabriel Garcia, 213
"Martin Heidegger at Eighty" (Arendt), 348n2
Marx, Karl: aesthetic theory and, 81–91; Arendt's objective in-between and, 145–47; on capitalist globalization, 2, 60–62, 192; on commodity fetishism, 66–77; critique of bourgeois normativity by, 7–8; Derrida's discussion of, 161; Hegel and, 46; Heidegger and, 122, 124–25; on labor, 66–77, 204; on modernity, 205–10; on production and time, 70–77, 220–21; on revolution, 196; on slavery, 216; on social force, 31, 336n36; on spatialization of global capitalism, 62–65, 89–91, 210–11, 341n10; world literature and work of, 7–11, 24, 77–91, 211
mass consumption: cosmopolitanism and, 261–67; cultural plurality and, 77–91
materialism: Arendt on, 149–54; decolonization and, 197–98; humanitarianism and, 284–89; inversion of spiritualism, 62–65; postcolonial reconfiguration of, 240–45; in world literature, 77–91, 191–93

Mau Mau uprising, 196
Mauss, Marcel, 18, 281, 289–95
McLuhan, Marshall, 329–31
media: Morichjhāpi refugee massacre
in, 247–50, 256–59; narrative of
Somalia in, 282–89
memory of the world: in Ghosh's fiction,
248–53; in Rosca's State of War, 320–24
Mercatorian space, conflation of globalization and, 30–32
messianic hope, Derrida's deconstruction and, 174–80, 191
metaphysics, Heidegger's worldliness
and, 109–12
middle-class consciousness, subaltern
environmentalism and, 260–67
Middle Passage, in postcolonial literature, 218–20, 236
Midnight's Children (Rushdie), 313
Mignolo, Walter, 200
militarized humanitarianism, 285–89
Military Bases Agreement, 315
Mill, John Stuart, 221–22
Mintz, Sidney, 221–22, 226
Miskito Indians, in Cliff's fiction, 235
Mo, Timothy, 13–15, 215, 314, 324–31
modernity: Arendt on alienation and,
155–60; cosmopolitanism and, 261–67;
heterotemporality and, 198–210;
homelessness of modern humanity
and, 120–22; local traditions of giving and reciprocity and, 292–95; loss
of world in, 95–130; precolonial past
and, 229–33
mondialisation, 42, 174–80
morality: environmentalism and, 259; in
Ghosh's Hungry Tide, 271–77
Moretti, Franco, 31, 34–38, 80, 313,
336n36, 337n37
Morichjhāpi: cosmopolitan consciousness concerning, 259–67; massacre
of refugees in, 247–50, 256–59,
272–77, 361n24

mortality, Arendt on, 133, 137–44
multilingual complexity: in Farah's
writing, 280–81; in Mo's Renegade,
327–31; world literature and,
268–70
multitemporality. See heterotemporality
mutual dependency, Heidegger's being-
with-others and, 105–7
mythology: heterotemporality and,
205–10; suspension of disbelief in,
302–9

Naipaul, V. S., 15, 213, 216, 243
Nancy, Jean-Luc, 351n26
narrative: Arendt's subjective in-
between and, 147–54; Derrida on,
184–86; Eurocentric form of, 313–14;
in Farah's Gifts, 296–300; gift of time
and, 304–9; humanitarianism promoted through, 286–89; media narratives of Somalia, 282–89; nature
imagery and, 253–59; postcolonial
emergence and, 12–13, 210–15; theory
of, 311–13. See also storytelling
natality: Arendt's discussion of, 136–44,
157–60, 172, 198; decolonization and,
198; Derrida on, 172–73
nationalism: anticolonialism and,
201–2, 239; dialectics of place and,
236–39; Hegel on, 55–59; postcolonial world literature and, 211–15
National Socialism, Heidegger's association with, 134–36, 349n6
natural law theory, Arendt on, 156–60
nature: biocentric view of, 253–59; dialectics of place and, 233–39; hostility
of, in Ghosh's fiction, 250–53
Nehru, Jawaharlal, 198
neocolonialism: humanitarianism and,
285–89; in Philippines, 315–31; post-
independence struggle against, 197;
precolonial past and, 227–33, 229–33;
tourism and, 224–27

neoliberal capitalist globalization, humanitarianism and, 283–89

Nettleford, Rex, 217–18

newness, Arendt's solution to alienation and, 155–60

Ngũgĩ wa Thiong'o, 269, 282

Nkrumah, Kwame, 197–98

Noli Me Tángere, 325

Non-Aligned Movement, 194

nongovernment organizations, 278–79, 283–89

nonhuman agency: Derrida on time and, 162–67; in Ghosh's fiction, 250–53, 257–59, 261–67; inhuman textuality and, 271–77; precolonial past and, 232–33

nontruth, literature as, 183–86

normativity: of capital, 69–77; deficit in world literature of, 31–38, 77–91; postcolonial world literature and, 210–15, 218–20; in world literature, 5–11, 38–45, 191–93, 310–31

No Telephone to Heaven (Cliff), 217–18, 224, 227, 233–34, 240–41

novel form: faith *vs.* reality in, 302–9; postcolonial literature and, 212–15

objective in-between, in Arendt's work, 145–47

objective reality, violence of, 97–103

Of Grammatology (Derrida), 173

Omaar, Rakiya, 286–87

"On the Essence of Ground" (Heidegger), 117–19, 142

ontology: Derrida's *différance* and, 168–73; Heidegger's worldliness and, 107–12

Operation Restore Hope, 278, 286–89

The Origin of the Work of Art (Heidegger), 8

The Origins of Totalitarianism (Arendt), 157

Other: action as response to, 167–73; time as gift of, 162–67

Ouisia and Gramme (Derrida), 163–65, 350n8

outsider, in world literature, 324–31

pan-Africanism, 198

Parmenides, 108

passage metaphor, in Cliff's fiction, 236–39

Pavel, Thomas, 4

performative language, Derrida on, 353n55

phenomenology: Derrida on, 168–73; in Ghosh's *Hungry Tide,* 272–77; of gifts, 296–300; of worldliness, 95–130; world literature and, 182–86

Philippine-American War, 318

Philippine Rehabilitation Act, 315

Philippines, postcolonial literature in, 215, 314–31

"Philology and *Weltliteratur*" (Auerbach), 24–25

Philosophy of Right (Hegel), 47–50

photojournalism, humanitarianism promoted through, 286–89

physical forces, 337n38

Physics (Aristotle), 163

place, postcolonial dialectics of, 233–39

plasticity of reason, 199–210

play, Derrida's concept of, 173–74

plurality: in Arendt's discussion of worldliness, 136–44; deep communication and, 268–70

poesis, 99–100

poetry: Arendt on, 153–54, 267; genocide and, 330–31; middle-class consciousness of subalternity and, 259–67; uncovering of worldliness and, 126–30

polarization, capitalist globalization and, 78–80

politics: in Farah's *Gifts,* 303–9; Hegel on world history and, 47–50; humanitarian aid in Somalia and, 278–79, 282; humanitarianism and, 283–89; local traditions of giving and reciprocity and, 289–95

postcoloniality: aporia of, 300–309; ecotourism and, 255–59; in Farah's *Gifts,* 281; feminist-maternal ontopology and, 233–39; Hegel's cultural hierarchy and, 57–59; heterotemporality and modernity and, 198–210; interpretive hypotheses for world literature and, 210–15; local traditions of giving and reciprocity and, 289–95; reconfiguration of time and space and, 239–45; sugar and tourism capital and, 220–27; temporality of decolonization and, 193–98; transnational literary power and, 33; uneven development and, 90–91; world literature and, 11–19, 191–215. *See also* colonialism; decolonization

pragmata, 99–100

Pramoedya Ananta Toer, 282

praxis, 99–100

precolonial past: Eurocentric colonial erasure of, 221–27; future projections from, 216–45; resurrection of, 227–33; in Rosca's *State of War,* 316–24

presence: Derrida's deconstruction of, 164–67, 350n2; in Ghosh's *Hungry Tide,* 262; Heidegger's privileging of, 164, 205–6, 350n2; in Rosca's *State of War,* 320–24; time as form of, 204–6

production: Arendt on, 149–54; capital's revolutionization of, 70–77

Project Tiger, 253–56

proletariat, as historical agent, 73–77

proper, loss of, 120–22; deconstructive critique of, 168

Provincializing Europe (Chakrabarty), 202

racialized hierarchies, tourism and, 224–27

radical finitude: Arendt's discussion of, 142–44; in Farah's *Gifts,* 300–309; Heidegger's concept of, 107–12; in Mo's *Renegade,* 329–31

Rancière, Jacques, 344n82

reality: Lefebvre's theory of space and, 86–91; literature and, 302–9; Lukács's theory of, 81–82

reason, decolonization and plasticity of, 199–210

reciprocity, local traditions in Somalia, 289–95

Refusal of Time, The (video installation), 1–2

reification: Arendt on literature and, 153–54; commodity fetishism and, 67–68, 88–91

religion: colonialism and, 314; deep ecology and, 254–59, 270; heterotemporality and, 205–10; local traditions of giving and reciprocity and, 292–95

Renegade or Halo Halo (Mo), 13, 314, 324–31

repetition, Arendt's discussion of worldliness, 144, 151–54

representational space, 85; dialectics of place and, 234–39; postcolonial reconfiguration of, 239–45

res corporea (Descartes), 98–99

res extensa, 101

retemporalization of world, commodities, time and capitalism, 65–77

revolutionary time: in Cliff's fiction, 220, 240–45; in postcolonial world literature, 13–19

reworlding, world literature and, 248–53

time: deep time in world literature, 267–70; Derrida on, 177–80, 350n8; gift of, in Farah's fiction, 303–9; human appropriation of, 206–10; inhuman otherness of, 161–87; modernity and consciousness of, 200–210; narrative and, 311–13; narrative theory and, 311–13; in Rosca's *State of War*, 317–24

tourism capital: ecotourism and, 253–59; postcoloniality and, 220–27, 241–45, 358n25; precolonial past and, 229–33; slavery and, 216–17

trade and industry: globalization and liberalization of, 216; Marx on, 67–68; in Philippines, 315

transcendence: Arendt on Heidegger's discussion of, 134–36; Derrida on, 174–75; Heidegger on force of world-ing and, 113–20

translation: in Ghosh's *Hungry Tide*, 272–77; Heidegger's being-with-others and, 104–7; middle-class consciousness of subalternity and, 265–67; of world literature, 39–45

transnationalism: humanitarian aid and, 278–79, 283–89; world literature and, 31–34

transregional networks, in Asia, 4–5

tribalism, in world literature, 324–31

Tydings-McDuffie Act, 314

Tydings War Damage Act, 315

understanding, worldliness and, 102–3

United Nations Operation in Somalia (UNOSOM), 278

United States: colonization of Philippines by, 314–16, 326–31; neocolonialist ideology of, 13; Somalian crisis and, 278, 286–89, 291–95

unlearning, in postcolonial literature, 220

unworlding: environmentalism and, 253–59; humanitarianism as, 278–309; modernity and, 121–22

value, objectivity of, 66–77; Heidegger and, 101–3; world as realm of, 97–103

Vargas Llosa, Mario, 367n19

Villa, Dana, 348n3

violence: of cultural imperialism, 209–10; of foreign aid, 290–95; in Ghosh's fiction, 250–53; Hegel on arts and role of, 51–55, 58–59, 191; of incorporation, 79–80; of objective reality, 97–103

Vorhandenheit, Heidegger's concept of, 97–100, 105, 346n10

vouloir dire, Derrida's concept of, 181, 353n47

Voyages (Hakluyt), 326

Walcott, Derek, 226–27

Wallerstein, Immanuel, 78–81, 193

Way in the World, A (Naipaul), 243

Wealth of Nations (Smith), 221

Weber, Max, 201, 316

wilderness preservation, commodification of nature and, 253–59

Wordsworth, William, 244

world cinema, critical theories of, 335n10

world history: as court of judgment, 51–55; culture and power in, 46–59; globalization and, 61–62; in Hegel's cultural hierarchy, 57–58; optic of, 47–50; spatialization of world market, 64–65; world literature and, 31

worlding: alterity and, 168–73; art and, 128–30; cosmopolitanism and, 122–25; deconstructive development of, 209–10; Derrida's discussion of, 175–80; "de-worlding" and, 98–99; Heidegger's concept of, 98–99, 103–7, 128–30; literature as tool for, 246–48;

loss of the proper and, 120–22; normative theory of world literature and, 6, 8–11; phenomenology of, 95–130; in Philippines, 314; poetry and, 126–30; postcolonial literature and, 13–19, 211–15; power of storytelling and, 300–309; spatialization and, 62–65; temporalization and, 191–93; transcendence and force of, 113–20

worldliness: Arendt's discussion of, 131, 136–44, 155–60; cosmopolitanism and, 122–25; deconstructive account of, 173–80; Derrida's discussion of, 161–87; globalization and, 28–38; Heidegger's concept of, 107–12; outsider worldliness, 324–31; phenomenology of, 95–97; poetry and uncovering of, 126–30; postcolonial reconfiguration of, 240–45; primary sense of, 97–103; as text, Derrida on, 167–73

world literature: Arendt's subjective in-between and, 147–54; cartographies of spatial world and, 3–5; comparative literature and, 23–28; cosmopolitanism and, 2–3; as deep communication, 267–70; defined, 28–29; dehumanization of humanitarian aid and, 285–89; Derrida's deconstruction and, 180–86, 353n51; eternal ideas in, 310; globalization and, 23–45, 191–93; Heidegger's philosophy and, 102–3; market metaphor and, 28–38; Marx's critique of, 63–65; normative theory of, 5–11; poetry and worldliness in, 117–20, 126–30; postcoloniality and, 11–19, 193–98, 210–15; power of global capitalism in, 69–77; temporal conceptualization of, 2; temporalization of decolonization and, 193–98

worldly ethics, in postcolonial world literature, 13–19, 214, 245, 324–27

world music, critical theories of, 335n10

World Social Forum, 12, 174

world-systems theory, 78–81, 193; capitalist globalization and, 199–210, 343n55; Latin American modernity and, 206–10; slavery and, 223–27

World Republic of Letters, The (Casanova), 31–33

World War II, decolonization after, 194

World Wildlife Fund (WWF), 257

Wretched of the Earth, The (Fanon), 196, 223–24

writing, Derrida on, 181, 353n48

Wuthering Heights (Brontë), 217

zonal inequality, materialist world literature and, 77–91

Zuhandenheit, Heidegger's concept of, 99–100, 346n10